THE JUSTICE FACTORY

Spend time at the International Criminal Court (ICC), and you will hear the familiar language of anti-impunity. Spend longer, and you will encounter the less familiar language of management – efficiency, risk, and performance, and tools of strategic planning, audit, and performance appraisal. How have these two languages fused within the primary institution of global justice? This book explores that question through a historical and conceptually layered account of management's effects on the ICC's global justice project. It historicises management, forcing international lawyers to look at the sites of struggle – from the plantation to the United Nations – that have shaped the court's managerial present. It traces the court's macro, micro, and meso scales of management, showing how such practices have fashioned a vision of global justice at organisational, professional, and argumentative levels. And it asks how those who care about global justice might engage with managerial justice at an institution animated by forms, reforms, and the promise of optimisation.

RICHARD CLEMENTS is Assistant Professor at Tilburg Law School and Faculty member at the Institute for Global Law & Policy, Harvard Law School.

CAMBRIDGE STUDIES IN INTERNATIONAL
AND COMPARATIVE LAW: 182

Established in 1946, this series produces high quality, reflective and innovative scholarship in the field of public international law. It publishes works on international law that are of a theoretical, historical, cross-disciplinary or doctrinal nature. The series also welcomes books providing insights from private international law, comparative law and transnational studies which inform international legal thought and practice more generally.

The series seeks to publish views from diverse legal traditions and perspectives, and of any geographical origin. In this respect it invites studies offering regional perspectives on core *problématiques* of international law, and in the same vein, it appreciates contrasts and debates between diverging approaches. Accordingly, books offering new or less orthodox perspectives are very much welcome. Works of a generalist character are greatly valued and the series is also open to studies on specific areas, institutions or problems. Translations of the most outstanding works published in other languages are also considered.

After seventy years, Cambridge Studies in International and Comparative Law sets the standard for international legal scholarship and will continue to define the discipline as it evolves in the years to come.

Series Editors

Larissa van den Herik
Professor of Public International Law, Grotius Centre for International Legal Studies, Leiden University

Jean d'Aspremont
Professor of International Law, University of Manchester and Sciences Po Law School

A list of books in the series can be found at the end of this volume.

THE JUSTICE FACTORY

Management Practices at the International Criminal Court

RICHARD CLEMENTS
Tilburg University

Shaftesbury Road, Cambridge CB2 8EA, United Kingdom

One Liberty Plaza, 20th Floor, New York, NY 10006, USA

477 Williamstown Road, Port Melbourne, VIC 3207, Australia

314–321, 3rd Floor, Plot 3, Splendor Forum, Jasola District Centre, New Delhi – 110025, India

103 Penang Road, #05-06/07, Visioncrest Commercial, Singapore 238467

Cambridge University Press is part of Cambridge University Press & Assessment, a department of the University of Cambridge.

We share the University's mission to contribute to society through the pursuit of education, learning and research at the highest international levels of excellence.

www.cambridge.org
Information on this title: www.cambridge.org/9781009153119
DOI: 10.1017/9781009153102

© Richard Clements 2024

This publication is in copyright. Subject to statutory exception and to the provisions of relevant collective licensing agreements, no reproduction of any part may take place without the written permission of Cambridge University Press & Assessment.

First published 2024

A catalogue record for this publication is available from the British Library.

Library of Congress Cataloging-in-Publication Data
Names: Clements, Richard, 1991- author.
Title: The justice factory : management practices at the International Criminal Court / Richard Clements, Tilburg University.
Description: Cambridge, United Kingdom ; New York, NY : Cambridge University Press, 2023. | Series: Cambridge studies in international and comparative law; csil | Includes bibliographical references and index.
Identifiers: LCCN 2023027773 (print) | LCCN 2023027774 (ebook) | ISBN 9781009153119 (hardback) | ISBN 9781009153096 (paperback) | ISBN 9781009153102 (epub)
Subjects: LCSH: International Criminal Court. | Criminal justice, Administration of. | Court administration.
Classification: LCC KZ7312 .C579 2023 (print) | LCC KZ7312 (ebook) | DDC 345/.01–dc23/eng/20230613
LC record available at https://lccn.loc.gov/2023027773
LC ebook record available at https://lccn.loc.gov/2023027774

ISBN 978-1-009-15311-9 Hardback

Cambridge University Press & Assessment has no responsibility for the persistence or accuracy of URLs for external or third-party internet websites referred to in this publication and does not guarantee that any content on such websites is, or will remain, accurate or appropriate.

CONTENTS

List of Figures   *page* vii
Acknowledgements   viii
List of Abbreviations   xi

1   Introduction   1
    1.1   A Tale of Two Tongues   1
    1.2   Management Defined   5
    1.3   Management Situated: The ICC *Dispositif*   12
    1.4   Management Situated: On International Legal Managerialism   18
    1.5   The Argument   28
    1.6   Outline and Style   30

2   A History of the International Criminal Court's Managerial Present   37
    2.1   Introduction   37
    2.2   Managing before Taylor: Plantation, Factory, War   40
    2.3   (International Legal) Management after Taylor   47
    2.4   The Third World as Managerial Problem   66
    2.5   A Situated Definition of Management Practices   80
    2.6   Conclusion   88

3   The Managerial Court: Macro-management   90
    3.1   Introduction   90
    3.2   Making the Institution Manageable   92
    3.3   Management in the Interim   102
    3.4   Efficiency in the Young Court   104
    3.5   Building the Managerial Scaffolding   108
    3.6   The Global Financial Crisis   119
    3.7   Internalising Critiques   124
    3.8   Conclusion   132

v

CONTENTS

4 The ICC Expert: Micro-management 135
4.1 Introduction 135
4.2 Becoming a Global Justice Professional 137
4.3 Settling Down 147
4.4 Keeping On 162
4.5 Moving Up 169
4.6 Conclusion 177

5 ICC Legal Argumentation: Meso-management 178
5.1 An Appalling Decision 178
5.2 The ICC's Argumentative Dilemmas 182
5.3 ... Always Already: Management and the Argumentative Dilemmas 185
5.4 The Flight to Management 223
5.5 Conclusion 226

6 'In a Technical and Political View': A Study of the ICC Registry's *ReVision* Project 228
6.1 Introduction 228
6.2 Contention, Discourse, Complexity 231
6.3 *ReVision*'s Flight to Management 238
6.4 From Politics to Technique: Narrowing through Expert Articulation 243
6.5 Management Technique as Politics 258
6.6 *ReVision* as Professional Comfort 274

7 Conclusion 277
7.1 Managerial Justice Continued 277
7.2 From Strategic Plan to Strategy of Rupture 280
7.3 A Strategy of Discomfort 284
7.4 (Not a) Conclusion 298

Select Bibliography 299
Index 331

Online Appendices available at the following link:
www.cambridge.org/9781009153119

FIGURES

3.1 Court Capacity Model *page* 114
3.2 ICC Strategic Plan 2013–2017 structure   128
4.1 *e*Recruitment search engine   140
4.2 *e*Recruitment job description   141
4.3 *e*Recruitment core competencies list   144
4.4 Core competencies diagram   157
4.5 Mid-term progress monitoring worksheet   164
4.6 Performance report objectives   166
6.1 Pre-*Re*Vision Registry structure   254
6.2 Post-*Re*Vision Registry structure   255
6.3 Registry Statements and Core Values   270

ACKNOWLEDGEMENTS

This book comes after six years of thinking, researching, and writing about the often nebulous, always surprising, and defiantly obscure topic of the International Criminal Court's managerial practices. Putting it all together and calling it a book is a lonely and often daunting experience: wishing to live up to the intellectual task inspired by others; working to make room for thought in a busy job, a busy world; and always the hope that the final draft will register with, maybe even spur, more than a few readers. On more than one occasion, in the midst of a pandemic, I have wondered whether it can all be done.

Against that backdrop, this book has been a wonderful pretext for meeting people, thinking with colleagues, travelling, and making the most of creative and political energies. More than once have I had to pinch myself for these and other privileges. In turn, the people this book brought together represent a motley crew of colleagues, friends, and family who may never meet but whose trace in this book is clear to me. It is in the spirit of making those traces visible that I thank everyone who advised, read, questioned, motivated, and supported me in this process.

This book originated at the Lauterpacht Centre for International Law at the University of Cambridge, under the steady guidance of Surabhi Ranganathan, my doctoral supervisor. I am deeply grateful to Surabhi for the freedom and rigour, as well as the enthusiasm and good humour, that made up those three years, and which continue today. The PhD was examined by Gerry Simpson and Sarah Nouwen. I could not have asked for a better discussion nor for better feedback. Their comments helped to turn a graduate dissertation into something more. So too did David Kennedy, whose intellectual guidance at the Institute for Global Law & Policy has spurred and challenged my thinking in equal measure, and whose advice has always come at the right time. Both Cambridges have offered a space for intellectual curiosity and for the slow boring of holes that writing often feels like. Despite the demands of teaching, Tilburg has also become a similar space for me, and conversations with colleagues

ACKNOWLEDGEMENTS

ix

have greatly enriched this book. Such relationships and spaces must continue to be defended against the managerial university.

Present conditions make it all the more moving that colleagues and friends have made time to read and comment on my work. I am particularly thankful to Nadia Lambek, Surabhi Ranganathan, Christine Schwöbel-Patel, Sergio Peña-Neira, Leila Ullrich, Augusto Bravo, and Latha Varadarajan for reading and offering invaluable advice on various chapters. The team at Cambridge University Press have been extremely supportive throughout the process, and I am grateful to them all, particularly Marianne Nield, and Tom Randall. Others have helped formulate good ideas, discourage bad ones, and otherwise inspire me to keep going, whether in the Lauterpacht Centre kitchen, the 'cave', Public Law & Governance, or elsewhere. They include Jean d'Aspremont, John Barker, Arnulf Becker Lorca, Luca Bonadiman, Cyra Choudhury, Megan Donaldson, Mark Drumbl, Guy Fiti Sinclair, Laurel Fletcher, Christopher Gevers, Leena Grover, Douglas Guilfoyle, John Haskell, Philipp Kastner, David Kennedy, Benedict Kingsbury, Jan Klabbers, Birju Kotecha, Mike Leach, Lucas Lixinski, Dimitri van den Meerssche, Matthew Nicholson, Sarah Nouwen, Sundhya Pahuja, Phillip Paiement, Marie-Catherine Petersmann, Ileana Porras, Francisco Quintana, Nik Rajkovic, Michiel Stapper, Catherine Turner, Latha Varadarajan, and Marina Veličković. Books are also a great excuse to talk, laugh, gossip, and conspire. Friends like Luíza, Orfeas, Ivan, Mrinalini, Scott, James, Nadia, Nafay, Löve, Matt, and John have done each at various times. I thank them all.

I had the opportunity to present my work in various places and am grateful to the organisers of those events. They include the LSA International Law and Politics Collaborative Research Network; Alternative Approaches to International Law Workshop, Graduate Institute, Geneva; American Society of International Law Interest Group; Bureaucracies in Transition workshop, Queen's University Belfast; Critical International Law Colloquium, SOAS & Durham Law School; OxonCourts Discussion Group, Oxford University; and the Cambridge International Law Conference. Participating in these events was financially possible thanks to Girton College, the UK Arts & Humanities Research Council Doctoral Training Programme, the Yorke Fund, the Institute for Global Law & Policy, and Tilburg Law School.

Themes informing this book appeared in 'Managerialism: The Before, During and After of Fragmentation in International Law' (2017) *Queen Mary Law Journal* 1–12, and '*Re*Visiting the ICC Registry's *Re*Vision

Project' (2019) 17 *Journal of International Criminal Justice* 259–284. An unrecognisable version of Chapter 3 was published as 'From Bureaucracy to Management: The International Criminal Court's Internal Progress Narrative' (2019) 32 *Leiden Journal of International Law* 149–167.

To be happy in one's work but to remember that there is a world beyond is a lesson my parents, Joe and Audrey, continue to impart, and I am grateful to them for all their support. The same for Cecil, Ida, Sadie, Diane, Mark, and Helen for reminding me what it's all about.

Lastly, I would like to thank AB. Enduring and encouraging my obsessions with management has come with kindness, love, and laughter, from Ocean Drive to The Hague. Unmanageable *in extremis*, this book is dedicated to him.

ABBREVIATIONS

ASP	Assembly of States Parties
AU	African Union
CBF	Committee on Budget and Finance
DEO	Division of External Operations
ECOSOC	Economic and Social Council
FIDH	International Federation for Human Rights
G77	Group of 77
ICC	International Criminal Court
ICTR	International Criminal Tribunal for Rwanda
ICTY	International Criminal Tribunal for the former Yugoslavia
ILO	International Labour Organization
ILOAT	International Labour Organization Administrative Tribunal
PMC	Permanent Mandates Commission
SCSL	Special Court for Sierra Leone
STL	Special Tribunal for Lebanon
UNDP	United Nations Development Programme
UNGA	United Nations General Assembly
UNSC	United Nations Security Council
VPRS	Victims Participation and Reparations Section
VWU	Victims and Witnesses Unit
WGLL	Working Group on Lessons Learnt

1

Introduction

A court of law is not a factory*

[T]he Court can be conceived of as producing certain outputs, or core activities ... The production line should be organized in such a way as to avoid both bottlenecks and overcapacities within the process.**

1.1 A Tale of Two Tongues

To engage with the International Criminal Court (ICC) is to encounter the familiar language of anti-impunity. This is the language of 'common bonds', the 'unimaginable atrocities that deeply shock the conscience of humanity', and the desire to end impunity for the perpetrators of the world's worst crimes.[1] This language describes the key events of international criminal law as genocide, war crimes, and crimes against humanity. It frames the everyday procedural terminology of an international criminal court established to investigate and prosecute grave atrocities: the concepts of jurisdiction, modes of liability, evidence, as well as victim participation and reparation. Ultimately, the language of anti-impunity is the sobering yet somehow inadequate expression and redemption of mass suffering, victimhood, conflict, violence, and death.

Spend time in the court's public gallery, offices, or hallways, and you are likely to hear this vocabulary spoken by officials, judges, and interns. Here, legal officers and judges convene to discuss whether charges should

---

* Report on the Special Court for Sierra Leone by the Independent Expert Antonio Cassese, 12 December 2006, para. 58, available at: www.rscsl.org/Documents/Cassese%20Report .pdf.
** ICC Report on the Court Capacity Model, ICC-ASP/5/10, 21 August 2006, paras. 14 and 25.
[1] Preamble, Rome Statute of the International Criminal Court (signed 17 July 1998, entered into force 1 July 2002) A/CONF.189/9 (Rome Statute).

2 INTRODUCTION

be confirmed against a suspect accused of grave crimes and find themselves debating whether reports and evidence gathered by the Office of the Prosecutor (OTP) establish 'substantial grounds to believe that the person committed each of the crimes charged'.[2] A legal assistant within the Victims Participation and Reparations Section consults their superior to determine whether an individual qualifies as a victim under the Rome Statute.[3] A research institute hosts a roundtable event to reflect on the challenges of prosecuting Vladimir Putin or the crime of ecocide. Spend long enough in these institutional spaces and expert circles, and you may find yourself speaking that same language. In fact, it is a marker of professional success that you do so confidently, flexibly, and with relative ease, or so I realised once I began to spend time in these spaces and circles.

Yet there is another less familiar language that one may not have expected to hear in the 'primary institution of global justice'. This is the language of management. These are the ideas of 'effectiveness and efficiency', spoken like a mantra by successive ICC presidents annually before the plenary session of the Assembly of States Parties. It is the talk of strategic planning, performance measurement, and lessons learnt exercises that populate the court's official documents. It is the concern for optimisation and value for money voiced by practitioners, scholars, and students in their speeches, articles, essays, and classroom interventions. Ideas and practices of management are much more ubiquitous and familiar once we begin to notice them. This, I also learnt during my brief time as an ICC intern. Legal advisers and officers would move from a judges' conference meeting about the latest interlocutory appeal to a performance review meeting with their supervisor. Or perhaps they would be reminded to keep gathering statistics for court-wide performance indicators or engage in the latest process for an updated strategic plan. Although I was unfamiliar with this vocabulary at the time, I was struck by the seamlessness with which colleagues transited from talk of anti-impunity, mass violence, and justice to efficiency, performance appraisal, and risk.

Confronting these two very different languages, I initially reacted with unease. How was it that a court which Kofi Annan had designated 'a gift

[2] Article 61(7) Rome Statute.
[3] Article 68 Rome Statute; Rule 85 International Criminal Court Rules of Procedure and Evidence, ICC-PIDS-LT-02-002/13_Eng (Rules of Procedure and Evidence).

1.1 A TALE OF TWO TONGUES

of hope to future generations' could so easily take up this banal lingo?[4] Was it possible for a criminal tribunal to fulfil its requirements of independence, impartiality, and legality in the face of management pressure to efficiently deliver positive results?[5] Where did this leave those in whose name the court purported to act? My unease reached its peak when I read that ICC officials ended a 'retreat on efficiencies' in Poland with a trip to the Nazi extermination camp at Auschwitz-Birkenau.[6] Surely the irony of visiting that horrifyingly efficient system of people management cannot have been lost on them?[7]

Putting aside the tone-deaf nature of such a visit, I began to rationalise that even the most utopian ideals demand some institutional fleshing-out. And building an 'entire administrative infrastructure from scratch' was no easy task.[8] Any institution charged with ending impunity and strengthening international justice would have to take regular stock of its performance, monitor progress, and engage in reform in order to fulfil such an ambitious mission. Given the rather staid and rigid qualities of law, were techniques of cost accounting, strategic planning, and human resources management not better avenues for court improvement? Officials and scholars seemed to think so.

My scepticism took a back seat as I ended my internship and left The Hague. But management kept on coming. The Assembly of States Parties approved several audits of court organs and their activities, while also placing funding aside for the recruitment of management consultants PricewaterhouseCoopers, Mannet, and others to evaluate internal performance. Institutional experiments around workflow procedures, the onboarding of personnel, and risk management came and went. All the

---

[4] 'Secretary-General Says Establishment of International Criminal Court is Major Step in March Towards Universal Human Rights, Rule of Law' (Press Release) L/2890 (20 July 1998), available at: www.un.org/press/en/1998/19980720.l2890.html.

[5] This concern was also articulated in Sara Kendall, 'Commodifying Global Justice: Economies of Accountability at the International Criminal Court' (2015) 13 *Journal of International Criminal Justice* 113–134.

[6] 'Judges of the ICC Visit Auschwitz-Birkenau at the End of their Retreat on Efficiencies' (Press Release) ICC-CPI-20170626-PR1314 (26 June 2017), available at: www.icc-cpi.int/news/judges-icc-visit-auschwitz-birkenau-end-their-retreat-efficiencies.

[7] Similar connections are made in Zygmunt Bauman, *Modernity and the Holocaust* (Polity Press 1989).

[8] Philippe Kirsch Address to the Assembly of States Parties, Assembly of States Parties 7th Session, 14 November 2008, 9, available at: https://asp.icc-cpi.int/NR/rdonlyres/EB40944C-C250-4466-B99A-2F5ACDC8C941/0/ICCASPASP7GenDebePresident_Kirsch.pdf.

4   INTRODUCTION

while, organ leaders and individual staff members were becoming the
'responsible managers of the funds which the States Parties have provided'.[9] Antonio Cassese's early claim that 'a court of law is not a factory'
fell victim to discussions on court 'production line[s]', 'bottlenecks',
'efficiency indicators', and 'demand'.[10] As some participants began to
label the court Eurocentric and neo-colonial, official desires to optimise
seemed only to grow. With this, so too did my suspicion about
management's role.[11]

This book is an attempt to confront and think through this suspicion.
It is concerned with the relationship between the anti-impunity apparatus of the ICC and the ideas and practices of management which are
now institutionally pervasive. The vast majority of practitioners and
scholars who have sought to articulate that relationship (and there are
not many) have often posited management as being in the service of the
court's anti-impunity efforts. In simplified form, management practices
are objective tools which help the ICC, its organs, processes, and professionals to function better. Yet this book not only challenges the immediate effectiveness of such tools but also opens up a range of much more
subtle effects that management generates for the institution and its
professionals. In brief, the relationship between these two languages
turns out to be much more complex and constitutive of the project of
global justice than previously thought.

The book therefore studies management's role and effects on the ICC
as the primary institution of global justice in the twenty-first century.
I begin by introducing management in isolation from the court. The
book is a rare attempt to bring management ideas and practices, as well

---

[9] Sang-Hyun Song Remarks to the 11th Session of the Assembly of States Parties, Assembly
of States Parties 11th Session, 14 November 2012, available at: www.icc-cpi.int/sites/
default/files/NR/rdonlyres/0EEEED0E-5BA8-4894-8AB5-3C2C90CD301B/0/
ASP11OpeningPICCSongENG.pdf.

[10] Report on the Special Court for Sierra Leone, para. 58. Cassese reasons that 'its output
and productivity cannot be accurately measured by counting either the number of items
it has produced or the number of hours or days it takes to produce them. While the
efficiency of a Court is one aspect of its overall impact, the true measure of a court is in
the quality, and not the speed, of its judgements'. The language of bottlenecks and
production is from the ICC Report on the Court Capacity Model, ICC-ASP/5/10,
21 August 2006, para. 25.

[11] On a 'hermeneutics of suspicion', see Paul Ricoeur, *Freud and Philosophy: An Essay on
Interpretation* (Yale University Press 1970) 356. See also Eve Kosofsky Sedgwick,
'Paranoid Reading and Reparative Reading, Or, You're So Paranoid, You Probably
Think This Essay is About You' in Eve Kosofsky Sedgwick, *Touching Feeling: Affect,
Pedagogy, Performativity* (Duke University Press 2003) 123–151.

1.2 Management Defined

as the heterodox literature on critical management studies (CMS), into conversation with the ICC and its scholarship. Rather than attempting a single definition, I conceptualise management by thinking with critical social theory, as well as CMS. Thereafter, I situate management within the contemporary ICC before looking to critical international law scholarship on managerialism, technocracy, and expertise to articulate the book's theoretical axioms. I then summarise the argument in brief. The introduction ends by outlining the book and its stylistic choices.

1.2 Management Defined

There are as many definitions of management as there are of international law. Management has been described as a 'delegation of ownership',[12] a set of tasks for directing and co-ordinating production, a practice of control by managers,[13] a powerful class,[14] a post-capitalist ideology,[15] a historical period in late capitalism,[16] and a language.[17] Management is also 'an academic discipline', with all the disciplinary skirmishes and cross-disciplinary borrowings that characterise scholarly research.[18] Certainly, management may be all of these things; as famed management theorist Peter Drucker put it, '"management" denotes both a function and the people who discharge it. It denotes a social position and authority, but also a discipline and a field of study'.[19] For the purposes of this book, these definitions may be divided into two broad camps: the 'managerialist' and the 'critical' approaches. The managerialist approach represents the 'mainstream' or common sense

[12] Peter Drucker, *Management: Tasks, Responsibilities, Practices* [1974] (Harper Collins 2008) 2.

[13] Harry Braverman, *Labour and Monopoly Capital: The Degradation of Work in the Twentieth Century* [1974] (Monthly Review Press 1998) 68.

[14] James Burnham, *The Managerial Revolution: What Is Happening in the World* (The John Day Company Inc. 1941).

[15] Thomas Klikauer, *Managerialism: Critique of an Ideology* (Palgrave 2013).

[16] Willard F. Enteman, *Managerialism: The Emergence of a New Ideology* (University of Wisconsin Press 1993) 156.

[17] Robert Protherough and John Pick, *Managing Britannia: Culture and Management in Modern Britain* (Imprint Academic 2003) 45–46.

[18] Martin Parker, 'Managerialism' in Mark Tadajewski et al. (eds.), *Key Concepts in Critical Management Studies* (SAGE Publishing 2011) 157. See also Nik Rajkovic, 'The Space between Us: Law, Teleology and the New Orientalism of Counterdisciplinarity' in Wouter Werner, Marieke de Hoon and Alexis Gálan (eds.), *The Law of International Lawyers: Reading Martti Koskenniemi* (Cambridge University Press 2017) 167–196.

[19] Drucker, 'Management' 3.

6   INTRODUCTION

understanding of management visible in the courses at Business Schools and the strategy meetings of large-scale organisations.[20] The critical approach, though popular in some pockets of academia, is rarely taken up institutionally but instead as a mode of theoretical engagement.

Mainstream understandings of management characterise it as an objective and positivist set of techniques, processes, and ideas designed to make organisations function effectively. This has led one of the leading textbooks on management thought to offer a definition of management as 'the activity whose purpose is to achieve desired results through the efficient allocation and utilization of human and material resources'.[21] While very few ICC practitioners or scholars have sought to conceptualise the term, this mainstream position is popularly accepted in such circles. As seen in later chapters, when ICC presidents, registrars, legal officers, and commentators invoke something called management, they largely adopt this position, studying and evaluating management's functional effects as a set of neutral tools.

The critical alternative, reflected in the major works of CMS, differs from the mainstream position in several respects. As Stokes defines it,

> critical management studies (CMS) challenges the normative and mainstream representations of the structures and assumptions of human experiences in relation to organisational and managerial contexts and environments. It aims to critique and point up shortcomings in mainstream portrayals of management.[22]

These representations and portrayals include the assumption that management works but also that it is objective and politically neutral.[23] Critical Management Studies comprises critical sociologists, economists, organisations theorists, and psychologists, and eclectically draws on the critical tradition in social theory, including Marxism, post-structuralism,

---

[20] Chris Grey, *A Very Short, Fairly Interesting and Reasonably Cheap Book about Studying Organisations* (SAGE Publishing 2005) 106.

[21] Daniel A. Wren and Arthur G. Bedeian, *The Evolution of Management Thought* (Wiley 2017) 3.

[22] Peter Stokes, *Critical Concepts in Management and Organisation Studies* (Palgrave 2011) 30.

[23] For an overview, see Chris Grey and Hugh Willmott, 'Introduction' in Chris Grey and Hugh Willmott (eds.), *Critical Management Studies: A Reader* (Oxford University Press 2005) 1–6. Critical management studies represents, reacts to, and seeks to counterbalance a crisis of faith in the 'rationalistic models of orthodox management studies . . . positivism and functionalism', Chris Grey, 'Towards a Critique of Managerialism: The Contribution of Simone Weil' (1996) 33 *Journal of Management Studies* 591–611, at 592.

1.2 MANAGEMENT DEFINED

feminist, and postcolonial approaches to organisations and management. Its chief aim is to 'challenge[] prevailing relations of domination – patriarchal, neo-imperialist as well as capitalist – and anticipate[] the development of alternatives to them'.[24] Under these influences, CMS offers a thick, contextualised, and troubling picture of management in modern institutions. I therefore elaborate these conceptual strands of CMS to offer a critical approach to management as the approach guiding this book. International lawyers will likely recognise many of these positions in the insights of critical legal theorists and their studies of international (criminal) law.

An initial critical reading of management sees it as a set of discourses and techniques of power/knowledge active in assembling, arranging, and dispersing contemporary institutions and their participants. To elaborate, I briefly consider the notions of power, techniques, and knowledge drawing principally on the work of Michel Foucault. It is true that mainstream thinking has much to contribute to these notions. Mainstream management thinkers are certainly not devoid of a theory of power. However, they often overlook power's diffuse, subtle, and changing manifestations. Mainstream examples of power include struggles between and within organisations over control and authority. This is best represented in the figure of the overweening manager exerting control over their subordinates.[25] In this analysis, power is reified as a coercive 'thing' capable of being possessed and wielded by one over another. This reading of power is familiar to international lawyers as the *realpolitik* of geopolitical life in which states, organisations, or governance regimes tussle to maximise their interests.[26]

---

[24] Mats Alvesson, Todd Bridgman and Hugh Willmott, 'Introduction' in Mats Alvesson, Todd Bridgman and Hugh Willmott (eds.), *The Oxford Handbook of Critical Management Studies* (Oxford University Press 2013) 1–28, at 1. For a poststructuralist account, see Philip Hancock and Melissa Tyler, '"MOT your Life!": Critical Management Studies and the Management of Everyday Life' (2004) 57 *Human Relations* 619–645, at 620. Anshuman Prasad (ed.), *Against the Grain: Advances in Postcolonial Organisation Studies* (Universitetsforlaget 2012) offers a postcolonial reading of organisations. On feminism within CMS, see Joan Acker, 'Hierarchies, Jobs, Bodies: A Theory of Gendered Organisations' (1990) 4 *Gender & Society* 139–158; Karen Lee Ashcraft, 'Gender and Diversity: Other Ways to "Make a Difference"' in Alvesson et al. (eds.), 'The Oxford Handbook of Critical Management Studies' 304–327, at 324-7 contains an excellent bibliography on feminist thinking in management and organisation studies.

[25] This approach is visible in Burnham's sociology of a new managerial class taking over the levers of state power in the New Deal United States, Burnham, 'Managerial Revolution'.

[26] Hedley Bull, *The Anarchical Society: A Study of Order in World Politics* (Springer 1977).

8INTRODUCTION

Foucault has challenged this account of power, most famously in volume 1 of *The History of Sexuality*, with another which he depicts as 'the multiplicity of force relations immanent in the sphere in which they operate and which constitute their own organisation'.[27] This multiplicity of relations includes processes, chains, systems, strategies, disjunctions, contradictions, networks, and assemblages that manifest institutional apparatuses such as the state, society, and law.[28] Power is not possessed but an effect threaded into the 'always local and unstable' relations between people, places, and institutions.[29] Similarly, this book refrains from denoting states, experts, or the ICC as bearers of power since power *effects* these entities in a complex assemblage of people, structures, and practices.

Decentring the bearer of power also decentres the manager as a key figure. Mainstream and critical theorists of management thought have often focused on a managerial class.[30] For managerialists, managers are crucial mediators between ownership and workers, ensuring that both communicate and work effectively to their mutual benefit. For Drucker, managers represent 'the basic resource of the organisational enterprise'.[31] Managers have also occupied an important place in the critical management literature. Here, they emerge as enforcers of capitalist relations of domination, or as an exploitative class in their own right.[32] Whether commended or reviled, managers often take centre stage in studies of organisations.[33]

This book brackets the figure of the manager, partly because the hierarchical structure of the ICC means that most people are managers of *someone* or *something* at one point or another, and are often *manager* and *managed* concurrently. It is not possible to identify such an isolated

---

[27] Michel Foucault, *The Will to Knowledge: The History of Sexuality Volume 1* [1976] (Penguin 1998) 92.

[28] Ibid., 92–3.

[29] Ole Jacob Sending and Iver B. Neumann, 'Governance to Governmentality: Analysing NGOs, States, and Power' (2006) 50 *International Studies Quarterly* 651–672.

[30] See Wren and Bedeian, 'Evolution of Management Thought'; Burnham, 'Managerial Revolution'.

[31] Drucker, 'Management' 235.

[32] Burnham, 'Managerial Revolution', 82–5; Braverman, 'Labour and Monopoly Capital', 403–404. See Robert R. Locke and J.-C. Spender, *Confronting Managerialism: How the Business Elite and Their Schools Threw Our Lives Out of Balance* (Bloomsbury Academic 2011) xi.

[33] Drucker, 'Management' 521. See Stefan Sveningsson and Mats Alvesson, *Managerial Lives: Leadership and Identity in an Imperfect World* (Cambridge University Press 2016).

1.2 MANAGEMENT DEFINED

group or *a priori* class in this institution. The *who* of management thus becomes less important than the *how*. Looking to this how and thus to managerial relations of power brings forth 'the complex of mundane programmes, calculations, techniques, apparatuses, documents and procedures' involved in governing.[34] This network Foucault termed 'governmentality', a thick and intersecting arrangement of power relations spanning micro and macro scales of governance.[35] Considering these arrangements of power, Foucault also pointed towards the 'range of multiform tactics' comprising it, which flow through myriad and minute spaces rather than the decisions of political or institutional leaders.[36] In a management register, these tactics include discourses of efficiency, performance, success, supply, and austerity, as well as specific practices or 'governmental technologies' of strategic planning, audit, performance indicators, performance appraisal, best practices, lessons learnt, organigrams, and restructuring.[37] These and more are the 'techniques of power' that form the ICC.[38] This book follows the life cycle of such practices, rather than their 'users' or 'the institution', to understand their various roles and effects.

Management's effects are not simply coercive but constitutive of individual subjectivities and the institution itself.[39] For the ICC lawyer – and other professionals – management helps mediate the efficient, committed technician of institutionalised global justice through human

---

[34] Nikolas Rose and Peter Miller, 'Political Power beyond the State: Problematics of Government' (1992) 43 *British Journal of Sociology* 173–205, at 175.

[35] Wendy Larner and William Walters, 'Introduction: Global Governmentality' in Wendy Larner and William Walters (eds.), *Global Governmentality: Governing International Spaces* (Routledge 2004) 1–20, at 2. See Michel Foucault, 'Governmentality', in Graham Burchell, Colin Gordon and Peter Miller (eds.), *The Foucault Effect: Studies in Governmentality* (University of Chicago Press 1991) 87–104. In international law, see Nik Rajkovic, '"Global Law" and Governmentality: Reconceptualizing the "Rule of Law" as Rule "through" Law' (2010) 18 *European Journal of International Relations* 29–52; Stephen Legg, '"The Life of Individuals as well as of Nations": International Law and the League of Nations' Anti-Trafficking Governmentalities' (2012) 25 *Leiden Journal of International Law* 647–664; Isobel Roele, *Articulating Security: The United Nations and its Infra-Law* (Cambridge University Press 2021).

[36] Foucault, 'Governmentality' 95. See Michael Barnett and Raymond Duvall, 'Power in International Politics' (2005) 59 *International Organisation* 39–75.

[37] Colin Gordon, 'Governmental Rationality: An Introduction', in Burchell, 'The Foucault Effect' 1–52, at 4.

[38] Michel Chauvière and Stephen S. Mick, 'The French Sociological Critique of Managerialism: Themes and Frameworks' (2011) 39 *Critical Sociology* 135–143, at 140.

[39] Michel Foucault, *Discipline and Punish: The Birth of the Prison* [1977] (Penguin Books 1991) 23.

resourcing practices of recruitment, probation, and appraisal.[40] On an organ level, management also arranges activities such as prosecutorial investigations and outreach programmes through capacity models, workflows, and strategic plans.[41] Finally, management also produces novel legal arguments as part of and response to the well-worn argumentative dilemmas facing the court and its lawyers. In these various ways, management fashions the ICC professional, the organisation, and its argumentative field.

Management produces the professional, the organisation, and its arguments through expert knowledge. This knowledge is devised and deployed by various actors within and beyond the court's walls, and can be understood as the sets of tools mentioned previously but also a shared professional attitude towards the court's anti-impunity problematic. Much like international law, then, management is a 'field of people sharing professional tools and expertise, as well as a sensibility, viewpoint, and mission'.[42] And such expertise is not the exclusive domain of lawyers or managers but is mediated by judges, investigators, interns, scholars, students, and policymakers, not to mention those most affected by mass atrocities. Foregrounding management allows us to redescribe what these actors are doing as *managerial* work, and to appreciate that they each manage the court's human, financial, and administrative resources in diverse ways.

While certain actors perform managerial work, as we will see, they continue to conduct their international legal work alongside.[43] Yet this legal work entails not only the application of normatively constraining yet apolitical rules. Law is also part of the *dispositif* and, as such, comprises its own set of discourses and techniques of rule to form a professional practice. Law is a tactic which is 'constantly growing as the

---

[40] Michel Foucault, 'The Subject and Power' (1982) 8 *Critical Inquiry* 777–795, at 781. Chapter 4 discusses these practices as forms of 'micro-management'.

[41] See Martin Parker, *Organisational Culture and Identity: Unity and Division at Work* (SAGE Publishing 2000) 69–70. See also Mats Alvesson and Stanley Deetz, 'Critical Theory and Postmodernism: Approaches to Organisation Studies' in Grey and Willmott, 'Critical Management Studies' 60–106, at 85; Andreas Georg Scherer, 'Critical Theory and its Contribution to Critical Management Studies' in Alvesson and Willmott, *Oxford Handbook of Critical Management Studies*, 29–51, at 37.

[42] David Kennedy, 'When Renewal Repeats: Thinking Against the Box' (1999–2000) 32 *NYU Journal of International Law and Politics* 335–500, at 340. See Jean d'Aspremont et al. (eds.), *International Law as a Profession* (Cambridge University Press 2017).

[43] Fleur Johns, *Non-Legality and International Law: Unruly Law* (Cambridge University Press 2013) 1.

1.2 MANAGEMENT DEFINED

exercise of power and the accretion of knowledge'.[44] As such, it goes beyond the text and application of the Rome Statute to encompass the arguments deployed by ICC lawyers, the theories of justice posited by scholars, and the practices of evidence-gathering, outreach, and reparation that comprise the everyday work of court professionals. The managerial work of organisational improvement thus appears alongside the international legal work of anti-impunity.

Often, managerial and legal work coalesce wherein one conditions, buttresses, and effects the other. Legal concepts, processes, and arguments frame management practices and motivate their application to a particular problem. The OTP must attempt to discharge its investigatory powers under the Statute despite certain budgetary limitations. Accordingly, it has devised workflow systems, methods of prioritisation and selection, and capacity models to funnel its resources. Yet the opposite dynamic of management effecting or shaping law is also visible. When ICC judges decided not to open an investigation into the situation in Afghanistan in 2019, their primary argument concerned organisational sustainability and the proper use of court resources.[45] Management discourse clearly affected judicial decision-making. In these examples, law and management become intertwined, reciprocally conditioning and constituting one another.

Under such circumstances, the question arises whether the distinction between law and management collapses altogether.[46] After all, both are professional and institutional practices that disperse arguments and resources institutionally. Building on this similarity, though, law and management are still received and deployed very differently within the ICC.[47] The distinction between them is laid down and policed by those

---

[44] Anthony Beck, 'Foucault and Law: The Collapse of Law's Empire' (1996) 16 *Oxford Journal of Legal Studies* 489–502, at 501. For law as tactic, see Foucault, 'Governmentality' 95.

[45] This decision forms the backdrop for a discussion on the ICC argumentative field as 'meso-management' in Chapter 5.

[46] This is a query raised in Frédéric Mégret, 'International Criminal Justice as a Juridical Field' (2018) 13 *Champ pénal* 1, at 3.

[47] Jens Meierhenrich, 'The Practice of International Law: A Theoretical Analysis' (2013) 76 *Law & Contemporary Problems* 1–83. Sinclair describes international law as 'a discipline, discourse, and practice of reform', Guy Fiti Sinclair, *To Reform the World: International Organisations and the Making of Modern States* (Oxford University Press 2017) 2. For a reading of institutional practice based on actor-network theory, see Dimitri van den Meerssche, *The World Bank's Lawyers: The Life of International Law as Institutional Practice* (Oxford University Press 2022).

INTRODUCTION

who invoke and apply them. Institutional officials often treat certain practices as law or law-like because of their source, the process of their creation, or purported normative force. Having different traits, pedigree, and purposes, management will often be received differently. In fact, management is often engaged with precisely because it is *not* read as law: management is said to be efficient, flexible, and apolitical where law is slow, rigid, and politicised. Without collapsing the law/management distinction, both can be viewed as professional practices subsumed under either category in light of the professional sensibilities of those working within and around the ICC as a particular institutional space. This may, of course, differ in other international legal spaces.

1.3 Management Situated: The ICC *Dispositif*

Highlighting the role of power, techniques, and knowledge means capturing the wider *dispositif,* or discursive apparatus, of anti-impunity.[48] The Rome Statute 'ecosystem' is a global justice apparatus consisting of the players, procedures, practices, arguments, and places of global justice. Global justice is a field oriented around various institutional assemblages operating under the rationale of closing the impunity gap.[49] This gap is framed, like other contemporary global issues, as a governance problem to be solved or minimised. Its actors and experts put themselves in the service of that aim daily. Their procedures and practices span investigations and prosecutions – the 'core' functions of international criminal tribunals – as well as more peripheral but no less important practices of stigmatisation, representation, translation, outreach, reparation, and marketing, which also shape the field.[50] Its chief argumentative dilemmas concern the selectivity of investigations, the relationship between

---

[48] Defined in Michel Foucault, 'Confessions of the Flesh' in Colin Gordon (ed.), *Power/ Knowledge: Selected Interviews and Other Writings 1972–1977 by Michel Foucault* (Pantheon Books 1980) 194–228.

[49] Zeid Raad Al Hussein et al., 'The International Criminal Court Needs Fixing', *New Atlanticist*, 24 April 2019, available at: www.atlanticcouncil.org/blogs/new-atlanticist/ the-international-criminal-court-needs-fixing.

[50] See, for example, Frédéric Mégret, 'Practices of Stigmatisation' (2013) 76 *Law & Contemporary Problems* 287–318; Sara Kendall and Sarah Nouwen, 'Representational Practices at the International Criminal Court: The Gap Between Juridified and Abstract Victimhood' (2013) 76 *Law & Contemporary Problems* 235–262; Leila Ullrich, 'Beyond the "Global–Local Divide": Local Intermediaries, Victims and the Justice Contestations of the International Criminal Court' (2016) 14 *Journal of International Criminal Justice* 543–568, at 557–563; Luke Moffett, *Justice for Victims before the International Criminal*

1.3 MANAGEMENT SITUATED: THE ICC *DISPOSITIF*

international authority and domestic sovereignty, co-operation, and defendant- versus victim-centred justice.[51] Its key sites are The Hague, sub-Saharan Africa, and historically Nuremberg and Rome.

The global justice architecture thus goes far beyond the conventional focus on the Rome Statute, judges, and their decisions. In an effort to construct anti-impunity as a regime and a governance problem, the ICC occupies a central place in the imaginary of global justice. Yet such a place remains unstable thanks to entrenched dilemmas about the version of justice the court renders. In the twenty years since it became operational, the court and its infrastructure have been the subject of wide-ranging interventions, ranging from the promotional to the oppositional. I briefly capture the discourse around and against the ICC to better frame management's relationship to this institutional project.

The principal vector of policy and scholarly engagement with the ICC project is that of effectiveness.[52] Despite its low conviction rate and high cost, the court is considered effective on multiple fronts.[53] It has prosecuted multiple individuals for serious crimes ranging from the conscription of child soldiers and mass murder to the destruction of cultural property. Beyond this central plank of its work, the court has also worked with national criminal justice systems to prevent crimes from going unpunished. This complementary role has seen the court intervene to prosecute where states are 'unwilling or unable' to do so but has also allowed it to provide technical assistance to local authorities or promote domestic law reform.[54] The court's innovative victims regime has

---

Court (Routledge 2014) 143; Christine Schwöbel-Patel, *Marketing Global Justice: The Political Economy of International Criminal Law* (Cambridge University Press 2021).

[51] For further details, see Chapter 5.

[52] Schwöbel-Patel describes this as 'effectiveness critique' in contrast to 'assumptions critique', see Christine Schwöbel, 'Introduction' in Christine Schwöbel (ed.), *Critical Approaches to International Criminal Law: An Introduction* (Routledge 2015) 1–14, at 1.

[53] David Davenport, 'International Criminal Court: 12 Years, $1 Billion, 2 Convictions', *Forbes*, 12 March 2014, available at: www.forbes.com/sites/daviddavenport/2014/03/12/international-criminal-court-12-years-1-billion-2-convictions-2/?sh=4d2e0b672405.

[54] See article 17 Rome Statute. Important scholarly contributions on complementarity include Sarah Nouwen, *Complementarity in the Line of Fire: The Catalysing Effect of the International Criminal Court in Uganda and Sudan* (Cambridge University Press 2013); Phil Clark, *Distant Justice: The Impact of the International Criminal Court on African Politics* (Cambridge University Press 2018); Christian de Vos, *Complementarity, Catalysts, Compliance: The International Criminal Court in Uganda, Kenya, and the Democratic Republic of Congo* (Cambridge University Press 2020); Patryk I. Labuda, *International Criminal Tribunals and Domestic Accountability: In the Court's Shadow* (forthcoming, Oxford University Press).

14   INTRODUCTION

permitted individuals and communities to participate in trial proceedings and to receive reparations for atrocities committed against them. The court has allowed historical and group narratives to be articulated in moments of individual and communal catharsis.[55] Such achievements of what remains an innovative institutional experiment are not to be dismissed.

Most critiques of the court challenge these achievements on their own effectiveness terms. For the billions of euros invested in it, the court's record remains underwhelming. Its procedures remain slow while various episodes, including the prosecutor's overreliance on intermediaries and the low quality of court jurisprudence, demonstrate a still infant institution.[56] But there are also those who query the court's underlying assumptions and possible consequences. Tallgren has shown how 'artificial' and 'ridiculous' the ICC's claims to international justice and ending impunity are, given the tools at its disposal.[57] Nesiah cautions further by recalling 'the intertwined history and legacy of impunity that has accompanied every attempt at international justice'.[58] Victor's justice and hence impunity, from Nuremberg to Bogoro, is a recurring feature of anti-impunity. Even the anti-impunity efforts of the court are heavily circumscribed and partial. The ICC is said to focus on individuals rather than structures, on recent rather than historical events and transgenerational patterns of violence, and on direct, physical acts rather than slow, structural, and colonial forms of domination. In creating such a picture of global anti-impunity, the court works to 'naturalize, to exclude from the political battle, certain phenomena which are in fact the preconditions for maintenance of the existing governance'.[59] Such an argument sees the court as both reproducing of and dependent upon conditions of subordination for its continued existence.

These critiques have arisen out of the court's encounters with situation countries over the past twenty years. While supporters have witnessed co-operation and complementary justice-seeking between the court and

---

[55] Barrie Sander, 'The Expressive Turn of International Criminal Justice: A Field in Search of Meaning' (2019) 32 *Leiden Journal of International Law* 851–872.

[56] Ullrich, 'Global–Local Divide'.

[57] Immi Tallgren, 'The Sensibility and Sense of International Criminal Law' (2002) 13 *European Journal of International Law* 561–595.

[58] Vasuki Nesiah, 'Doing History with Impunity' in Karen Engle, Zina Miller and D.M. Davis (eds.), *Anti-Impunity and the Human Rights Agenda* (Cambridge University Press 2016) 95–122, at 96.

[59] Tallgren, 'Sensibility and Sense' 594–5.

1.3 MANAGEMENT SITUATED: THE ICC *DISPOSITIF*   15

national authorities, others highlight the dominating effects of the court's relationship with states parties, particularly for those caught up in mass atrocities. In Uganda, for example, former ICC prosecutors have 'uncritically taken on the point of view of one side' in the conflict between government and rebel forces, thereby downplaying government oppression of Ugandan citizens.[60] This has arguably consolidated authoritarian state apparatuses to the court's benefit.[61] Moreover, applying its penal lens, the ICC has been said to reduce complex dynamics of conflict, and political and economic relations to matters of individual guilt or innocence, and to an inherent vulnerability of 'victim communities'.[62] This focus on individual responsibility has prioritised institutional interests, often at the expense of ongoing national efforts. This was a particular concern levelled against the court in its interventions in Sudan while peace negotiations were in process.

Many such critiques revolve around the court's ostensible reproduction of colonial relations between Western actors and communities of the Global South long after the end of formal decolonisation. The vast majority of the court's activities concern the African continent, and it has only ever convicted Africans in its twenty-year history. Even ardent supporters are forced to confront such allegations, attempting to play down the possibility of an 'anti-African bias'.[63] The greatest concern has come from African states themselves. Despite early optimism among various African signatories to the Rome Statute, the court's pursuit of certain persons and types of criminality has led to frustration that Africa is being unfairly targeted, or that the court is simply designed to produce such outcomes. A sustained campaign by African states parties and the African Union to prompt mass withdrawal from the ICC has only recently abated.[64]

---

[60] Mahmood Mamdani, 'The New Humanitarian Order', *The Nation*, 29 September 2008, available at: www.thenation.com/article/new-humanitarian-order/.

[61] For a summary, see Richard Clements, 'Near, Far, Wherever You Are: Distance and Proximity in International Criminal Law' (2021) 32 *European Journal of International Law* 327–350.

[62] Adam Branch, 'Uganda's Civil War and the Politics of ICC Intervention' (2007) 21 *Ethics & International Affairs* 179–198; Mahmood Mamdani, *When Victims Become Killers: Colonialism, Nativism and the Genocide in Rwanda* (Princeton University Press 2001).

[63] Rachel López, 'Black Guilt, White Guilt at the International Criminal Court' in Matiangai Sirleaf (ed.), *Race and National Security* (Oxford University Press 2023).

[64] African Union Assembly decision 622(XXVIII), Decision on the International Criminal Court, Doc. EX.CL/1006(XX), Twenty-Eighth Ordinary Session of the Assembly of the Union, 30–31 January 2017, para. 6, available at: https://au.int/sites/default/files/deci

16   INTRODUCTION

This combination of achievement, scepticism, and opposition forms the terms of debate for the court. Court officials often rebuff such criticism as either pessimistic or as conducive to current and would-be perpetrators. On the charge of an anti-African bias, the court has entirely rejected the analysis and demands of its detractors. Former prosecutor, Luis Moreno-Ocampo has likened peddlers of the bias argument to Holocaust deniers.[65] While extreme, such rebuttals are also visible in less rhetorical interventions within mainstream scholarship. While largely accepting critiques of the court's effectiveness, such scholars reject claims of bias. In doing so, they 'largely forget[] to consider the complicity of international criminal law in injustices in the world'.[66]

Lastly, the court's *dispositif* also encompasses alternative interpretations of the organisation and its work. Many critical interventions have sought to read the court 'against the grain' as a mode of argumentation, deconstruction, and political action. Scholars have therefore interpreted the court variously as a distribution centre for stigma;[67] a sphere for political contestation through historical narrative; a body that acts on the basis of local choice and conditions;[68] an 'open, democratic and

---

sions/32520-sc19553_e_original_-_assembly_decisions_621-641_-_xxviii.pdf. See also Max du Plessis and Chris Gevers, 'The Sum of Four Fears: African States and the International Criminal Court in Retrospect – Part I', Opinio Juris blog, 8 July 2019, available at: http://opiniojuris.org/2019/07/08/the-sum-of-four-fears-african-states-and-the-international-criminal-court-in-retrospect-part-i/.

[65] Luis Moreno-Ocampo, 'From Brexit to African ICC Exit: A Dangerous Trend', Just Security blog, 31 October 2016, available at: www.justsecurity.org/33972/brexit-african-icc-exit-dangerous-trend/. Cf. the response to Ocampo in Itamar Mann and Ntina Tzouvala, 'Letter to the Editor: Response to Luis Moreno Ocampo on Comparisons to Holocaust Denial', Just Security blog, 1 November 2016, available at: www.justsecurity.org/34016/letter-editor-conflating-icc-african-bias-holocaust-denial-polarizing-dangerous-irresponsible/.

[66] Christine Schwöbel, 'The Comfort of International Criminal Law' (2013) 24 *Law & Critique* 169–191, at 183.

[67] Mégret, 'Practices of Stigmatisation'. See also Frédéric Mégret, 'What Sort of Global Justice Is "International Criminal Justice"?' (2015) 13 *Journal of International Criminal Justice* 77–96.

[68] Cf. Vasuki Nesiah, 'Local Ownership of Global Governance' (2016) 14 *Journal of International Criminal Justice* 985–1009. This form of complementarity would be residual as opposed to 'burden-sharing', see Padraig McAuliffe, 'From Watchdog to Workhorse: Explaining the Emergence of the ICC's Burden-Sharing Policy as an Example of Creeping Cosmopolitanism' (2014) 13 *Chinese Journal of International Law* 259–296.

1.3 MANAGEMENT SITUATED: THE ICC *DISPOSITIF* 17

participatory' process for establishing accountability;[69] a public good;[70] a 'transitional justice mechanism';[71] a development or anti-development agency;[72] a 'security court' for those living insecurely,[73] including, among others, women and gender non-conforming groups;[74] an anti-racist institution;[75] and a people's tribunal.[76]

It is this ICC *dispositif* to which management ideas and practices relate. Management shapes and is shaped by this discourse of global justice. Although the book's primary aim is to demonstrate the connection between the two, it can also be read as a story about why it is so

---

[69] Antony Anghie and B. S. Chimni, 'Third World Approaches to International Law and Individual Responsibility in Internal Conflict' (2003) 2 *Chinese Journal of International Law* 77–103, at 92.

[70] Kendall, 'Commodifying Global Justice' 118.

[71] Obiora Okafor and Uchechukwu Ngwaba, 'The International Criminal Court as a "Transitional Justice" Mechanism in Africa: Some Critical Reflections' (2014) 9 *International Journal of Transitional Justice* 90–108, at 106.

[72] See Helen Clark, Keynote Address to the 11th Session of the Assembly of States Parties to the International Criminal Court: Human Development and International Justice', 19 November 2012, available at: https://asp.icc-cpi.int/sites/asp/files/NR/rdonlyres/E10A5253-DA2D-46CE-90B8-7497426E9C39/0/ICCASP11_COMPKeynote_Remarks_HCENG.pdf; Errol Mendes, 'The important role of the IMF and external creditors in case of arrest warrants from the ICC – the Case of Sudan', OTP Guest Lecture Series (2009). Contemporary development projects and development thinking have been subject to much critical intervention in recent years; see Sundhya Pahuja, *Decolonising International Law: Development, Economic Growth and the Politics of Universality* (Cambridge University Press 2011); Celine Tan, *Governance through Development: Poverty Reduction Strategies, International Law and the Disciplining of Third World States* (Routledge 2011); Luis Eslava, *Local Space, Global Life: The Everyday Operation of International Law and Development* (Cambridge University Press 2015). Nouwen and Werner hint at this role by referring to ICL as 'redistribution', Sarah M. H. Nouwen and Wouter G. Werner, 'Monopolising Global Justice: International Criminal Law as Challenge to Human Diversity' (2015) 13 *Journal of International Criminal Justice* 157–176, at 170.

[73] George P. Fletcher and Jens David Ohlin, 'The ICC – Two Courts in One?' (2006) 4 *Journal of International Criminal Justice* 428–433, at 428–31.

[74] Christine Chinkin, *Women, Peace and Security and International Law* (Cambridge University Press 2022).

[75] López, 'Black Guilt, White Guilt' 10. See also Frédéric Mégret and Randle DelFalco, 'The Invisibility of Race at the ICC: Lessons from the US Criminal Justice System' (2019) 7 *London Review of International Law* 55–87.

[76] Dianne Otto, 'Beyond Legal Justice: Some Personal Reflections on People's Tribunals, Listening and Responsibility (2017) 5 *London Review of International Law* 225–249; Sara Dehm, 'Accusing "Europe": Articulations of Migrant Justice and a Popular International Law' in Andrew Byrnes and Gabrielle Simm (eds.), *Peoples' Tribunals and International Law* (Cambridge University Press 2017) 157–181; Ayça Çubukçu, *For the Love of Humanity: The World Tribunal on Iraq* (University of Pennsylvania Press 2018).

18   INTRODUCTION

difficult to formulate and effect these alternative imaginaries – and thus
distributions – of ICC justice. The following discussion of international
legal managerialism offers the building blocks for such an account.

1.4   Management Situated: On International Legal Managerialism

With this account of the ICC project in place, it is worth considering the
tools already available to the international lawyer seeking to make sense
of management ideas and practices.[77] Management may be a relatively
under-theorised concept for international lawyers, but managerialism is
not. Over the past thirty years, a consistent stream of critical scholarship
has investigated the 'managerialism' of international law and its governance regimes.[78] I draw on these strands to fashion four axioms about
international legal expertise that can be relied upon for the study of
management. Together these axioms problematise the assumptions on
which expertise (and management) rests, namely that it works, that it is
objective, that its power is exclusively functional, and that it is
largely ahistorical.

The term 'managerialism' has multiple meanings in international law
and scholarship: as a flexible model for enhancing rule compliance,[79] a
style of judicial activism,[80] a concern with the effectiveness of law,[81] and a
tool for minimising jurisdictional overlap between courts.[82] For others,
'managerialism' captures much of what is wrong with contemporary
international law. Koskenniemi diagnoses it as a form of 'unreflective

---

[77] As detailed later in Chapter 2, the newness of management is a product of management
thought which occludes its own past uses and historical patterns. The novelty of management is also refuted by the academic experience of the managerial university, see David
West, 'The Managerial University: A Failed Experiment?, *Demos Journal*, 14 April 2016,
available at: http://demosjournal.com/article/the-managerial-university-a-failed-experi
ment/.

[78] Beginning with Martti Koskenniemi, *From Apology to Utopia: The Structure of
International Legal Argument* (Reissued with a new epilogue, Cambridge University
Press 2005).

[79] Abram Chayes and Antonia Handler Chayes, *The New Sovereignty: Compliance with
International Regulatory Agreements* (Harvard University Press 1995) 3.

[80] Judith Resnik, 'Managerial Judges' (1982) 96 *Harvard Law Review* 374–448, at 376.

[81] Hersch Lauterpacht, *The Function of Law in the International Community* [1933]
(Oxford University Press 2011) 354.

[82] Laurence Boisson de Chazournes, 'Plurality in the Fabric of International Courts and
Tribunals: The Threads of a Managerial Approach' (2017) 28 *European Journal of
International Law* 13–72.

1.4 MANAGEMENT SITUATED

pragmatism' by international lawyers,[83] while Kennedy equates it to the global rule of experts.[84] These and other scholars offer a rich sociology and genealogy of expertise even if they have not directly engaged with the practices discussed in this book. Conversely, mainstream scholars, particularly those involved in the ICC project, have often grappled with the mechanics of select management practices without employing the same analytic of power. The point, then, is to bring existing international law critiques of managerialism to the critique of management through the former's insights on expertise.

Axiom 1: Expertise May Not Do What It Claims

A first critical insight is that expertise may not do what it claims to do. This may be because projects such as the ICC are systematically unable to deliver on their ambitious goals. One frequent achievement the court lays claim to is its deterrent effect on would-be perpetrators. Yet the verifiability of such a speculative claim is suspect, with scholars disagreeing over whether such a hypothetical claim can ever be proven.[85] The goal of rendering justice, whether to victims or suspects, is equally difficult to measure, given the instability and multivalence of the concept.[86] The court has sought to shed light on these terms, as in the OTP Strategic Plan for 2012–2015, which lists specific sub-goals of ending impunity as 'prevention of crimes, complementarity achieved, justice (seen to be) done, etc'.[87] Yet none are prioritised, nor are 'prevention' or 'justice done' further defined. Determining whether a goal has been met is a difficult task when the goal itself is always open to contestation and reinterpretation.

---

[83] Koskenniemi, 'From Apology to Utopia' xiv.

[84] David Kennedy, *A World of Struggle: How Power, Law, and Expertise Shape Global Political Economy* (Princeton University Press 2016).

[85] Compare Courtney Hillebrecht, 'The Deterrent Effects of the International Criminal Court: Evidence from Libya' (2016) 42 *International Interactions* 616–643, at 628, with Yvonne Dutton and Tessa Alleblas, 'Unpacking the Deterrent Effect of the International Criminal Court: Lessons from Kenya' (2017) 91 *St. John's Law Review* 105–175, at 108.

[86] Sarah M. H. Nouwen, 'Justifying Justice' in Martti Koskenniemi and James Crawford (eds.), *Cambridge Companion to International Law* (Cambridge University Press 2012) 327–351.

[87] Office of the Prosecutor Strategic Plan June 2012–2015 (OTP Strategic Plan 2012), 11 October 2013, para. 95, available at: www.legal-tools.org/doc/954beb/pdf/.

20   INTRODUCTION

A further basis for this axiom lies in the difficulty of rendering empirical judgment of any kind within such a complex institution.[88] These critiques have been raised before. Some scholars point to the partiality of expertise arising from its predominant reliance on measurable data. The picture rendered by expert analysis omits the historical, structural, or affective traces impacting individuals and communities.[89] The ICC is particularly susceptible to this critique, given the nature of its work with complex crimes and victim groups. Furthermore, the partiality of expertise comes to shape understandings of the context, problems, and possible solutions. As Nouwen puts it, '[W]hen what matters is what is countable, what is countable determines what matters'.[90] Rather than gradually forming a more comprehensive picture, expertise tends to prioritise evaluations based on what can be evaluated, and solutions for what can be measured. Over time, expertise conditions its own object of study.

Finally, one noticeable quality of management expertise is its rapid implementation cycle. This, too, militates against evaluations of its effectiveness. Court officials have noted that since efficiency is 'an ongoing process', it is difficult to take a snapshot of management's effects in isolation.[91] The volume of managerial practices introduced within the ICC over its first two decades attests to this never-ending character of reform. As techniques are proposed, introduced, implemented, altered, discarded, or audited, new ones are quickly layered on top. The ICC's Committee on Budget and Finance is particularly susceptible to proposing new reforms even while previous processes and techniques are being implemented. Such breathlessness offers little hope of measuring the effectiveness of management expertise.

---

[88] Max Horkheimer, 'Traditional and Critical Theory', in Max Horkheimer, *Critical Theory* (Continuum 1972, trans. Matthew J. O'Connell et al.) 188; Theodore Adorno et al. (eds.), *The Positivist Dispute in German Sociology* (Heinemann Books 1977).

[89] Kevin Davis, Benedict Kingsbury and Sally Engle Merry, 'Indicators as a Technology of Global Governance' (2012) 46 *Law & Society Review* 71–104, at 74–5.

[90] Sarah Nouwen, '"*As You Set Out for Ithaka*": Practical, Epistemological, Ethical, and Existential Questions about Socio-Legal Empirical Research in Conflict' (2014) 27 *Leiden Journal of International Law* 227–260, at 230.

[91] Comprehensive Report on the Reorganisation of the Registry of the International Criminal Court, Registry, ICC, August 2016, x, available at: www.icc-cpi.int/sites/default/files/itemsDocuments/ICC-Registry-CR.pdf.

1.4 MANAGEMENT SITUATED

Axiom 2: Expertise Is Not Politically Neutral

Many ICC practitioners and scholars maintain that neither the court nor the Rome Statute framework is 'political' but is concerned only with questions of law. Interestingly, the few ICC practitioners who have written about management maintain a similar distinction between politics and management, which appears as a politically neutral means of enhancing organisational performance.[92] In this reading, expertise has no stake one way or the other in a certain set of distributive outcomes but may be put to whatever objectives are laid out for it.

Interestingly, this claim has been challenged by international criminal courts themselves. In June 2017, Co-Investigating Judges at the Extraordinary Chambers in the Courts of Cambodia (ECCC) requested submissions on a possible stay of proceedings resulting from budgetary underfunding. Having implemented the management tool of 'results-based budgeting' to monitor court spending, the ECCC was confronted with a financial shortfall. 'As a measure of success and/or progress', the judges found this budgeting tool 'incompatible with judicial independence'.[93] The judges also surmised that the ICC's uptake of similar tools displayed a tension between the 'managerialist demands around effectiveness and efficiency from the donor community' and 'fair trial principles'.[94] They warned that 'applying managerial criteria to the core judicial activity is either bound to end as an exercise in futility or risks making dangerous inroads to the judicial self-perception'.[95] Management

---

[92] Philipp Ambach and Klaus Rackwitz, 'A Model of International Judicial Administration?: The Evolution of Managerial Practices at the International Criminal Court' (2013) 76 *Law & Contemporary Problems* 119–161; Philipp Ambach, 'The "Lessons Learnt" Process at the International Criminal Court – A Suitable Vehicle for Procedural Improvements?' (2016) 12 *Zeitschrift für Internationale Strafrechtsdogmatik* 854–867; Silvia Fernández de Gurmendi, 'From the Drafting of the Procedural Provisions by States to their Revision by Judges' (2018) 16 *Journal of International Criminal Justice* 341–361; Osvaldo Zavala, 'The Budgetary Efficiency of the International Criminal Court' (2018) 18 *International Criminal Law Review* 461–488; Sam Sasan Shoamanesh, 'Institution Building: Perspective from within the Office of the Prosecutor of the International Criminal Court' (2018) 18 *International Criminal Law Review* 489–516.

[93] Combined Decision on the Impact of the Budgetary Situation on Cases 003, 004, and 004/2 and Related Submissions by the Defence for Yim Tith, Office of the Co-Investigating Judges of the Extraordinary Chambers in the Courts of Cambodia, 004/2/07-09-2009-ECCC-OCIJ (11 August 2017) para. 35, available at: www.eccc.gov.kh/sites/default/files/documents/courtdoc/%5Bdate-in-tz%5D/D349_6_EN.PDF (ECCC Combined Decision).

[94] Ibid., para. 37.

[95] Ibid., para. 43.

22   INTRODUCTION

practices may therefore carry within them a capacity to prioritise the interests of certain donors or alter how institutional actors discharge core activities.

Aside from this cautionary tale, critical international lawyers have also taken aim at the objectivity of legal expertise. Interventions by Martti Koskenniemi, Hilary Charlesworth, Christine Chinkin, and Antony Anghie expose the politics of international law from various angles.[96] There have also been efforts, by Koskenniemi in his notion of 'structural bias' and Kennedy in his idea of 'background norms', to further apply these insights to expertise. For example, Koskenniemi identified the 'structural bias' characteristic of international law's governance regimes.[97] It is this bias, Koskenniemi claims, that explains why the same arguments and actors consistently win out despite international law's indeterminacy. While governance regimes such as 'human rights' appear to be neutral as to their outcome, Koskenniemi posits that each tilts in favour of certain priorities to the exclusion of others. In that example, the human rights regime favours political and civil over socio-economic rights. There is thus a political bent to how such regimes prioritise the arguments of their experts.

The idea of an in-built bias has been reproduced in critical scholarship on international criminal justice as a challenge to the field's objectivity: the anti-impunity regime prefers individualised over collective responsibility or immediate over transhistorical violence. The anti-African bias is a similar argument about the imbalanced co-ordinates of the regime. Yet the notion of bias tends to fix the parameters of a given regime too rigidly in time and place, when regimes themselves are also acts of professional world-building.[98] This is where Kennedy's notion of 'background norms' helps visualise global governance regimes as the result of expert articulation.[99]

---

[96] Koskenniemi, 'From Apology to Utopia'; Hilary Charlesworth and Christine Chinkin, *Boundaries of International Law* (Manchester University Press 2000); Antony Anghie, *Sovereignty, Imperialism, and the Making of International Law* (Cambridge University Press 2004).

[97] Martti Koskenniemi, 'International Law: Constitutionalism, Managerialism and the Ethos of Legal Education' (2007) 1 *European Journal of Legal Studies* 8–24, at 10–11. The shift is elaborated upon in Martti Koskenniemi, 'The Politics of International Law – 20 Years Later' (2009) 20 *European Journal of International Law* 7–19, at 9.

[98] Cf. B.S. Chimni, *International Law and World Order* (Cambridge University Press 2017) 317.

[99] See David Kennedy, 'Background Noise?: The Underlying Politics of Global Governance' (1999) 21 *Harvard International Review* 52–57, at 52.

1.4 MANAGEMENT SITUATED

Kennedy uses the term "background" to capture 'the suspicion that something that purported to be the result of foreground deliberation was actually the product of less visible background forces'.[100] In global affairs, this means looking to the expert and their legal arguments, rather than to political leaders, to understand the shape of the field.[101] Despite disavowing politics, experts working in the background are involved in narrating, invoking, and contesting the expert claims of others, to obvious distributive effect. A trade lawyer may read a toxic chemical spillage differently to an environmental lawyer, but the vocabulary of trade law – comparative advantage, trade barriers, social protection, and so on – will also have to be deployed as arguments in different arrangements with differing outcomes for the actors and habitats involved.[102]

At the ICC, ideas of complementarity, co-operation, and legitimacy affect the prosecutor's decision whether or not to open an investigation. By framing those terms through a context, experts like the prosecutor fashion the world of global justice as state based and state dependent, demanding proximity to governmental and often authoritarian structures. By such expert arguments, OTP officials govern atrocity situations, bringing some actors into the discussion, such as national security forces, while devaluing others, such as those proximate to atrocities themselves.[103] The solutions available – to have the ICC deal with criminality or its domestic equivalent – foreclose other avenues of political and social justice-seeking. Such dynamics of articulation, interpretation, narrowing, and exclusion are the politics of expertise.

Axiom 3: The Power of Expertise Lies Elsewhere than in Its Effectiveness

Expertise is overwhelmingly assessed against its effectiveness in achieving its aims. As noted earlier, the focus on effectiveness also permeates ICC practice and scholarship.[104] But it also occludes the constitutive or

---

[100] David Kennedy, 'Challenging Expert Rule: The Politics of Global Governance' (2005) 27 *Sydney Law Review* 1–24, at 3.

[101] Ibid., 6.

[102] Kennedy, 'World of Struggle' 139. This example adapts Koskenniemi's in 'The Politics of International Law – 20 Years Later' 11.

[103] Kennedy, 'Background Noise?' 57.

[104] For a selection of this effectiveness turn, see Cedric Ryngaert (ed.), *The Effectiveness of International Criminal Justice* (Intersentia 2009); Yuval Shany, *Assessing the Effectiveness of International Courts* (Oxford University Press 2014); Linda Carter, Mark Ellis and

24 INTRODUCTION

productive power of experts as they fashion the people, institutions, and arguments of global justice. Critical legal scholars have adopted this lens to map the mechanics of international legal expertise. The expert does not only propose and effect institutional reforms but articulates an institutional context and set of problems, a relevant legal infrastructure, and a range of policy solutions. Koskenniemi gives an insight into how profound this redescription of the field can be. With international law's fragmentation into functional regimes, the 'generalist' language of rules, government, and responsibility was substituted by the language of regulation, governance, and compliance. Indeed, even conflict and contestation are no longer recognised as 'disputes' but as 'management problems'.[105]

Managing problems, Koskenniemi's international lawyer 'looks behind rules and institutions' to 'assess costs and benefits. Streamline, balance, optimize, calculate'.[106] They are not rigidly concerned with a consistent jurisprudence, but 'context-sensitive, short-term, market-oriented and ad hoc'.[107] The lawyer becomes a 'cog in the regime-machine'[108] deploying their expertise to secure concrete results and 'smooth the prince's path'.[109] This managerial style makes the uptake of management ideas and tools less surprising, given the shared will to optimise, contextualise, and smooth institutional pathways. Similarly, Kennedy's experts 'aggregate interests, resolve conflicts, manage risks, address common problems,

Charles Chernor Jalloh, *The International Criminal Court in an Effective Global Justice System* (Edward Elgar 2016).

[105] Martti Koskenniemi, 'Constitutionalism as Mindset: Reflections on Kantian Themes about International Law and Globalization' (2007) 8 *Theoretical Inquiries in Law* 9–36, at 14; Martti Koskenniemi, *The Gentle Civilizer of Nations: The Rise and Fall of International Law 1870-1960* (Cambridge University Press 2001) 485.

[106] Koskenniemi, 'Ethos of Legal Education' 13.

[107] Martti Koskenniemi, 'Between Commitment and Cynicism: Outline for a Theory of International Law as Practice' in Martti Koskenniemi, *The Politics of International Law* (Hart Publishing 2011) 271–293, at 280. The growing connections between international law and international relations from the 1980s onwards has also influenced the uptake of this language in combination with those of microeconomics, including notions of 'stakeholders', 'firms', and 'transaction costs', see Robert Keohane, 'The Demand for International Regimes' (1982) 36 *International Organisation* 325–355, at 330–337; Allen Buchanan and Robert Keohane, 'The Legitimacy of Global Governance Institutions' (2006) 20 *Ethics & International Affairs* 405–437. For an overview, see Dennis Dijkzeul and Yves Beigbeder, 'Introduction' in Dennis Dijkzeul and Yves Beigbeder (eds.), *Rethinking International Organisations* (Berghahn 2006) 1–23, at 7–11.

[108] Koskenniemi, 'Ethos of Legal Education' 17.

[109] Koskenniemi, 'Politics of International Law' – Twenty Years Later' 16.

1.4 MANAGEMENT SITUATED

and promote prosperity'.[110] They are trained to think in terms of 'best practice, practical necessity [and] efficiency' as a form of 'intellectual and practical work'.[111] The expert governs (or constitutes) 'when what is articulated comes to pass'.[112] Both accounts of expertise signal its constitutive capacity. They also beg the question that if experts govern via a 'modest practice of eclectic social and institutional management',[113] then how does management itself fit in?

Alongside these interventions, the socio-legal literature on managerial judging, spearheaded by Judith Resnik, offers an insight into the constitutive role of management vis-à-vis court proceedings and judges. Writing in the context of increased litigation within US courts in the 1980s, Resnik identified a shift in how federal judges were responding to such changes.[114] They had graduated from 'uninformed, passive umpires' relatively unconcerned with issues of scheduling, documentation control, and speed into 'active managers' who took control over their calendars and sought out alternative dispute settlement avenues in order to reduce their docket and increase court efficiency.[115] These 'trappings of the efficiency era' may or may not have sped up proceedings, but for Resnik they crucially changed litigants' self-understanding as collaborators in judicial efficiency as *adjudication* became *administration*.[116]

A similar shift was marked internationally, at the Yugoslavia Tribunal, by Langer and Doherty. They revealed how a mix of legal and managerial tools, including the use of *ad litem* judges, case management plans, and pre-trial conferences impacted the Tribunal's work in subtle yet far-reaching ways.[117] This managerial judging style created 'different

---

[110] José María Beneyto and David Kennedy (eds.), *New Approaches to International Law: The European and the American Experiences* (TMC Asser Press 2012) v; David Kennedy, 'The Mystery of Global Governance' (2008) 34 *Ohio Northern University Law Review* 827–860. See Johns, 'Unruly Law' 17.

[111] David Kennedy, 'The Politics of the Invisible College: International Governance and the Politics of Expertise' (2001) 5 *European Human Rights Law Review* 463–497, at 471; Kennedy, 'World of Struggle' 110.

[112] Kennedy, 'World of Struggle' 9.

[113] Kennedy, 'Invisible College' 472.

[114] Resnik, 'Managerial Judges' 374. See also Judith Resnik, 'Managerial Judges and Court Delay: The Unproven Assumptions' (1984) 23 *Judges Journal* 8–11 and 54–55.

[115] Maximo Langer, 'The Rise of Managerial Judging in International Criminal Law' (2005) 53 *American Journal of Comparative Law* 835–910, at 836.

[116] Resnik, 'Managerial Judges' 445.

[117] Maximo Langer and Joseph Doherty, 'Managerial Judging Goes International but Its Promise Remains Unfulfilled: An Empirical Assessment of the ICTY Reforms' (2011) 36 *Yale Journal of International Law* 241–305, at 291.

26 INTRODUCTION

structures of interpretation and meaning through which the participants in the criminal adjudication process (prosecutors, judges, defence attorneys, etc.) understand criminal procedure and their respective roles'.[118] Adopting such practices, they 'become part of actors' internal dispositions' and shape their 'legal identities'.[119]

Axiom 4: Expertise Is Neither Ahistorical Nor Progressively Linear

Mainstream accounts of the connection between expertise and history embody a paradox. At one level, expertise and its effects are often intentionally studied as if outside history. The historical vacuum in which management emerges and operates extends only to the immediate institutional context, rendering wider trends and external dynamics irrelevant. In this account, the historical context and emergence of expert tools and arguments are also irrelevant. At another level, however, practitioners and scholars of disciplines such as international law are constantly 'doing history'.[120] This kind of work is often on show at the ICC, whether in the construction of historical narratives of atrocity, or in symbolic invocations of the Nuremberg legacy. The international criminal lawyer situates their expertise, deploying history and narrative to celebrate, justify, or warn. History is also deployed in the narration of the field's institutional maturation from flawed, skeletal mechanism at Nuremberg to the more robust but still temporary ad hoc Tribunals to the end story

---

[118] Langer, 'Rise of Managerial Judging' 849.

[119] Ibid. International law and international relations scholarship on international bureaucracy touch on the cultures that spring up within them. See Michael Barnett and Martha Finnemore, *Rules for the World: International Organisations in Global Politics* (Cornell University Press 2004) 18–19: 'rules can be constitutive of identity, particularly of the identity of the organisation ... Bureaucratic rules thus shape the activities, understandings, identity, and practices of the bureaucracy and consequently help to define the bureaucratic culture'. International law scholars have traced the effects of bureaucratic culture within certain 'normative orders'; see Touko Piiparinen, 'Law versus Bureaucratic Culture: The Case of the ICC and the Transcendence of Instrumental Rationality' in Jan Klabbers and Touko Piiparinen (eds.), *Normative Pluralism and International Law: Exploring Global Governance* (Cambridge University Press 2013) 251–283, at 252–253.

[120] Barrie Sander, *Doing Justice to History: Confronting the Past in International Criminal Courts* (Oxford University Press 2021); Janne Nijman, 'An Enlarged Sense of Possibility for International Law: Seeking Change by Doing History' in Ingo Venzke and Kevin Jon Heller (eds.), *Contingency in International Law: On the Possibility of Different Legal Histories* (Oxford University Press 2021) 92–110.

1.4 MANAGEMENT SITUATED

of the permanent ICC.[121] The upshot of this paradoxical view of expertise and history is that supporters of the ICC project find themselves constantly looking to history to explain and expand the enterprise whose 'time has come' even while they assert the timelessness of the tools deployed to realise it.

Critical scholarship pinpoints a more significant role for history in analysing expertise, and for the role of expertise in the past. Scholars have pointed to the continuity and contingency of international legal arguments and concepts, locating these in time and place in order to render them politically contestable.[122] As well as bracketing the question of historical progress, such accounts also demonstrate the importance of history to expertise. Koskenniemi's historical account of international law from its late-Victorian rise to its 'fall' in the 1960s pinpoints the specific historical conditions of international legal managerialism. The decline of the field is attributed to its instrumentalisation for political ends during the Cold War.[123] Thereafter, the discipline 'never really recovered'[124] and became what it remains today: a specialist, technical craft put to the ends of global rulership.[125] Once the field began to fragment in the 1990s, expertise was further put to the task of proffering efficient solutions to the global challenges of the post-Cold War era.[126] Since then, legal expertise has 'slowly vanished behind its utilitarian reasons', according to Koskenniemi.[127] Far from being isolated from history, expertise, particularly international legal managerialism, is partly conditioned by, partly responsible for disciplinary undulations.

Historically entangled with professional sensibilities, expertise also exhibits the scars of the institutional struggles and skirmishes in which

---

[121] See, for example, Philippe Sands, *From Nuremberg to The Hague: The Future of International Criminal Justice* (Cambridge University Press 2009).

[122] Roberto Unger, *False Necessity* (Cambridge University Press 1988); cf. Susan Marks, 'False Contingency' (2009) 62 *Current Legal Problems* 1. For an example, see Karen Knop, 'The Tokyo Women's Tribunal and the Turn to Fiction' in Fleur Johns, Richard Joyce and Sundhya Pahuja (eds.), *Events: The Force of International Law* (Routledge 2010) 145–164.

[123] Koskenniemi, 'Gentle Civilizer of Nations' 3.

[124] Ibid., 3.

[125] Ibid., 413.

[126] Martti Koskenniemi, 'The Fate of Public International Law: Between Technique and Politics' (2007) 70 *Modern Law Review* 1–30, at 4.

[127] Martti Koskenniemi, 'Global Governance and Public International Law' (2004) 37 *Kritische Justiz* 241–254, at 252.

INTRODUCTION

it was forged.[128] Expertise is both the register in which political contestation takes place institutionally and the spoils of victory won from it. As noted in Chapter 2, management expertise thus appears as the 'truth effects' of such contestation, papering over the cracks and conflicts that define its very terms. Hence, the expertise surfacing in ICC discourse cannot be viewed in isolation from that institution, nor indeed from other prior institutions in which management ideas and practices were forged internationally. To understand management at the ICC, it is thus important to trace its pre-lives, particularly in the United Nations, as is done in Chapter 2.

These four axioms provide a starting point for the study of management in international institutions by resisting some common assumptions about expertise. It brackets the question of management's effectiveness and contests its claim to political neutrality. It also looks to the world-making effects of expertise, particularly as it appears in specific institutional milieux. With these axioms in mind, I briefly summarise the arguments of this book as they relate to management before outlining the book's structure and style.

1.5   The Argument

The four axioms above are only a starting point for the analysis conducted in this book. Having studied the ICC's management apparatus, these axioms can be further refined. Instead of rehashing arguments from each chapter, I connect them here in rudimentary form to the four axioms, indicating the chapters in which such arguments are elaborated:

- Management ideas and practices are important features of international legal expertise, such that international law is not *all* that international lawyers do;[129]

---

[128] Jochen von Bernstorff and Philipp Dann (eds.), *The Battle for International Law: South–North Perspectives on the Decolonisation Era* (Cambridge University Press 2019). See Martin Clarke et al., 'Cold War International Law', Oxford Bibliographies, 28 October 2020, available at: www.oxfordbibliographies.com/view/document/obo-9780199796953/obo-9780199796953-0214.xml; see also Pahuja, 'Decolonising International Law'; Luis Eslava, Michael Fakhri and Vasuki Nesiah (eds.), *Bandung, Global History, and International Law: Critical Pasts and Pending Futures* (Cambridge University Press 2017).

[129] To paraphrase Koskenniemi, 'From Apology to Utopia' 612.

1.5 THE ARGUMENT

- Management ideas and practices are not universal and timeless but particular to the (largely Western, European, American) experience of governing spaces and peoples institutionally. This experience can be traced to the management of slavery through the plantation to the organisation of war and the running of the (American) factory. More recently, management has been part of the effort to establish international institutional projects relating to those living under and breaking with colonial rule, whether in the League of Nations or, later, the postcolonial United Nations (Chapter 2);
- Management forms and reforms the institutional co-ordinates and characters of global justice rather than simply improving extant structures and processes. Discourses of efficiency, strategy, risk, and workload and techniques of strategic planning, audit, performance appraisal, onboarding, indicators, workflow, best practices, and organigrams produce an institutional imaginary and a professional sensibility (Chapters 3, 5 and 6);
- Management ideas and practices have facilitated the radical closure of institutional and emancipatory possibilities, from the G77's New International Economic Order at the UN to African states' desire for decolonial global justice at the ICC. That process does not play out in identical terms wherever management is found. At the level of large-scale organisational reform, it turns the ICC organisation into the outer limits of justice-seeking (Chapter 3) and of professional/political action (Chapter 6). In day-to-day professional interactions of staff, it encourages and rewards a concern for the institution above other priorities (Chapter 4). And within the ICC's legal discourse, it occasions a flight from the dilemmas and complexities comprising the argumentative field (Chapter 5);
- Management is less a 'force for good' smoothing the path towards global justice than part of the expert and institutional architecture that narrows the terms of global justice to what the ICC can offer, discounts contestations of ICC-style justice and alternative imaginaries thereof, and excludes those in whose name the court purports to act from its decision-making processes;
- Management's various effects can be neither reformed away nor entirely removed but can be targeted only at the level of professional discourse. A posture or strategy of discomfort admits to the politics of management, the choices it engenders, and the possibility of taking a break from the will to manage (Chapter 7).

30   INTRODUCTION

In sum, management is a pervasive discourse, set of arguments and practices which implicates the ICC from the macro- to the micro-level. Management implicates the ICC in ways not altogether benign but helps explain why political alternatives within the court are so radically foreclosed and ignored by those at the centre of this project.[130] Management's force therefore lies not in its problem-solving potential for a gradually improving court but its productive and indeed subordinating potential as against the court's alternative interpretations. This cannot be represented as a homogeneous set of traits but is traceable instead across multiple scales of operation from large-scale organisational reform to everyday professional work to the ICC's argumentative field. Nonetheless, the commonality between the ideas and practices deployed across these scales is to narrow, exclude, and invisibilise the political contestations and argumentative dilemmas that comprise the project.

1.6   Outline and Style

This book traces a concerted flight to management resulting from two decades of institution building and rebuilding, professional improvement, and argumentative innovation. In addition to the (in)visibilising and in/exclusionary effects of the court's managerial machinery, management has also foreclosed the contestations, complexities, and dilemmas that comprise the ICC project. Together, such effects of management render 'thinking otherwise' not only difficult but also susceptible to condemnation. These insights come through a series of different interventions over the course of five substantive chapters and a conclusion.

These chapters gradually compile a picture of management and the ICC through the layering of different argumentative styles or methods. Rather than limiting the mechanics of these chapters to the notion of method, I also take account of other devices, including pace, intimacy, irony, and audience in offering a series of management studies across and between various scales of operation. I treat these styles as fragments 'lying about that we can use quite instrumentally, pragmatically, and

[130] Balakrishnan Rajagopal, *International Law from Below: Development, Social Movements and Third World Resistance* (Cambridge University Press 2000) 543.

1.6 OUTLINE AND STYLE

disloyally'.[131] This is not a supermarket sweep of pre-packaged methods but an effort to think with and against certain styles and methods to overcome the will to make method an agent or actor in the story while also allowing them to render management's effects differently when approached from alternative angles.[132] Some will appeal more than others, and I encourage hypertextual rather than linear readings of the book and its chapters.[133]

Chapter 2 starts from the premise that in order to understand management's effects on the ICC project, it is crucial first to consider how and under what circumstances management ideas and practices have come to appear self-evident, authoritative and universally applicable 'at all'.[134] This chapter therefore looks to history to 'trace the forces that gave birth to our present-day practices ... and identify the historical conditions upon which they still depend'.[135] This genealogical style allows us to trace

> how contemporary practices and institutions emerged out of specific struggles, conflicts, alliances, and exercises of power, many of which are nowadays forgotten. It thereby enables the genealogist to suggest ... by presenting a series of troublesome associations and lineages – that institutions and practices we value and take for granted today are actually more problematic or more "dangerous" than they otherwise appear.[136]

Genealogy thus makes the ICC and its expert tools look strange, even unrecognisable.[137] It helps answer the question I began this book with: how could terms such as 'audit', 'appraisal', and 'performance' fit so seamlessly with terms such as 'atrocity', 'victims', and 'global justice'?

---

[131] Janet Halley, *Split Decisions: How and Why to Take a Break from Feminism* (Princeton University Press 2006) 7.

[132] Following Martti Koskenniemi, 'Letter to the Editors of the Symposium' (1999) 93 *American Journal of International Law* 351–361, at 352.

[133] This form of reading is captured in the IGLP 'Crunching the Core' seminar series and, to an extent, reflects the lawyer's mode of engaging with treaty texts.

[134] Raymond Geuss, 'Genealogy as Critique' (2002) 10 *European Journal of Philosophy* 209–215, at 212.

[135] David Garland, 'What Is a "History of the Present"? On Foucault's Genealogies and Their Critical Preconditions' (2014) 16 *Punishment & Society* 365–384, at 373. The 'original' contribution is from Michel Foucault, 'Nietzsche, Genealogy, History' in Paul Rabinow (ed.), *The Foucault Reader* (Pantheon Books 1984) 76–100.

[136] Garland, 'What Is a "History of the Present"?' 372.

[137] Anne Orford, 'In Praise of Description' (2012) 25 *Leiden Journal of International Law* 609–624, at 617–618.

32 INTRODUCTION

Problematising a classic understanding of management from a former ICC president, this chapter replaces a decontextualised yet progressive management with one that has appeared in institutional settings ranging from the plantation to the postcolonial United Nations. In those spaces – and in the ICC of today – management's self-evidence and popularity became possible through repeated efforts to depoliticise and dehistoricise it. These traits were attached to management under deeply political conditions, whether in the factory relations between workers and managers in late nineteenth-century New England or the struggles between North and South over the United Nations from the 1960s onwards. The spoils of victory that followed such struggles were the discursive possibilities of describing and pursuing political agendas via the seemingly scientific and apolitical register of efficiency, planning, cost-effectiveness, and performance. Genealogy highlights the power of management at the ICC through these earlier institutional snapshots.

The third to fifth chapters are studies of management at the ICC. These studies take place across three different scales: macro, micro, and meso. I divide the analysis in light of the multiple layers of institutional power relations. Foucault often characterised power spatially as 'near and far', 'side-by-side', and 'dispersed'.[138] There are 'general conditions ... organised into a more-or-less coherent and unitary strategic form' – otherwise called 'global strategies' – and there are 'dispersed, heteromorphous, localised procedures of power'.[139] To this may be added the plane of legal argumentation. These three layers are arranged grid-like, even if they are not hermetically sealed off from one another. They offer points of entry for viewing management from above (macro-level organisational reform), across or diagonally (meso-level field of argumentation), and individually (micro-level professional engagements over the course of one individual career).

Chapter 3 thus studies management at the macro-architectural level, tracing its emergence within the court as a central ordering language for the new permanent institution. This chapter also begins to map the actors, arguments, and meanings ascribed to management ideas and

---

[138] Michel Foucault, 'Of Other Spaces: Utopias and Heterotopias' (1984) *Architecture/Mouvement/Continuité* (trans. Jay Miskowiec) 1–9.

[139] Michel Foucault, 'Power and Strategies' in Colin Gordon (ed.), *Power/Knowledge: Selected Interviews and Other Writings 1972–1977 by Michel Foucault* (Pantheon Books 1980) 134–145, at 142. See Ben Golder, *Foucault and the Politics of Rights* (Stanford University Press 2015) 121.

1.6 OUTLINE AND STYLE

practices as the court's workload expanded. Such macro-analysis reveals how the parameters of global justice were narrowed through the deployment of management and its interpretations of success, failure, performance, and risk. This chapter attempts to redescribe the organisation from the perspective of these practices. This means, to quote Orford, reading 'expert documentation on international institutional arrangements with the care and rigour that we are used to seeing given to the pronouncements of European philosophers'.[140] In attempting this redescription, it necessarily includes and excludes in an effort to train a lens on specific discourses and practices, rather than the key court cases and political shifts that normally take centre stage.[141]

Chapter 4 moves to the micro-scale to consider how management ideas and practices implicate the ICC professional, specifically the ICC lawyer. At their most benign, management practices are made available to professionals to guide the application of their knowledge and skills and to facilitate self-optimisation. Yet within that vision of individual micro-management lies the capacity to delimit the conditions of possibility by limiting the professional imaginary of global justice. From the point at which the would-be employee begins to fill out an application for an ICC position, to when they are onboarded on day one, to their annual performance appraisals, and finally until they leave, the ICC professional is mediated through management ideas and tools that constrain and discourage confrontation with the ICC's politics, contestations, and complexities.

The style of this chapter is based on an ethnography of documents inflected with personal observation during my time as an ICC intern.[142] Managerial practices mostly take a material form whether as plans, reports, or forms. Like other techniques of rule, these documents bring into being that which they represent, both in their content and in their material form as pieces of paper.[143] Managerial

---

[140] Orford, 'In Praise of Description' 620.

[141] On the (colonial) politics of archives, see Ann Stoler, 'Colonial Archives and the Arts of Governance' (2002) 2 *Archival Science* 87–109. In international law, see Madelaine Chiam et al., 'Introduction: History, Anthropology and the Archive of International Law' (2017) 5 *London Review of International Law* 3–5, at 5.

[142] On an ethnographic 'way of seeing', see Harry Wolcott, *Ethnography: A Way of Seeing* (AltaMira Press 1999) 66 and 68. In international law, see Eslava, 'Local Space, Global Life', and Johns' 'quasi-ethnography' in 'Unruly Law' 31.

[143] Matthew Hull, 'Documents and Bureaucracy' (2012) 41 *Annual Review of Anthropology* 251–267, at 253.

34 INTRODUCTION

documents enforce certain rules of engagement, capture and direct individual activity, and establish their own lifecycles.[144] I thus rely on Annelise Riles' definition of (managerial) documents as 'paradigmatic artifacts of modern knowledge practices'.[145] Seeing ethnographically allows one not only to 'describe what the people in some particular place or status ordinarily do', but also to understand 'the meanings they ascribe to what they do', thereby revealing the sentiments on which the project relies.[146]

Among international legal scholars, documents have only recently been subjected to the ethnographic lens normally reserved for groups and communities.[147] The ICC's managerial documents, like any other, demand engagement, communication, transportation, verification, filing, and storage by a range of actors within and without the institution. Many of the aesthetic features of documents help produce and sustain the institution through crests, letterheads, organigrams, tables, flowcharts, boxes, lists, and bullet points.[148] Appreciating the material qualities of managerial documents and professional encounters with them also foregrounds the more subtle discursive effects missed by a macro-level analysis or interviews and trains the gaze back on the metropole and its official practices.

---

[144] Carol Bacchi and Jennifer Bonham, 'Reclaiming Discursive Practices as an Analytic Focus: Political Implications' (2014) 17 *Foucault Studies* 173–192, at 184.

[145] Annelise Riles, 'Introduction: A Response' in Annelise Riles (ed.), *Documents: Artifacts of Modern Knowledge* (University of Michigan Press 2006) 1–40, at 2.

[146] Wolcott, 'Ethnography: A Way of Seeing' 68.

[147] The most notable exceptions include Richard Harper, *Inside the IMF: An Ethnography of Documents, Technology and Organisational Action* (Routledge 1998); Annelise Riles, 'Models and Documents: Artefacts of International Legal Knowledge' (1999) 48 *International & Comparative Law Quarterly* 805–825; Annelise Riles, *The Network Inside Out* (University of Michigan Press 2001); Bruno Latour, *The Making of Law: An Ethnography of the Conseil d'État* (John Wiley & Sons 2010); Julie Billaud, 'Keepers of the Truth: Producing "Transparent" Documents for the Universal Periodic Review' in Hilary Charlesworth and Emma Larking (eds.), *Human Rights and the Universal Periodic Review: Rituals and Ritualism* (Cambridge University Press 2015) 23–84, at 63. For a more recent 'turn' to artefacts and objects in international law, see the London Review of International Law special issue on 'History, Anthropology and the Archive of International Law' (2017) 5 *London Review of International Law* 3–196; Jessie Hohmann and Daniel Joyce (eds.), *International Law's Objects* (Oxford University Press 2019).

[148] See Riles, 'Documents', esp. chapters by Don Brenneis and Marilyn Strathern; Nayanika Mathur, *Paper Tiger: Law, Bureaucracy, and the Developmental State in Himalayan India* (Cambridge University Press 2016), chapter 4.

1.6 OUTLINE AND STYLE 35

Between the macro and micro lies management and indeed law as a 'discursive field' of arguments.[149] That field emerges in the course of professional practice but is also capable of orienting expert debate and action as Pierre Bourdieu has shown. Chapter 5 therefore positions management alongside the legal arguments structuring the ICC as a professional field. As Simpson and others have demonstrated, the ICC field is largely constructed as 'a set of dilemmas' or dyadic oppositions – law versus politics, international versus domestic, accused versus victim and so on – that facilitate arguments without ever finally resolving them.[150] This chapter engages a mode of deconstruction similar to Simpson, Koskenniemi, and others in seeking to unearth a pattern in the invocation of management to deal with these legal dilemmas. Within this legal terrain, management operates as a mechanism deployed by arguers to escape these dilemmas (even while it displaces critical engagement with them). It is in such instances that management's function as professional salve is most apparent as it conditions a flight from the professional responsibility to confront the theoretical and political contradictions of the ICC project.

Chapter 6 takes one notable reform moment at the ICC – the *Re*Vision project to reorganise the Registry – as a sounding of management ideas and practices running through and effecting this reorganisation.[151] It shows how management expertise relates to politics in two ways. It depoliticises through its terms of engagement and reform techniques, while simultaneously enacting managerial reform as the extent of the court's politics. The zeal with which management is taken up and obsessed over institutionally can be described as the draw of an apolitical politics. This chapter takes up the mode of redescription once again while also engaging with the network of documents that justified and diagnosed *Re*Vision. It is a more synchronic sounding of the court's managerial layers as displayed in previous chapters but here offered as a means for thinking through the relationship of politics and technocracy.

Together these chapters offer a vision of an institutional project saturated and conditioned by management ideas and practices. In large

---

[149] Gerry Simpson, *Law, War and Crime: War Crimes, Trials and the Reinvention of International Law* (Wiley 2007) 2.

[150] Ibid., 4.

[151] Joseph H. H. Weiler, 'The Geology of International Law – Governance, Democracy and Legitimacy' (2004) 64 *Zeitschrift für Ausländisches Öffentliches Recht und Völkerrecht* 547–562.

part, these prove to have exclusionary effects for the field and its professional consciousness. The conclusion therefore asks how management and ICC-style managerial justice might be confronted, resisted, or broken with. Rather than the reactionary move of posing solutions, the conclusion offers the possibility of adopting a professional posture – *a strategy of discomfort* – to confront management and the iteration of global justice it presently supports. Engaging dialogically with the writings of Jacques Vergès, Max Weber, and decolonial thinkers, I end this book by invoking the strategy of rupture and the ethic of responsibility. The strategy of discomfort is intended for various participants in the ICC project and may occasion quite different avenues for critical engagement if taken up.

2

A History of the International Criminal Court's Managerial Present

As an institution with a mandate to end impunity for the most serious crimes known to mankind, the Court must stand firm and remain committed to this cause. This is part of the burden of the Court's success. Nevertheless, the Court does not exist in a vacuum. In recognition of the need to work to achieve its goals as efficiently and effectively as possible, the Court has recently undertaken a series of reform initiatives. These are not mere cost-cutting exercises, but are part of the natural evolution of the ICC as a judicial institution into a fully-fledged, functioning international court.[1]

2.1 Introduction

In 2016, then-International Criminal Court (ICC) president and drafter of its core texts, Silvia Fernández de Gurmendi, made the above statement in a popular practitioner's text on the Rome Statute. The epigraph begins with a familiar message that continues to have extraordinary purchase. Fernández invokes the language of the Rome Statute preamble, recalling the 'unimaginable atrocities that deeply shock the conscience of humanity' and the 'delicate mosaic' of humanity, which 'may be shattered at any time'. The 'cause' to which Fernández refers is 'to put an end to impunity', which now manifests in 'an independent permanent International Criminal Court'. Such a court is also a symbolic achievement. As Fernández states elsewhere, its creation 'marked a culminating point in the surge of idealist cosmopolitan doctrines in the 1990s, a decade which favoured questions of human security over state security,

---

[1] Silvia Fernández de Gurmendi, 'Introductions to the Third Edition' in Otto Triffterer and Kai Ambos (eds.), *The Rome Statute of the International Criminal Court: A Commentary* (3rd ed., C. H. Beck Hart Nomos 2016) xvi–xvii, at xvi.

38   A HISTORY OF THE ICC'S MANAGERIAL PRESENT

and considered justice and the rule of law as indispensable conditions for achieving peace'.[2]

Following this invocation, though, Fernández already begins to paint a very different picture. From the idealism of the global anti-impunity movement, the tone and focus shift to its institutional embodiment and pragmatic organisational management. Where before, international criminal justice was a wide vista of possibility, now it is about the court's 'reality', its hard choices, and the need to meet lofty expectations. And yet, despite these constraints and expectations, Fernández is confident that the challenge can be met.

How? Through constant, quotidian work on the institution: by orienting the court towards results or 'goals', by reflecting inward as part of 'reform initiatives' that will crystallise into 'lessons learnt' for the future, and by retaining the institutional ideal of a 'fully-fledged' and 'functional' court. Fernández elaborates on this ideal in practice. 'ReVision', the name given to the restructuring of the ICC Registry in 2014–2015, exemplifies the 'streamlining' of internal structures. A 'strategic plan' has been devised by the Office of the Prosecutor to organise its work and 'utilise its resources in the most effective manner'. 'Lessons Learned' exercises are optimising judicial processes and developing 'best practices'. At the time, Fernández was also involved in devising performance indicators for the court.[3] However utopian its mission, says Fernández, the court must be pragmatically managed. This represents a 'natural evolution' in the story of the ICC and the fight against impunity.

The question that animates this chapter is how a view such as this has become possible. Specifically, how has it become possible for international (criminal) lawyers like Fernández to utter the language of mass atrocity or global justice in the same breath as efficiency, strategic planning, and reform? While common answers may be found in organisational necessity, or in the need to link theory to practice, this chapter posits an alternative rationale for the proximity of anti-impunity and management as professional vocabularies. I argue that such proximity

---

[2] Silvia Fernández de Gurmendi, 'Final Reflections: The Challenges of the International Criminal Court' in Hector Olásolo (ed.), *Essays on International Criminal Justice* (Hart Publishing 2012) 194–198, at 194.

[3] Report of the Court on the Development of Performance Indicators for the International Criminal Court, ICC, 12 November 2015, available at: www.icc-cpi.int/sites/default/files/itemsDocuments/Court_report-development_of_performance_indicators-ENG.pdf.

2.1 INTRODUCTION

results from two common yet powerful assumptions about management, also visible in Fernández's account. The first assumption is that management is a discipline without a history, or at least a timeless truth whose history plays no part in contemporary efforts to apply it institutionally. And the second is that law and management are separate bodies of professional knowledge or fields of engagement. It is these two assumptions, namely that management is a timeless, scientific truth, and that it exists at a remove from law, that undergird engagement with management by ICC professionals. Since these assumptions affirm management's power and self-evidence at the ICC, this chapter problematises both.

Fernández's 'reform initiatives' are often treated as 'recent' phenomena, spurred by necessity and the desire for self-improvement but occupying a 'perpetual present' of innovation and novelty.[4] However, as this chapter demonstrates, management's timelessness (and its immunity from time's accumulations and contextualisations) is difficult to sustain. In different iterations, management has featured across organisational settings over the past 150 years. What Fernández treats as new innovations are but the legacies of past organisational struggles. As Orford notes, '[p]articular ideas come to dominate public discourse, not because they are accurate or logical, but as a result of struggle'.[5] They are the result of more or less successful efforts within a range of organisations, whether as techniques for making slavery more efficient in the Antebellum South or as a strategy for undermining Third World democratisation of the United Nations. The tools that ICC officials look upon as clean and clear solutions contain traces of these encounters. It is part of the success of management that what Fernández sees when observing management today is timeless truth and novelty, when these are but the truth or novelty effects of prior struggles.

---

[4] This 'perpetual present' is described as 'a state characterized by an abundance of frequently changing language and "buzzwords", by frequent discussions of new approaches that promise better chances of success than those currently in use, and by a strong – and in many ways understandable – sense of wanting to look forward rather than back', D. Lewis, 'International Development and the "Perpetual Present": Anthropological Approaches to the Re-Historicization of Policy' (2009) 21 *European Journal of Development Research* 32–46, at 33. See also Pierre Bourdieu, 'The Force of Law: Towards a Sociology of the Juridical Field' (1987) 38 *Hastings Law Journal* 805–853.

[5] Anne Orford, 'Muscular Humanitarianism: Reading the Narratives of the New Interventionism' (1999) 10 *European Journal of International Law* 679–711, at 708.

40 A HISTORY OF THE ICC'S MANAGERIAL PRESENT

Similarly, Fernández relies on management's separateness to law as justification for applying it institutionally. Management is often ascribed many of law's missing virtues: it is practical, flexible, and untainted by politics where law is slow, rigid, and susceptible to politicisation. This assumption, too, is challenged by the episodes where legal arguments, doctrines, and discourses have been combined with management tools as a form of politics. Hence, it was not only legal arguments that powered the early International Labour Office but latent 'scientific management' which sought to govern and discipline certain populations. And when the United States reacted against Third World voices within the 1970s United Nations, the reaction was framed in terms of not only human rights and development but duplication, bureaucracy, and efficiency. Management and law have thus synergistically shaped global institutions long before the arrival of the ICC. In tracing these connections, this chapter puts paid to Fernández's assumption that lawyers have not frequently relied upon the language and techniques offered by management to intervene in global affairs. I begin this genealogy by looking to several legal-managerial institutions of the nineteenth century.

2.2   Managing before Taylor: Plantation, Factory, War

The conventional history of management, however unfamiliar to international lawyers, traces a line from pre-modern craft to modern professional practice. Frederick Winslow Taylor and the advent of 'scientific management' often appear as a fulcrum in that progression. Yet, rather than follow that linear story, this chapter takes snapshots of several legal-managerial institutions spanning the pre-Taylor/Taylor divide. This de-emphasises such a divide and reveals the continuities across diverse times and places in how management and law have been combined to govern society. This section considers three such institutions: the plantation, the factory, and war, before moving to Taylorism and some corresponding institutional moments at the global level.

2.2.1   Managing the Plantation

The sugar plantations of Jamaica and the cotton plantations of the southern United States were productive sites of legal and managerial innovation. Historically, management's plantation past has been

2.2 MANAGING BEFORE TAYLOR: PLANTATION, FACTORY, WAR 41

downplayed by scholars as much as international law's colonial one.[6] The business historian Alfred Chandler described the plantation overseer as possibly the 'first salaried manager'.[7] And yet Chandler and many other management historians are keen to designate plantation management as an 'ancient form of large-scale production' – one that is far away enough in its violence from the civilising effect of modernity and modern management tools to be labelled a purely historical phenomenon.[8]

Nonetheless, studies of plantation life evince the importance of management and accounting in establishing plantations as viable and brutal modes of production.[9] These include the arrangement of plantation hierarchies 'akin to the multidivisional form' of large post-war organisations. This early version of the multi-divisional or M-form 'combined the strategic functions of a central office with the operating efficiency of smaller divisions', allowing for easy comparison and strategic allocation of resources.[10] Plantations were, in Rosenthal's words, a 'brutal preview' of the modern M-form.[11]

Task-work design and bonus schemes were also important pillars of plantation management.[12] Henry Gantt of the eponymous chart was the son of a Maryland slaveholder. He hoped that the incentive system devised under slavery would not be abolished after the civil war but 'adapt[ed] to modern needs'.[13] Indeed, Gantt 'liked to say that scientific management marked a great step forward from slave labour' rather than its repudiation.[14] The plantation was thus a thoroughly modern space, with its organisational division, worker productivity schemes, and well-designed layouts.[15] Such management tools allowed for observation but

---

[6] Bill Cooke, 'The Denial of Slavery in Management Studies' (2003) 40 *Journal of Management Studies* 1895–1918.

[7] Alfred D. Chandler Jr, *The Visible Hand: The Managerial Revolution in American Business* (Harvard University Press 1977) 64–67.

[8] Ibid.; Caitlin Rosenthal, *Accounting for Slavery: Masters and Management* (Harvard University Press 2018) 6. Thanks to Jason Jackson for pointing me towards this literature.

[9] R. Keith Aufhauser, 'Slavery and Scientific Management' (1973) 33 *Journal of Economic History* 811–824.

[10] Rosenthal, *Accounting for Slavery* 16–17.

[11] Ibid., 48.

[12] Aufhauser, 'Slavery and Scientific Management' 815.

[13] Rosenthal, *Accounting for Slavery* 201.

[14] Ibid., 202, quoting Carol Kennedy, *Guide to the Management Gurus* (Random House 2012) 15.

[15] The world's first proposal for a business school was made in 1750 'for the sons of American planters', Rosenthal, *Accounting for Slavery* 73.

42   A HISTORY OF THE ICC'S MANAGERIAL PRESENT

also provided the language for fashioning the plantation as a sphere of organised violence.[16]

That the ICC, like many modern organisations, deploys similar practices today is unsurprising. In particular, the ICC's effort to manage atrocities and atrocity spaces resembles the plantation's creative 'synthesis of field and factory'.[17] Plantation owners located in England could easily 'see' the plantation from afar through work ledgers and the organisational chart. Such practices facilitated a proximity between the source of raw materials and the place for their refinement in ways that had until then been difficult to maintain for remote owners. Likewise, the ICC has had to confront the physical distance of the Hague-based courtroom from sites of atrocity.[18] To that end, it has used management tools such as outreach strategies, organisational charts, and data collection methods to construct its own notions of 'the field'. Plantations are thus an important antecedent for the management of space and peoples across vast distances.[19]

The plantation was not only a managerial but also a legal space. Inventories and account books were crucial sources of authority within the legal regime of the slave trade. As Rosenthal notes,

> the law offered a flexible tool that supported markets for complex and expensive property like slaves. Rather than undermining commodity markets for the enslaved, special rules made them more efficient, enabling buyers and sellers to make certain assumptions about transactions and to expect some protection in court when they were not met.[20]

Management became a stabilising influence on an otherwise volatile market. The possibility of legal disputes with other slaveowners turned overseers into assiduous bureaucrats of the plantation, documenting a slave's accumulating and depreciating value or the quality of the goods they produced. In contrast, management also served legal reformers of the slave trade. Deficit pounds of cotton picked were recorded in work logs and used to calculate the number of lashes to be administered to

---

[16] Ibid., 78.

[17] Sidney Mintz, *Sweetness and Power: The Place of Sugar in Modern History* (Viking 1985) 46–47.

[18] Clements, 'Near, Far, Wherever You Are'.

[19] Rosenthal, *Accounting for Slavery* 50; Derek H. Alderman and G. Rebecca Dobbs, 'Geographies of Slavery: Of Theory, Method, and Intervention' (2011) 39 *Historical Geography* 29–40, at 34.

[20] Rosenthal, *Accounting for Slavery* 143.

2.2 MANAGING BEFORE TAYLOR: PLANTATION, FACTORY, WAR   43

under-performing slaves. Ameliorationists relied on this raw data to build the case for a more humane system by regulating 'the number of lashes that could be inflicted, by whom, and under what conditions'.[21] Law reformers here relied on management techniques, and they did so to advocate not the abolition of slavery but its more humane continuation as an effective site of production. Reformers hoped to 'reduce the brutality of slavery but also to strengthen the larger system',[22] and in doing so put management to the task of optimising slavery.

The eventual abolition of slavery in the United States did not spell the end for such tools. Rather, contracts between planters and freed slaves maintained the logic of the slave ledger. The only difference was that a new column for wages had to be added. The contract, alongside the M-form, work logs, and incentive schemes, thus stabilised the post-slavery plantation. The work of Chandler and others has been to sever these violent cases of management from its modern scientific claims.

2.2.2   Managing War

Plantations are less familiar as legal institutions than state armed forces. One important moment in the legal-managerial production of imperialism was the reorganisation of the US Army in 1901. This reorganisation was undertaken by US Secretary of War Elihu Root.[23] Root was appointed US War Secretary in 1899 and contributed to important shifts in US foreign policy occasioned by the Spanish-American War and the invasion of the Philippines. By his own admission, Root identified as a 'lawyer first and all the time'. This disposition went hand in hand with a reformist zeal. While practising as an attorney in New York, Root had spearheaded a plan to reorganise the state's judicial system.[24] Similarly, as new anti-trust legislation was introduced in the

---

[21] Ibid., 81.

[22] Ibid.

[23] Root's reorganisation has been labelled '[t]he first conscious and systematic application of "management principles"' in Peter Drucker, *Management Challenges for the Twenty-First Century* (Harper 2001) 7. Root himself deplored the term 'Taylor system' precisely because such techniques attributed to Taylor were already being trialed in the US Ordnance Bureau as early as the 1840s; see David W. Holden, 'Managing Men and Machines: US Military Officers and the Intellectual Origins of Scientific Management in the Early Twentieth Century', submitted PhD thesis (2016) (on file with author), 118.

[24] Philip Jessup, *Elihu Root*, Volume 1 [1938] (Archon 1964) 176–177.

44   A HISTORY OF THE ICC'S MANAGERIAL PRESENT

1890s, he advised several clients on how to rearrange their corporate structures to ensure regulatory compliance.[25] Drawing on these experiences, Root took up the War portfolio in 1899 'to perform the lawyer's duty upon the call of the greatest of all our clients, the Government of our country'.[26]

How Root approached the US Army of 1901 offers some insight into the reformist sensibility of later diplomats and international lawyers. Root began by positioning the US Army in the context of American expansionist aspirations. He believed that the US victory in the Spanish-American War had been a stroke of luck and that 'with a better prepared enemy, the defects of our system would have been made more glaring'.[27] Root was thus preparing for a new age in US foreign policy in which a militia based on British imperial practices would be replaced with a modern and well-structured, hierarchical, and appropriately staffed fighting force. This was driven by the 'demands of colonial government' brought on by the 'new insular possessions ... administered by the army'.[28] With his reorganisation plans, Root wished to 'la[y] the foundations for a state of preparedness for war on the part of the United States which ha[d] hitherto been unknown'.[29]

Root's lack of military or administrative training seemed to be more of an asset than an obstacle as he surveyed the task ahead. One contemporary believed Root's non-military training 'induced him to apply his great mind to the study, not only of the details of military affairs, but to all the higher questions of military administration'.[30] This resulted in 'painstaking care' being taken over the reorganisation plan. Root targeted overlapping processes that slowed down the army machinery.[31] Moreover, the exigencies of war warranted new battalion staff officers and the creation of a chief of staff structure close to the president.[32] It also required a military information division and expanded military training at West

---

[25] Ibid., 184.

[26] Ibid., 215.

[27] William H. Carter, 'Elihu Root: His Services as Secretary of War' (1904) 178 *North American Review* 110–121, at 111.

[28] Jessup, *Elihu Root* 240–241.

[29] Carter, 'Elihu Root' 117.

[30] Ibid.

[31] James E. Hewes Jr, *From Root to McNamara: Army Organisation and Administration, 1900–1963* (Center of Military History 1975) 6.

[32] Army Appropriations Act 1901.

2.2 MANAGING BEFORE TAYLOR: PLANTATION, FACTORY, WAR 45

Point. In reforms contained in the 1901 Army Appropriations Act, Root revealed himself to be 'a person of large executive and administrative ability'.[33]

In the army as in the plantation, regulation of complex organisations was both a legal and a managerial enterprise. And for lawyers like Root, restructuring of state armed forces dovetailed with ideas about wider global reordering. Once promoted to Secretary of State, Root instructed US delegates to the 1907 Hague Conference to spotlight a new international court for the settlement of disputes. Once hostilities were under way in Europe, Root called for both victory over Germany and a future reorganisation of the world designed to minimise the waging of aggressive war. He called for 'a new birth of the law of nations' and wrote to Lassa Oppenheim that 'the more I reflect upon the possibilities of the future ... the more certain I become that the establishment of adequate law is the essential of every proposal for a new condition of international affairs better than the old'.[34] The connection for Root was that 'at the basis of every community lies the idea of *organisation* to preserve the peace'.[35] Root's vision pointed to the organisational role of law, where experimental ideas of renovation and management could be applied beyond one army to the family of nations.[36]

2.2.3 Managing the Factory

While the plantation and war are key episodes in management history, the factory is the central site of the story managers tell themselves about the emergence of their field. The factory, as a new mode of production but also a moment of 'cultural rebirth', represents the divide between pre-rational and rational, informal and formal, and ancient and modern methods.[37] The factory's birth is put down to sheer necessity. Technological innovation had made mass manufacturing possible, which had, in turn, allowed production to be conceived on a hitherto unimaginable scale. Production was no longer confined to the small-scale and artisanal back shop but would instead arrange hundreds of workers, flooding in from the countryside, according to the exigencies of the

---

[33] Jessup, *Elihu Root* 240.
[34] Ibid., 375.
[35] Ibid., 377.
[36] David Kennedy, 'Move to Institutions' (1987) 8 *Cardozo Law Review* 841–988.
[37] Daniel A. Wren and Arthur G. Bedeian, *The Evolution of Management Thought* (Wiley 2017) 21.

production line. As part of this story, the 'separation of hand and brain' occasioned by the division of labour and the complexity of factory supervision required more oversight and expertise than what the factory owner could offer. Hence, management's modern origin story pinpoints the delegation of responsibility, sometime around 1780, to a middleman.[38]

Although far from professional in the modern sense, these middlemen mediated the relationship between workers and owners. The conflict between labour and capital became the driving force behind managers' interventions as they sought to resolve disputes and locate 'win–win' situations for both groups. This demanded much of the manager. It meant tackling the labour shortages afflicting early English factories and persuading existing labourers to stick it out in the face of urban distractions. Confronting these early obstacles, managers also redefined issues of population upheaval as questions of labour and the 'problem' of the reluctant worker.

Management practices foregrounded issues of labour supply and workers' laziness. Laws were passed on uniform working hours designed to make labour supply more constant and predictable.[39] And managers began to assess and reward workers for tasks as an incentive for staying in their job and stabilising uprooted lives.[40] From this, the work supervisor soon morphed into a sociologist concerned with recording and imbibing thrift and moral discipline. This idea of the manager as not only a supervisor but a moral guide strikes a chord with those pursuing later moralising projects. In various statements, Fernández invokes management as a position within the organisational hierarchy and a value-set for professionals to live by. Such connection to morality harks back to the proselytising of factory managers.[41]

These three pre-Taylorite episodes reveal a situated practice of pre-professional managing. Such episodes inaugurated aspects of management later inherited by the ICC. From the plantation experience, it

---

[38] This has been designated the 'primordial act' in the creation of a corporate structure; see Philip Selznick, 'Foundations of the Theory of Organisation' (1948) 13 *American Sociological Review* 25–35.

[39] In Britain, the Health and Morals of Apprentices Act 1802 applied a working cap of twelve hours per day to apprentices. This was later extended to all factory workers in the Factory Act 1833.

[40] Wren, 'Evolution of Management Thought' 50.

[41] Principally Robert Owen, *A New Vision of Society, or Essays on the Principle of the Formation of the Human Character* [1813].

2.3 (INTERNATIONAL LEGAL) MANAGEMENT AFTER TAYLOR   47

became possible to view 'remote' places from afar with the aid of organisational charts and statistics. Internationally minded reformism connecting organisations to peace and justice emerged through the move to institutions after 1918. And management was not just a functional but a moral guide for how the managed should live. These assumptions reveal the political and legal connections of management even before it became 'scientific'.

2.3   (International Legal) Management after Taylor

Even at the outbreak of war in 1914, management was, at best, a small collection of methods applied by engineers in a handful of New England factories. Yet by the Wall Street Crash of 1929, management was being touted as 'indispensable'.[42] For the authors of the 1931 organisations text, *Onward Industry!*, management had become the brain to the organisational body, 'which actuates, directs, and controls the plans and procedure of organisation'.[43] The popularity of management in the ICC a century later arose partly from this professionalisation of management into a scientific practice and set of theories. Through its apparent objectivity and distance from politics, management became a powerful language for the articulation of political, economic, and social projects in the United States and beyond. This section highlights the innovations of 'scientific management' and its successor movement, the 'human relations' school. It then looks to how those schools of thought shaped two important interwar institutions: the International Labour Office and the League of Nations Permanent Mandates Commission. It then pre-empts a discussion on the postcolonial United Nations in the next section by considering the UN's move to planning in the 1950s.

2.3.1   *Scientific Management as 'an Effort of the Imagination'*

Had his eyesight been better, Frederick Winslow Taylor may have been remembered as an obscure mortgage lawyer in his father's Philadelphia law firm. Instead, Taylor entered the Midvale Steel Works in 1878 as a machinist before ascending the ranks to chief engineer only six years

---

[42] Wren, 'Evolution of Management Thought' 3.

[43] Alan Campbell Reiley and James D. Mooney, *Onward Industry!: The Principles of Organisations and Their Significance to Modern Industry* (Harper & Bros 1931) 10.

48　　A HISTORY OF THE ICC'S MANAGERIAL PRESENT

later.[44] In the course of this rapid rise, Taylor studied the behaviour of his fellow workmen. By the time he had risen to chief engineer, he had become obsessed with the blight of 'soldiering', a practice adopted by workers to cap individual productivity and thereby prevent them from being held to higher performance standards. Rather than seeing soldiering as a legitimate tactic for withholding labour, Taylor drew on popular tropes about worker laziness to point to the loss of earnings they caused. Because such 'awkward, inefficient, or ill-directed movements of men, however, leave nothing visible or tangible behind them', '[t]heir appreciation call[ed] for an act of memory, an effort of the imagination'.[45] In this imaginary, Taylor visualised 'the waste of material things', which he saw as more damaging to national prosperity than vanishing forests or depleted coal reserves.

A key reason behind this great waste of things, for Taylor, lay in how the problem had been addressed until then. All nineteenth-century American factory owners and men of capital were out searching for 'the ready-made, competent man; the man whom some one else has trained'.[46] This was the wrong approach, said Taylor. Rather it was the duty of businessmen to 'systematically cooperat[e] to train and to make this competent man'.[47] Hence, 'the first object of any good system must be that of developing first-class men; and under systematic management the best man rises to the top more certainly and more rapidly than ever before'.[48] However nefarious was national waste, it would only be resolved through the minute supervision and recalibration of individual workers.

While drawing on existing techniques, Taylor also sought to convert these from rules of thumb into a science. He believed that 'the best management is a true science, resting upon clearly defined laws, rules, and principles' applying 'to all kinds of human activities, from our simplest individual acts to the work of our great corporations'.[49] These scientific techniques included motion study (to determine the optimal movements of workers), time study (establishing standardised schedules

---

[44] Stephen Cummings et al., *A New History of Management* (Cambridge University Press 2019) 84–5.

[45] Frederick W. Taylor, *Principles of Scientific Management* [1911] (Dover Publications 1998) iii.

[46] Taylor, 'Principles' iii.

[47] Ibid., iv.

[48] Ibid.

[49] Taylor, 'Principles' iv.

2.3 (INTERNATIONAL LEGAL) MANAGEMENT AFTER TAYLOR   49

and targets), planned work layouts and task management, and costing analysis linking production to budgeting. It also required improved working conditions, such as better lighting, tool design, and posture to eliminate fatigue and maintain consistent levels of output.[50] These practices were later implemented by Taylor at Bethlehem Steel Company. In *Principles*, Taylor spends much time explaining the effect of these techniques on a German pig-iron handler called Schmidt, and he estimates that such 'fundamental principles' would save the company around $75,000 a year.[51]

In reality, Taylor's science was little more than a collection of rules of thumb applied to greater effect in plantations and the military decades before. His tale of Schmidt has also been famously debunked as a myth,[52] while his 'rough talk' with workers belied a sense of intellectual (and racial) superiority over the 'mentally sluggish type[s]'.[53] Moreover, the effects of scientific management on other factories in Philadelphia, and famously during the Watertown strikes of 1911, point towards management as a cause of unrest.[54] Striking workers derided Taylorism as a way for bosses to exert control over their lives, and the stopwatch and clipboard 'reduce[d] workers to virtual slavery', recalling Gantt's intent, and further restricted workers' freedom over the deployment of their labour.[55] A major congressional inquiry took place in the wake of the Watertown strikes, to which Taylor was called to testify.[56]

---

[50] Ibid., 67–68; Tony Morden, *Principles of Management* (McGraw-Hill 1996) 5–6.

[51] Taylor, 'Principles' 35–36.

[52] Charles Wrege and Amedeo Perroni, 'Taylor's Pig-Tale: A Historical Analysis of Frederick W. Taylor's Pig-Iron Experiments' (1974) 17 *Academy of Management Journal* 6–27; Jill Hough and Margaret White, 'Using Stories to Create Change: The Object Lesson of Frederick Taylor's "Pig-Tale"' (2001) 27 *Journal of Management* 585–601.

[53] Taylor, 'Principles' 21.

[54] Mike Davis, 'The Stopwatch and the Wooden Shoe: Scientific Management and the Industrial Workers of the World' in James Green (ed.), *Workers' Struggles, Past and Present: A "Radical America" Reader* (Temple University Press 1983) 83, at 83.

[55] James O'Connell, Official Circular No. 12, Office of the International President, International Association of Machinists, 26 April 1911 (reprinted in *Hearings to Investigate the Taylor System, Volume 2*, 1222–1223). French activist Simone Weil drew similar conclusions after spending time at the Renault factory in France, Simone Weil, *Oppression and Liberty* [1933] (Routledge 1988) 9.

[56] Robert Hoxie, *Scientific Management and Labour* (Appleton-Century-Crofts 1915) Appendix II, 140–149.

50   A HISTORY OF THE ICC'S MANAGERIAL PRESENT

While Taylor's stated aim was the 'maximum prosperity for the employer, coupled with the maximum prosperity for each employee',[57] the political economist Harry Braverman argued that the 'separation of hand and brain' occasioned by Taylorism was 'the most decisive single step in the division of labour taken by the capitalist mode of production'.[58] Workers became alienated from their outputs as 'craftsmanship [was] destroyed and ... the remaining ties, already tenuous and weakened, between the working population and science [were] more or less completely broken'.[59] This was coupled with the very deskilling Taylor and others sought to confront. For Braverman, management was less scientific method than 'the representative of management masquerading in the trappings of science'.[60] It was, in his Marxist reading, class war 'by other means'.[61] But before Braverman could launch such critiques, management continued to assert itself as a science. By his death in 1915, Taylor had acquired a crowd of disciples committed to his 'gospel of efficiency'.[62] Deploying Taylorism, they began articulating a new vocabulary for analysing the organisation from its workflow processes to its individual human components.

These disciples were also of the time and spirit of twentieth-century progressivism.[63] By 1914, the spirit of American progressivism had taken hold in public discourse. Public officials, social reformers, and captains of industry had come to view ideological party politics as quaint and ill-suited to the problems of the modern world. They surveyed the complex and overlapping issues faced by burgeoning city populations, such as

---

[57] Taylor, 'Principles' 1.

[58] Harry Braverman, *Labour and Monopoly Capital: The Degradation of Work in the Twentieth Century* [1974] (Monthly Review Press 1998) 87. Braverman read Marx as a management theorist, prompting organisations scholars to study the labour process in greater depth. See David Knights and Hugh Willmott (eds.), *Labour Process Theory* (Macmillan 1990); David Spencer, 'Braverman and the Contribution of Labour Process Analysis to the Critique of Capitalist Production – Twenty-Five Years On' (2000) 14 *Work, Employment & Society* 223–243. Labour process analysis largely paved the way for CMS. Others saw management as a 'system of social control'; see Judith Merkle, *Management and Ideology: The Legacy of the International Scientific Management Movement* (University of California Press 1980) 86.

[59] Braverman, 'Labour and Monopoly Capital' 90.

[60] Ibid., 59.

[61] John Foster, 'Introduction' in Braverman, 'Labour and Monopoly Capital' ix–xxiv, at xiv.

[62] Wren, 'Evolution of Management Thought' 118.

[63] Sinclair offers a concise overview of the progressive zeitgeist in Guy Fiti Sinclair, *To Reform the World: International Organisations and the Making of Modern States* (Oxford University Press 2018) 55.

2.3 (INTERNATIONAL LEGAL) MANAGEMENT AFTER TAYLOR 51

public sanitation, mass education, and urban planning, and saw the sciences, including management, as appropriate means for studying and minimising social upheaval without the nuisance of political interference. For their part, Taylor's followers saw management as one of the disciplines that would redefine political life away from 'terms of good and evil' and towards 'knowledge, efficiency, and scientific planning against ignorance, error, and economic waste'.[64]

Management represented the organisational wing of this progressive movement. New management consultants staked out a position between public policy analysis on one side, and sociology on the other.[65] They connected ideas of individual responsibility and geo-political competition, detailed surveillance and government institutions, in ways that had not been done before. This was deemed a matter of national concern: Taylor had opened *Principles* with an address by Teddy Roosevelt stating '[t]he conservation of our national resources is only preliminary to the larger question of national efficiency'.[66] Taylor thus pointed to the 'great loss which the whole country is suffering through inefficiency in almost all of our daily acts'.[67] There was no question that management would allow managers to optimise the 'first-class man' for the national benefit.

Similarly, management was being connected to the emerging global status of the United States. 'The elimination of "soldiering"', says Taylor, 'would so lower the cost of production that both our home and foreign markets would be greatly enlarged, and we would compete on more than even terms with our rivals'.[68] Taylor saw this as a win–win situation, stating that 'the larger profit would come to the whole world in general'.[69] Nonetheless, he was in little doubt as to the proper beneficiaries: 'the English and American peoples'.[70] For Taylor, any American who fears the removal of the under-performing worker 'should realise that the one element more than any other which differentiates civilised from uncivilised countries – prosperous from poverty-stricken peoples – is that the average man in the one is five or six times as productive as the

---

[64] Edward Purcell Jr, *The Crisis of Democratic Theory: Scientific Naturalism and the Problem of Value* (University Press of Kentucky 1973) 15.

[65] James Smith, *The Ideas Brokers: Think Tanks and the Rise of the New Policy Elite* (Free Press 1993) 52–55.

[66] Taylor, 'Principles' iii.

[67] Ibid., iv.

[68] Ibid., 4.

[69] Ibid., 73.

[70] Ibid., 76.

52 A HISTORY OF THE ICC'S MANAGERIAL PRESENT

other'.[71] In the toss-up between unmotivated American workers and the unproductive 'other', scientific management would help racial superiority to win out.[72]

These desires gave the manager at the centre of Taylor's theory incredible power. They would of course be standing over each worker, stopwatch in one hand, clipboard in the other. But they were also now placed in the larger project of American renewal envisioned by Taylor to traverse the factory, government, and global political rivalries. Managers were to become 'preeminent knowledge brokers'.[73] In this, they became reliant on lawyers and brought their own expertise to the legal issues of the time. Not least of these issues was that of the railroad monopolies. And there is no better embodiment of management's crossovers with law at the time than Louis Brandeis.

The same age as Taylor, Brandeis proposed the name 'scientific management' to Taylor as an authoritative slogan for his approach. The name, Brandeis explained, would 'appeal to the imagination'.[74] It may be surprising to find the railroad baron-busting 'people's lawyer' Brandeis in league with one so frequently derided by the American Labor Union. Yet like other progressives, Brandeis saw himself as a 'mediator between capitalists and workers ... apply[ing] his reformist skills to improve conditions for both parties through the use of progressive workplace concepts'.[75] This role was on display in the 1910 *Eastern Rate* case. In that case, Brandeis argued against a proposed rate hike by the Eastern Railroad Company by pointing to the possibility of one million dollars in efficiencies being achieved a day through the application of Taylorism.[76] In these situations, Brandeis saw 'a perfect

---

[71] Ibid., 75.

[72] For a racialised account of management, see David Roediger and Elizabeth Esch, *The Production of Difference: Race and the Management of Labor in US History* (Oxford University Press 2012), esp. chapter 5. See also Elizabeth Esch, *The Color Line and the Assembly Line: Managing Race in the Ford Empire* (University of California Press 2018).

[73] Christopher McKenna, *The World's Newest Profession: Management Consulting in the Twentieth Century* (Cambridge University Press 2006) 16.

[74] Brandeis letter to Drury (31 January 1914), in Leslie Oakes and Paul Miranti Jr, 'Louis D. Brandeis and Standard Cost Accounting: A Study of the Construction of Historical Agency' (1996) 21 *Accounting, Organisations and Society* 569–586, at 578.

[75] David Savino, 'Louis D. Brandeis and His Role Promoting Scientific Management as a Progressive Movement' (2009) 15 *Journal of Management History* 38–49, at 40.

[76] Oscar Kraines, 'Brandeis' Philosophy of Scientific Management' (1960) 13 *Western Political Quarterly* 191–201; Walter Lippmann, *Drift and Mystery* (Mitchell Kennerly 1914) 10–11.

2.3 (INTERNATIONAL LEGAL) MANAGEMENT AFTER TAYLOR 53

opportunity to bring together his legal ability [and] his knowledge of efficient work methods' to benefit freight operators.[77]

Brandeis was as keen an experimenter of management as Fernández a century later. He admiringly recalled Colbert's famous line: 'Accountancy – that is government'.[78] And by the time of his election to the US Supreme Court, he was articulating scientific management in his opinions. Dissenting from the majority in *New State Ice Co. v. Liebmann* (1932), he again adopted a Taylorist diagnosis. Citing publications of the Taylor Society, he reasoned

> that through improved methods of manufacture, made possible by advances in science and invention and vast accumulation of capital, our industries had become capable of producing from thirty to one hundred per cent more than was consumed even in days of vaunted prosperity.[79]

This recalled the waste and opportunity imagined by Taylor. At the heart of Brandeis' management style lay 'experimentation'.[80] He argued in *Liebmann* that '[t]here must be power in the States and the Nation to remould, through experimentation, our economic practices and institutions to meet changing social and economic needs'.[81] This was a 'grave responsibility' for those tasked with finding new solutions. Foreshadowing the models of the New Deal era, Brandeis speculated that 'a single courageous State may, if its citizens choose, serve as a laboratory; and try novel social and economic experiments without risk to the rest of the country'.[82] This favoured a creative deployment of legal and management arguments to address social conflict and foregone profits.[83] The turn to 'human relations' built on Brandeis' vision of management as a mode of social uplift, something that would prove useful to international officials after the Great War.

---

[77] Savino, 'Louis D. Brandeis' 41.

[78] Oakes and Miranti, 'Standard Cost Accounting' 569.

[79] *New State Ice Co. v. Liebmann* 285 US 262 at 308 (1932).

[80] Ibid., 310.

[81] Ibid., 311.

[82] Ibid., 311. See Savino, 'Louis D. Brandeis' 45.

[83] Lawrence Freedman, *Strategy: A History* (Oxford University Press 2013) 464. Brandeis was often challenged for his faith in scientific management, not least by workers themselves who preferred to call it 'scientific driving', see Jill Lepore, 'Not So Fast', *The New Yorker*, 12 October 2009, available at: www.newyorker.com/magazine/2009/10/12/not-so-fast.

54   A HISTORY OF THE ICC'S MANAGERIAL PRESENT

2.3.2   Interbellum Experiments with Labour

'[T]he discipline of "international institutions" has made much of 1918', says Kennedy.[84] International institutional law takes the armistice and the war/peace break, as its 'origin', much in the way management takes Taylorism as its own. Like international institutional law, management was also fuelled by the desire to bring order to chaos. Under that interpretation, the irrational Great War had left the world 'disorganized', prompting lawyers like Elihu Root to advocate for global reorganisation.[85] Those within institutions like the International Labour Office also saw themselves on the vanguard of this reorganisation, based on aspirations towards moral and social uplift after the fractures of war.

The International Labour Organization (ILO), established under Part XIII of the Treaty of Versailles, captured and facilitated this new management approach. As documented by Guy Sinclair, ILO officials 'articulated a functionalist vision of their organisation as an apolitical agency of international administration'.[86] They quickly took up the Taylorist (and progressive) aim of minimising conflict between capital and labour. The very basis of the ILO – 'the wellbeing, physical, moral and intellectual, of industrial wage-earners' – also reflected a shift from Taylorism towards a new concern for worker welfare.[87] With this newfound stance of the international, ILO officials saw management as a way to 'fan the Promethean sparks into flames to light the path of progress to be followed by mankind in a spirit of practical idealism'.[88]

Sinclair documents the emergence of this bilingual speaker of law and management at the ILO. The organisation's mandate set the boundaries for action in the realm of worker welfare and social engineering. It was therefore 'an ideal setting for the confluence of individuals with diverse kinds of scientific knowledge and know-how, including public administration, social security, management science, economics, and law'.[89] In management, as in related fields, scientific rationality and methods

---

[84] David Kennedy, 'Move to Institutions' 841.

[85] Francis Walters, *A History of the League of Nations* [1952] (Praeger 1986) 3; Kennedy, 'Move to Institutions' 845.

[86] Sinclair, 'To Reform the World' 108.

[87] Peter Miller and Ted O'Leary, 'Accounting and the Construction of the Governable Person' (1987) 12 *Accounting, Organisations and Society* 235–265, at 252.

[88] Hugo Haan, 'Scientific Management and Economic Planning' (1933) 166 *Annals of the American Academy of Political and Social Science* 66–74, at 74.

[89] Sinclair, 'To Reform the World' 108.

2.3 (INTERNATIONAL LEGAL) MANAGEMENT AFTER TAYLOR 55

would prove an ideal register through which to establish the Office as an 'apolitical agency'.[90]

The ILO's reliance on management emanated from its wish to implement mutually beneficial labour relations policies for owners and workers. This idea already lay at the heart of progressivism and was a firm basis on which to speak to and draw from management experts. In the mid-1920s, the ILO sent some of its officials to the United States to discuss scientific management with leaders in industry in an effort to apply such techniques to their own work. The ILO published the outcome of these meetings in 1927 as a report entitled 'Scientific Management in Europe' and in the same year lent its support to the creation of an International Management Institute (IMI) in Geneva.[91]

The IMI, which the ILO maintained strong ties with, helped organise the World Economic Conference in 1927, and later the World Social Economic Planning Congress. These contributed to a new vocabulary of 'rationalisation' based on 'international cooperation, coordination, and planning'.[92] The purchase of management was apparent to leading officials within the early IMI, such as Lyndall Urwick, director from 1928 until its closure in 1933.[93] As Sinclair describes, Urwick backed the rationalisation turn globally, contending that 'Taylor's "mental revolution" must take place in international affairs as well as individual businesses and that the principles of management must be applied "to the management of national economies and of the world economy"'.[94] This endeavour was greatly assisted by the creation of new Business Schools and the rise of management consulting as a profession.[95]

The management Urwick and the ILO officials took up was not, however, pure Taylorism. Taylor's followers had already judged that scientific management failed to account for the worker themselves: their state of mind and cohesion with others. Taylor's encounters with the

---

[90] Ibid., 108.

[91] Antony Alcock, *History of the International Labour Organisation* (Macmillan 1971) 121.

[92] Sinclair, 'To Reform the World' 92.

[93] Thomas Cayet, 'The ILO and the IMI: A Strategy of Influence on the Edges of the League of Nations, 1925–1934' in Jasmien van Daele et al. (eds.), *ILO Histories: Essays on the International Labour Organisation and Its Impact on the World during the Twentieth-Century* (Peter Lang 2010) 251–270, at 257–258.

[94] Sinclair, 'To Reform the World' 93 quoting Urwick.

[95] McKenna, 'World's Newest Profession' 8. There is a large literature on the history of the Business School; see, for example, Rakesh Khurana, *From Higher Aims to Hired Hands: The Social Transformation of American Business Schools and the Unfulfilled Promise of Management as a Profession* (Princeton University Press 2007).

56   A HISTORY OF THE ICC'S MANAGERIAL PRESENT

mythical Schmidt evinced a theory of the obedient worker who submits body and soul to recalibration. Difference and deviation were the enemies of efficiency. The post-Taylorites of the 'human relations' school sought to update that analysis. If Taylorism 'dominate[d] the world of production', according to Braverman, then 'the practitioners of "human relations" and "industrial psychology" [were] the maintenance crew for the human machinery'.[96] The individual worker had to be studied similarly to the wider labour process. Elton Mayo, a key part of that shift, took aim at the 'anomie ... of the industrial worker' and by the early 1920s was looking for a way to reconcile 'the worker's need for belongingness with the conflicting allegiances of the complex world he now finds himself in'.[97]

Once Mayo and others began their experiments, they were surprised to find that it was not physical layout or monitoring that affected productivity but informal variables such as group cohesion. From these experiments, 'the feeling of security and certainty' became key determinants of worker attitudes and hence productivity.[98] Hereafter, managers began to focus on worker contentment and their daily environment to continue making the productive worker. This new set of concerns shifted 'the study of the habituation of workers to their work ... from the plane of psychology to that of sociology'.[99]

But this was not an easy transition. It required managers to access the 'biological and social facts' of workers' lives beyond the organisation and the wider social milieu that conditioned them. From here a concern for worker welfare translated to the production of data about their needs, interests, and desires, at work, at home, and in their community. This dovetailed with social reforms geared towards securing the 'chronic contentment' of the worker, a productivity-increasing and union-busting strategy.[100] Already latent in Taylor's improvement of lighting and other conditions, these efforts included pension plans, unemployment insurance, and small schemes of profit sharing.[101] This was the spirit of Henry

---

[96] Braverman, 'Labour and Monopoly Capital' 60.

[97] William H. Whyte, *The Organisation Man* (Simon & Schuster 1961) 33.

[98] Ibid., 35.

[99] Braverman, 'Labour and Monopoly Capital' 100. See Mary Parker Follett, 'The Giving of Orders' in Henry Metcalf and Lyndal Urwick (eds.), *Dynamic Administration: The Collected Papers of Mary Parker Follett* (Harper & Brothers Publishers 1942) 23–45.

[100] Whyte, 'Organisation Man' 37–38.

[101] Richard Hoffman, 'Corporate Social Responsibility in the 1920s: An Institutional Perspective' (2007) 13 *Journal of Management History* 55–73, at 60.

2.3 (INTERNATIONAL LEGAL) MANAGEMENT AFTER TAYLOR   57

Ford's 'five-dollar-day', welfarism, and the turn to 'the social'.[102] Ford himself was also notorious for implementing the study of workers through his company's Sociological Department, which sent experts to workers' homes in order to gauge their marital relations, alcohol consumption, and spending patterns.

These innovations in psychology, sociology, and statistical collection were noticed by international administrators at the ILO as they first encountered management. A Scientific Division was created within the ILO to compile and disseminate information on various labour topics. As Sinclair recounts, '[i]n undertaking independent and impartial studies . . . the Scientific Division's work frequently paved the way for a more direct and practical engagement with those issues'.[103] An institutional infrastructure was constructed to facilitate this but also to deal with and act on the information received to devise labour standards for eventual codification.[104]

Practically, management helped to 'specify and calculate risks, to prepare actuarial estimates, and to levy and collect contributions'.[105] It also helped to imaginatively connect the otherwise dislocated ideas of labour supply concerns and the care of populations through rational international guidance:

> Through a combination of chance opportunities, ad hoc improvisations, and deliberate action, this accumulation of expert knowledge and experience gradually led the ILO into providing technical assistance to help countries set up social insurance schemes.[106]

More robust prototypes followed in other institutions. This deployment of legal, scientific, and managerial knowledges to render disparate constituencies epistemologically legible would become a key modality of governance in later institutions. It is not only the ICC that has had to confront the immense logistical task of identifying, reaching, and documenting communities and complex events at a distance. The Permanent Mandates Commission (PMC) was among the first to fuse law and administration in attempting to regulate distant populations.

---

[102] Duncan Kennedy, 'The Three Globalisations of Law and Legal Thought: 1850–2000' in David M. Trubek and Alvaro Santos (eds.), *The New Law and Economic Development: A Critical Appraisal* (Cambridge University Press 2006) 19–73, at 37–56 on 'the social'.

[103] Sinclair, 'To Reform the World' 60.

[104] Ibid.

[105] Ibid., 65.

[106] Ibid., 65.

The League Covenant establishing the PMC ascribed a supervisory role to the Commission. Article 22 of the Covenant established the 'sacred trust of civilisation' between 'those colonies and territories' and 'the States which formerly governed them'. That trust was grounded in the understanding that these colonies were 'not yet able to stand by themselves under the strenuous conditions of the modern world'. Their 'tutelage' became the responsibility of 'advanced nations'. And the machinery of supervision and improvement would be made to last only so long as these less advanced nations were themselves capable of acting independently.[107] Many of the assumptions and aspirations in Taylor's management manifesto, from making the competent man to the responsibilities of the benevolent manager, appear also in this international legal text.

The PMC followed the ILO in its endorsement of management. It took seriously other forms of expertise, particularly public administration, which soon fed into practices of colonial administration. This 'alliance between law and administration', according to Antony Anghie, placed the PMC 'in a unique position to engage in an ongoing and evolving process of receiving, assimilating, and synthesizing information from the mandate territories and then using this information to develop more appropriate and effective standards'.[108] This knowledge would be 'gathered from the furthest peripheries and consolidated by the League' in reports and committees, before prompting administrative guidelines and legislative proposals.[109]

The PMC combined Taylorism with human relations and notions of welfarism to shape the societies in which mandate powers intervened. 'The promotion of "efficient communities" was a major preoccupation of the Mandate System' according to Quincy Wright, US international lawyer and key architect of the PMC. Placing Taylorism on an international footing, Wright 'envisage[d] communities, efficiently governed and utilising their natural and human resources to the full'.[110] Much as Taylorism had cast the worker as an optimisable unit in production, the

---

[107] Ntina Tzouvala, *Capitalism as Civilization: A History of International Law* (Cambridge University Press 2021).

[108] Antony Anghie, 'Colonialism and the Birth of International Institutions: Sovereignty, Economy, and the Mandate System of the League of Nations' (2002) 34 *NYU Journal of International Law & Policy* 513–634, at 576.

[109] Ibid., 614.

[110] Ibid., 587, quoting Quincy Wright.

2.3 (INTERNATIONAL LEGAL) MANAGEMENT AFTER TAYLOR 59

global gospel of efficiency led 'colonial powers to view natives in terms of the labour and economic wealth they represented'.[111]

Beyond Taylorism, this project represented 'the native' as both unit of production and psychological being.[112] The League of Nations Draft Convention on Slavery articulates this human relations approach to colonial peoples. As Anghie recounts of the Convention, 'colonial labour legislation [was] framed with a view to ensuring not merely the well-being of the native, but also his physical and moral development, and at the same time furthering the economic progress of the country'.[113] The PMC was thus 'a happy (if always-improving) unity between welfare on the one hand, and productivity and economic efficiency on the other'.[114] The human relations school further fused those strands of governance together.

Interbellum international institutions comprised an alloy of management theories, administrative practices, and legal infrastructures for the management of workers and colonial populations. Management helped ILO and PMC officials to frame the problem of 'the worker' and the 'native', to collect relevant data, and ask questions about moral uplift and social values. This combination of scientific management and work psychology proved a potent mix, outlasting the short-lived League experiment and finding its way into the governing rationale of the UN Trusteeship Council after 1945. Yet by then, management was changing again, allowing officials not only to supervise disparate communities but to plan organisations and their environments on a global scale.

2.3.3 Planning the Post-War World

In 1946, not long after states had assembled to establish the United Nations Organisation in San Francisco, one US official reflected on the magnitude of the architectural task. Donald Stone, a public administration expert, was by then the Assistant Director of Administrative Management in the US Bureau of the Budget. Stone combined his theoretical study of public administration, particularly public works, with

---

[111] Ibid., 589.
[112] Ibid., 589, quoting Quincy Wright.
[113] Ibid., 592–593.
[114] Ibid., 593.

60 A HISTORY OF THE ICC'S MANAGERIAL PRESENT

practice, establishing the American Public Works Association in 1937.[115] He was also interested in applying management principles to public administration. In his 1939 book, *The Management of Municipal Public Works*, he 'attempt[ed] to trace the essentials of management – principles, procedures, and techniques which have emerged as valid for application to governmental affairs – and to translate them into terms of municipal public works administration'.[116] Stone became a key figure in American wartime and post-war organisation, assisting in the restructuring of the US executive in 1939 and subsequently in assembling US occupation plans of Europe once war broke out.[117] However, it was Stone's role in designing both the post-war Marshall Plan and United Nations that revealed his management expertise and fused such ideas with international law and governance.

By the 1930s, a new mode of managerial intervention was already in circulation. Chester Barnard had developed a theory of the organisation as a system of co-operation between 'investors, suppliers and customers' rather than as an inward-looking black box.[118] These co-operative systems were to be judged on their effectiveness and efficiency in attaining set objectives and satisfying the 'individual motives' of stakeholders.[119] The 'ever-present conflict' of organisational and individual motives had to be synchronised if organisations were to be successful.[120] Managers were lynchpins for co-ordinating and communicating between these stakes and stakeholders, not just workers and owners. This effort to 'bridge the requirements of the formal organisation with the needs of the socio-human system was a landmark in management thought'.[121]

Systems thinking allowed officials such as Stone to directly link the organisation and its field of intervention.[122] But it was the American

---

[115] Donald C. Stone, 'Administrative Management: Reflections on Origins and Accomplishments' (1990) 50 *Public Administration Review* 3–20, at 8.

[116] John Edy, 'The Management of Municipal Public Works. By Donald C. Stone' (1939) 1 *Journal of Politics* 444–445, at 445.

[117] Stone, 'Administrative Management' 11.

[118] Wren, 'Evolution of Management Thought' 258.

[119] Ibid., 267.

[120] Ibid., 273.

[121] Ibid., 267.

[122] In ICC parlance, this is frequently characterised as an 'ecosystem'; see Independent Expert Review of the International Criminal Court and the Rome Statute System: Final Report, ICC, 30 September 2020, para. 19, available at: https://asp.icc-cpi.int/sites/asp/files/asp_docs/ASP19/IER-Final-Report-ENG.pdf.

2.3 (INTERNATIONAL LEGAL) MANAGEMENT AFTER TAYLOR   61

experience of the New Deal that crystallised ambitious efforts towards large-scale thinking and planning. The projects instigated by President Franklin Roosevelt followed the progressivist desire to 'depoliticise normally charged political issues and render them amenable to rational resolution'.[123] This also shaped 'the US vision of the postwar international economic order ... recasting political conflicts as "neutral" problems of efficiency and productivity'.[124] The New Deal thus offered the possibility of a 'constitutional revolution through pragmatic action'.[125]

The Tennessee Valley Authority (TVA) embodied the New Deal spirit. It also exemplified management's role in large-scale administrative projects prior to the UN. The TVA was 'to improve the navigability and to provide for the flood control of the Tennessee River; to provide for reforestation and the proper use of marginal lands in the Tennessee Valley [and] to provide for the agricultural and industrial development of said Valley'.[126] Experts thus identified market instability and the diminishing fertility of the land and decided to intervene technocratically across several US states through the introduction of hydroelectric power and new soil fertilisers.[127] This inaugurated a 'managerial class' as a new force in US political life.[128]

The TVA embodied much contemporary management thinking: the technical deployment of expertise through an administrative organisation and a concern for the wider social milieu.[129] It applied a systems lens: 'budgeting in the TVA is planning, planning is done by those

---

[123] Anne-Marie Slaughter-Burley, 'Regulating the World: Multilateralism, International Law, and the Projection of the New Deal Regulatory State' in John Ruggie (ed.), *Multilateralism Matters* (Columbia University Press 1993) 125–156, at 140.

[124] Ibid.

[125] David Mitrany, *A Working Peace System* (National Peace Council 1946) 3.

[126] Tennessee Valley Authority Act 1933, 48 Stat. 58–59, 16 USC, s. 831.

[127] See Timothy Mitchell, *Rule by Experts: Egypt, Techno-Politics, Modernity* (University of California Press 2002) chapter 1. For more on the Tennessee Valley Authority, see Erwin Hargrove, *Prisoners of Myth: The Leadership of the Tennessee Valley Authority, 1933–1990* (Princeton University Press 1994) 80; Philip Selznick, *TVA and the Grass Roots: A Study in the Sociology of Formal Organisation* (University of California Press 1949) 29–37.

[128] James Burnham, *The Managerial Revolution: What Is Happening in the World* (The John Day Company Inc. 1941) 192.

[129] Peter Drucker, *Management: Tasks, Responsibilities, Practices* [1974] (Harper Collins 2008) 134.

62 A HISTORY OF THE ICC'S MANAGERIAL PRESENT

responsible for operations'.[130] The TVA itself had an organisational structure that the UN specialised agencies would later adopt, including a directorate, a consolidated office of general management combining planning, budgeting, information, and employment, while the technical tasks of the TVA were divided into specialised offices and divisions.[131] The TVA was uniquely 'program-centred', meaning that 'basic management patterns spanned the usual dichotomy separating adjective administration from substantive policy'.[132] Administration and policy were fused. This model heavily influenced Stone and others in their blueprints of the Marshall Plan and the UN.[133] Slaughter-Burley even labels the post-war international order 'a macrocosm of the New Deal regulatory state'.[134]

The TVA model, particularly its reliance on management expertise, was most visibly replicated in the Marshall Plan's Technical Assistance Program (TAP). The TAP was an exercise in rebuilding European industry through American know-how. Plan administrators therefore brought 'European managers, trade unionists, politicians, and bureaucrats to the industrial centers of the United States', in the hope that 'these visitors would go back home sufficiently impressed to think of introducing, in their own enterprises, some of the institutions and practices they had seen across the Atlantic'.[135] Many did, with Factory Performance Reports and Productivity Councils being implemented across German factories. By 1948, 700 French industrialists and managers had made this transatlantic crossing to learn from 'the most modern American industrial practices'.[136]

---

[130] Albert Lepawsky, 'Technical Assistance: A Challenge to Public Administration' (1956) 16 *Public Administration Review* 22–23, at 29.

[131] Jeffery Shelton, 'Tennessee Valley Authority: The Establishment of a System for the Development of Agency Objectives', Unpublished MPA thesis, Atlanta University, July 1981, 18–19 (on file with author).

[132] Lepawsky, 'Technical Assistance' 29.

[133] So too would the functionalism of political scientists such as David Mitrany, for whom the TVA was an 'outstanding example' of functionalism, see David Mitrany, 'The Functional Approach to World Organisation' (1948) 24 *International Affairs* 350–363, at 354.

[134] Slaughter-Burley, 'Regulating the World' 125.

[135] Volker Berghahn, 'The Marshall Plan and the Recasting of Europe's Postwar Industrial Systems' in Eliot Sorel and Pier Carlo Padoan (eds.), *The Marshall Plan: Lessons Learned for the 21st Century* (OECD 2008) 29–42, at 34.

[136] Solidelle Wasser and Michael Dolfman, 'BLS and the Marshall Plan: The Forgotten Story', *Monthly Labour Review*, June 2005 44–52, at 44.

2.3 (INTERNATIONAL LEGAL) MANAGEMENT AFTER TAYLOR 63

Management expertise was not only used for material benefit but strategic advantage against the USSR in the first days of the Cold War. It helped to effect a capitalist vision of post-war Europe and keep socialist influence over France and Italy at bay.[137] One British treasury official lamented this strategy: 'the Americans want an integrated Europe looking like the United States – "God's own country"'.[138] By framing political and economic instability as a set of technical problems, American management experts could zero in on outmoded organisational methods and apply their own knowledge to update them. But it also set the stage for growing US–Soviet tension by inculcating American capitalist development against its alternatives.[139]

From the Marshall Plan, Stone became involved in the 'second major effort in recent times to organize the international community to work for the prevention of global war'.[140] Managerial experts moved seamlessly from the US executive to planning the war effort to post-war reconstruction, and now to a replacement for the League. At the US Bureau of the Budget, Stone oversaw these efforts and by late 1944, his staff had expanded 'to deal with problems of post-war requirements and organisation', as well as the US State Department's future role in a post-war world. To that end, he 'published an unofficial paper on lessons to be learned from the League of Nations and the criteria for a post-war United Nations organisation'.[141] Reflecting on these efforts, Stone acknowledged that such discussions and papers infused administrative management 'in the organisational and financial development of the evolving international system'.[142]

Such influence was visible in the UN structure. Replicating the New Deal model, problems were functionally separated and regulated via autonomous and specialised institutions. They took the form of 'specialised agencies' dealing with food, agriculture, and public health. These agencies were 'folded into the UN system [but] had independent

---

[137] Michael Hogan, *The Marshall Plan: America, Britain and the Reconstruction of Western Europe, 1947–1952* (Cambridge University Press 1987) 429.

[138] Robert Hall, quoted in Laurence Kaplan, *The United States and NATO: The Formative Years* (University Press of Kentucky 1984) 131.

[139] According to Drucker, 'the success of the Marshall Plan made management a bestseller. Suddenly everybody talked management, everybody studied management', Drucker, 'Management' 13.

[140] Stone, 'Administrative Management' 12.

[141] Ibid., 11.

[142] Ibid., 11.

64 A HISTORY OF THE ICC'S MANAGERIAL PRESENT

identities and decision-making procedures to carry out a variety of functions'. While Stone's managerial style reflected a desire to construct an organisation that could deal with such complex issues, it also set a premium against the expert governance of populations much like the TVA.[143]

The new UN head as 'Secretary-General' also assumed a central role as chief administrative officer.[144] Stone argued that it would take 'an exceptional amount of executive leadership and skill to make the UN work from a purely administrative standpoint'.[145] This leader-manager had to be involved in 'planning and directing its work', 'recruiting and managing the staff', 'organising the financial services', and 'establishing reporting facilities'.[146] On top of these, the Secretary-General would have to 'develop an effective working environment and tradition for the Secretariat and insure high moral purpose, good will, and loyalty to the organisation on the part of all the persons on the staff'.[147] The Secretary-General also had to embody a new international spirit. For Stone, '[t]he way in which he performs this job will have an important effect on the organisation's standing, for in the eyes of the world, the Secretary-General personifies the United Nations'.[148] Unlike the League secretaries, the UN head was intended to be not only an administrative officer but a global manager of international issues. That managerial status would be taken up by many heads of international institutions in the years to come, not least successive presidents of the ICC as managers of anti-impunity and international justice.

Once the UN became functional, Stone's technical assistance experience filtered into agency operations in various parts of the world, notably the Global South. Officials relied on ideas of public administration and management to assess 'under-developed' countries, much as the PMC had done some years prior. A Special Committee on Public Administration Problems was created for this purpose. The Committee's priorities demonstrate the effort to spread a certain vision of liberal democracy and capitalism. In its 'Standards and Techniques of Public Administration' for under-developed states, the Committee stated that

---

[143] Slaughter-Burley, 'Regulating the World' 135.
[144] Donald C. Stone, 'Organising the United Nations' (1946) 6 *Public Administrative Review* 115–129, at 118.
[145] Ibid., 115.
[146] Ibid., 118.
[147] Ibid.
[148] Ibid.

2.3 (INTERNATIONAL LEGAL) MANAGEMENT AFTER TAYLOR   65

'[a]n effective system of public administration must be founded on a policy which tends to broaden the range of personal freedom, economic and social opportunity, and political democracy'.[149] 'This norm may be regarded as a basic standard for good public administration', said the Committee, meaning that management techniques should be 'directed towards the improvement of the material and cultural achievements of an increasing number of groups and individuals'.[150]

Public administration was designed to work alongside capitalist forms of economic development and social welfare in reshaping societies of the Global South.[151] Such assistance involved 'equipping governments for the formulation and implementation of development plans' as well as 'basic surveys of resources and building up of administrative services'.[152] The 1950 UN mission to Bolivia demonstrates the UN's expanded mandate as well as the combined reliance on management, policy, economics, and law. As one commentator noted, 'besides formulating recommendations in the economic and social fields on a wide front … [officials] recommended a priority attack on the public administration of the country as a whole'.[153] The head of the UN mission worked closely with the Bolivian president, who was then attempting to stem economic decline and social unrest. The mission arranged an audit of the country's public finances to determine weaknesses.[154] It was not enough, though, and in 1952 the sitting president was deposed in a revolutionary coup. Nevertheless, the UN continued to send personnel to serve as 'international technicians'[155] and were frequently 'called upon to act on subjects involving overall management or policy formulation'.[156] This pattern of deploying management experts to inculcate management practices domestically spread to other parts of Latin America, and further afield.[157]

The role of Donald Stone from US public works expert to UN architect exemplifies the common threads of management thought and practice

---

[149] Lepawsky, 'Technical Assistance' 23.
[150] Ibid.
[151] Ibid.
[152] Sixth Report of the Technical Assistance Board, ECOSOC, 18th Session, E/2566E/TAC/REP.3, 24 (1954).
[153] Lepawsky, 'Technical Assistance' 25.
[154] Milton Bracker, 'UN Unit in Bolivia Makes Inventory', *New York Times*, 12 July 1950.
[155] Lepawsky, 'Technical Assistance' 26.
[156] Ibid.
[157] Ibid.

66   A HISTORY OF THE ICC'S MANAGERIAL PRESENT

that ran throughout these mid-century governance projects. This was an amalgam of management ideas and tools drawing on Taylorism, human relations psychology, and notions of planning. But these were hardly apolitical enterprises. Management was relied upon alongside law and other disciplines to establish an anti-communist Europe at the outset of the Cold War, and within the UN to discipline Third World states under a liberal, capitalist model. The next section shows how management could equally be relied upon to thwart Third World ambitions even after formal decolonisation.

2.4   The Third World as Managerial Problem

Perhaps surprisingly, the immediate precursor to management's deployment by the ICC is the postcolonial UN from the 1960s. This period saw a general uptake of management tools and ideas by a range of state and UN officials. In keeping with previous sections, that period also saw the articulation and subsequent routing of Third World political claims within the UN through management. That crucial 'battle' for international law, though waged in multiple settings and understood as a political and legal struggle, should also be seen as a managerial struggle between competing ideas of global order.[158]

This section begins by considering the background against which Third World arguments for UN democratisation emerged. Prior to the founding of the G77, the UN was already beginning to frame the trickle of newly independent states into the organisation as a problem to be managed. This already limited the space within which Third Worldists could articulate an alternative institution. I then trace the confrontation between the Third World vision of UN democracy contemplated in the New International Economic Order (NIEO), and the counter-strategy launched by the United States and others to retain the status quo arrangement of Western hegemony. This, too, was framed in managerial terms, meaning management had a clear set of political stakes, winners and losers, even if these remain occluded in the mainstream account of management at the ICC.

As newly independent states began to enter the UN in the 1950s, they were already being approached through a management lens. The Expanded Programme of Technical Assistance – precursor to the UN

---

[158] Jochen von Bernstorff and Philipp Dann (eds.), *The Battle for International Law: South–North Perspectives on the Decolonisation Era* (Cambridge University Press 2019).

2.4 THE THIRD WORLD AS MANAGERIAL PROBLEM 67

Development Programme – had been set up to embed this lens as a way to read 'under-developed' new members. Moreover, a 1948 General Assembly resolution captured how the UN's founding members interpreted the confluence of factors characterising these societies. They bore 'low standards of living', which not only affected the populace directly but 'the world as a whole'. These sub-optimal economic conditions were a threat to regional stability, 'prejudicial to the maintenance of peaceful and friendly relations among nations and to the development of conditions of economic and social progress'.[159]

The General Assembly therefore requested the Economic and Social Council (ECOSOC) to address the 'whole problem of the economic development of under-developed countries in all its aspects'.[160] Other institutions joined ECOSOC in addressing underdevelopment as a problem including the ILO and the International Bank for Reconstruction and Development, which the General Assembly asked to 'adopt all reasonable measures to facilitate the early realization of development loans, particularly those in areas economically under-developed'.[161] The policy work of the Secretariat, under Trygvie Lie, also emphasised the 'provision of technical assistance to economically backward countries'.[162] Such interpretations fashioned entire peoples and countries as a problematic.

As the UN's mandate expanded, new members found that the task of managing the UN itself would occupy considerable time and resources. One of Lie's acts was thus to form a decentralised 'committee structure and new organisational entities and policies'.[163] Eight departments were established, from Security Council Affairs to Legal Affairs and Administrative Services. The Secretariat's hierarchical position in relation to these committees and the new specialised agencies largely resembled the multi-divisional or M-form. With its earliest expression in the American plantations of the nineteenth century, the M-form was

---

[159] United Nations General Assembly Resolution (UNGA Res.) 198 (III) (4 December 1948) para. 1.

[160] Ibid., para. 3. The fusion of international peace and security agendas with development logics would re-emerge in the ICC in the early 2000s; see Christine Schwöbel-Patel, *Marketing Global Justice: The Political Economy of International Criminal Law* (Cambridge University Press 2021).

[161] UNGA Res 198 (III) para. 4.

[162] Development of a Twenty-Year Programme for Achieving Peace through the United Nations, UN General Assembly, A/1525, 17 November 1950.

[163] Joachim Müller (ed.), *Reforming the United Nations: A Chronology* (Brill Nijhoff 2016) 13.

68 A HISTORY OF THE ICC'S MANAGERIAL PRESENT

experiencing a revival by the 1950s, comprising a large part of the advice issued by a new body of management consultants offered to organisations such as Royal Dutch Shell.[164] Translated to the UN, this structure saw specialised agencies operating as 'separate and semiautonomous divisions' subordinate only to budgeting decisions.[165] The M-form created a split between the strategy work of the Secretariat and the operational mandate of the agencies. It also meant that despite inter-agency co-ordination, issues arising would be dealt with from within functional silos.

The M-form became a powerful form for the co-ordination of large-scale UN efforts, such as the 1960 peacekeeping mission in the Congo. As Sinclair recalls, the mission was a milestone for the application of 'modern governing practices'.[166] This was partly because of the scale of applying such practices to large populations and partly because such a mission helped to piece together the early threads of humanitarianism and development. It is unlikely the UN would have succeeded in its efforts in the Congo were it not for planning tools such as the M-form. The mission sought to remake state institutions 'including the state bureaucracy, army, and school system', and in doing so read the Congolese peoples as a manageable populace seeking self-improvement.[167]

Applying management to the problems of the Global South also required that the Secretary-General become a 'competent technocrat'.[168] Dag Hammarskjold embodied this managerial style, fusing it with his own vision of law. According to Oscar Schachter, Hammarskjold 'regarded himself as a man of law', believing that 'the processes of law, and, as he put it, the principles of justice were crucial to the effort to avert disaster and to achieve a secure and decent international order'.[169] And yet, as Schachter also acknowledged, Hammarskjold 'made no sharp distinction between law and policy'.[170] Law was not mere technique but 'the authoritative expression of principles that determine the goals and

---

[164] McKenna, 'World's Newest Profession' 170.

[165] Wren, 'Evolution of Management Thought' 210.

[166] Sinclair, 'To Reform the World' 114.

[167] Ibid., 155 and 172.

[168] Müller, 'Reforming the United Nations' 16.

[169] Oscar Schachter, 'Dag Hammarskjold and the Relation of Law to Politics' (1962) *American Journal of International Law* 1–8, at 1.

[170] Ibid., 2.

2.4 THE THIRD WORLD AS MANAGERIAL PROBLEM 69

direction of collective action'.[171] This approach to law as principled goal-seeking would make it highly susceptible to 'management by objectives', an emerging trend in American management circles at the time.[172] It also ordained the Secretary-General as a 'political technician who was required from time to time to deal with specific problems'.[173]

After Hammarskjold's untimely death in 1961, the managerial style nonetheless started to permeate other UN offices. Hammarskjold's replacement, U Thant, dramatically expanded the UN development infrastructure to encompass a Conference on Trade and Development and an industrial relations organisation. Management expertise was deployed within these mandates, both as practice and as a body of trained experts. Given the American context for management consultancy, it is unsurprising that this led to a political economy of expertise favouring Western and northern-trained experts. As one architect of the UN Industrial Development Organisation described it, the organisation needed to 'secure personnel of a different type from those generally found in international organisations', especially 'practitioners of industry, on proven organisers, practical technologists, and managerial talent'.[174] He reckoned that 'such personnel will obviously have to be found primarily in the plants and establishments of industrialised countries'.[175]

This organisational growth was not without cost. By the early 1960s, some US officials were already expressing their disquiet over the development mandate, complaining that Thant's expanded apparatus created 'inefficiencies, duplications and overlapping of activities'.[176] To this end, the General Assembly established an expert committee to examine UN financing in 1964. It resulted in UN budgetary reform, new systems for performance reporting, and long-term planning.[177] Thereafter, budgets were approved annually and included long-term planning estimates. A Joint Inspection Unit (JIU) was also established to 'investigate all matters having a bearing on the efficiency of services and proper use of funds'.[178] By the time a new vision of global order was being voiced by

---

[171] Ibid.
[172] Drucker, 'Management' 126.
[173] Schachter, 'Dag Hammarskjold' 3.
[174] Walter Kotschnig, 'The United Nations as an Instrument of Economic and Social Development' (1968) 22 *International Organisation* 16–43, at 36.
[175] Ibid., 36–37.
[176] Müller, 'Reforming the United Nations' 19.
[177] Ibid.
[178] Ibid.

70   A HISTORY OF THE ICC'S MANAGERIAL PRESENT

Third World states, then, they were already being read as a problem to be managed, and the UN as a potential problem too.

2.4.1   Management as Emancipatory Tool

Despite comprising a numerical majority within the General Assembly by the mid-1960s, former colonial states operated under the shadow of prior management ideas and concerns from the preceding decade. While they sought to articulate an alternative future for the UN, one that prioritised the experiences and needs of Third World peoples, representatives nonetheless framed their agenda within this institutional milieu. Yet as they engaged with existing members, bloc groupings, and civil servants, Third World actors saw how their entry into the UN was being narrated as a set of 'new constitutional, political and organisational problems' both domestically and within the UN itself.[179]

One of the first major reforms of a UN body reflected this concern about dysfunction in light of growing membership. The UN Development Programme was originally established differently to other agencies by having much greater control over strategic, as well as operational, issues. This decision to relax the M-form created potential overlap between the United Nations Development Programme (UNDP) and the UN Secretariat in their strategic advancement of the UN development mandate. This and similar issues led the UNDP Governing Council to commission an investigation into the effectiveness of UNDP and the wider development mandate.[180] Led by Sir Robert Jackson, the panel and its subsequent capacity report of 1969 framed the situation as a managerial problem demanding management solutions.[181]

Jackson diagnosed that the growth in the UN's development mandate had turned the organisation into 'probably the most complex organisation in the world'.[182] UNDP had become too decentralised, and many of its projects operated too independently to mount an effective response to multi-layered development issues. 'Who controls this "Machine"?',

---

[179] Sinclair, 'To Reform the World' 143, quoting Dag Hammarskjold.

[180] United Nations Development Programme: Report of the Governing Council, Sixth Session, E/4545, 11–28 June 1968, available at: https://digitallibrary.un.org/record/1298171?ln=en.

[181] A Study of the Capacity of the United Nations Development System, Volume 1, United Nations, DP/5, 1969, available at: https://digitallibrary.un.org/record/695860?ln=en (Capacity Report).

[182] Ibid., iii.

2.4 THE THIRD WORLD AS MANAGERIAL PROBLEM   71

Jackson asked.[183] His own assessment was that UNDP had 'become unmanageable ... slower and more unwieldy, like a prehistoric monster'.[184] He also pointed to how few modern management methods were in place, such as performance appraisal systems or standardised recruitment policies.[185] Jackson proposed to strengthen co-ordination within and between bodies making up the UN's development mandate. These bodies should have the capacity to 'oversee structural management changes and new management techniques' such as a UN Development Cooperation Cycle for centralising and streamlining information flows.[186] As Franda observes, 'this was among the first of many UN reports that specifically focused on the UN bureaucracy itself, seeking answers to world problems in the design of more modern and professional managerial techniques'.[187]

Yet Jackson's analysis glossed over the political contours of this growing apparatus. Once the G77 was created in June 1964, the General Assembly began to shift from 'an instrument of empire into an anti-colonial forum'.[188] The 1955 Bandung conference had already brought Third World leaders together in a historic meeting a decade before, but that lineage was now being extended into UN agencies. According to Gupta, the United Nations Conference on Trade and Development (UNCTAD) was an 'institutional child' of Bandung and 'the launching pad of the New International Economic Order'.[189] Such a forum 'embod[ied] an

---

[183] Ibid., iii.

[184] Ibid., iii.

[185] Jackson was not the only international official to turn to management as part of development. The World Bank President, Robert McNamara, saw poverty reduction in the 'developing' world as a primary goal to be confronted with 'technology, scientific management, and beneficent leadership', see Sinclair, 'To Reform the World' 241. McNamara, as Sinclair points out, was a convert to Taylorism, and its successor movements focused on planning, in his efforts to restructure the US federal government. In a continuation of Stone's work, McNamara applied the '"calculative apparatus" of costing, budgeting, and establishing controls on public expenditure', Sinclair, 'To Reform the World' 241.

[186] Mark Franda, *The United Nations in the Twenty-First Century: Management and Reform Processes in a Troubled Organisation* (Rowman & Littlefield Publishers 2006) 168.

[187] Ibid., 168.

[188] Mark Mazower, *No Enchanted Palace: The End of Empire and the Ideological Origins of the United Nations* (Princeton University Press 2009) 25.

[189] Priya S. Gupta, 'From Statesmen to Technocrats to Financiers: Development Agents in the Third World' in Luis Eslava, Michael Fakhri and Vasuki Nesiah (eds.), *Bandung, Global History, and International Law: Critical Pasts and Pending Futures* (Cambridge University Press 2017) 481–497, at 490. See also Balakrishnan Rajagopal, *International*

72 A HISTORY OF THE ICC'S MANAGERIAL PRESENT

alternative school of thought and power structure'.[190] From its creation in 1964, UNCTAD therefore symbolised the participatory, solidaristic themes of Bandung 'both institutionally and theoretically'.[191] Here and elsewhere, the G77 posed an alternative vision of global economic development under the banner of an NIEO.

Jackson's report can be read in light of these North–South dynamics. As such, it seemed to offer a timely boost to the NIEO agenda. He found that 'too many leaders in the affluent states now appear to believe that the plight of two-thirds of mankind can be safely swept under the political rug and left there'.[192] In place of such indifference, Jackson asserted that the development framework 'could do a remarkable job in co-operating with the Third World, but the prospects are not very promising unless the machine can be brought under control'.[193] The best solution as he saw it was

> for governments to transform UNDP into a strong and effective organisation, and for UNDP, in turn, by the exercise of enlightened managerial and financial procedures, to secure the co-operation of the Agencies in bringing the machine under reasonable control and, by doing so, facilitating improved co-operation with the Third World.[194]

Thereafter, the G77 offered the fullest expression of an alternative UN in their 1974 Declaration on the Establishment of a New International Economic Order and Programme for Action. The declaration posited that the system as presently conceived had made it 'impossible to achieve an even and balanced development of the international community'.[195] Economic crisis and widening inequality 'necessitate[d] the active, full and equal participation of the developing countries in the formulation and application of all decisions that concern the international community'.[196] The NIEO was therefore to be built upon the sovereign equality of states and permanent sovereignty over natural resources. It demanded

---

Law from Below: Development, Social Movements, and Third World Resistance (Cambridge University Press 2003) 79.

[190] Gupta, 'From Statesmen to Technocrats' 490.

[191] Ibid., 491.

[192] Capacity Report x.

[193] Ibid., vi.

[194] Ibid.

[195] United Nations General Assembly Declaration on the Establishment of a New International Economic Order, General Assembly Sixth special session, 3201(S-VI), 1 May 1974, para. 1, available at: https://digitallibrary.un.org/record/218450?ln=en.

[196] Ibid., para. 2.

2.4 THE THIRD WORLD AS MANAGERIAL PROBLEM 73

restitution for those under occupation or colonial domination, as well as just and equitable trading links, scientific and technological access, and other key drivers of economic equity.

While centred on the global economy, the 1974 declaration also places the United Nations at the heart of efforts towards economic redistribution. It states that '[t]he United Nations as a universal organisation should be capable of dealing with problems of international economic cooperation in a comprehensive manner and ensuring equally the interests of all countries'.[197] Accordingly, '[i]t must have an even greater role in the establishment of a new international economic order'[198] and the declaration calls upon all states to 'exert maximum efforts with a view to securing the implementation of the present Declaration' as 'one of the principal guarantees for the creation of better conditions for all peoples to reach a life worthy of human dignity'.[199] Appreciating the institutionalised nature of contemporary global inequality, the G77 thereby sought to rely on the UN for its alternative agenda. In doing so, they not only took up the language of restructuring and management but also confronted the hegemonic reliance on management that had prevailed among Western states and UN officials until then. This brought the politics of management into the open.

2.4.2 Management as Terrain of Institutional Struggle

Until newly independent states started acquiring UN membership, states of the Global North had come to rely upon the UN and its agencies as a 'more than adequate mechanism' for the defence of imperialism.[200] But with decolonisation and the 1974 declaration, northern representatives and policymakers began to express their discontent with the organisation.[201] United States motions were increasingly being voted down, and the NIEO agenda provided a consistent source of alternative ideas for a postcolonial body.[202] One high-profile official embodied this discontent and sought to form an alternative US-led agenda against the NIEO, one that also relied much more explicitly on ideas and tools of management.

---

[197] Ibid para. 6.
[198] Ibid.
[199] Ibid.
[200] Mark Mazower, 'No Enchanted Palace' 17.
[201] Mark Mazower, *Governing the World: The History of an Idea* (Penguin 2012) 308.
[202] Ibid.

74   A HISTORY OF THE ICC'S MANAGERIAL PRESENT

Daniel Patrick Moynihan was appointed US ambassador to the UN by President Ford in 1975. Only months into the position, Moynihan was decrying the 'failure of American diplomacy' to deal with the new reality of a Third World UN majority.[203] Rejecting calls to boycott or withdraw from the UN, Moynihan acknowledged 'that there was no escaping involvement in the emergent world society', meaning the United States would instead have to 'understand what has been going on'.[204] In his analysis, Moynihan quickly attributed the UN's problems to the explicitly ideological stance of the G77. Third World states had co-ordinated 'points of systematic attack' against the UN as part of the 'international liberalism' that had failed them.[205] Recognising the potency of such attacks, Moynihan proposed that the United States and its allies conduct a counter-offensive along similar lines by showcasing how 'international liberalism and its processes have enormous recent achievements to their credit'.[206]

In order to adequately advocate this political stance, Moynihan proposed that the United States 'go into opposition' at the UN against the G77. This would be a 'painful' choice in the short-term but 'liberating' for long-term Western interests.[207] Management featured explicitly within this political counter-strategy, as institutional politics by other means. One of the chief exhibits for international liberalism, he noted, was the 'multinational corporation which, combining modern management with liberal trade policies, is arguably the most creative international institution of the twentieth century'.[208] Already Moynihan's reading of management in the service of capital contrasted with management in service of democratisation. The strategy became an 'intellectual and multitiered American response to decolonisation and its consequences', with management as one of its flanks.[209]

Moynihan forced an open political confrontation of North and South.[210] His proposal crystallised northern alliances and brought them

---

[203] Daniel P. Moynihan, 'The United States in Opposition', *Commentary*, March 1975, available at: www.commentarymagazine.com/articles/the-united-states-in-opposition/. See further Mazower, 'Governing the World' 309–310.

[204] Ibid.

[205] Ibid.

[206] Ibid.

[207] Ibid.

[208] Ibid.

[209] Mazower, 'Governing the World' 310.

[210] Ibid.

2.4 THE THIRD WORLD AS MANAGERIAL PROBLEM   75

to seeing the UN as a renewed site of struggle. Hereafter, the counter-offensive to the NIEO took on several forms.[211] Principally, it entailed efforts to decentralise and diffuse the power of development bodies such as UNDP and ECOSOC that Third World states were increasingly at risk of controlling via a majority vote. As one commentator summarised the policy, 'a more fragmented United Nations system was seen as increasing their influence on the governance of the system' as opposed to a unified and restructured set of mechanisms favouring Third World interests.[212] Alongside this fragmentation, northern states also redoubled their efforts to have international economic and trade issues dealt with by the institutions in which they exerted greater influence, namely the World Bank and International Monetary Fund.[213]

An important reform exercise commissioned in the same year as the NIEO declaration began to exhibit this North–South conflict. The General Assembly commissioned an expert panel on UN-wide reform, led by US diplomat Richard Gardner. Gardner was sympathetic to Third World calls for economic welfare and was eager to improve the UN's functioning in light of recent diplomatic challenges, such as the Middle East crisis in 1967. Yet Gardner joined Jackson and Moynihan in his diagnosis of the UN as an ill patient, as set out in a *Foreign Affairs* article some years prior. It is worth summarising Gardner's diagnosis, given how prominently ideas of politicisation and institutional mismanagement featured within his UN reform efforts.

According to Gardner, ideological engagement with the UN by Third World states was a major cause of institutional inertia. He despaired at the 'decline in third-party attitudes and a marked increase in the tendency to vote, not on the merits of a question, but with regard to bloc affiliation and the protection of other interests'.[214] Gardner was not blind to regional political allegiances. Yet he believed that '[f]or the world organisation to work more effectively, its members will have to give greater priority to their long-term interests in building a civilised system of world order than to short-term considerations of national, ideological

---

[211] See generally Umut Özsu, 'Neoliberalism and the New International Economic Order: A History of "Contemporary Legal Thought"' in Justin Desautels-Stein and Christopher Tomlins (eds.), *Searching for Contemporary Legal Thought* (Cambridge University Press 2017) 330–347, at 339.

[212] Müller, 'Reforming the United Nations' 14.

[213] Özsu, 'Neoliberalism and the New International Economic Order' 341.

[214] Richard Gardner, 'Can the United Nations Be Revived?', *Foreign Affairs*, July 1970, available at: www.foreignaffairs.com/articles/1970-07-01/can-united-nations-be-revived.

or racial advantage'.[215] Rather than reading the NIEO as a guarantor of such world order, Gardner was heavily invested in the structures established in 1945 with some modification. Here, maintaining status quo arrangements was a non-ideological stance as compared to the clear political opportunism of the NIEO.

Gardner's second move was to foreground the lack of institutional accountability, underperformance, and poor allocation of resources. This, too, came in the form of a pragmatic management towards improved performance. It involved streamlining the procedures of the General Assembly and 'reducing the gap between voting power and real power'.[216] The UN also had to 'develop a modern planning, programming and budget system'.[217] This meant that instead of assessing the UN in terms of 'inputs', it should be assessed in terms of results and the 'delivery of specific services to members in the form of peacekeeping, human rights and development programs'.[218] Focusing on 'service delivery' meant ensuring the budget was being spent on those projects yielding the best results, a calculation that placed a premium on the concerns of the UN's largest financial contributors. This coincided with the plan to match voting power to 'real power' assessed in terms of gross domestic product.

Another concern that fused management concerns to the US agenda related to the quality of UN staff. Gardner claimed that the 'objectivity and impartiality' of UN staff had declined just as the number of officials from Third World countries was increasing.[219] Despite the clear racial undertone, Gardner again looked to a solution in management: moving away from career appointments and towards a higher UN salary scale, both of which would attract more personnel from developed countries. This was also consistent with Gardner's view that 'US input into the system – political, intellectual and financial – has been essential to every successful UN action in the last 25 years'.[220] Through his diagnosis, Gardner put management at the service of a Global North agenda even as he used such language to castigate the overtly politicised tactics of the G77.

[215] Ibid., 663.
[216] Ibid., 666.
[217] Ibid., 671.
[218] Ibid.
[219] Ibid., 670.
[220] Ibid., 672.

2.4 THE THIRD WORLD AS MANAGERIAL PROBLEM   77

These ideas found a home in the expert panel led by Gardner in 1974. The report adopted the language of 'institutional restructuring' and 'meaningful reform of the system', proposing improved working methods for the General Assembly and strengthened co-operation of states through an increasingly Third Worldist ECOSOC.[221] At first glance, the Gardner report takes seriously the concerns of the NIEO agenda. It proposes a new Office for Programme Planning and Coordination inside ECOSOC and a Director-General mandate for Development and International Economic Cooperation.[222] These proposals were made with a view towards rendering the UN 'a more effective instrument for the establishment of a new, more rational, and just international economic order'.[223]

Nonetheless, the World Bank and other regional banks were deemed the best route for Third World financing, and the new DG for Development sought to 'promote improved system-wide co-operation'[224] based on the desire of Western actors to 'harmonise economic development activities within the UN system'.[225] Yet for Third Worldists, harmonising UN bodies and prioritising efficient allocation of resources was 'a way of fragmenting the consideration of [the G77's] overall claims, thus jeopardising the already fragile cohesiveness among its members'.[226] Gardner's staffing ideas also appeared in the report, proposing standardised recruitment through examinations and training, as well as measures to 'eliminate unproductive staff'.[227] These proposals seemed to be in keeping with the demand for US expertise as well as the 'American tradition of "apolitical pragmatism that stresses efficiency above all"'.[228]

The United States was buoyed by the success of the Moynihan-informed counter-strategy. Despite also contributing to 'institutional

---

[221] A New United Nations Structure for Global Economic Co-operation: Report of the Group of Experts on the Structure of the United Nations System, E/AC.62/9, 28 May 1975, at iii and 2 (Gardner Report).

[222] Joachim Müller, *Reforming the United Nations: New Initiatives and Past Efforts, Volume 1* (Brill 1997) I/24.

[223] Gardner Report, 3–4.

[224] Ibid., 95.

[225] Ronald Meltzer, 'Restructuring the United Nations System: Institutional Reform Efforts in the Context of North–South Relations' (1978) 32 *International Organisation* 993–1018, at 996.

[226] Ibid., 1012.

[227] Müller, 'New Initiatives and Past Efforts' I/28.

[228] Stanley Hoffmann, 'No Choices, No Illusions' (1976–77) 25 *Foreign Policy* 97–140, at 123.

78   A HISTORY OF THE ICC'S MANAGERIAL PRESENT

sprawl', US officials labelled new economic and social programmes 'wasteful and unsystematic, lacking meaningful evaluation procedures and modern management techniques'.[229] In 1977, the US Comptroller-General conducted a study into US participation in a range of international organisations, including the UN. He found that '[m]anagement problems within the international organisations themselves keep the US from participating more'.[230] To assuage US concerns, said the Comptroller, the UN had to 'increase the organisation's efficiency and effectiveness'.[231] He therefore requested that the UN provide more information on programme planning and performance to the US government to increase transparency. He also asserted that 'immediate steps must be taken to strengthen and improve financial management, including evaluation and external audit'.[232]

Such demands placed upon the UN came to a head when Ronald Reagan became US president. Having internalised the Moynihan strategy, and relying heavily on the small state ideology of the conservative Heritage Foundation, the Reagan administration weaponised its financial contributions to force further UN concessions. In 1980, Congress opted to reduce its contribution to the UN budget by 20 per cent until the UN implemented a system of weighted voting based on national economic output.[233] Such financial brinkmanship was designed to gut several bodies and programmes and reinstate Western preferences over budgetary allocations.[234] During this time, claims of 'rampant budgetary mismanagement' went hand in glove with accusations of UN 'politicisation' and 'anti-Western bias'.[235]

---

[229] Meltzer, 'Restructuring the UN System' 996.

[230] US Comptroller-General, U.S. Participation in International Organisations, ID-77–36, 24 June 1977, iv, available at: www.gao.gov/assets/120/119000.pdf.

[231] US Participation in International Organisations: Report to the Congress by Elmer B. Staats, Comptroller General, ID-77–36, 24 June 1977, 1, available at: www.gao.gov/assets/id-77-36.pdf.

[232] Ibid., 22.

[233] Foreign Relations Act 1985 (Kassebaum amendment). For further detail, see Richard Nelson, 'Current Developments: International Law and U.S. Withholdings of Payments to International Organisations' (1986) 80 American Journal of International Law 973–983, at 974–976; Paul Taylor, 'The United Nations System under Stress: Financial Pressures and Their Consequences' (1991) 17 Review of International Studies 365–382.

[234] Gene Lyons, 'Review Essay: The UN and American Politics' (1999) 5 Global Governance 497–511.

[235] Brett Schaefer, 'Look Before Leaping to Rejoin UNESCO', Heritage Foundation, 7 May 2001, available at: www.heritage.org/report/look-leaping-rejoin-unesco.

2.4 THE THIRD WORLD AS MANAGERIAL PROBLEM 79

The fruits of this sustained counter-strategy were reaped in a 1985 expert panel (the 'group of 18') appointed to 'conduct a thorough review of the administrative and financial matters of the United Nations, with a view to identifying measures for further improving the efficiency of its administrative and financial functioning'.[236] In an apolitical register, the group of 18 drew on a decade and a half of institutionally embedded ideas about how best to manage the organisation. They suggested that the UN budget be passed via consensus rather than a positive vote, effectively giving major financial contributors a de facto veto.[237] They also endorsed an 'audit culture' by then visible in state bureaucracies throughout Europe and the United States.[238] Auditors would assess performance at a program level and through 'monitoring, evaluation and inspection' of personnel in periodic evaluation reports and a staff rating system.[239] The group further recommended a new Office of Human Resources Management, which was duly set up.[240]

Such proposals embodied many of the efficiency concerns raised by Global North actors throughout the 1970s and effectively neutered G77 ambitions towards a more radical restructuring. Management ideas of efficiency, audit, and performance had successfully erased the traces of the NIEO agenda under the guise of 'depoliticisation' even as it bore clear distributive consequences for both the West and the rest.[241] Management's power was to elide reform with apolitical recalibration while fracturing an alternative political vision of international economic governance.

---

[236] UNGA Res 40/237 (18 December 1985) para 2(a).

[237] Franda, 'The UN in the Twenty-First Century' 200.

[238] Michael Power, *The Audit Society: Rituals of Verification* (Oxford University Press 1997); Marilyn Strathern, *Audit Cultures: Anthropological Studies in Accountability, Ethics and the Academy* (Routledge 2000).

[239] Group of High-Level Intergovernmental Experts to Review the Efficiency of the Administrative and Financial Functioning of the UN (Group of 18 Report), General Assembly Official Records 41st Session, Supplement No. 49, A/41/49, 15 August 1986. See recommendations 9, 12, 14–15, 50–51, and 63–67.

[240] Ibid., recommendations 41 and 50. Recommendation 67 also proposed that external auditors 'put more emphasis on management audits'.

[241] One Secretariat official noted that '[t]he reforms of the late 1980s could also be seen as a first phase in the discussion and implementation of effective management and leadership concepts in the Organisation in the new post-Cold War era', Tapio Kanninen, 'Developing the UN Retrenchment, Reorganisation and Reform Strategy during the 1986–1988 Financial Crisis' in Chris de Cooker (ed.), *International Administration: Law and Management Practices in International Organisations* (Martinus Nijhoff 2009) 227–260, at 254.

2.5 A Situated Definition of Management Practices

These episodes of UN management frame the ICC's managerial present. In particular, the UN of the late 1970s has left a mark on future efforts towards international organisation, given the emergence of anti-impunity and the human rights agenda. That period also saw an increased reliance on planning, efficiency, and performance discourses in the context of North–South conflict. Such a historical conjunction helps explain their proximity in the speeches of ICC presidents. The postcolonial UN demonstrated the distributional stakes of management despite its reliance on an apolitical language to frame and legitimise those distributions. Management's success was to rout the NIEO agenda and obscure the political projects of its detractors. Management became a tabula rasa, bearing no mark of the historical gains and losses it helped to bake into the UN project. That apolitical trait would make it an attractive source for institutional experiments of anti-impunity in the 1990s.

Nonetheless, the familiar practices of ICC management, including performance measurement and strategic planning in public settings, were only introduced in the UN during the 1980s as part of the 'New Public Management' turn. New Public Management (NPM) was a set of discourses and practices deployed by European politicians and policymakers to apply the seemingly corporate tools of management in domestic public sectors, including schools, prisons, and healthcare.[242] NPM drew from the various organisational, human relations, and planning traditions of earlier management theory. It was famously labelled the 'organisational' wing of neoliberalism for promoting privatisation, outsourcing, and entrepreneurial values within the public sector.

NPM also marked a shift in political rationality.[243] Linked to neoliberalism, it shirked the idea of the small state in favour of deeper and more diverse forms of organisational and professional governance. These techniques would play a significant role in 'encasing' the market,

---

[242] For a full account of NPM's emergence, see Donald Kettl, *The Global Public Management Revolution: A Report on the Transformation of Governance* (Brookings Institution Press 2000). For NPM's effects on higher education, see Cris Shore and Stephen Roberts, 'Higher Education and the Panopticon Paradigm: Quality Assessment as "Disciplinary Technology"' (1995) 27 *Higher Education Review* 8–17; Anthony Bradney, 'The Quality Assurance Agency and the Politics of Audit' (2001) 28 *Journal of Law & Society* 430–442, at 432.

[243] Nikolas Rose and Peter Miller, 'Political Power beyond the State: Problematics of Government' (1992) 43 *British Journal of Sociology* 173–205, at 198.

2.5 A SITUATED DEFINITION OF MANAGEMENT PRACTICES   81

much in the way legal concepts and practices were doing.[244] Its most common practices were performance accountability and appraisal, auditing, strategic planning, and streamlining all of which brought many facets of the organisation – its administrative structure, individual staff members, external stakeholders, and long-term goals – into productive relation with one another to optimise, report, appraise, and motivate. Crucially, the UN solidified these techniques within the creative arsenal of international officials.

The UN Joint Inspection Unit was an important vehicle for NPM techniques beginning in the mid-1970s. General Assembly resolution 31/192 (1976) establishing the JIU invested it with investigation powers over 'all matters having a bearing on the efficiency of the services and the proper use of funds' with the aim of 'improving management and methods'.[245] The JIU was run by public administration and management experts, such as Maurice Bertrand, who served in the Unit until 1985. Throughout his time there, Bertrand penned 'well over 200 reports, dealing with administrative, financial, and structural aspects' of the UN system.[246] The frame the inspectors adopted was one of institutional dysfunction, which, against the backdrop of US financial brinkmanship, prompted a search for more effective working processes, use of finances, and productive personnel.[247]

The JIU was concerned to minimise institutional risks of various kinds and sought out evidence that might enhance the UN's exposure to risk. They exhibited a trend that scholars were already identifying as the 'audit society'. Audit relied upon 'independence from the matter being audited;

---

[244] Quinn Slobodian, *Globalists: The End of Empire and the Birth of Neoliberalism* (Harvard University Press 2018).

[245] Article 5 Statute of the Joint Inspection Unit, UNGA Res 31/192 (22 December 1976) Annex. The JIU was created as an experiment in 1966 but was only placed on a statutory footing a decade later.

[246] Maurice Bertrand, 'The Historical Development of Efforts to Reform the UN' in Adam Roberts and Benedict Kingsbury (eds.), *United Nations, Divided World: The UN's Roles in International Relations* (2nd edn., Clarendon Press 1993) 420, at 423.

[247] Klaus Hüfner, 'Financing the United Nations: The Role of the United States' in Dennis Dijkzeul and Yves Beigbeder (eds.), *Rethinking International Organisations: Pathology and Promise* (Berghahn Books 2003) 29–53, at 41. Bertrand was under no illusion as to the politics of US management claims, stating that for Reagan, 'it was not a question of improving the functioning of the World Organisation through a process of management or to increase its efficiency, but solely a matter of regaining control over the United Nations and thereby preventing them from being able to continue serving as a propaganda forum against the United States and against Reagan' (Klaus, 'Financing the UN' 41).

technical work in the form of evidence gathering and the examination of documentation; the expression of a view based on this evidence [and] a clearly defined object of the audit process'.[248] As practised by the JIU, audit sanitised the political choices of the postcolonial UN. Audit and auditors embodied Gardner's professional values of independence and neutrality in gathering evidence of institutional liabilities. Applying their expert judgment, auditors like Bertrand established a 'style of evaluation' where the UN 'emerge[d] as legitimate, safe, efficient, cost-effective'.[249] This style also proved reasonably immune to critique. Ineffective or poor auditing rarely occasioned a loss of confidence in auditing itself but seemed to offer opportunities or 'lessons learnt' for the next cycle. By this token audit 'supplies its own rationale [and] regenerates itself in the face of apparent failure'.[250]

Beyond legitimising itself and the organisation, audit also creates its own object of inquiry. As staff members are audited, they become 'depersonalised units of economic resource whose productivity and performance must be constantly measured'.[251] The same can be said of whole divisions or organs. Audit and auditors are concerned with the identification, classification, regulation, and redistribution of risk, denoted as 'doubt, conflict, mistrust and danger'.[252] This constitutive work is visible in the JIU's surveys of UN operations. It highlighted the administrative and financial risks to organisational effectiveness, thereby characterising structures and personnel as liabilities with pathologies that needed to be managed better in future operations. The JIU did not seek to instantiate a risk-free zone but sought to inculcate risk as a professional mindset to be adopted by managers and policymakers as they executed their mandates.

This attempt to internalise risk was further embedded within the UN from 1990. After General Assembly resolution 45/237, the JIU inspectors took 'a more selective approach in drawing up its work programme to give greater attention to management, budgetary and administrative

---

[248] Power, 'The Audit Society' 5.

[249] Ibid.

[250] Marilyn Strathern, 'Bullet-Proofing: A Tale from the United Kingdom' in Annelise Riles (ed.), *Documents: Artifacts of Modern Knowledge* (University of Michigan Press 2006) 181–205, at 190.

[251] Cris Shore and Susan Wright, 'Coercive Accountability: The Rise of Audit Culture in Higher Education' in Strathern, 'Audit Cultures' 57–89, at 62.

[252] Power, 'Audit Society' 1.

2.5 A SITUATED DEFINITION OF MANAGEMENT PRACTICES   83

issues'.[253] In a follow-up resolution in 1993, states asked the JIU to 'put more emphasis on inspection and evaluation to ensure optimum use of funds'.[254] The effect was to read the UN and its operations as a series of managerial risks. One 1995 JIU report characterised the UN as 'a growing web of administrative controls and mandates that have enveloped the government bodies, leadership and staff of the United Nations in bureaucratic gridlock without providing the intended managerial culture'.[255] Through auditing, the JIU promoted a risk-aware managerial culture to confront organisational and professional liabilities.

The JIU was not alone in embedding a UN audit infrastructure. The Office of Internal Oversight Services (OIOS) was established by the General Assembly in 1994. The OIOS was proposed by the Clinton administration as part of the effort to reinvent government. Influenced by NPM, Clinton sought to replace a slow and ineffective UN bureaucracy with a lean and flexible version of modern governance infused with entrepreneurial ideas of ownership and responsibility.[256] In the OIOS, Clinton envisaged an 'American style' Inspector General's Office designed to 'promote efficiency and effectiveness in the administration, ensure systematic evaluation of programs, and identify and root out alleged bureaucratic waste, fraud and abuse'.[257] The OIOS also housed an Investigative Section to 'check into reported cases of corruption, mismanagement, and wastage, and that can be reached via a "hot line" on a twenty-four hour basis'.[258] Within ten years, the Office had published hundreds of reports and issued thousands of recommendations to UN bodies, including the Secretariat and the High Commissioner for Human Rights. Kofi Annan, as a staunch supporter of the OIOS, saw it as 'one of the [UN's] main instruments for ensuring effective internal oversight and accountability'.[259]

---

[253] UNGA Res 45/237 (21 December 1990) para. 2.

[254] Ibid., para. 4.

[255] Management in the United Nations: Work in Progress, Joint Inspection Unit, JIU/REP/95/8, 4 August 1995, v.

[256] Denis Saint-Martin, 'How the Reinventing Government Movement in Public Administration Was Exported from the US to Other Countries' (2001) 24 *International Journal of Public Administration* 573–604, at 574. See David Osborne and Ted Gaebler, *Reinventing Government: How the Entrepreneurial Spirit is Transforming the Public Sector* (Penguin 1993).

[257] Müller, 'Reforming the United Nations' 56.

[258] Franda, 'The UN in the Twenty-First Century' 206.

[259] Kofi Annan, 'Internal Oversight – A Key to Reform at the United Nations' (2003) 30 *International Journal of Government Auditing* 1–10, at 9–10. By the 1990s, the OIOS was

84   A HISTORY OF THE ICC'S MANAGERIAL PRESENT

Another key management practice for the UN was restructuring. Restructuring entails rearranging 'financial, physical, human, [and] information assets' within an organisation.[260] At the UN, this manifested in different ways. Where Third World states had advocated large-scale democratisation of UN agencies to challenge Western primacy, this vision had lost its purchase by the late 1970s. According to one UN commentator, '"reform" became synonymous [with] "cost-cutting"'.[261] To back this up, a new position of Under-Secretary-General for administration and management was created in the early nineties, occupied first by former head of PricewaterhouseCoopers, Joseph Connor. Pursuant to US calls for a 'no-growth budget', Connor proposed major cuts to UN staff in 1996. In a similar vein, an Efficiency Board was also created to constantly identify and implement efficiency measures.[262]

Yet restructuring goes beyond redistribution of resources. It contemplates the 'complete strategic transformation intended to change an organisation's design, its work processes, corporate culture, values, attitudes, and mission'.[263] It offers a 'stocktaking' opportunity for actors reflecting on the organisation's future. These discursive dimensions of restructuring were understood by Kofi Annan and others who extolled 'management culture' and values of leadership, vision, and performance.[264] These were intended to guide the UN as the new millennium approached. The International Civil Service Commission (ICSC), which was already moving towards a system of human resource management by the 1980s, began advocating mission statements as a way

---

exposing a steady stream of minor dysfunctional practices, which Western journalists were only too happy to lay at Secretary-General Boutros-Ghali's feet. Barbara Crossette, 'In War on Corruption and Waste, UN Confronts Well-Entrenched Foe', *New York Times*, 3 November 1997; 'The Scandal of the UN's "Lost" Millions', *Sunday Times*, August 1993. Franda describes how those opposed to Boutros-Ghali also framed him as a bad manager, see Franda, 'The UN in the Twenty-First Century' 72.

[260] Wayne Cascio, 'How Does Downsizing Come About?' in Cary L. Cooper, Alankrita Pandey and James Campbell Quick (eds.), *Downsizing: Is Less Still More?* (Cambridge University Press 2012) 51–75, at 51–52.

[261] Dirk Salomons, 'Good Intentions to Naught: The Pathology of Human Resources Management at the United Nations' in Dijkzeul and Beigbeder, 'Rethinking International Organisations' 111–139, at 127.

[262] Müller, 'Reforming the United Nations' 56.

[263] Cascio, 'How Does Downsizing Come About?' 51–52.

[264] Renewing the United Nations: A Programme for Reform: Report of the Secretary-General, A/51/950, 14 July 1997, 6 and Action 18. See also, Human Resources Management Reform: Report of the Secretary-General, A/55/253, 3 August 2000, para. 58.

2.5 A SITUATED DEFINITION OF MANAGEMENT PRACTICES   85

to foster 'performance-related culture'.[265] Such cultural shifts sought to redefine the UN official not as bureaucrat but as productive manager of their tasks and themselves.[266]

A third relevant set of practices relate to performance management. In a 1979 report, the ICSC sought to prioritise the 'efficient and effective utilisation of human resources'.[267] Subsequently, it proposed new tools for performance appraisal, individual work plans, and additional staff training. Not only would these tools increase staff productivity, but they were also intended to generate 'a sense of affiliation with the organisation' and 'fulfil the individual's need to retain a sense of control over his/ her personal destiny in the increasingly complex and impersonalised modern industrial society'.[268] Proponents of performance management were thus attuned to the self-disciplining and self-improvement possibilities for staff. It enhanced productivity while also configuring the employee as a committed, efficient professional.

Performance management is an individualised cycle for measuring and evaluating staff performance according to criteria pre-agreed between the appraisee and their supervisor.[269] But as the ICSC attests with its desire for self-improvement, such tools do not only describe staff performance. The exercise itself forms and reforms professional subjectivities according to a wider set of organisational ideals.[270] Performance appraisal produces a cast of characters including appraisees, appraisers,

---

[265] Towards a New System of Performance Appraisal in the United Nations Secretariat: Resources for Successful Implementation, Joint Inspection Unit Report, JIU/REP/94/5, June 1994, para. 142, available at: https://documents-dds-ny.un.org/doc/UNDOC/GEN/ GL9/904/68/pdf/GL990468.pdf?OpenElement.

[266] Glenn Morgan and André Spicer, 'Critical Approaches to Organisational Change' in Mats Alvesson, Todd Bridgman, and Hugh Willmott (eds.), *Oxford Handbook of Critical Management Studies* (Oxford University Press 2013) 251–266, at 253–254; see Paul Leonardi and Michele H. Jackson, 'Technological Determinism and Discursive Closure in Organisational Mergers' (2004) 17 *Journal of Organisational Change Management* 615–631, at 625.

[267] Report of the International Civil Service Commission, General Assembly 34th Session, Supplement No. 30, A/34/30, 4 October 1979, para. 212, available at: https://icsc.un.org/ Resources/General/AnnualReports/AR1979.pdf. This also came as part of the discontent with the effects of growing membership on individual performance; see Robert Jordan, 'What Has Happened to Our International Civil Service?' (1981) 41 *Public Administration Review* 236–245.

[268] Report of the International Civil Service Commission, para. 213.

[269] See further Chapter 4.

[270] See Barbara Townley, 'Performance Appraisal and the Emergence of Management' (1993) 30 *Journal of Management Studies* 221–238.

supervisors, and human resources officers. These subjects are bound together by the appraisal cycle, which positions the appraisee at its core. Given that most staff, whether entry-level or managerial, are appraised, the appraisal network becomes an interstitial web of knowledge spanning the organisation.

As discussed in Chapter 4, the appraisal web is made in the documentary paper trail of probation reports, competency models, missions, and appraisal forms, all of which attempt to capture the employee in what Foucault calls a 'network of writing', which can then be archived in the personal file.[271] Through documents and face-to-face meetings, appraisal becomes the 'ceremony of power, and the form of the experiment, the deployment of force and the establishment of truth'.[272] The subject is mediated as a series of skills, competencies, achievements, and ratings. And because these qualities are not empty but acquire meaning in light of previously struggled-over organisational preoccupations and aims, they offer a map (and the outer limits) for professional action, in accordance with what is organisationally right, sensible, effective, and necessary.[273] Kofi Annan captured this sensibility when proposing management training for UN officials. For him, (self-)appraisal would 'help field staff to think more strategically, take greater responsibility, manage teams and stand accountable for allocating resources and achieving results'.[274]

A final practice or process is the replacement of inter-organ co-ordination with holistic and long-term 'strategic planning'. Strategic planning took off during the rise of management consulting in the 1960s, as a framework for allowing consultants to take stock of the organisational whole via a common vocabulary of goals, resources, indicators, risks, and opportunities.[275] In corporate settings, it involves 'long-range planning of a firm in relation to its market, competitors, technology, management, resources, funding, and so on', resulting in a strategic plan spanning

---

[271] Michel Foucault, *Discipline and Punish: The Birth of the Prison* [1977] (Penguin Books 1991) 184.

[272] Ibid.

[273] Christopher Grey, 'Career as a Project of the Self' (1994) 28 *Sociology* 479–497, at 489.

[274] Renewing the United Nations: A Programme for Reform: Report of the Secretary-General, A/51/950, 14 July 1997, 6 and Action 18. Towards a New System of Performance Appraisal in the United Nations Secretariat, para. 94.

[275] McKenna, 'World's Newest Profession'; Freedman, 'Strategy'.

2.5 A SITUATED DEFINITION OF MANAGEMENT PRACTICES   87

several years against which progress is tracked.[276] The strategic plan and the process of devising it are important sites for expert imagination. It brings together structural components of the organisation such as hierarchies and reporting lines with non-structural aspects, such as culture and staffing. In casting a wide net, strategic planning defines, orders, and evaluates facets of organisational life in relation to external realities.[277]

Like other management techniques, strategic planning effaces its own politics and redistributions. It is not only created within a historical milieu but also necessarily fashions a context out of an organisational past and present. The roadmap formed within this context 'project[s] solidarity of purpose'.[278] Yet it can only capture one version of the world, however complex, designate it as reality, and deploy this as a rationale for future decision-making. The conditions of organisational possibility become apparent: what *is* strategically planned becomes what *should* be planned. Activities and decisions legible according to the plan are refined and prioritised while those incommensurable with institutional improvement are left out of the text.

Strategic planning is the technique that most clearly bridges 1990s UN reform with anti-impunity's 'new tribunalism' in the same decade.[279] Kofi Annan was appointed Secretary-General in 1996, having previously served as Assistant Secretary-General for Human Resource Management. Annan was part of the team that created the OIOS and, once elected as UN head, began to centralise managerial decision-making in the hands of a Senior Management Group comprising the heads of various UN departments and programmes. In addition to instilling a management culture among staff, Annan hoped to create a strategic planning hub within the Secretariat. Until then, strategic planning had amounted to information gathering and speech writing.[280] But in August 1998 – only a month after the Rome Statute was finalised – Annan established the UN

---

[276] Nicholas Terry and Peter Moles, *Oxford Handbook of International Financial Terms* (Oxford University Press 2005).

[277] Alvesson and Willmott term this 'strategy talk'; see Mats Alvesson and Hugh Willmott, *Making Sense of Management* (SAGE Publications 2012) 149; Nelson Phillips and Sadhvi Dar, 'Strategy' in Alvesson et al., *Oxford Handbook of CMS* 414–432, at 419.

[278] Ibid., 151–152.

[279] Thomas Skouteris, 'The New Tribunalism: Strategies of (De)Legitimation in the Era of International Adjudication' (1999) 17 *Finnish Yearbook of International Law* 307–356.

[280] Abiodun Williams, 'Strategic Planning in the Executive Office of the UN Secretary-General' (2010) 16 *Global Governance* 435–449, at 436.

88 A HISTORY OF THE ICC'S MANAGERIAL PRESENT

Strategic Planning Unit. It was to identify the Secretary-General's priorities, prepare policy documents for dissemination, and ensure the effective realisation of UN goals.[281] Later, the Unit helped formulate instruments such as the Global Compact on corporate social responsibility and the Millennium Declaration.[282] The Unit also prepared Annan's report, *In Larger Freedom: Towards Development, Security and Human Rights for All*. Strategic planning thus opened up new problem frames and opportunities for centralised UN action at the turn of the millennium.

2.6   Conclusion

Techniques of audit, restructuring, performance management, strategic planning, and related management tools epitomise modern management within international institutions. They are not timeless scientific tools but the result or 'truth effects' of considerable professional work by UN civil servants, lawyers, politicians, commentators, and scholars over the course of the past fifty years. Their presence and persistence today attest to the struggle over meaning that ensued in institutions from the ILO to the UN, and the dynamics that saw efficiency and effectiveness win out over radical restructuring. Rather than operating solely as time capsules for past struggles, these practices continue to shape the concerns and priorities of institutional actors. This chapter has shown the variety of management's uses: reducer of distance in the southern plantations, disciplinarian of workers, vehicles of mass information about remote populations, facilitator of US imperial expansion, and conciliator of capital and labour. In the international context, management has also reconfigured colonial places and peoples, been used as a weapon for radical democratisation, and been employed as a method of counter-revolution.

In this chapter's epigraph, a former ICC President extols the virtues of management reform. The Office of the Prosecutor, says Fernández, 'has developed its new strategic plan for the coming years to discharge its duties and utilise its resources in the most effective manner'.[283] Strategic planning, large-scale reorganisation, lessons learnt exercises, and performance indicators erupt in a perpetual managerial present, separate

---

[281] Williams, 'Strategic Planning in the Executive Office of the UN Secretary-General' 437.
[282] Ibid., 439.
[283] Triffterer, 'Rome Statute of the International Criminal Court' xvi.

2.6 CONCLUSION

to law, in which the court must respond to effectiveness challenges through expert reform. This chapter has sought to reveal the genealogical linkages between management and law as complementary modes of professional world-building. It is this blending of knowledges that partly explains management's self-evidence today.

The other reason for management's self-evidence, according to this account, lies in its capacity to constantly efface its own historical and political baggage. Whatever Fernández's concerns about management's efficacy and implementation, there is no sense in which management might bear the scars of previous institutional skirmishes, never mind repeating them in future ones. Yet against Fernández and others, this chapter attests to management's presence as a professional-political discourse and practice during efforts to maintain slave labour, expand the American empire, govern colonial peoples, and oppose Third World emancipation. By the time one reads Fernández and accepts management as right and sensible, one has had to unsee all these uncomfortable episodes. This is the real 'power' of management tools and discourses for the great justice experiment that would begin in Rome.

3

The Managerial Court

Macro-management

3.1 Introduction

The genealogy offered in Chapter 2 reveals much about the context within which management would later be invoked by International Criminal Court (ICC) architects and experts once that project gathered steam. As the extended example of the UN demonstrates, management practices have often been deployed by lawyers and diplomats on the basis of some broad appeal to scientific expertise and as an apolitical language of efficiency. Yet this invocation often masks the historically embedded nature of management in institutions and denies management's political stakes. Chapter 2 also shows how, by the 1990s – the 'Decade of International Law' – managerial practices were ubiquitous at the UN, in institutional practice and scholarly writing as tools to confront a growing set of global aims.[1] This chapter brings this story into the more recent past by showcasing and critiquing the deployment of management practices within the ICC, one of the most celebrated achievements of twenty-first-century liberal cosmopolitanism.

In tracing the growth of the ICC's managerial infrastructure from 1998 until roughly twenty years later, the chapter makes two broad contributions. First, it shows how, from the drafting stage of the Rome Statute until the court's most recent engagements, management ideas of efficiency, and practices such as strategic planning, risk assessment exercises, and performance indicators, have been important components of the court's working life. Management ideas and practices have been invoked by court experts and external supporters to confront certain challenges facing the organisation and, in a relatively short time span, have evolved into an important professional dialect. Although this first

---

[1] The UN was not the only such fora; see, for example, Richard Harper, *Inside the IMF: An Ethnography of Documents, Technology and Organisational Action* (Routledge 1997).

3.1 INTRODUCTION

contribution appears largely descriptive, it also serves to rebuff arguments levelled against the court that it is insufficiently or only partially managed. The management architecture suggests otherwise.

A second contribution is based on the long survey of management ideas and practices, which is to show that its primary effect has been to narrow professional and institutional markers of success, failure, risk, and opportunity for the global justice project down to that which is deemed institutionally possible. Hence, the discourse of 'strategy' and tools of strategic planning have centralised the ICC within the global justice project while also confining that project to the ICC's institutional co-ordinates based on concepts of results, resources, and time. Models, plans, and reports have turned court experts into labourers in a justice factory – gathering materials, calculating capacity, and calibrating it to 'demand'. The audit apparatus of risk assessment has foregrounded institutional risks, occluding the vulnerabilities of those in whose name the court ostensibly acts. This second contribution thus shows what is gained and lost by adopting this new professional toolkit.

The chapter proceeds chronologically, both to give a sense of management's growth over time and to reveal the various narrowings ICC experts have enacted through management. I begin with the preliminary debates that set the discursive parameters for negotiating a permanent international criminal court. While those debates show delegates' relative indifference to questions of management, they nonetheless illustrate the key conditions under which management emerged as a viable and necessary language for court architects. Initially, the discussion often lay between a permanent or an efficient institution, but these were quickly fused in a bid to countenance a permanent court that could nonetheless be well-managed. Debates around the court's funding arrangements and the shadow of mismanagement at the ad hoc tribunals only sharpened architects' resolve to create a permanent, efficient court.

Once the court was established, various actors from inside the court and out became involved in the project of constructing a managerial body. Some of these have deeply affected the parameters of the court's own perception of its work and ambitions, including the move to strategic planning or risk assessment. And as the managerial infrastructure expanded, efforts to limit or counter it often fell short. In this cartography, I show how management operated less as a bolt-on to optimise extant institutional structures and more as a reflexive narrowing device for the aims and ambitions of the project itself. In narrowing the court's parameters of operation, management occludes complex, structural

92　THE MANAGERIAL COURT: MACRO-MANAGEMENT

dynamics of global justice that implicate a wide range of groups, not least those most proximate to mass atrocities. Rather than arguing that management should respond by becoming more attuned to such complexity, this chapter instead shows how difficult management has made it for ICC experts to think and do exactly that.

3.2　Making the Institution Manageable

The institutionalised project of global justice is an invention of the last thirty years.[2] Commentators have frequently pointed to the role played by domestic courts and other institutional experiments as the precursor to the permanent and universal international criminal court of today. They project backwards a patchwork of disparate but common efforts towards anti-impunity, ranging from the 1474 trial of Peter von Hagenbach to the Klaus Barbie trial for Nazi war crimes in 1987, and many episodes in between.[3] There is a sense among commentators that such efforts, though laudable, were deficient for their parochial reach and for states' inability to fashion a more stable and universal set of mechanisms at the international level.

This is one of the historical imaginaries into which the agenda for a permanent ICC is said to emerge and respond. Within this historical understanding, the ICC represents not only a next step in the march of human progress but also the further institutionalisation of a project to end global impunity. Despite its brief history, this institutionalised version of global justice has become remarkably successful as the dominant mode of confronting global injustice. How management has played a role in securing this pre-eminent position for the ICC as a 'primary

---

[2] Thomas Skouteris, 'The New Tribunalism: Strategies of (De)Legitimation in the Era of International Adjudication' (2006) 17 *Finnish Yearbook of International Law* 307–356, at 308–309. Christine Schwöbel-Patel links this trend to the rise of humanitarianism as a post-Cold War discourse, Christine Schwöbel-Pabel, *Marketing Global Justice: The Political Economy of International Criminal Law* (Cambridge University Press 2021) 77–78.

[3] Kevin Jon Heller and Gerry Simpson (eds.), *The Hidden Histories of War Crimes Trials* (Oxford University Press 2013). For similar efforts to render alternative histories of ICL, see, for example, Neil Boister and Robert Cryer, *The Tokyo International Military Tribunal: A Reappraisal* (Oxford University Press 2008); Morten Bergsmo, Cheah Wui Ling and Yi Ping (eds.), *Historical Origins of International Criminal Law, Volume 1* (Torkel Opsahl Academic EPublisher 2014); Gerry Simpson, 'The Conscience of Civilisation, and Its Discontents: A Counter History of International Criminal Law' in Philipp Kastner (ed.), *International Criminal Law in Context* (Routledge 2018) 11–27.

3.2 MAKING THE INSTITUTION MANAGEABLE 93

institution' of global justice is the subject of this chapter, beginning with the early institutionalising efforts of the International Law Commission (ILC) and, in the 1990s, through the efficiency concerns of drafters at the Rome Conference.

3.2.1 Pre-Rome Debates

After the establishment of the ILC in 1947, its members were almost immediately authorised by the UN General Assembly to examine the topic of an 'international criminal jurisdiction'.[4] The ILC drew from the extensive and innovative work carried out as part of the effort to prosecute Nazi war criminals, first at the International Military Tribunal at Nuremberg, and subsequently during the Nuremberg trials. It codified the so-called Nuremberg Principles in 1950, while trials of lower-ranking Nazi officials were still being conducted in post-war Germany. Later the ILC broached the 'desirability and possibility of establishing an international judicial organ for the trial of persons, charged with genocide or other crimes'.[5] This was the beginning of an effort to approach mass atrocities institutionally, not only internationally.

ILC members proposed various types of institutional models, one being the Criminal Chamber of the International Court of Justice (ICJ).[6] This idea proposed an amendment to the ICJ Statute to add a criminal branch to the world court, placing such activities on a permanent institutional footing and ensuring access to considerable UN resources and personnel. Ultimately, the idea was not endorsed as members feared the model would be impractical.[7] Other designs also conceived of a permanent or semi-permanent organisation, with features of judicial organs and jurisdictional parameters not unlike the ad hoc tribunals that emerged decades later.

Despite these blueprints, the ILC's proposals were shelved for forty years as the General Assembly deferred consideration of a code of crimes.[8] Only in the early 1990s was the ILC seized of the topic again, by which point several scholars had already rallied behind the idea of a

---

[4] United Nations General Assembly Resolution (UNGA Res) 260B (III) (9 December 1948).
[5] Report of the International Law Commission on the Work of its 2nd Session, A/CN.4/34, Volume II.IV, 5 June–29 July 1950, para. 128 (ILC Report 1950).
[6] Ibid.
[7] Ibid., paras. 137–139.
[8] UNGA Res 898 (IX) (14 December 1954).

94   THE MANAGERIAL COURT: MACRO-MANAGEMENT

permanent international criminal court.[9] The establishment of the ad hoc international criminal tribunals for Yugoslavia and Rwanda provided a glimpse into how an institutional response to mass atrocity might work by putting a cadre of international criminal lawyers to work in building a nascent jurisprudence and institutional apparatus.[10] By the time the ILC reprised the topic of international criminal jurisdiction in 1992, it had become much easier to conceive of global justice as a permanent and institutional endeavour.

When the ILC established a working group on the topic in 1992, a treaty-based international criminal court was listed as one of the possible mechanisms for prosecuting international crimes. Yet rather than being a 'standing full-time body', the proposed mechanism was intended to 'be called into operation as and when required'.[11] There was some disagreement among delegates as to this lean mechanism. Some delegates questioned the feasibility and, ultimately, the effectiveness of such a model. Others regarded national prosecutions and the ratification of universal jurisdiction laws as more effective ways to tackle impunity.[12] Despite these concerns, the working group adopted a preference for a 'flexible facility at the international level'.[13]

With flexibility as the watchword, discussions within the ILC turned on questions of practicality and effectiveness. According to the working group, the principal paradox was whether to opt for the more 'practical solution of a non-standing permanent body' or 'the more desirable alternative of a full-time organ'.[14] Some delegates saw flexibility as necessary for effective and timely investigations and prosecutions. This remained the dominant position when James Crawford became chair of

---

[9] See Ben Ferencz, *An International Criminal Court: A Step to World Peace* (Oceana Publications 1980); M. Cherif Bassiouni, 'From Versailles to Rwanda in Seventy-Five Years: The Need to Establish a Permanent International Criminal Court' (1997) 10 *Harvard International Law Journal* 11–62; John Dugard, 'Obstacles in the Way of an International Criminal Court' (1997) 56 *Cambridge Law Journal* 329–342.

[10] Roy S. Lee, 'Introduction: The Rome Conference and Its Contribution to International Law' in Roy S. Lee (ed.), *The International Criminal Court: The Making of the Rome Statute* (Kluwer Law International 1999) 1–40, at 6.

[11] Report of the Working Group on the Question of an International Criminal Jurisdiction, Report of the International Law Commission on the Work of its 44th Session, A/47/10, Volume II.II, 4 May–24 July 1992, Annex, para. 4(e) (ILC Working Group Report).

[12] Ibid., paras. 33–36.

[13] Ibid., para. 41.

[14] Report of the Commission to the General Assembly on the Work of Its 46th Session, A/CN.4/SER.A/1994/Add.1, 2 May–22 July 1994, Volume II.II, para. 49 (ILC Report 1994).

3.2 MAKING THE INSTITUTION MANAGEABLE

the ILC working group. He affirmed in 1994 that the envisaged court 'will not have a large infrastructure or a permanent staff'.[15] Yet increasingly, concerns about effectiveness led the working group to seek out a 'workable structure for a permanent court'.[16] The ILC's 1994 draft Statute reflected a compromise. It sought to 'combine the two approaches by providing for the present realistic and pragmatic arrangement, while at the same time envisaging the possibility of the court remaining permanently in session in the long term as a way of encouraging uniformity and further development of the law'.[17] This amalgam formed the background against which discussions for an international criminal court began.

At the Ad Hoc Committee, '[a]lmost all the delegations that spoke to this question thought so [i.e. that the court should be permanent] but believed that it should sit only when it was needed'.[18] Yet efficiency rationales began to creep into the thinking of delegates.[19] During one session in April 1995, the United Kingdom implored delegates to 'constantly bear in mind this question: is it the best use of limited resources to undertake international investigations and prosecutions with all the difficulties and duplication of personnel that that involves...?'[20] The UK instead preferred national prosecutions and efficiency over international action by a permanent body.[21] US delegates scrutinising the 1994 draft Statute were equally suspicious about the lack of accountability mechanisms for the new body, reflecting a position they had earlier staked out at the UN. They worried that the draft Statute 'contain[ed] no provisions regarding the budget and administration of the court'.[22] Yet

---

[15] James Crawford, 'The ILC Adopts a Statute for an International Criminal Court' (1995) 89 *American Journal of International Law* 404–416, at 408–410; ILC Report 1994, para. 49.

[16] Crawford, 'The ILC Adopts a Statute for an ICC' 408–410; ILC Report 1994, para. 49.

[17] ILC Report 1994, para. 49.

[18] Fanny Benedetti, Karine Bonneau, and John Washburn, *Negotiating the International Criminal Court: New York to Rome, 1994–1998* (Martinus Nijhoff 2014) 29.

[19] Provisional Estimates of the Staffing, Structure and Costs of the Establishment and Operation of an International Criminal Court, Preliminary Report of the Secretary-General, Ad Hoc Committee for an International Criminal Court, A/AC.244/L.2, 20 March 1995, para. 5.

[20] Summary of Observations Made by the Representative of the United Kingdom of Great Britain and Northern Ireland on 3, 4, 5, 6, and 7 April 1995, Ad Hoc Committee on the Establishment of an International Criminal Court, Press Release no. 32/95, 7 April 1995, 11–12.

[21] Ibid., 12.

[22] Comments of the United States of America, comments received pursuant to paragraph 4 of General Assembly Resolution 49/53 on the Establishment of an International

THE MANAGERIAL COURT: MACRO-MANAGEMENT

their approach tacitly accepted the need for an institution to deal with mass atrocities.[23] Although their commitment to a future court remained tentative, the US delegation was adamant that 'to provide for effective functioning and adequate oversight, a number of such matters must be addressed'.[24] Cost-effectiveness was 'of the highest priority in the consideration of the draft Statute'.[25]

From these interventions, delegates to the Ad Hoc Committee began to contemplate a permanent *and* efficient institution. This approach was most apparent in the deliberations on draft article 4(1) establishing the court as a permanent institution acting 'when required':

> The approach reflected in article 4, paragraph 1, of the draft statute ... was described as an acceptable compromise which sought to strike a balance between, on the one hand, the requirements of flexibility and cost-effectiveness in the operation of the court and, on the other hand, the need to promote, as an alternative to ad hoc tribunals, a permanent judicial organ, able to ensure uniformity and consistency in the application and further development of international criminal law.[26]

The drafters' thinking had moved on from mutually exclusive categories of permanence and efficiency towards a model accommodating both. As with the ILC working group, the Ad Hoc Committee's consensus around a model of permanent yet efficient justice allowed other details to be fleshed out. Further details, including the structure of the court itself and its funding arrangements, were also guided by concerns over efficiency. As preparations began for the Rome Conference, the debates and the context surrounding them thrust efficiency to the forefront of delegates' minds.

3.2.2 Managerial Concerns at Rome

Once the Ad Hoc Committee completed its work, the Preparatory Committee for the Rome Conference took up several previously unaddressed issues. Among these was the court's funding arrangements, to

---

Criminal Court', Report of the Secretary-General, Ad Hoc Committee for an International Criminal Court, A/AC.244/1/Add.2, 31 March 1995, para. 3.

[23] Ibid., para. 3.

[24] Ibid.

[25] Ibid., para. 74.

[26] Report of the Ad Hoc Committee on the Establishment of an International Criminal Court, UN General Assembly, A/50/22, 7 September 1995, para. 18.

3.2 MAKING THE INSTITUTION MANAGEABLE

which the Preparatory Committee turned in spring 1998. Delegates were aware of the implications of different funding models. Concerns about the court's independence from funders had to be balanced against the need for institutional stability, and there was a 'general understanding that its authority would be undermined if hampered by a lack of adequate, long-term and secure funding'.[27] This 'common concern' about financing and its impact on court effectiveness underpinned many interventions at the Preparatory Committee.[28]

Since permanence and efficiency were both sought by delegates, discussions frequently devolved to weighing up competing priorities. Halff, Tolbert, and Villacis recall that

> [t]he discussion in the Preparatory Committee therefore focused on finding a mechanism that would be able to guarantee the independence and impartiality of the Court, while at the same time avoiding the situation in which the prospective financial burden could be a prohibitive factor for States considering accession to the Statute.[29]

As this observation reveals, independence and stability were not the only factors driving the discussion. In fact, the court's funding arrangement had important political and economic implications for states. Preferences over the funding model were divided between the future court's largest financial donors and those less well-placed to contribute. These two broad categories of states found themselves divided, with wealthier states largely from the Global North favouring a self-funded institution and less wealthy states of the Global South advocating a court financed through the UN. That debate replicated the North–South dynamic that had characterised earlier UN struggles.

Large donor states – including Germany, the United States, and the United Kingdom – recommended a self-funded court unlike the UN-funded ad hoc tribunals. In their analysis, such an institution would not only be more self-sufficient but would also be more financially accountable to its members. In contrast, they saw a UN-funded court raising the prospect of outside influence being exerted by a wealthy UN member who remained outside the court's statute, potentially disrupting court

---

[27] Maarten Halff, David Tolbert, and Renan Villacis, 'Article 115: Funds of the Court and of the Assembly of States Parties' in Otto Triffterer and Kai Ambos (eds.), *The Rome Statute of the International Criminal Court: A Commentary* (3rd edn., C.H. Beck Hart Nomos 2016) 2253–2262, at 2255.

[28] Ibid., 2255.

[29] Ibid.

98   THE MANAGERIAL COURT: MACRO-MANAGEMENT

investigations into their own conduct. Such actors might begin to attach conditions to their UN contributions, putting the ICC's work at risk.

Conversely, states of the Global South were not convinced by the self-funded model. They warned (prophetically so) that a self-funded court would be equally susceptible to financial brinkmanship. They were already familiar with attempts to hold the UN to ransom in the 1980s and early 1990s and feared a similar strategy at the new court. These fears were not allayed by the secretary to the Rome Conference, who candidly remarked that 'to secure the financial health of the Court, the support of major financial contributors was crucial and hence the concerns of the major contributors should be looked at more sympathetically'.[30] In response, the head of the Indian delegation at Rome worried that a self-funded court would spend much time and energy appeasing major donors, occasioning a two-tier system of membership.[31] These states were also concerned about having to pick up a heavy financial burden should wealthier states opt to remain outside the court.

Based on these concerns, various Asian, African, and Latin American delegates, as well as civil society groups, proposed that the court be funded via the UN common budget. This was designed to insure them against the financial risks arising from non-participation of wealthy states. It also better reflected the court's universal aspirations. Amnesty International stated that '[i]t is appropriate to have the General Assembly fund the court as part of the regular UN budget since [it] will be acting on behalf of the entire international community'.[32] As Kendall outlines, delegations that supported UN financing believed that such an arrangement would 'make it possible for all States to initiate proceedings without financial burdens'.[33] Removing any possibility of using financial pressure to influence case selection would make the court more representative and

[30] Mahnoush Arsanjani, 'Financing' in Antonio Cassese, Paola Gaeta and John R.W.D. Jones (eds.), *The Rome Statute of the International Criminal Court, Volume 1* (Oxford University Press 2002) 315, 320.

[31] Rao, 'Financing the Court' 402.

[32] Amnesty International, 'The International Criminal Court: Making the Right Choices – Part IV: Establishing and Financing the Court and Final Clauses', March 1998, available at: www.amnesty.org/en/library/asset/IOR40/004/1998/en/6b9d9776-f000-40e2-ae29-2006d9785e2c/ior400041998en.html.

[33] Summary of Proceedings of the Ad Hoc Committee during the Period 3–13 April 1995, A/AC.244.L.2, 136; see Sara Kendall, 'Commodifying Global Justice: Economies of Accountability at the International Criminal Court' (2015) 13 *Journal of International Criminal Justice* 113–134, at 120.

3.2 MAKING THE INSTITUTION MANAGEABLE 99

accessible 'to all UN member states regardless of their financial circumstances, and thus more "global" in its orientation and possible interventions'.[34]

Despite this divide, states favouring a UN-funded court came around to the idea of self-funding once they were assured that wealthy states would sign up to the court. That assurance quickly collapsed, and fears vindicated, when the United States decided not to sign the final text. Yet to many signatories, it was accepted that 'most major donor States would support the Statute', and this fact, coupled with possible UN funding in the case of a Security Council referral 'removed opposition to placing the burden of financing the Court on the shoulders of States Parties'.[35]

Final article 115 of the Statute detailing the court's funding arrangements bears the marks of these struggles and ambivalences. It provides that the court be funded via state party contributions and potentially by the UN when referring situations to the court (a mechanism that has not been deployed despite several UN Security Council referrals). The Statute also allows for voluntary contributions by governments, international organisations, and private persons.[36] States parties are in charge of setting the court's annual budget,[37] while the court's finances are subject to annual independent audit.[38] The level of state party contributions is calculated according to the UN scale of assessment, itself based on gross domestic product.[39] Such a scale effectively placed greatest financial responsibility and thus influence in the hands of wealthy states parties. The court became financially independent of the UN while becoming dependent on Western states parties in a way that would give their efficiency concerns greater argumentative force as the institution sought to remain economically viable.

Alongside funding, efficiency anxieties greatly affected the Rome Conference due to the underperformance of ad hoc tribunals, notably the International Criminal Tribunal for Rwanda (ICTR). In June 1996, the UN General Assembly asked the then Under-Secretary-General for Internal Oversight, Karl Paschke, to 'identify[] problems and recommend[]

---

[34] Kendall, 'Commodifying Global Justice' 120.

[35] Arsanjani, 'Financing' 323.

[36] Article 116 Rome Statute of the International Criminal Court (signed 17 July 1998, entered into force 1 July 2002) A/CONF.189/9 (Rome Statute).

[37] Article 115 Rome Statute.

[38] Article 118 Rome Statute.

[39] Article 117 Rome Statute.

100   THE MANAGERIAL COURT: MACRO-MANAGEMENT

measures to enhance the efficient allocation of resources' at the ICTR.[40] His findings, issued only eighteen months before the opening of the Rome Conference, made for a sobering read.[41] The report identified 'serious operational deficiencies in the management of the Tribunal' and 'frequent violations of the United Nations rules and regulations'.[42] It concluded that 'not a single administrative area of the Registry (Finance, Procurement, Personnel, Security, General Services) functioned effectively'.[43]

Paschke's indictment of the ICTR cast a long shadow over discussions in Rome. Central to his diagnosis was the mismanagement of the tribunal.[44] By characterising the problem as one of management, Paschke suggested that the ICTR's problems – like the UN's in previous years – lay in 'poor management, ineptitude or lack of expertise'.[45] These findings were intended as 'a giant step towards the creation of an international criminal court of justice' that would avoid the same management mistakes.[46]

Paschke's findings offered delegates a checklist of what not to do, while instilling anxiety about inefficiency and underperformance. His report singled out the ICTR registrar as responsible for rifts between other organs and for defying requests by judges and prosecutors. '[A]ware of this statutory weakness and of the resulting threat of inefficiency, the drafters of the Rome Statute supplied statutory provisions entrusting the Presidency with the responsibility for the proper administration of the Court' under article 43(2) of the Statute and provided that the registrar be elected by the judges under article 43(4).[47] The final structure of the ICC Registry laid down in article 43 of the Statute was 'largely due to the impact of the Paschke Report and tales, whether justified or not, of

---

[40] UNGA Res 50/213C (7 June 1996).

[41] Report of the Office of Internal Oversight Services on the Audit and Investigation of the International Criminal Tribunal for Rwanda, A/51/789, 6 February 1997 (Paschke Report).

[42] Paschke Report, Summary and 1.

[43] Ibid., 9.

[44] Press Briefing by Under-Secretary-General for Internal Oversight Services, 12 February 1997, available at: www.un.org/press/en/1997/19970212.paschke.html.

[45] Ibid.

[46] Ibid.

[47] Philipp Ambach and Klaus Rackwitz, 'A Model of International Judicial Administration?: The Evolution of Managerial Practices at the International Criminal Court' (2013) 76 Law & Contemporary Problems 119–161, at 136.

3.2 MAKING THE INSTITUTION MANAGEABLE 101

Registry mismanagement at the ICTR'.[48] Beyond the Registry, the decision to create a pre-trial phase of proceedings for authorising investigations and confirming charges against suspects was also influenced by efficiency concerns, namely to 'streamline the functioning of Chambers to ensure that they are able to manage and conduct cases as expeditiously as possible'.[49]

Once negotiations ended, the ad hoc experience continued to frame institutional developments at the new court. In 2001, International Criminal Tribunal for the former Yugoslavia (ICTY) registrar Hans Holthuis posited that administrative flexibility should become the 'cornerstone of [the ICC's] modus operandi'.[50] Ralph Zacklin, writing as UN Assistant-Secretary-General for Legal Affairs in 2004, described the ad hoc tribunals as 'mammoth bureaucracies'.[51] Recalling how their 'insuperable administration and managerial difficulties ... became apparent' soon after their creation, he hoped the ICC would avoid the same fate by placing efficiency atop its list of priorities.[52]

This ICC pre-history shows how concerns about efficiency and management shaped early discussions on a permanent international criminal court, despite early signs that efficiency and permanence seemed mutually exclusive traits. The Ad Hoc Committee's deliberations, as well as debates over the court's funding model and the shadow of mismanaged ad hoc tribunals, framed many discussions both during and after the Rome Conference about how best to structure and run the new court. Like many court advocates since, delegates who celebrated the Statute in July 1998 saw a natural fusion of ideas about global justice and the discourse of efficient management and optimal performance. The delegation from the Philippines captured that sensibility in articulating the

---

[48] John R.W.D. Jones, 'The Registry and Staff' in Cassese et al., 'Rome Statute of the ICC' 280.

[49] Karim Khan, 'Article 34: Organs of the Court' in Triffterer and Ambos, 'The Rome Statute of the International Criminal Court' 1197–1203, at 1200. See Articles 34 and 57 Rome Statute.

[50] 'Flexibility Must be Cornerstone of Administration of International Criminal Court, Preparatory Commission Told', Press Release L/2976, 6 March 2001, available at: www .legal-tools.org/uploads/tx_ltpdb/doc41976.htm.

[51] Ralph Zacklin, 'The Failings of Ad Hoc International Tribunals' (2004) 2 *Journal of International Criminal Justice* 541–545, at 543.

[52] Ibid. Scholars mirrored this position, with Bassiouni stating '[i]f the lessons of the past are to instruct the course of the future, then the creation of a permanent system of international criminal justice with a continuous institutional memory is imperative', Bassiouni, 'From Versailles to Rwanda' 12–13.

102   THE MANAGERIAL COURT: MACRO-MANAGEMENT

'dream of an international criminal court that shall be an efficient and effective dispenser of justice'.[53]

3.3   Management in the Interim

If the efficiency discourse played out in Rome, its effects were already visible after the Statute's adoption. The four years between the end of the Rome Conference and the Statute's entry into force are generally remembered as the time in which the Rules of Procedure and Evidence and Elements of Crimes were agreed upon by the Preparatory Commission (PrepCom).[54] Alongside the Statute, such texts formed the applicable law necessary for prosecutors and judges to discharge their mandates. Yet this interim period also witnessed a shift from theoretical discussions about future court structures to practical questions about how to make the court a functioning reality. The court's architects frequently invoked efficiency as part of this transition.

In December 1999, the Working Group on the Rules of Procedure and Evidence were discussing a proposed Victims and Witnesses Unit to be housed within the Registry. The Unit would have a mandate to assist victims seeking legal advice and provide protective measures to both victims and witnesses, and the working group was eager to 'ensure the efficient and effective performance of its work'.[55] To that end, it proposed that prosecution and defence services within the Unit remain separate and that staff receive adequate training and maintain a high degree of confidentiality. Others linked efficiency to adequate funding. The first president of the Assembly of States Parties (ASP), Zeid Al Hussein, stated in 2004 that the court 'cannot be considered – no matter what its eventual size or the extent of its budget – as too expensive'.[56] For him, as for others at the time, '[w]hat would be too expensive, are the consequences of having no Court at all'.[57] Efficiency was equated to providing

---

[53] Statement by His Excellency Lauro L. Baja to the Rome Conference, 16 June 1998, 1.

[54] William Schabas, *An Introduction to the International Criminal Court* (Cambridge University Press 2017) 21–22.

[55] Discussion paper submitted by the Coordinator concerning Part 4. Organisation and composition of the Court, ICC Preparatory Commission Working Group on Rules of Procedures and Evidence, PCNICC/1999/WGRPE(4)/RT.2/Add.1, 14 December 1999, 3.

[56] Address by Prince Zeid Raad Zeid Al Hussein President of the ASP, Assembly of States Parties 3rd Session, 6 September 2004, 2, available at: https://asp.icc-cpi.int/iccdocs/asp_docs/library/asp/060904_PZ_ASP_English.pdf.

[57] Ibid.

3.3 MANAGEMENT IN THE INTERIM 103

the resources required to carry out the court's functions effectively, while questions of accountability or strategic oversight took a backseat.

Despite these different iterations, early architects began to construct a managerial infrastructure within the new court. The draft Financial Regulations of early 2002 introduced the vocabulary of financial accountability, audit, and internal controls into the everyday practices of court officials.[58] The ideal promoted within the Regulations was 'effective financial administration and the exercise of economy'.[59] To that end, court funds were to be rigorously recorded and carefully disposed of 'to ensure ... [t]he economical use of the resources of the Court' while accounts were to be audited annually.[60] Concurrently, a Committee on Budget and Finance (CBF) was established by the ASP. The CBF comprised twelve geographically diverse members drawn from the fields of economics, public administration, and diplomacy, many of whom had built their careers within national bureaucracies and audit offices.[61] Karl Paschke, author of the UN report on ICTR mismanagement, was elected as the Committee's first chair in 2003.

The CBF was provided with extensive internal powers. These included the power to review the annual budget proposed by the registrar and make appropriate recommendations to the ASP. The CBF also has the power to scrutinise the court's audit reports and transmit these to the ASP with additional comments. In monitoring court spending, the CBF has access to 'any document submitted to the Assembly that contains financial or budgetary implications or any other matter of a financial, budgetary, or administrative nature'.[62] These expansive powers give the CBF considerable leeway to investigate almost all areas of court activity.[63]

Finally, the interim period saw a nascent audit regime put in place. The Financial Regulations established an Office of Internal Audit to 'conduct independent audits of the financial transactions and the administrative

---

[58] Draft Financial Regulations, ICC Preparatory Commission, PCNICC/2001/1/Add.2, 8 January 2002, available at: www.legal-tools.org/doc/396a35/pdf/.

[59] Regulation 1.3. Financial Regulations and Rules, ICC-ASP/1/3, adopted 9 September 2002.

[60] Regulation 10.1(c)(iii) Financial Regulations and Rules.

[61] Committee on Budget and Finance webpage, https://asp.icc-cpi.int/en_menus/asp/CBF/Pages/default.aspx.

[62] Assembly of States Parties Resolution (ASP Res) 1/4 (3 September 2002) Annex, para. 3.

[63] When interviewed, some ICC officials took a dim view of the CBF's extensive access to all such documents. One ICC staff member described the CBF's involvement as less micro-management than 'nano-management', ICC Interview 002, 13 July 2018 (on file with author).

104 THE MANAGERIAL COURT: MACRO-MANAGEMENT

systems' in accordance with international auditing standards.[64] The ASP appointed an auditor with powers to 'make observations with respect to the efficiency of the financial procedures, the accounting system, the internal financial controls and, in general, the administration and management of the Court'.[65] Like the CBF, the auditor would have 'free access to all books, records and other documents ... necessary for the performance of the audit'.[66] Such expertise became an important vector for standards of quality control and embedding a concern for financial accountability within the infant court.

3.4 Efficiency in the Young Court

Many drafters were involved in assembling the court's management infrastructure from 1998. Yet various interventions framed the institution in management terms. Chief among these was the court's first prosecutor, Luis Moreno-Ocampo. Ocampo adopted the mindset of an entrepreneurial manager within a start-up in establishing the initial structures and procedures of the Office of the Prosecutor (OTP). During his last days as a visiting professor at Harvard University before assuming his new post, Ocampo asked for some management advice from Fernando Oris de Roa, a friend in the Argentinian agribusiness. He asked Roa 'for some advice on how to use the private sector efficiency to build an international organisation'.[67] Roa described the nascent institution as a kind of 'startup', asked Ocampo about its 'mission', and focused his advice on 'what I know: management'.[68] In response, Ocampo noted, 'I have the chance to build the most efficient public office', and took Roa's advice with him to The Hague.[69]

Within Ocampo's new Office, a preparatory team of 'institution-builders' consulted widely with national and international criminal justice experts on the most appropriate structures and procedures for

---

[64] Rule 110.1(a) Financial Regulations and Rules.

[65] Regulation 12.3 Financial Regulations and Rules.

[66] Rule 110.1(c) Financial Regulations and Rules.

[67] Luis Moreno-Ocampo, 'The International Criminal Court' in David Crane, Leila Sadat, and Michael Sharf (eds.), *The Founders: Four Pioneering Individuals Who Launched the First Modern-Era International Criminal Tribunals* (Cambridge University Press 2018) 94–125, at 112.

[68] Ibid., 113–115.

[69] Ibid., 116.

3.4 EFFICIENCY IN THE YOUNG COURT

conducting complex criminal investigations.[70] The OTP's internal structure was separated into functional divisions and units dealing with investigations, complementarity, prosecutions, and trials. The preparatory team also drafted key documents outlining the OTP's composition, duties, and relationship to other organs.[71] In a 2003 Policy Paper, Ocampo described how the experiences of the OTP in its 'first few months have guided it in shaping the most effective structure to carry out its mission'.[72] This vision of a justice start-up, while in keeping with the structures of the ad hoc tribunals, sought to deviate from the traditional bureaucratic structures common within domestic criminal justice systems. In a 2003 draft Policy Paper, the OTP claimed that '[o]nly a project-oriented as opposed to a static organisational model can bring the desired results'.[73] To that end, 'post levels and fixed hierarchies' were considered to be 'counter-productive'.[74] This flexible structure chimed with the permanent yet efficient ideal envisaged by the Statute's drafters.

Ocampo had a sense of what efficient justice entailed even before any investigations were opened. Preliminary examinations were expected to be 'process focused and cost-effective' while investigations would follow an 'open, horizontal organisation ... with very short vertical lines of authority'.[75] Ocampo also promoted the complementary role of the court vis-à-vis national courts. He believed that the best-case scenario for the ICC would be 'zero case. Because zero case means there's no genocide, or if there's a genocide, the national court will do it, and as a system we should respect national courts'.[76] Where the court did have to step in – when states were either unwilling or unable to investigate or prosecute grave crimes – the OTP's role would simply be to 'fill the gap created by

---

[70] Morten Bergsmo, 'Institutional History, Behaviour and Development' in Morten Bergsmo, Klaus Rackwitz, and Song Tianying (eds.), *Historical Origins of International Criminal Law, Volume 5* (Torkel Opsahl Academic EPublisher 2017) 1–36, 1.

[71] Morten Bergsmo et al., 'A Prosecutor Falls, Time for the Court to Rise' (2017) 86 *FICHL Policy Brief Series* 1–4, at 2.

[72] Paper on Some Policy Issues before the Office of the Prosecutor: Referrals and Communications, Office of the Prosecutor, September 2003, Annex, 5.

[73] Draft Paper on Some Policy Issues before the Office of the Prosecutor for Discussion at the Public Hearing in The Hague on 17 and 18 June 2003, Office of the Prosecutor, 18 June 2003, 7.

[74] Ibid.

[75] Ibid., 9 and 11.

[76] Todd Benjamin, Interview with Luis Moreno Ocampo, International Bar Association, 1 February 2013, available at: www.ibanet.org/Article/NewDetail.aspx?ArticleUid= 81213DCF-0911-4141-AD29-A486F9B03D37.

106 THE MANAGERIAL COURT: MACRO-MANAGEMENT

the failure of States to satisfy their duty to investigate'.[77] In these instances, too, the Office was expected to 'exercise its investigative powers with firmness and efficiency'.[78]

Early attempts to fine-tune court organs occasionally involved more comprehensive restructuring exercises. These were frequently conducted in the language of efficiency. In 2004, the OTP 'examined its rudimentary structure to find ways to increase integration and efficiency'.[79] It restructured several divisions 'to adapt to needs that came to light as it became operational' and created an OTP Executive Committee to centralise strategic decision-making, drawing on a similar move at the UN Secretariat some years before.[80] Yet Ocampo remained adamant that this did not amount to bureaucratisation. It was part of the 'ICC model' of start-up justice to separate strategic decisions from operational activity to ensure clear lines of authority and rapid deployment of resources within project-based situations.[81] So resolute was Ocampo's enthusiasm for this model he advocated that it be packaged and exported 'to manage all the conflicts, all the problems'.[82] Alongside the court's substantive contribution to anti-impunity, then, lay its equally important organisational contribution of efficient, entrepreneurial justice.

Other organs contributed to making the court an 'independent and credible institution of international criminal justice'.[83] The Presidency and Registry drafted administrative policies on personnel, prefacing the court-wide turn to human resource management in later years. During this establishment phase, the organs focused on aligning staff regulations with those of the UN common system and introduced a rudimentary appraisal process to track staff performance. These policies were also guided by the court's desire to 'affirm fiscal responsibility to the states parties' by proving that staff were competent and efficient. The Registry's Human Resources Section therefore conducted a job evaluation exercise in July 2004 to review each position's compliance with the UN common

---

[77] Draft Paper on Some Policy Issues, 5. See Article 17(1)(a) Rome Statute.

[78] Draft Paper on Some Policy Issues, 5.

[79] Report on the Activities of the Court, ICC-ASP/3/10, 22 July 2004, para. 44.

[80] Ibid., paras. 46–47.

[81] Luis Moreno-Ocampo, 'The International Criminal Court: Seeking Global Justice' (2007) 40 *Case Western Reserve Journal of International Law* 215–225, at 216.

[82] Ocampo asked rhetorically, '[c]an we transfer this idea to all the areas like copyright or others? Probably yes', Interview with Luis Moreno Ocampo 1 February 2013.

[83] Report on the Activities of the Court 2004, para. 3.

3.4 EFFICIENCY IN THE YOUNG COURT 107

system and to 'establish a sense of equity in the work environment'.[84] Also in keeping with the UN, new management procedures were introduced within the Registry in 2004 and an Office of Internal Audit formed to conduct periodic and ad hoc reviews of court administration.

These internal efforts to construct and narrate the court were matched by the external work of court leaders. As they did so, they found much to commend the institution only after two years in operation. By 2005, while experts grappled with constructing the court 'from scratch', the OTP was already investigating alleged war crimes and crimes against humanity in both Uganda and the Democratic Republic of the Congo (DRC). The evidence collected in Uganda allowed the prosecutor to issue arrest warrants against high-ranking members of the Lord's Resistance Army and by the end of 2005, the OTP had also issued a warrant against Thomas Lubanga for the conscription and use of child soldiers in the DRC conflict. In the same year, another investigation opened into the Darfur genocide after the UN Security Council referred the situation to the court.

Speaking at the ASP's fourth session in 2005, Ocampo recalled these positive results to states parties. Nonetheless, he was frank about the OTP's inability to keep up with growing demand. In addition to its active situations, the OTP was planning additional field missions to Côte d'Ivoire and the Central African Republic. To deal with this growing demand (and despite the OTP also controlling the 'supply' of situations), Ocampo instead proposed a better internal allocation of resources and assured states that cost-effectiveness remained a 'basic principle' for his Office.[85] At a diplomatic gathering in Brussels, the court's first registrar, Bruno Cathala, similarly acknowledged that 'we must adapt our working methods on a case-by-case basis: we have to plan our projects according to constantly differing political and cultural contexts ... In this drive to adapt to the requirements of the field, we are constantly looking for the most efficient use possible of our budgetary resources'.[86]

---

[84] Ibid., para. 66.
[85] Statement by Luis Moreno-Ocampo, Prosecutor of the International Criminal Court, Assembly of States Parties 4th Session, 28 November 2005, 1, available at: www.icc-cpi .int/NR/rdonlyres/0CBFF4AC-1238-4DA1-9F4A-70D763F90F91/278514/LMO_ 20051128_English.pdf.
[86] Speech by the Registrar of the International Criminal Court Bruno Cathala, Brussels, 8 June 2005, 6, available at: www.icc-cpi.int/NR/rdonlyres/ECD36817-DE8D-4F2B- A75F-DA282FED1AA1/278492/DB200506_BC_En.pdf.

108   THE MANAGERIAL COURT: MACRO-MANAGEMENT

As these efforts suggest, the court's first priority was to transform an idea on paper into an efficient yet 'fully functional judicial institution'.[87] This was achieved by creating basic managerial processes oriented towards the cost-effective delivery of court services, and by promoting the court's efficiency credentials to states parties. Having laid the foundations, the court proceeded to adopt more detailed and long-term management practices in its efforts to confront atrocity situations. The remaining sections of this chapter map this expanding terrain of management practices, as well as its consequences.

3.5   Building the Managerial Scaffolding

Despite its early successes, the infant court still suffered from 'teething problems' according to the international judge and scholar, Antonio Cassese.[88] The CBF noted that the court had not yet reached its full capabilities while also failing to offer clear and measurable objectives. Moreover, despite procedures to record organ-wide performance, implementation was patchy and results often vague or incomplete. Some organs collected no performance data at all.[89] The CBF recommended that to set overarching objectives, the court should link budgetary resources to expected outputs. This practice of 'results-based budgeting' was already popular in national settings, not to mention the Khmer Rouge tribunal, and sought to connect capabilities to results.[90]

The budget-to-results link was further embedded some months after by the court's Strategic Planning Project Group, set up in 2004–2005. The Project Group accepted the CBF's budgeting recommendation by proposing a strategic planning process that would allow the court to track its progress, matching 'long-term goals' to 'short-term action'.[91] The process would lead to the formation of a strategic plan, as a 'key management

---

[87] 'International Criminal Court "Now a Fully Functional Judicial Institution", Assembly of States Parties Told as It Begins One-Week Session', Press Release no. ASP2004.003-EN, 6 September 2004, available at: https://asp.icc-cpi.int/iccdocs/asp_docs/library/asp/ICC-ASP20040906.003-E.Rev.21.pdf.

[88] Antonio Cassese, 'Is the ICC Still Having Teething Problems?' (2006) 4 *Journal of International Criminal Justice* 434–441.

[89] Report of the Committee on Budget and Finance on the Work of Its 3rd Session, ICC-ASP/3/18, 13 August 2004, paras. 43–45.

[90] Ibid., paras. 45–46. See Chapter 1.

[91] Report of the Committee on Budget and Finance on the Work of Its 4th Session, ICC-ASP/4/2, 15 April 2005, para. 40.

3.5 BUILDING THE MANAGERIAL SCAFFOLDING 109

instrument' for directing resources to results. In response, the CBF was satisfied with this planned process and continued to emphasise the need for a 'meaningful set of interrelated strategic goals, expected accomplishments and performance indicators'.[92] This turn to strategic planning prompted a new mode of governing the relationship between the court and the wider global justice project.

3.5.1 The 'Strategic Planning' Turn

After internal consultation, including with the CBF, the ICC's first strategic plan was published in August 2006. The plan sets out the court's multiple goals and priorities for future years and offers some detail on the timeframes and resources required to achieve these goals. Despite its mundane tone and content, the plan is more than a mere outline of the court's expected activities. It also frames the court and its objectives in new ways. First, it carves out a pre-eminent position for the court within the wider global justice project. In this way, it understands the anti-impunity project to be a largely technocratic and institutionalised endeavour. Second, it iteratively redescribes the court's extant mandate and objectives through priority lists and the language of results, time spans, and resources. Through such redescription, the 2006 Strategic Plan begins to narrow the co-ordinates of global justice. The globally desirable comes to be equated with the institutionally possible, while the institutionally possible is fixed by calculations of results, time, and resources.

The plan's drafters deem the document 'instrumental to the Court's success'.[93] It 'provides a common framework for the Court's activities over the next ten years' and 'sets out the clear direction and priorities that will guide the Court'.[94] The plan is also intended to 'assist the Court in taking a proactive role in shaping its future'[95] and operates as the basis for dialogue between the court and states, international organisations, and civil society.[96] It also fosters a particular relationship between the court and the anti-impunity project.

---

[92] Ibid., para. 41.
[93] Strategic Plan of the International Criminal Court, ICC-ASP/5/6, 4 August 2006, para. 2.
[94] Ibid., para. 3.
[95] Ibid., para. 18.
[96] Ibid., para. 3.

110   THE MANAGERIAL COURT: MACRO-MANAGEMENT

From its first pages, the plan positions the ICC at the heart of global anti-impunity. It praises the achievements of the court's architects and external supporters for 'turn[ing] the words of the Statute into a functioning, permanent judicial institution', while reminding them of the international community's 'high aspirations' for the court.[97] It has become a 'working reality' within 'an emerging system of international justice involving States, international organisations, other international courts and non-governmental organisations'.[98] That multi-actor regime not only extends to criminalisation of individual perpetrators but also to the 'broader system of international law concerned with the peace, security and well-being of the world'.[99] According to the plan, the court takes on a 'particular, central role' at the intersection of these 'system[s] of international justice'.[100]

By binding the ICC to global justice, the plan performs a slippage by placing global justice within an institutional frame. Rather than the ICC contributing to a wider external project, the project of global justice is internalised and ultimately bound to the fate of the court itself, which must function effectively if justice is to be done. And since the ICC and global justice are so heavily imbricated (and because of the importance of efficiency), the globally desirable comes to be equated to what is deemed institutionally possible. This elision within the strategic plan is visible in the mediation of global justice through the terms of institutional constraints, resources, and strategic objectives – a managerialisation of global justice as professional reimagination. Accordingly, court success and failure equate to the success or failure of the wider project, while institutional risk and opportunity comprise the extent of the project's own liabilities and possibilities.

This elision begins with objectives, which the plan reformulates from an unstable, inter-connected, and politically contested global agenda into ascertainable, isolated, and agreed bullet points or 'strategic goals'. The vague pretext for the court's establishment, previously captured by the Statute's preamble, is now read as a fixed and agreed 'mission' guiding officials. The court's aims are to 'fairly, effectively and impartially investigate, prosecute and conduct trials of the most serious crimes', 'act transparently and efficiently', and 'contribute to long lasting respect for

[97] Ibid., para. 20.
[98] Ibid., paras. 1 and 20.
[99] Ibid., para. 20.
[100] Ibid., para. 21.

3.5 BUILDING THE MANAGERIAL SCAFFOLDING 111

and the enforcement of international criminal justice, to the prevention of crime and to the fight against impunity'.[101] Although no less vague than the preamble, these mission aims then form the backdrop for several strategic goals, including improving the quality of justice, creating a well-recognised and adequately supported institution, and becoming a model of public administration.[102] In the last two of these, the centrality of the ICC to global justice becomes clear.

Aside from reducing complex categories such as justice and impunity down to bite-sized slogans, the framing of 'strategic goals' has other effects. The goals are listed and numbered, but the plan does not rank them in order of priority. Rather, each operates as a standalone goal, with 'quality of justice' ranking equally to the goal of making the court a 'model of public administration'.[103] The connections between the strategic goals become frayed in an effort to isolate them from each other, even as they assume mutual reinforcement. For example, the wish that the court act according to 'high legal standards' to protect the rights of court participants may demand precisely the kind of legalist, bureaucratic culture that the court seems to rebuff in its quest to become a non-bureaucratic model of public administration. Moreover, the requirement to itemise into manageable goals makes it more difficult for court experts to witness the possible contradictions between effective prosecutions and preventing crime or tackling impunity. Although the court's investigative efforts may in fact hamper and delay local peace-building efforts – as has been documented by scholars[104] – the list represses such contradictions and dark sides, as well as the dissenting voices making this point.

The most far-reaching effect of the plan's reformulation, however, is the downgrading of ambitions to a set of organisational tick-boxes. The goals of creating 'a well-recognised and adequately supported institution' and making the court 'a model of public administration' must be pursued with the same intensity as efforts to improve the 'quality of justice' meted out by the court.[105] To become an 'adequately supported institution', the court will consider neither the reception of its policies among communities it intervenes in nor the structural conditions that go to producing

---

[101] Ibid., para. 18.
[102] Ibid para. 24.
[103] Ibid.
[104] Phil Clark, *Distant Justice: The Impact of the International Criminal Court on African Politics* (Cambridge University Press 2018).
[105] Strategic Plan 2006, para. 24.

112 THE MANAGERIAL COURT: MACRO-MANAGEMENT

atrocity situations.[106] Instead, it will 'enhance awareness of, effect a correct understanding of and increase support for the Court'.[107] This both portends to a single, correct understanding authoritatively rendered by the institution, while shifting responsibility for lack of support onto those who deviate from this understanding. It also limits the court's own responsibility to campaigning and promoting itself among relevant stakeholders rather than to confronting differing understandings of the court and its role in situation countries.

The 'judicial goal' of enhancing quality of justice shows what this means in practice. Since global justice and institutional functionality are fused, high-quality justice amounts to 'four to six new investigations into cases', 'a system to address all security risks', and completing a 'Court Capacity Model' to track the upper limit of the court's activities. This conception of justice is not only narrow in an individual, criminalised sense but also now as a set of technical tasks by experts. Justice becomes synonymous with what the institution deems plausible and palatable within the discourse of financial and organisational constraint. The possibility that quality of justice might be enhanced by assessing plausibility or risk from the perspective of local communities, through rendering fewer cases, or by withdrawing from situations entirely, is not countenanced.

Within this new frame of evaluation, it becomes easy, and encouraged, for court experts to read what is good for the court as what is good for global justice.[108] The Court Capacity Model offers an illustration. The model was devised as part of the court's response to the strategic goal of enhancing the quality of justice, and a detailed report on the model was published only a few weeks after the court's first strategic plan. According to the report, the model is a 'planning tool that allows the Court to determine the resources needed to achieve a certain output over a given period of time and to optimise the use of its resources'.[109] In order to forecast demand, the model relies upon 'comprehensive data from all of the Court's activities' and takes into account the contextual challenges

---

[106] Ibid.

[107] Ibid.

[108] This elision is discussed further in Sarah M.H. Nouwen and Wouter G. Werner, 'Monopolizing Global Justice: International Criminal Law as Challenge to Human Diversity' (2015) 13 *Journal of International Criminal Justice* 157–176.

[109] Report on the Court Capacity Model, ICC-ASP/5/10, 21 August 2006, Executive Summary, 3.

3.5 BUILDING THE MANAGERIAL SCAFFOLDING   113

and contingencies that might arise to alter these variables.[110] These known unknowns are labelled 'dependency factors' and include the smooth conduct of investigations, and the number of communications or witnesses involved in investigations and trials.[111]

The model is then effectively put to work, with the aforementioned inputs being combined with 'assumptions' about the average length of proceedings, volume of work, and complexity of activities to predict outputs.[112] The report gives a clear indication of the model's flexibility and the desire that it be experimented with to calibrate the best allocation of resources. As the report states, 'the Model can be used to align, through an optimisation process, all of the Court's activities at desired levels'.[113] The fine level of detail demanded by such calculations is visible in Figure 3.1, taken from the report.

The model explicitly relies upon imaginaries of the factory. As the report notes, 'the integration of all of the Court's activities into a production line facilitates the identification and review of areas that either have overcapacity or lack resources'.[114] Since the product is no less than justice itself, the model's advantage is to help remove 'bottlenecks in its production line'.[115] Global justice as contested political vision is replaced with justice as a factory capable of calibrating its inputs, assumptions, and outputs to global demand.[116]

Much is lost in that process. What the model excludes can be deduced from the inputs it accounts for, namely individual personnel allocated to tasks, isolated activities, and time. Although the plan's drafters sought to account for certain unknowns such as the level of state co-operation in the court's 'dependency factors', this too is reduced to a set of input variables. The unmeasurable includes work that cannot be conducted by court personnel, or that is often expected from victims and witnesses, work that is necessarily longer-term such as societal rebuilding, and work that has no foreseeable or measurable 'impact'.[117] The model excludes

---

[110] Ibid.

[111] Ibid., Figure 2.

[112] Ibid., para. 21.

[113] Ibid., para. 24.

[114] Ibid., para. 25.

[115] Ibid.

[116] Similar imaginaries of calibration appear in scholarship, see Mikaela Heikkilä, 'The Balanced Scorecard of International Criminal Tribunals' in Cedric Ryngaert (ed.), *The Effectiveness of International Criminal Justice* (Intersentia 2009) 27–54.

[117] Report on the Court Capacity Model, para. 31.

Court Capacity Model

Dependency Factors (DF)

SR	3	Situation-related	No. situations
INV	4	Investigation-related	Cases under investigation
ODF	1	Other dependency factors	
MGT	1	Management	No dependency factor
TR	0	Trial-related	No. simultaneous trials
WpT		Witness per trial	
COMM	1000	Communications/year	

Organ	Section	Category	Functions	Ref	Dependency Factor (DF1)	Dependency Factor (DF2)	FTE/DF	Optimized FTE*DF	2005 Resource Diff		2006 Resource
OTP	PIU	OS	Case-related communications and outreach	F1	SR		0.75	2.25	1.5	-0.75	1.5
OTP	PIU	OS	External communications	F1	ODF		0.95	0.95	0.95	0	0.95
OTP	PIU	OS	General media network devpt.& analysis	F1	ODF		0.45	0.45	0.45	0	0.45
OTP	PIU	Admin	Management	F1	MGT		0.10	0.1	0.1	0	0.1
OTP	KBU	Admin	Development of information systems	F2	ODF		2.50	2.5	2.5	0	2.5
OTP	KBU	Admin	Application support	F3	ODF		1.00	1	1	0	1
OTP	KBU	OS	Judicial process/support	F4	INV		0.30	1.2	0	-1.2	2
OTP	KBU	OS	Court room support	F5	TR		1.00	0	0	0	0
OTP	KBU	Admin	Management	F2	MGT		0.50	0.5	0.5	0	0.5
OTP	ISAU	OS	Analytical support to investigations	F6	SR		1.15	3.45	4.45	1	3.45
OTP	ISAU	OS	Crime monitoring	F6	ODF		2.50	2.5	2.5	0	2.5
OTP	ISAU	OS	Methodolgy development & research	F6	ODF		1.50	1.5	1.5	0	1.5
OTP	ISAU	Admin	Other	F6	MGT		1.55	1.55	2.55	1	1.55
OTP	OSU	OS	Mission support/witness protection	F7	INV		1.00	4	2.95	-1.05	3
OTP	OSU	OS	Security rules and regs/compliance	F7	ODF		0.50	0.5	0.5	0	0.5
OTP	OSU	OS	Data entry - transcription	F8	SR		5.80	17.4	3.15	-14.25	8.15
OTP	OSU	OS	Data entry - meta data	F8	SR		2.50	7.5	3.15	-4.35	7.15
OTP	OSU	Admin	Management	F9	ODF		0.25	0.25	0.25	0	0.2
OTP	OSU	Admin	Administration	F10	ODF		1.0	1	1	0	1
OTP	IEU	Core	Register communications		COMM		0.00	0.5	0.5	0	0.5
OTP	**IEU**	**OS**	**Mission support**		**SR**		**0.80**	**2.4**	**2**	-0.4	**5**
OTP	IEU	OS	Registration of evidence		SR		1.80	5.4	4.5	-0.9	4.5
OTP	IEU	OS	Evidence custody		ODF		1.00	1	0	-1	1
OTP	IEU	Admin	Application support		ODF		1.00	1	1	0	1
OTP	IEU	Admin	Other		MGT		1.00	1	0	-1	

	Optimized	2005		2006
Total FTE Core	#N/A	0.5	0	0
Total FTE Operational Support (OS)	58.2	36.4	-21.8	49.15
Total FTE Admin	9.2	9.2	-2.22E-16	9.15
Total	#N/A	46.1	-21.8	58.9

Figure 3.1 Court capacity model

3.5 BUILDING THE MANAGERIAL SCAFFOLDING 115

the work being done by other actors, notably those most proximate to atrocities, whether as victims, witnesses, or indeed suspects. Scholars have pointed to the key dynamic of intergenerational harm arising from colonial domination and exploitation for making sense of and engaging atrocity spaces, particularly in contexts such as the DRC and Uganda.[118] The psycho-social condition of victims and victim communities also affect the speed, depth, and viability of court investigations, but these, too, fall outside the scope of 'dependency factors'.[119] Such layered and unstable dynamics defy categorisation as input variables, with the effect that such dynamics are rendered invisible by the model even as it relies upon them to pursue certain suspects and criminal acts. The factory-inspired model requires that these problematics be excluded from professional view.[120]

Both the plan and the model evince what is won and lost in the turn to strategic planning. The terms of global justice, its successes, failures, aspirations, and limits, become those of institutional success, failure, aspiration, and constraint. Through this slippage, court experts and even outside supporters become labourers in a justice factory, collecting more raw data and materials, clarifying assumptions, and gaining more detail on contextual challenges, before processing them into strategic goals that maintain the institution as a 'construction site for more justice'.[121] In engaging with such equipment, court experts also ignore and discard

---

[118] Antony Anghie and B.S. Chimni, 'Third World Approaches to International Law and Individual Responsibility in Internal Conflict' (2003) 2 *Chinese Journal of International Law* 77–103, at 88; Kamari Clarke, 'Rethinking Africa through Its Exclusions: The Politics of Naming Criminal Responsibility' (2010) 83 *Anthropological Quarterly* 625–651.

[119] Franz Fanon has written of the psychological dynamics of colonialism: Franz Fanon, *The Wretched of the Earth* (Grove Press 1963).

[120] Simply adopting a 'long-term vision' to counteract this factory mindset, as Human Rights Watch has advocated, would not undo its limitations. The raison d'etre of the Model is to plan up to a decade into the future. When HRW laments, therefore that the court's Strategic Plan 'places too much emphasis on management and organisational issues' to the detriment of 'the court's long-term vision', it ignores how such a managerial orientation is itself designed to blueprint the future court as a well-oiled machine, Human Rights Watch, The Strategic Plan of the International Criminal Court: A Human Rights Watch Memorandum, July 2006, 2, available at: www.hrw.org/sites/default/files/related_material/The%20Strategic%20Plan%20of%20the%20ICC.pdf.

[121] Hans-Peter Kaul, 'The International Criminal Court: Current Challenges and Perspectives' (2007) 6 *Washington University Global Studies Law Review* 575–582, at 576.

116 THE MANAGERIAL COURT: MACRO-MANAGEMENT

the unquantifiable as unusable (and therefore unnecessary) for institutional improvement.

3.5.2 Implementing the Strategic Plan

Once formulated, the strategic plan was presented to states parties, who quickly endorsed the framework. Some states parties, particularly major donors including Germany, Canada, Australia, and New Zealand, welcomed the plan as a move towards critical 'self-examination'.[122] The implementation of the plan was secured through state support but also budgetary allocation. In 2007, the court's budget proposal allocated resources along the plan's three strategic goals. With funding secured, the court was expected to devise indicators to track their progress as well as conduct risk assessment and performance reviews.[123]

The institutional/global elision inaugurated by the strategic plan proved attractive, not least for its narrowing of goals. It also operated to allocate responsibility among actors inside the court and out, whether to officials carrying out day-to-day activities, managers overseeing spending, or states buttressing investigations. The strategic framework was soon applied to more specialised areas of court activity, such as the court's outreach mandate for victim communities. The 2006 Strategic Plan for Outreach articulated the court's aims and methods for communicating to victim communities on the basis that justice needed to be 'done and seen to be done'.[124] Much like the court-wide plan, the Outreach Strategy also reconfigured the court's aspirations from justice being done to justice being 'seeing to be done'.

The Outreach Strategy aimed 'to ensure that affected communities can understand and follow the Court' and 'enable the Court to better understand [their] concerns and expectations'.[125] To this end, the strategy identified target groups for outreach, including NGOs, civic leaders, women, children, and academic communities,[126] and outlined several

---

[122] Statement on behalf of Germany by Dr Georg Witschel, Assembly of States Parties 5th Session, 23 November 2006, 2, available at: https://asp.icc-cpi.int/sites/asp/files/asp_docs/library/asp/ICC-ASP5_Statement_germany.pdf. See also ASP Res 5/2 (1 December 2006), para. 1 welcoming the plan, although only two African states explicitly welcomed it in their ASP statements.

[123] Strategic Plan 2006, para. 56.

[124] Strategic Plan for Outreach, ICC-ASP/5/12, 29 September 2006, para. 2.

[125] Ibid., paras. 2–3.

[126] Ibid., paras. 18.

3.5 BUILDING THE MANAGERIAL SCAFFOLDING 117

'message themes' for court staff to communicate to these audiences.[127] Outreach personnel had to highlight the court's 'judicial role, the fairness, efficiency and impartiality of its proceedings, and the fact that the Court is mindful of the context in which it is active, and is responsive to victims'.[128] According to the strategy, 'communication should serve first of all to increase the confidence of those communities in the international criminal justice system, since they will be better informed about the Court and its role'.[129] The goal was to 'maximise understanding' of the court's work, 'so that it could respond more effectively and clarify, where necessary, any misconceptions that might exist, particularly on the question of how local and international justice mechanisms work together'.[130]

The strategic approach to outreach implied that the court remained the primary interlocutor for creating and mediating public understanding of its role and impact in situation countries while affected communities would be consulted when deemed fit to fill gaps in knowledge. This approach also focused on improving understanding and in correcting misunderstandings about its work among victim communities. Both assumptions treated the knowledge of such communities as invalid until mediated through field and outreach officers. Groups targeted through outreach are read as information poor, demanding appropriate communication and educational tools to rectify this ostensible deficiency.[131] Here, hidden actors including victim groups become the raw material for the outreach machinery to draw upon and refine into ICC-informed interpreters of their own suffering through 'the norms of individual criminal responsibility, fair trial standards, and so on'.[132]

Despite successfully putting the court's resources into operation, these strategic frameworks also demanded more data collection and performance measurement. There was thus ample opportunity to extend the managerial infrastructure in the wake of these strategies. In 2007, the CBF lamented that the court had yet to fully implement results-based

---

[127] Ibid., para. 46.

[128] Ibid.

[129] Ibid., para. 4.

[130] Ibid., para. 3.

[131] Nicole de Silva, 'International Courts' Socialisation Strategies for Actual and Perceived Performance' in Theresa Squatrito et al. (eds.), *The Performance of International Courts and Tribunals* (Cambridge University Press 2018) 288–323, at 304; Birju Kotecha, 'The Art of Rhetoric: Perceptions of the International Criminal Court and Legalism' (2018) 31 *Leiden Journal of International Law* 939–962, at 946–947.

[132] De Silva, 'Socialisation Strategies' 315–316.

budgeting and performance indicators. It proposed that the court follow the 'SMART' model familiar in other public and private organisations to render them 'specific, measurable, achievable, relevant and time-bound'.[133] As with the Court Capacity Model, SMART performance criteria reinforced a vision of justice that was *institutionally* detailed, costed, and realistic but vague on broader patterns of activity relevant to the court, including multi-causal, overlapping, and long-term causes of subordination that underpinned the mass atrocities it concerned itself with.[134]

Lastly, the strategic planning process catalysed the court's audit regime and a strategic approach to human resources. In 2007, the CBF expressed some concern that the internal auditor had adopted a 'hybrid of internal and external audit roles', which had 'diminished the effectiveness of the internal audit function'.[135] It recommended that 'the internal audit function should be adjusted in the light of experience to strengthen the contribution that the Internal Auditor could make to the efficient running of the Court'.[136] The strengthened auditor offered 'independent assurance and advice to the registrar, as accounting officer, on the effectiveness of the Court's control and management systems'.[137] This expanded audit infrastructure occasioned greater interest in the itemisation of risk and institutional liability.

Simultaneously, the CBF was promoting a 'strategic approach to managing the court's most crucial assets, its human resources'.[138] In the court's setup phase, the Human Resources Section had been tasked with 'the speedy recruitment of qualified external candidates' and accordingly adopted the Staff Rules and Regulations.[139] As its apparatus grew, the court had to look beyond '"basic" organisational human resources functions' to 'explor[e] a more dynamic and complex set of human resources management practices'.[140] A 2008 Human Resources Strategy

---

[133] Report of the Committee on Budget and Finance on the Work of its 8th Session, ICC-ASP/6/2, 29 May 2007, para. 16.

[134] Nouwen and Werner, 'Monopolizing Global Justice' 165 and 170.

[135] Report of the Committee on Budget and Finance on the Work of its 9th Session, ICC-ASP/6/12, 28 September 2007, para. 22.

[136] Ibid.

[137] Ibid.

[138] Development of a Human Resources Strategy: Progress Report, ICC-ASP/7/6, 26 May 2008, para. 2.

[139] Ibid., para. 4.

[140] Ibid., para. 5.

3.6 THE GLOBAL FINANCIAL CRISIS

therefore inaugurated a performance appraisal system to standardise performance evaluation across the organs.[141] These practices subsequently effected a new professional consciousness.

By 2008, the court had made 'good progress' in implementing the 2006 Strategic Plan.[142] Various managerial offshoots had been devised and implemented under the same strategic terms as the plan itself, and such processes reveal the extent of the supporting apparatus required to construct a court-wide strategic framework. But like the plan, they confined the project of global justice to the bounds of institutional possibility, framed as they were by the desire for efficiency and results. In slipping from the global to the institutional, the court centred its own goals, concerns, and understandings of its work while placing others beyond institutional need and desire. These conditions of institutional possibility were further implanted by the global financial crisis.

3.6 The Global Financial Crisis

According to then-registrar, Silvana Arbia, 2008 marked a 'historic moment for international criminal justice', as states parties celebrated a decade of the Rome Statute.[143] Six cases were already before the court, while four persons were detained in the ICC's Detention Unit. Supporters hoped that a fifth detainee would soon arrive after the issuance of an arrest warrant against President Omar Al Bashir of Sudan. But in addition to celebrating a decade since Rome, the court was also lauding the construction of an 'entire administrative infrastructure from scratch'.[144]

With the ICC entering a busier period, court experts were eager to continue the strategic and optimising work begun in 2006. In fact, the

---

[141] Ibid., para. 7.

[142] Report of the Bureau on the Strategic Planning Process of the ICC, ICC-ASP/7/29, 6 November 2008, para. 1.

[143] Silvana Arbia Registrar Address to the Assembly of States Parties, Assembly of States Parties 7th Session, 17 November 2008, 2, available at: https://asp.icc-cpi.int/NR/rdon lyres/6FFBBDCD-313D-4765-A603-0CCE900B4B83/0/ ICCASPASP7StatementRegistrar.pdf.

[144] Judge Philippe Kirsch Address to the Assembly of States Parties, Assembly of States Parties 7th Session, 14 November 2008, 9, available at: https://asp.icc-cpi.int/NR/rdon lyres/EB40944C-C250-4466-B99A-2F5ACDC8C941/0/ ICCASPASP7GenDebePresident_Kirsch.pdf.

120   THE MANAGERIAL COURT: MACRO-MANAGEMENT

CBF remained concerned about meagre results, high costs, and slow procedures. In 2008, it suggested that a 'rigorous examination of possibilities to increase productivity would yield significant cost savings given that many inefficient bureaucratic policies had been adopted in the early years'.[145] Continuing to locate the court's problems in the organisation itself, the CBF recommended that the court 'undertake a review of administrative procedures with the aim of eliminating red tape'.[146]

Although the court's organs and the CBF were instrumental to the efficiency drive, major financial contributors also tried to foster financial prudence. This pressure was visible in wealthy states' endorsement of the court's strategic plan and was raised with greater frequency from 2008 onwards. A further important development in late 2007 was Japan's ratification of the Rome Statute, whereupon it became the court's largest donor. It pledged to 'faithfully fulfil' its obligation to contribute 22 per cent of the court's budget.[147] But mirroring the sentiments of other large donors, Japan predicated the court's viability upon its efficiency. Speaking at the ASP annual session, the foreign minister committed Japan to 'pursu[ing] the efficient management of the ICC so that it can deliver maximum results within its limited resources'.[148]

Alongside these changes, the global financial crisis of October 2008 precipitated a renewed state interest in court management, particularly among large donors. In November, the ASP held its seventh session in The Hague, and during the general debate, representatives of wealthy states parties outlined a new economic common sense. The French spokesperson noted that '[t]he current economic and financial climate requires us to ensure that the development of the Court's activities is based on a financial scenario which is compatible with what Member States can provide'.[149] Beyond budgetary concerns, efficiency savings were also needed. Delegates lauded the 'excellent analytical work' of the CBF 'without which many aspects of the Court's work would remain

---

[145] Report of the Committee on Budget and Finance on the Work of Its 11th Session, ICC-ASP/7/15, 31 October 2008, para. 56.

[146] Ibid.

[147] Statement of the Government of Japan, Assembly of States Parties 6th Session, 3 December 2007, 2, available at: https://asp.icc-cpi.int/iccdocs/asp_docs/library/asp/Japan_gd_statement_en_6thasp.pdf.

[148] Ibid.

[149] Ibid 9.

3.6 THE GLOBAL FINANCIAL CRISIS

little known'.[150] As a result of such work, states parties had '[a] better understanding of the constraints on the Registry and a better knowledge of the financial, material and human resources available to the Court'.[151] This concerted effort by states, court organs, and experts was needed if states were to 'continue to justify to their parliaments and their public opinion the resources sought by the court'.[152]

Senior court officials responded swiftly in recommitting the court to the search for efficiencies. Registrar Arbia took a committed stance:

> I am conscious of the fact that resources allocated by the States Parties need to be used efficiently and cost-effectively ... The Court will spare no effort in ensuring optimum administrative and management actions in order to secure the best results with minimum costs without in any way jeopardising the quality and efficiency of justice.[153]

All aspects of the court's work were to be rigorously reviewed, including the number of trials, funding of defence activities, and the protection of victims and witnesses. An important and early effect of the financial crisis, then, was to bring additional core legal activities within the ambit of managerial evaluation and subject them to the same cost-cutting lens as non-judicial tasks. Court experts were also expected to become more efficient. Arbia acknowledged that 'the Court owes its success to its dedicated and committed staff'.[154] It therefore intended to appraise staff performance and train managers in performance measurement 'to ensure the proper functioning of a modern, transparent and non-bureaucratic organisation'.[155]

Risk acquired significant traction in the wake of the financial crisis. Arbia described risk management as the practice of identifying and evaluating risks 'in terms of likelihood and impact'.[156] External consultants were employed to assess these risks, after which the court 'select[ed] priority risks and envisage[d] actions to address them accordingly'.[157] In keeping with its strategic approach, the identification and

---

[150] Déclaration de M. Jean-François Blarel (France), Assembly of States Parties 7th Session, 14 November 2008, para. 13, available at: https://asp.icc-cpi.int/iccdocs/asp_docs/library/asp/ICC-ASP-ASP7-GenDebe-France-ENG.pdf.

[151] Ibid.

[152] Ibid., para. 9.

[153] Registrar Address 17 November 2008, 5–6.

[154] Ibid., 22.

[155] Ibid.

[156] Ibid., 25.

[157] Ibid.

122   THE MANAGERIAL COURT: MACRO-MANAGEMENT

prioritisation of risk was an expert task that foregrounded institutional liabilities. The degree of risk was evaluated according to the audit measures of institutional and financial stability and reputation rather than wider vulnerabilities involving, for example, atrocity spaces, communities, or suspects. As for the risks arising from the global financial crisis itself, the CBF identified these in a similarly limited fashion. Instead of considering the possible ramifications of funding reductions for victim application procedures, or investigations, the CBF identified the 'banking risk' to the court's financial holdings then located in several Dutch banks.[158]

This risk regime also extended beyond audit reporting. The court implemented a 'comprehensive enterprise risk management exercise'.[159] The report that resulted from this exercise detailed some of the risk measures taken to date, including the creation of a 'system of Court-wide administrative issuances', a Coordination Council, and a strategic plan. To this risk regime, the court now added a Corporate Governance Statement, an expanded Audit Committee, and efforts to redesign internal procedures through 'business process re-engineering'.[160]

These risk and audit practices not only foregrounded management expertise but also calibrated risk as a set of technical deficiencies capable of being rectified through careful management and co-ordination. The 2010 Corporate Governance Statement similarly located risk in the overlap between organ functions and the potential damage caused to prosecutorial and judicial independence. There was also a risk in requiring seemingly independent organs to co-operate on common issues. Within these terms, the court proposed to clarify the roles and responsibilities of the organs and to centralise responsibility in the Presidency.

Shortly after, the ASP established an Independent Oversight Mechanism (IOM) under article 112(4) of the Statute with powers to investigate, evaluate, and inspect court organs, functions, and policies with the aim of enhancing 'efficiency and economy'. The IOM was modelled along the lines of the UN Office of Internal Oversight Services (OIOS) and officials from that office offered assistance to the

---

[158] Report of the Committee on Budget and Finance on the Work of Its 12th Session, ICC-ASP/8/5, 13 May 2009, para. 32.

[159] Report of the Court on Measures to Increase Clarity on the Responsibilities of the Different Organs, ICC-ASP/9/34, 3 December 2010, para. 4 (Clarity Report).

[160] Ibid., 32–34.

3.6 THE GLOBAL FINANCIAL CRISIS

start-up team at the IOM once it became operational in 2011.[161] Like the OIOS, the IOM was populated by audit personnel who began to collect data on the court to diagnose a range of managerial and personnel deficiencies.

As with other managerial technologies, audit restricted the frame of professional analysis of the court, this time through the concept of risk. When applying the lens of risk *to* the institution, the risks posed *by* the institution are obscured. These risks have already been well-documented by scholars. Some have pointed to the risks faced by victims and witnesses, whether in terms of their safety in co-operating with the court, or the risk of not receiving justice from the court. To this may be added the risks associated with unintended consequences should the court deliver justice, such as the possibility of rekindling intra-community conflict in the event that it prosecutes only part of the conflict and its actors. Relatedly, the wider risks of court involvement are also excluded from view. ICC-style justice has been shown to obstruct peace negotiations in situation countries, and the effort to focus only on direct and immediate physical violence risks exacerbating the wider conditions underpinning atrocities.[162] Since the co-ordinates of the audit regime are limited to what the institution currently does and can do, the ability to work wider risks into expert analysis is considerably reduced.[163]

This survey of measures taken in the wake of the global financial crisis evince the additional pressures incumbent upon the court and its various experts as states and other external actors sought to enact a politics of austerity within the institution. Spurred by large donors, the embedding of management was led by court experts deploying their technical tools and frames of strategy and risk. Undoubtedly, senior court officials were attuned to management's ability to 'resonate more with states parties', and their deployment reflected a willingness on the part of court leaders to retain good relations with its major funders.[164] The other advantage was to recalibrate the markers of success and failure for the court at a time when results remained lacklustre. Management could not only

---

[161] Report of the Bureau on the Establishment of an Independent Oversight Mechanism, ICC-ASP/8/2, 15 April 2009, para. 4.

[162] Kamari Maxine Clarke, '*Kony 2012*, the ICC, and the Problem of the Peace-and-Justice Divide' (2012) 106 *American Society of International Law Proceedings* 309–313, at 312.

[163] Clarity Report, para. 33; Presidential Directive on Audit Committee, ICC/PRESD/G/2009/1, 11 August 2009, para. 4.1.

[164] Jonathan O'Donohue, 'Financing the International Criminal Court' (2013) 13 *International Criminal Law Review* 269–296, at 283.

124 THE MANAGERIAL COURT: MACRO-MANAGEMENT

downplay complex and often uncontrollable forces but also place the extra-institutional entirely beyond the professional frame.

3.7 Internalising Critiques

In December 2011, as the court neared the end of its first case, President Sang-Hyun Song reflected on its achievements thus far.[165] The number of ongoing investigations and trials had grown from the previous year, 'amounting to well over a thousand hours of court sittings since January'.[166] The number of applications to participate as victims in the court's proceedings had risen to 5,865 by November 2011, and the number of victim applications for reparations had increased eightfold on the previous year to 6,254.[167] Closing statements had already been presented in the case against Thomas Lubanga, with Trial Chamber I soon to issue the court's first judgment.

Yet these statistics seemed to gloss over a more contested narrative. By 2011, the situation in Afghanistan, which notably implicated the US armed forces and the US Central Intelligence Agency in war crimes, had been under preliminary examination for four years with little sign of conclusion. In contrast, after the UN Security Council voted unanimously to refer 'an old enemy', Muammar Gaddafi to the ICC in February 2011, the OTP opened an investigation within only one month.[168] That decision caused consternation among African states parties concerned about the lengths to which the court would go to be seized of a case, even at the risk of jeopardising ongoing peace negotiations. It was therefore unsurprising to find some directing their discontent towards the very efficiency-mindedness the court had been fostering since the outset. Yet those critiques were quickly subsumed into a refined management.

Officially, management continued to be part of the solution for long-term improvement. In 2011, President Song declared before the ASP that '[i]f we are seriously committed to building a system of universal justice,

---

[165] Judge Sang-Huyn Song Remarks to the Assembly of States Parties, ASP 10th Session, 12 December 2011, 2, available at: https://asp.icc-cpi.int/iccdocs/asp_docs/ASP10/Statements/ASP10-ST-Pres-Song-Remarks-ENG.pdf.

[166] Song Remarks to ASP, 2.

[167] Ibid.

[168] Makau Mutua, 'Africans and the ICC: Hypocrisy, Impunity, and Perversion' in Kamari Maxine Clarke, Abel S. Knotterus and Eefje de Volder (eds.), *Africa and the ICC: Perceptions of Justice* (Cambridge University Press 2016) 47–60, at 54.

3.7 INTERNALISING CRITIQUES

a system of equal justice for all, we must maintain the effectiveness of the Court'.[169] He reassured states parties that '[t]he Court is fully committed to seeking maximum economy and efficiency in its operations' and that while '[s]ome important efficiencies have already been achieved ... more will be needed in 2012'.[170] To continue the effort, the court began to submit annual efficiency reports to keep track of efficiency efforts across all court organs and functions. By 2012, it was submitting its seventh report and had devised a co-ordinated strategy dedicated solely to identifying efficiencies.[171] Efficiency had become a 'critical matter' for the court.[172]

Despite its popularity, efficiency did not go unchallenged as a framework of evaluation. Defence practitioners and NGOs were concerned about the potentially damaging effects of an efficiency mindset, particularly for the fairness of court proceedings. The International Bar Association's (IBA) 2011 report on 'Enhancing Efficiency and Effectiveness of ICC Proceedings' replicated some of these concerns.[173] As an organisation concerned largely with defence issues, the IBA considered the negative effect of 'the protracted pace of judicial proceedings' on defence rights.[174] Whilst supporting the court's efforts to find organisational efficiencies, the IBA nonetheless acknowledged the limits of this focus.[175] It noted how '[t]he Court may well become a model of administrative and procedural efficiency yet fail to have an impact on victims and affected communities or to stem the tide of impunity for egregious crimes'.[176] In a similar vein, Human Rights Watch noted that 'the ICC's mandate will not be fulfilled solely by conducting efficient, effective

---

[169] Song Remarks to ASP, 2.

[170] Ibid.

[171] Seventh Status Report on the Court's Progress Regarding Efficiency Measures, ICC-ASP/11/9, 4 May 2012, para. 4.

[172] Ibid., para. 47.

[173] International Bar Association, 'Enhancing Efficiency and Effectiveness of ICC Proceedings: A Work in Progress', January 2011. Similar concerns were raised by scholars; see Yvonne McDermott, *Fairness in International Criminal Tribunals* (Oxford University Press 2016) 46, 66 and 90.

[174] Ibid., 8.

[175] The Study Group on Governance was designed to facilitate dialogue between the Court and States Parties 'with a view to strengthening the institutional framework of the Rome Statute system and enhancing the efficiency and effectiveness of the Court', ASP Res 9/2 (10 December 2010) para. 1. For an overview of the Group's activities, see Report of the Bureau on the Study Group on Governance, ICC-ASP/10/30, 22 November 2011, para. 3.

[176] IBA Report, 16.

126   THE MANAGERIAL COURT: MACRO-MANAGEMENT

investigations' but that it must 'prioritise efforts to make international criminal justice accessible and meaningful to local populations'.[177]

For its part, the court often acknowledged the potential conflict between efficiency and fairness. Yet instead of setting up a paradox between efficiency and fairness, the court framed them as balancing factors, making itself the authoritative balancer in reaching an optimal solution. In its seventh efficiency report the court indicated that while '[t]he cost-effectiveness of the Court is related to all aspects of its mandate [including] preliminary examination, investigation, trial, appeals and reparations', each of these phases 'has been designed to respect fairness towards all parties'.[178] The report recognised that fairness was not anathema to the concept of efficiency because 'in the long term [fairness] is the measure that will produce a most efficient institution'.[179] This interpretation placed fairness within rather than against designs for an efficient court.

Having accounted for fairness within the efficiency mindset, the court reiterated its existing priorities, namely 'implementing transparent and relevant benchmarks for its activities'.[180] Counteracting the fairness concerns it had just acknowledged, the report proposes a 'reengineering exercise' to 'assess whether every activity or output is needed, and if there are more efficient ways of performing them'.[181] This exercise extended to 'activities directly related to the judicial process' and reviewed 'areas where judicial decisions have had a significant cost impact in the past'.[182] Not only does the court appear to repudiate the primacy of fairness, then, but it also manages to do so under the pretext of a reasonable balance between fairness and efficiency.

Another counter to efficiency, this time by dissatisfied African states parties, had a different effect. Rather than being subsumed within the

---

[177] Human Rights Watch Memorandum, 2.

[178] Seventh Report on Efficiency Measures, para. 5.

[179] Ibid. See Adrian Fulford, 'The Reflections of a Trial Judge' (2011) 22 *Criminal Law Forum* 215–223, at 223.

[180] Seventh Report on Efficiency Measures, para. 6. Scholarly interventions dealing with the fairness-efficiency debate often settle on the need for a balance, see Hirad Abtahi and Shehzad Charania, 'Expediting the ICC Criminal Process: Striking the Right Balance between the ICC and States Parties' (2018) 18 *International Criminal Law Review* 383–425, at 405; Annika Jones, 'A Quiet Transformation? Efficiency Building in the "Fall" of International Criminal Justice' (2019) 19 *International Criminal Law Review* 445–474, at 447.

[181] Seventh Report on Efficiency Measures, para. 8.

[182] Ibid.

3.7 INTERNALISING CRITIQUES

discourse of efficiency, the priorities of African states parties were cast beyond the scope of an effective institution altogether. By 2013, the court had begun to face several challenges to its legitimacy. The African Union (AU) challenged the court's interventions in Sudan and then Kenya, when the prosecutor brought charges against the president and vice-president. The immediate concern was the court's disregard for head-of-state immunity, which many African states saw as foundational to international law. States were also concerned that the court was simply unwilling to look beyond Africa in its investigations and prosecutions. Some interpreted the dynamic as reminiscent of colonialism, and the AU pursued a protracted withdrawal campaign to resist such power dynamics.[183] African states also engaged in other tactics, requesting a deferral of proceedings against the two Kenyan suspects in the hope of pursuing dialogue at the ASP about the court's 'consequences on peace and stability and reconciliation'.[184] Nevertheless, the indictments proceeded, confirming African members' 'sense of lack of consideration of a whole continent'.[185]

Despite these confrontations, the court's management texts offer no sign of such wider debates nor of the contestation of the court's mission, goals, and methods. Instead, 2013 represented the successful end to the court's first managerial cycle as the old strategic plan was replaced with a new plan for 2013–2017. Whatever the dynamics of dissent elsewhere, the 2013 Strategic Plan attempted to mobilise a consensus among structures and staff towards agreed objectives. Moreover, the new plan provided a more comprehensive picture of this managerial apparatus calibrating goals, priorities, and expected results while accounting for future contingencies (see Figure 3.2).

---

[183] 'African Countries Back Away from ICC Withdrawal Demand', *Sudan Tribune*, 10 June 2009, available at: www.sudantribune.com/spip.php?article31443.

[184] Indictment of sitting Heads of State and Government and Its Consequences on Peace and Stability and Reconciliation: Informal Summary by the Moderator, Assembly of States Parties, ICC-ASP/12/61, 27 November 2013.

[185] African Union Assembly Decision on the Progress Report of the Commission on the Implementation of the Decision on the International Criminal Court, Assembly/AU/Dec.493(XXII), 30–31 January 2014, para. 8. Mahmood Mamdani, 'The New Humanitarian Order', *The Nation*, 29 September 2008, available at: www.thenation .com/article/new-humanitarian-order/; Thabo Mbeki and Mahmood Mamdani, 'Courts Cannot End Civil Wars', *New York Times*, 5 February 2014. See also Asad Kiyani, 'Al-Bashir and the ICC: The Problem of Head of State Immunity' (2013) 12 *Chinese Journal of International Law* 467–508, at 493–497.

Structure

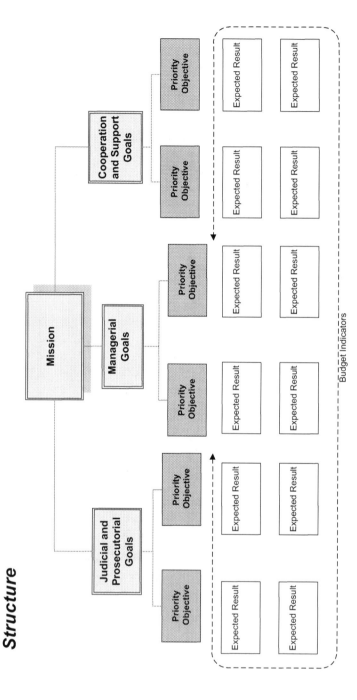

Figure 3.2 ICC strategic plan 2013–2017 structure
© ICC-CPI

3.7 INTERNALISING CRITIQUES

The flowchart in Figure 3.2 located global justice in the careful, internal arrangement of the ICC's mission, goals, indicators, and results. Results, whether expected, unexpected, or unfulfilled, allow the court to proceed with implementing the indicators, prioritising certain objectives, and fulfilling its mission. Indeed, the particular layout renders 'expected results' less important than objectives, goals, and mission: they appear small and unconnected to the other components of the flowchart. Consistent with the global/institutional slippage, the institutional priorities and mission are prioritised over results. Whether expectations are confirmed or not has little effect on the strategic framework of the institution.

Substantively, the judicial goal of ensuring 'adequate and meaningful participation and representation of victims' illustrates how the 2013 Strategic Plan establishes institutional co-ordinates while rejecting politically contested aspects of its mandate.[186] Through the global/institutional elision, meaningful participation and representation of victims equate with what can reasonably be achieved by the court under conditions of financial and organisational constraint. This corresponds with the action points under this goal. The court intends to '[r]evisit the victim application system', '[i]mplement [a] Revised Strategy in Relation to Victims', '[i]mplement the revised legal aid system relating to victims', and offer training to counsel.[187] What 'adequate and meaningful participation' might mean to victims and other groups subject to the court's work is not contemplated.

In addition, results are phrased in terms of institutional action rather than their consequences. Hence, such measures will create a 'deeper understanding of the lessons learnt and the challenges faced to date' and achieve a 'more sustainable, effective and efficient victim application system' with an '[i]ncreased sensitivity to the requirements of victims broadly'.[188] Gradually, an expectation of victim-oriented participation meaningful on victims' terms is diluted down to the court's capacity to revise its internal procedures and publish an internal strategy document. The same effect is visible with goal of expeditious judicial proceedings (conducting an 'in-depth "lessons learnt" exercise') and guaranteeing the

---

[186] International Criminal Court Strategic Plan 2013–2017, 13 April 2013, 3.
[187] Strategic Plan 2013, 5.
[188] Ibid., 5.

130 THE MANAGERIAL COURT: MACRO-MANAGEMENT

rights of the defence (translating to a revised, cost-effective, and monitored legal aid system).[189]

The value ascribed to management knowledge is visible in the plan's managerial goals. Unlike judicial goals, which give a sense of connecting the institution to relevant actors, managerial goals are designed to be purely internal. To deliver coherent governance, the court will '[r]e-examine and adapt the structure, staffing and resources of the Court in the light of practical experience, promoting efficiency and effectiveness'.[190] To enhance budgeting and planning, the court will refine its risk management processes and 'improve the performance measurement and evaluation of the Court'.[191] Having reduced the programme to a desk-based exercise, the court's managerial improvements are easiest to frame, measure, and realise.

The updated plan evinces a doubling-down on current trajectories and the cost-effectiveness concerns of wealthier states parties. Performance indicators exemplified that move. The plan aspired to improve the 'strategy-budget-performance indicators' link.[192] Subsequently, the ASP asked the court to 'intensify its efforts to develop qualitative and quantitative indicators that would allow the Court to demonstrate better its achievements and needs, as well as allowing States Parties to assess the Court's performance in a more strategic manner'.[193] The four initial indicators tracked the fairness of court proceedings, effective leadership/management, security and risk to actors engaging with the court, and victims' access to court.[194] These performance indicators prompted data to be gathered across the organs, building up a picture of the court's strengths and weaknesses, and precipitating policy shifts to address any institutional defects.[195]

---

[189] Ibid., 4.

[190] Ibid., 6.

[191] Ibid., 7.

[192] Ibid., 6–7.

[193] ASP Res 13/5 (17 December 2014) Annex 1, para. 7(b).

[194] Report of the Court on the Development of Performance Indicators for the International Criminal Court, 12 November 2015, para. 7, available at: www.icc-cpi.int/sites/default/files/itemsDocuments/Court_report-development_of_performance_indicators-ENG.pdf.

[195] This is also the mainstream reading of indicators; see Philipp Ambach, 'Performance Indicators for International(ised) Criminal Courts – Potential for Increase of an Institution's Legacy or "Just" a Means of Budgetary Control?' (2018) 18 *International Criminal Law Review* 426–460.

3.7 INTERNALISING CRITIQUES

In devising this list, the court acknowledged the difficulty of selecting accurate and comprehensive performance criteria. The list was a 'work in progress' to be refined over time as more data offered a clearer picture.[196] To that end, in April 2016, senior court officials attended a Swiss retreat on performance indicators and a month later the Hague Institute for Global Justice held a forum on performance indicators attended by court staff, academics, and civil society.[197] While recognising the limitations of performance indicators, they nonetheless reproduced many of the court's prior imperatives. The indicators told a particular story about what was required to realise global justice, namely expeditious court proceedings, effective court management, security of individuals, and victims' access to court. Only the latter of these could be said to directly impinge on events and actors beyond the court itself, with the others placing the focus firmly on the institution. In addition, the kinds of data the court collected was heavily influenced by the need to be efficient in the amassing of such information. The court therefore began by considering 'mainly quantitative indicators which stakeholders will recognise as reflecting key aspects of the Court's performance, and which can be measured over time'.[198]

The data relied upon shows the partial picture of court performance that African states also sought to challenge. The fairness of proceedings was calculated by the percentage of court findings on fair trial violations and the number of successful appeals on such grounds, rather than upon engagements with suspects and victims. Access to court was captured by the time taken to decide on victim applications and the percentage of the victim population reached through outreach activities rather than on structural and material obstacles to victim engagement. Similarly, in recognising the high impact of external factors on performance such as local security, limited data, and lack of state co-operation, the court

---

[196] Report on the Development of Performance Indicators, para. 6. See Birju Kotecha, 'The ICC's Office of the Prosecutor and the Limits of Performance Indicators' (2017) 15 *Journal of International Criminal Justice* 543–565, at 549.

[197] Second Court's Report on the Development of Performance Indicators for the International Criminal Court, ICC, 11 November 2016, paras. 11–14, available at: www.icc-cpi.int/sites/default/files/itemsDocuments/ICC-Second-Court_report-on-indicators.pdf. See also Third Court's Report on the Development of Performance Indicators for the International Criminal Court, 15 November 2017, available at: www.icc-cpi.int/sites/default/files/itemsDocuments/171115-Third-Report-performance-indicators-ENG.pdf.

[198] Report on the Development of Performance Indicators, para. 11.

132 THE MANAGERIAL COURT: MACRO-MANAGEMENT

limited its initial selection of indicators to cover 'issues which are essentially under the control of the institution itself'.[199] As these data reveal, indicators could only tell a story about the internally controllable and statistically measurable features of global justice, ignoring external and remote actors and experiences. The data collected then reinforced the institutional co-ordinates of the global justice project. The situation faced by the ICC as a result of these tools is aptly summarised by Nouwen:

> When what matters is what is countable, what is countable determines what matters: the availability of datasets rather than the importance of issues begins to set the research agenda. Empirical research that is limited to indexing, quantifying, and counting thus risks misrepresenting an inherently political concept such as "justice" as a value-neutral unit that can be multiplied by the application of technical expertise.[200]

Unlike statistics about fair trial violations or timeframes for processing victim applications, unquantifiable and immeasurable data such as the wider context of violence, the multiple layers of subordination experienced by those located in atrocity spaces, and the particular understandings of justice by those proximate to atrocity were absent. This created a picture of court performance that equated what lay beyond its own capabilities as beyond the concern of global justice.

3.8   Conclusion

The foregoing chronological mapping exercise reveals several notable points about management ideas and practices as invoked and deployed in the International Criminal Court. Some of these points may be more surprising than others. First, management ideas of efficiency, strategy, and risk, and practices of strategic planning, audit, performance indicators and more, have featured prominently throughout the ICC's short history. Management was present in early attempts to formulate the institution and remains at the forefront of efforts to improve court

---

[199] Ibid., para. 9.

[200] Sarah Nouwen, "'As You Set Out for Ithaka": Practical, Epistemological, Ethical, and Existential Questions about Socio-Legal Empirical Research in Conflict' (2014) 27 *Leiden Journal of International Law* 227–260, at 230. See Ruth Buchanan, Kimberley Byers and Kristina Mansveld, "'What Gets Measured Gets Done": Exploring the Social Construction of Globalised Knowledge for Development' in Mosche Hirsch and Andrew Lang (eds.), *Research Handbook on the Sociology of International Law* (Edward Elgar 2018) 101–121.

3.8 CONCLUSION 133

functioning in recent times.[201] It has also expanded its reach considerably from the early paeans to cost-efficiency and is now capable of bringing core legal activities within its evaluative lens as a result of work by court experts including senior officials, the CBF, NGOs, and commentators. This has, perhaps unsurprisingly, occasioned a major expansion of the court's managerial infrastructure.

More surprising, however, is that such an expansion has also enacted a contraction in discursive terms. Although primarily justified as optimising existing structures and goals, management practices have considerably altered the frame of reference for global justice professionals and supporters alike. Rather than being a small fragment of a large and changing agenda for justice, the institution is now conceived by diplomats, lawyers, and others as the very outer limit of that project. Although this may not register at the rhetorical level, where references are frequently made to national prosecutions or institutional experiments beyond the ICC,[202] at the level of the court's quotidian tools, an institutionally bounded project has become the dominant mode for imagining global justice. The institution, through management practices, now acts as the raison d'être of court experts and sets the limits of the professional imagination in global justice circles.[203]

As Kamari Clarke has noted, 'new technologies of knowledge generation have guided the development of a new international domain dependent on the viability of its supranational disciplinary institutions'.[204] Management can also be understood in such terms. As this chapter shows, the viability of the ICC as an institution has become part of the professional sensibility of the global justice community. In that uptake, much is lost in the way of professional imagination and political contestation. Short-term, measurable, and realistic proposals become the

---

[201] Richard Clements, '"Efficiency Is Paramount in This Regard": The Managerial Role of the ICC Presidency from Kirsch to Fernández' (2022) 21 *Law and Practice of International Courts & Tribunals* 342–368.

[202] See proposals for a special tribunal to prosecute atrocities arising from the Russia-Ukraine War, 'United Nations, Law Not War: A Special Tribunal for the Crime of Aggression', 25 October 2022, available at: https://media.un.org/en/asset/k1q/k1qyewjw26.

[203] Frédéric Mégret, 'International Criminal Justice: A Critical Research Agenda' in Christine Schwöbel (ed.), *Critical Approaches to International Criminal Law* (Routledge 2015) 17–53, at 42.

[204] Kamari Maxine Clarke, *Fictions of Justice: The International Criminal Court and the Challenge of Legal Pluralism in Sub-Saharan Africa* (Cambridge University Press 2010) 68.

only viable option for an institution seeking to enact its mandate and keep funders on side.[205] At the same time, the possibility of thinking otherwise – about long-term effects and conditions of violence, the immeasurable realities of colonialism and its modern iterations, vulnerabilities and potentialities for those most proximate to atrocity spaces – become not only difficult to articulate within a new vocabulary but professionally discouraged. Having identified these macro trends over the course of the court's brief history, the following chapter turns to the micro-effects such practices have upon the professional life and imagination of court experts.

[205] Warner Ten Kate and Sarah M.H. Nouwen, 'The Globalisation of Justice: Amplifying and Silencing Voices at the ICC' in Jeff Handmaker and Karin Arts (eds.), *Mobilising International Law for 'Global Justice'* (Cambridge University Press 2019) 46–62.

4

The ICC Expert

Micro-management

4.1 Introduction

Managerial practices waxed throughout the International Criminal Court (ICC) from an early penchant for efficiency to a more recent and comprehensive rationalisation of all court activities. In constructing a managerial court, senior officials have identified the court's staff members as pivotal to institutional success. As former registrar Silvana Arbia emphasised to states parties in 2008, 'the Court owes its success to its dedicated and committed staff'.[1] She elaborated that the court's

> high quality results could not have been achieved without the commitment, determination and strong motivation of the Court's staff members who have brought their competence, creativity and tireless efforts to the service of international justice.[2]

Arbia's conviction – echoed by others[3] – has been borne out in a range of staff-focused managerial practices to optimise individual performance. Among these practices are the human resourcing tools associated with recruitment, performance appraisal, and career advancement. They also include more general frameworks for collective accountability such as audit and independent oversight. Together these practices are designed to

---

[1] Silvana Arbia Registrar Address to the Assembly of States Parties, Assembly of States Parties 7th Session, 17 November 2008, 2, available at: https://asp.icc-cpi.int/NR/rdonlyres/6FFBBDCD-313D-4765-A603-0CCE900B4B83/0/ICCASPASP7StatementRegistrar.pdf.

[2] Ibid., 4.

[3] In the wake of the Registry's reorganisation, Registrar Herman von Hebel expressed his 'gratitude to all ICC staff for their constant commitment to and sacrifice for defending the principles underpinning the Rome Statute', Registrar Herman von Hebel Remarks to the 14th Session, Assembly of States Parties 14th Session, 21 November 2015, 11, available at: https://asp.icc-cpi.int/iccdocs/asp_docs/ASP14/ASP14-BDGT-REGISTRAR-ST-ENG-FRA.pdf.

136 THE ICC EXPERT: MICRO-MANAGEMENT

optimise the court's deployment of human resources in order to contribute to its 'proper functioning [as] a modern, transparent and non-bureaucratic organisation'.[4]

In reinforcing the connection between individual staff, the modern organisation, and global justice, practices of human resource management also help produce global justice as an office-based endeavour conducted by professional experts through elite institutions. Whereas the dominant view is that the decision by the international community to opt for an institutionalised and expert-driven version of global justice has precipitated vital practices of professional optimisation, in fact the opposite is the case. The introduction of management ideas and practices designed to record, rate, and shape the ICC employee has further narrowed the professional imagination of those dealing with global atrocity and injustice down to the institutionally practical and professionally palatable. Practices of professional optimisation thus reinforce the co-ordinates of global justice discussed in Chapter 3.

As I show in this chapter, though, management operates not only at the level of large-scale organ restructuring or strategic frameworks but also immediately and constantly upon the individual employees, including lawyers, who work at the court. This is not a matter of management determining professional identity but of 'active identity work' on the part of professionals, where ideas and practices are mediated through professionals themselves.[5] Practices of socialisation and self-discipline occlude, expunge, fix, and responsibilise the court professional in particular ways as they get in, settle down, keep on, and move up within this modern organisation of global justice.[6] As this chapter demonstrates, these patterns of self-identification become part of the professional sensibility and the expectations of the field, and accrue from their repeat encounters with management practices ostensibly designed to improve performance.[7]

---

[4] Registrar Address 17 November 2008, 24.

[5] Mats Alvesson and Hugh Willmott, 'Identity Regulation as Organisational Control: Producing the Appropriate Individual' (2002) 39 *Journal of Management Studies* 614–644, at 621.

[6] See Nuremberg Academy, 'Power in International Criminal Justice: Towards a Sociology of International Justice', Instituto degli Innocenti, 28–29 October 2017, 5, available at: www.nurembergacademy.org/fileadmin/user_upload/170912_Programme_and_concept_note_Florence_conference_20171028-29.pdf.

[7] Kirsten Campbell, 'The Making of International Criminal Justice: Towards a Sociology of the "Legal Field"' in Mikkel Christensen and Ron Levi (eds.), *International Practices of Criminal Law: Social and Legal Perspectives* (Routledge 2017) 149–169.

4.2 BECOMING A GLOBAL JUSTICE PROFESSIONAL

This micro-level account of the ICC's managerial practices largely comprises the court's managerial archive of reports, documents, forms, and charts. Despite their non-legal qualities, these documents build a picture of the professional lawyer within the ICC as they are gradually enmeshed in an institutional apparatus. I arrange these documents as they would be encountered and experienced by the future and then actual employee. I also spoke with several court professionals to enrich this account. Such documents not only offer a story of professional management (one that is likely familiar to the law-firm lawyer or university academic), they also centre office life as the locus and lodestar of global justice.

4.2 Becoming a Global Justice Professional

Given that there is no 'outside' the discourse of global justice, by the time the prospective employee decides to apply for a position at the court, they will already have a particular vision of what the project means and how to achieve it. This will have been influenced by certain geographical, educational, and cultural factors. As a student of law, criminology or forensics, they may have been drawn into the small sub-field of international criminal law (ICL) due to its novelty, cosmopolitan ethos, ethical commitment, or sheer spectacle.[8] They may have seen a future in ICL that allowed them to 'assuage[] the moral hunger for a response to visible yet unimaginable human suffering'[9] without giving up on the desire for a 'respectable career'.[10] As they progressed through their studies, reading textbooks and articles,[11] seeing the ICC in the news, in

---

[8] Elies van Sliedregt, 'International Criminal Law: Over-Studied and Underachieving?' (2016) 29 *Leiden Journal of International Law* 1–12, at 1–4. Christine Schwöbel, 'Spectacle in International Criminal Law: The Fundraising Image of Victimhood' (2016) 4 *London Review of International Law* 247–274.

[9] Sarah M.H. Nouwen, 'Justifying Justice' in Martti Koskenniemi and James Crawford (eds.), *Cambridge Companion to International Law* (Cambridge University Press 2012) 327–351, at 330. See also David Koller, 'The Faith of the International Criminal Lawyer' (2013) 40 *NYU Journal of International Law & Policy* 1019–1069.

[10] Samuel Moyn, 'Anti-Impunity as Deflection of Argument', in Karen Engle, Zina Miller and D.M. Davis (eds.), *Anti-Impunity and the Human Rights Agenda* (Cambridge University Press 2016) 68–94, at 79.

[11] Mikkel Christensen, 'Preaching, Practicing and Publishing International Criminal Justice: Academic Expertise and the Development of an International Field of Law' (2016) 17 *International Criminal Law Review* 1–20, at 10.

138   THE ICC EXPERT: MICRO-MANAGEMENT

documentaries,[12] on film,[13] in bestselling books, or when visiting the court as tourist or intern,[14] they will have found themselves taking up much of the professional doxa or common sense of ICL.[15] A project of anti-impunity, directed towards the criminal punishment of individuals in certain violent pockets of the world and driven by ideas of the rule of law and human rights. Because of their exposure to the court, the ICC will likely stand in as substitute or heuristic for the project and its values. It may even be this representation that prompts the outsider to apply for a job there. By the time that decision is made, perhaps after conversations with friends or with an inside contact, the idea that global justice is institutionally driven is already part of the professional's understanding of the field.

4.2.1   Job Application

For its part, the ICC encourages these perceptions. As seen in the strategic plan, the court seeks to render itself a recognisable and well-publicised institution of anti-impunity. But at the level of professional career, an important initial encounter between the potential employee and the court takes place beyond the building and its plans in the court's online recruitment system. The ICC '*eRecruitment*' portal is where the applicant will land in searching for an ICC job. The portal contains all

[12] Wouter Werner, 'Justice on Screen – A Study of Four Documentary Films on the International Criminal Court' (2016) 29 *Leiden Journal of International Law* 1043–1060.

[13] Kirsten Ainley, Stephen Humphreys and Immi Tallgren, 'International Criminal Justice on/and Film' (2018) 6 *London Review of International Law* 3–15.

[14] Campbell, 'The Making of International Criminal Justice'.

[15] On the profession of ICL and related fields, see Mikkel Christensen, 'The Emerging Sociology of International Criminal Courts: Between Global Restructurings and Scientific Innovations' (2015) 63 *Current Sociology Review* 825–849; Christensen, 'Preaching, Practicing and Publishing International Criminal Justice'; Mikkel Christensen and Ron Levi, 'Introduction: An Internationalized Criminal Justice: Paths of Law and Paths of Police' in Christensen and Levi, 'International Practices of Criminal Justice' 1–15; Yves Dezalay and Bryant G. Garth (eds.), *Lawyers and the Construction of Transnational Justice* (Routledge 2012); Frédéric Mégret, 'Thinking About What International Humanitarian Lawyers "Do": An Examination of the Laws of War as a Field of Professional Practice' in Wouter Werner, Marieke de Hoon and Alexis Gálan (eds.), *The Law of International Lawyers: Reading Martti Koskenniemi* (Cambridge University Press 2017) 265–296; Frédéric Mégret, 'International Criminal Justice as a Juridical Field' (2018) 13 *Champ pénal* 1. See also the 'profession' of international law, Jean d'Aspremont et al. (eds.), *International Law as a Profession* (Cambridge University Press 2017); Friedrich Kratochwil, 'Practising Law' in Wouter Werner et al., 'Law of International Lawyers' 225–264, at 228.

4.2 BECOMING A GLOBAL JUSTICE PROFESSIONAL 139

relevant recruitment information and documents for the applicant to make their application from anywhere in the world.[16] The portal allows applicants to search, save, and track vacancies, as well as apply directly. For this, the applicant will create a candidate profile with information about their education, training, work experience, language proficiency, and other skills. There is also space to upload a CV and cover letter. As with any prospective job, it is easy for the applicant to begin imagining themselves into the post. Indeed, such self-situating behaviour as detailing their 'fit' for the post and describing their motivations in a cover letter is encouraged by the court. Through this digital encounter, the applicant is brought – and brings themselves – into relation with the institution through ideas not of global anti-impunity but professional competence and aspiration.

As applicants spend time on the website, they begin to become comfortable in the court's 'organisational world' and will become acquainted with the organisation's own ideas of itself.[17] That world may feel extremely familiar irrespective of how geographically removed the applicant might be from The Hague. The portal's search functionality offers a sense of the organisation. Although the applicant may be applying for a legal position – and let us assume that they are – they will find many other 'functional areas' with vacancies being advertised, such as 'auditing', 'controlling/accounting/finance', 'customer service', 'general management', and 'sales and marketing' (see Figure 4.1). At first, the applicant might baulk at the strangeness of such positions before recalling that, after all, the court is a complex, modern organisation like any other.

Getting back on track, the applicant finds the position they were looking for: Legal Officer (P-3) in the Gender and Children Unit (Investigation Division) of the Office of the Prosecutor (OTP).[18]

---

[16] ICC eRecruitment website: https://career5.successfactors.eu/career?company=1657261P& site=&lang=en_GB.

[17] Robert Cooper and Gibson Burrell, 'Modernism, Postmodernism and Organisational Analysis: The Contribution of Michel Foucault' in Alan McKinlay and Ken Starkey (eds.), *Foucault, Management and Organisation Theory* (SAGE Publishing 1998) 14–28, at 25.

[18] All the information about this position is drawn from relevant documents posted on the ICC eRecruitment portal on 31 January 2018; see ICC, Job Description for Legal Officer (P-3), ID 18084 (posted 31 January 2018) (on file with author). This post was selected partly at random, partly because it is a position familiar to the lawyers likely to read this book, and partly to impress upon readers the force of management as a discourse and set of tools in any area of court activity, including those areas labelled as 'core'.

Figure 4.1 *e*Recruitment search engine
© ICC-CPI

Clicking on the listing, the applicant arrives at the main job description, which contains much of the relevant information one would expect from a job advertisement, including the contract duration, salary, and application deadline (see Figure 4.2). The listing of 'duty station' (The Hague) is a reminder of the transnational nature of the court's work and the location of many of its employees 'in the field'. Yet this hint at the court's global reach is quickly dampened by the remainder of the job specification, which details the post's structural location within the organisation or 'organisational context', as well as the successful candidate's 'duties and responsibilities'.[19] Essential qualifications tell the applicant whether they are suitably qualified for the post, while 'ICC Core Competencies' listed at the end of the advertisement imagine the values and traits of the ideal candidate. I return to these competencies later.

Reading through their prospective duties, the applicant will see that they will be expected to provide 'legal and advisory support to the Office in the implementation of the Sexual and Gender-Based Crimes Policy and the Policy on Children', draft implementation reports, offer legal

[19] Job Description for Legal Officer, 1.

Job Title: Legal Officer (P-3)

Job Req ID 18084 - Posted 31/01/2018 - Professional - Investigation and Analysis - The Hague - NL

Deadline for Applications:	28/02/2018
Organizational Unit:	Gender and Children Unit, Office of the Prosecutor
Duty Station:	The Hague - NL
Type of Appointment:	Fixed Term Appointment
Minimum Net Annual Salary:	€69,511.00
Contract Duration:	General Temporary Assistance (GTA), 6 months

A roster of suitable candidates may be established for this post as a result of this selection process for fixed-term appointments against both established posts and positions funded by general temporary assistance (GTA).

Figure 4.2   eRecruitment job description
© ICC-CPI

advice to investigation teams, conduct legal and policy research on sexual and gender-based crimes, offer legal expertise and training on vulnerable witnesses to staff members, and 'liaise with external networks' on such issues.[20] From the comfort of their own home, the relationship that the applicant has opened up between themselves and the court now results not only in the applicant reflecting on whether they could perform such functions but also in an attempt to convey through the application their capacity to do so. In seeking to persuade the recruitment panel of this, the applicant is careful to adopt their expectations and assumptions as part of the applicant's own professional attitude. As Grey has observed, such application documents as the CV are 'a powerful technique for stating what one was, is and will be and for giving a narrative of the self'.[21] The applicant will thus read these duties as crucial components for achieving the court's mission.

Other sections of the job advertisement do even more to construct the organisational lifeworld for the applicant.[22] This is precisely the impact of the section entitled 'organisational context', which positions the applicant within the court's management structures even before their

---

[20] Ibid., 1.
[21] Christopher Grey, 'Career as a Project of the Self' (1994) 28 *Sociology* 479–497, at 495.
[22] Edmund Husserl, *The Crisis of European Sciences and Transcendental Phenomenology* [1936].

142 THE ICC EXPERT: MICRO-MANAGEMENT

application has been seen by the recruitment panel. It is worth reproducing this segment as the applicant reads it:

> The Investigation Division (ID), under the overall management of its Director and management team, provides the investigative component of the integrated team which conducts the Office's investigations and prosecutions under the responsibility of PD's [Prosecution Division's] Senior Trial Lawyer. ID recruits, trains and monitors the performance of investigators, analysts and data inputters within the integrated team.[23]

What does this contextual paragraph tell the applicant? It informs them, if they did not already know, that they will not only work for 'the ICC', even less for 'global justice'. Rather, they will exist in relation to various hierarchical structures 'under' a management team, which will intermittently assess their performance. Although this structure seems unchanged since Weber's iron cage, the hierarchy is already deemed to exist not only as a layer for the successful candidate to slot into but as a constant relationship between manager and managed throughout their time working there. This contextual paragraph thus sets the future employee's lines of authority and, crucially, the extent and limits of professional action. They must fulfil their own responsibilities to certain standards, and not deviate from them. Responsibility means simply operating within particular organisational confines.

The 'duties and responsibilities' section further clarifies the future employee's understanding of responsibility as meeting the job specification or operating within certain professional expectations. This is where the institution stands in for the wider project, and where the success of the former equates to the latter. By 2018, when this job advertisement was posted, management ideas and practices had considerably rearranged understandings and imaginaries of global justice both inside the court and out, as traced in Chapter 3. The job specification reflects that shift towards global justice as a set of technical, bullet-pointed tasks. It is not that drafting implementation reports, preparing filings, or conducting staff trainings on witness vulnerability *replace* global justice but that, as far as the applicant can see, they *are* global justice. The applicant knows that while justice may be a many-splendoured thing, when trainings are delivered, reports drafted, and expertise offered, their part in the project is being realised. Even complex notions of 'gender', which seem to defy all classification, become simply a 'Unit' within an

---

[23] Job Description for Legal Officer, 1.

4.2 BECOMING A GLOBAL JUSTICE PROFESSIONAL 143

office. Such framings help to invoke in the applicant the experience and the comfort that complex realities can and should be mediated expertly and institutionally.[24]

The final subject-producing moment in the job advertisement is also its most managerial, namely the list of 'ICC Core Competencies'. Core competencies were introduced by management theorists Prahalad and Hamel in a 1990 article of the *Harvard Business Review*. In trying to make sense of the achievements of a large American corporation, Prahalad and Hamel put its success down to its own self-perception: 'not a collection of strategic business units, but a portfolio of core competencies'.[25] A competency is 'a measurable pattern of skills, knowledge, abilities, behaviours and other characteristics needed to perform and fulfil one's job responsibilities'.[26] Much like in any other modern organisation, at the ICC, employees are expected to embody various predefined competencies in order to fulfil their role and the court's wider mission. The applicant's relationship to these core competencies will similarly be as a hope that they can embody them and as guide or blueprint for describing themselves to the recruitment panel.

The job advertisement lists seven core competencies.[27] As the applicant reads it, the successful candidate is expected to demonstrate 'dedication to the mission and values', 'professionalism', 'teamwork', 'learning and developing', 'handling uncertain situations', 'interaction', and 'realising objectives'.[28] Under each of these competencies, the job description lists more 'concrete' and 'expected' behaviours and skills (see Figure 4.3).[29]

For example, dedication to mission and values means 'act[ing] consistently in accordance with the mission and values of the Organisation', 'maintain[ing] confidentiality', 'show[ing] commitment', and 'present[ing]

---

[24] Christine Schwöbel, 'The Comfort of International Criminal Law' (2013) 24 *Law & Critique* 169–191.

[25] C.K. Prahalad and Gary Hamel, 'The Core Competence of the Corporation', *Harvard Business Review*, May–June 1990, 1–15.

[26] Elaine Schilling, 'Core Competencies and Their Role in Performance Appraisals', Webchat Presentation on Performance Management, University of California Merced, 3 May 2016, 3, available at: https://hr.ucmerced.edu/files/page/documents/webchat_slide_-_core_competencies.pdf.

[27] These have since been updated slightly, but the main structure of competency with listed behaviours remains unchanged.

[28] Job Description for Legal Officer, 2.

[29] Ibid., 2.

ICC Core Competencies

Dedication to the mission and values
- Acts consistently in accordance with the mission and values of the Organisation;
- Maintains confidentiality, acts with integrity and shows respect for diversity;
- Shows commitment to the organisation;
- Presents a positive image of the organisation during external discussions.

Professionalism
- Applies professional and technical expertise;
- Keeps abreast of organisational issues;
- Produces workable solutions to a range of problems;

Teamwork
- Listens, consults and communicates proactively;
- Handles disagreements with tact and diplomacy;
- Recognises and rewards the contribution of others;

Learning and developing
- Identifies development strategies needed to achieve work and career goals and makes use of developmental or training opportunities;
- Learns from successes and failures;
- Seeks feedback and gives feedback to others to increase organisational effectiveness;
- Seeks opportunities for improvement of work;
- Has an open mind and contributes to innovation.

Handling uncertain situations
- Adapts to changing circumstances;
- Deals with ambiguity, making positive use of the opportunities it presents;
- Plans activities and projects well in advance and takes account of possible changing circumstances;
- Manages time effectively.

Interaction
- Expresses opinions, information and key points of an argument clearly;
- Handles contacts with diplomacy and tact;
- Communicates in a transparent and open way with internal and external contacts while complying with confidentiality requirements.

Realising objectives
- Accepts and tackles demanding goals with enthusiasm;
- Keeps to agreements with others;
- Focuses on client needs;
- Takes responsibility for actions, projects and people;
- Monitors and maintains quality and productivity.

Figure 4.3   *e*Recruitment core competencies list
© ICC-CPI

a positive image of the organisation during external discussions'.[30] This will be important when engaging with external networks, as one of the successful candidate's duties. The candidate may also have to collaborate with colleagues in drafting reports, offering expertise or training, and as such 'listens, consults, and communicates proactively', 'manages time effectively', and 'focuses on client needs'. Self-sufficiency, responsibility for one's own work, and adaptability are important themes of the core competencies. The successful candidate therefore 'learns from successes and failures', 'seeks feedback and gives feedback to others to increase organisational effectiveness', 'takes responsibility for actions, projects and

[30] Ibid.

4.2 BECOMING A GLOBAL JUSTICE PROFESSIONAL 145

people', and 'monitors and maintains quality and productivity'.[31] In addition to being confined to the organisation and to professional tasks, the core competencies restrict the employee's responsibilities to fostering these competencies, traits, and skills within their own professional selves.

Moreover, in the applicant's desire to embody and portray their embodiment of the competencies to the recruitment panel, questions about the list's suitability, necessity, or peculiarity are disengaged. How closely do the 'mission and values of the Organisation' correlate with the desires and ethos of the diverse communities that are subject to court intervention? Would it be appropriate to 'accept and tackle demanding goals with enthusiasm' when the goal runs the risk of silencing or distorting the voices of women, genderqueer people, or children? How comfortable is the applicant with labelling those who rely on the Gender and Children Unit's work 'clients', or how much should the court be about 'produc[ing] workable solutions to a range of problems'? These probing questions, however fleetingly they may pass through the applicant's mind, are sidelined and forgotten in the need to ingratiate themselves with the recruitment panel. The self-disciplining work of completing the application, finally clicking 'Apply', and logging out is mediated by the various organisational but also managerial technologies of the self, including the court's management structures and the core competencies list. Although the recruitment panel will understandably interpret our candidate (and all others) as a potential competent and committed employee, the candidate will have arranged their professional self similarly in the run-up.

4.2.2 Recruitment

Once the deadline has passed, the recruitment panel begins its engagement with the applicant. As the ICC's Recruitment Guidelines state, the Human Resources Section will be the first to review all applications having drafted the job advertisement in the first instance.[32] Thereafter, a three-member interview panel will be established, and while this panel will largely consist of the applicant's would-be colleagues or supervisor in

---

[31] Ibid.
[32] International Criminal Court Recruitment Guidelines for Established Posts (entered into force 2 November 2009, unclassified 22 November 2012), paras. 3.2 and 6.1 (Recruitment Guidelines).

the Investigation Division, at least one of the panel 'should represent the Human Resources Section and coordinate the process'.[33] In addition to the terms of the job advertisement, the panel will be mindful of the need to 'ensure the highest standards of efficiency, competence, and integrity' in recruitment according to article 44(2) of the Statute. ASP resolution 1/10 (2002) distinguishes this requirement as a 'general principle' applicable to all staff.[34]

The interview panel will further refine the applicant and their sense of professional self. To begin, our applicant's completed application, available digitally but possibly printed in hard copy, will capture their professional identity as a bundle of knowledge, skills, competencies, and motivations.[35] For the recruitment panel, the job advertisement now moves from an applicant's blueprint to a recruitment checklist for aligning organisational demand to candidate supply. Although it will again be unsurprising to find the panel focusing on competencies and the ideal candidate, the applicant will also be required to speak the same language and present themselves persuasively. Persuasion happens partly through articulation, partly through self-identification.

In seeking to draw out the organisationally competent professional self,[36] the panel may decide to conduct interviews as well as written tests or role plays to allow interviewees to momentarily embody their future position.[37] Interviews usually follow a 'competency-based' format according to the Recruitment Guidelines, which is designed to ascertain – in an 'objective and measurable' way[38] – the candidate's ability to deploy their skills in real-life scenarios.[39] The requirement of measurability creates the same constraints as other management tools described in Chapter 3, albeit here at the individual level. It prevents certain traits and skills beyond the competencies list from being assessed and valued. By this, the court expresses disinterest in the applicant's capacity for reflecting on the

---

[33] Recruitment Guidelines, para. 5.1.

[34] ASP Res 1/10 (9 September 2002), para. 1. See also the additional 'core values' outlined in Regulations 1.2–1.3, Staff Regulations for the International Criminal Court, adopted in ASP Res 2/2 (12 September 2003).

[35] Recruitment Guidelines, para. 7.1.

[36] On the production of the managerial subject, see Barbara Townley, *Reframing Human Resource Management: Power, Ethics and the Subject at Work* (SAGE Publishing 2014) 114–115.

[37] Recruitment Guidelines, para. 7.

[38] Ibid., para. 7.1.

[39] Ibid., para. 7.3.

political ramifications of their own work or the contradictions and contentions of ICC-style justice. Such traits are neither necessary nor desirable within the institutionalised project of global justice.

Like the list of competencies or roleplaying, the competency-based interview requires the applicant to imagine themselves into a future yet timeless, hypothetical workplace in order to resolve a particular challenge that might arise in their work or among colleagues. This imaginative experiment further establishes the organisational limits of the employee's role and gets them to make sense of the task of, in this case, enhancing protections for women and children as facing obstacles of workflow problems, time pressures, or lack of team collegiality. When the applicant demonstrates a capacity to overcome these imagined obstacles, they also show they can play their part in allowing the court to do its work while appearing to protect the vulnerable groups it engages with. Interviewers will take notes to this effect before reviewing and comparing applicants with one another once the interviews are complete.[40] An interview report is produced, possibly alongside a 'rating sheet' to rank candidates in order of preference.[41]

The combination of these managerial recruitment techniques – the job advertisement, the application form, interview questions, and panel reports and rankings – initiate a record of the future employee as a competent, efficient professional of global justice. The creation of the managerial self is both an organisational and an individual endeavour, with one constantly relating ideas of professionalism, commitment, and responsibility back to the other in order to fashion an ideal global justice worker.[42] If our applicant is lucky enough to be recruited after this months-long process, this is the discursive basis upon which they will relate to the organisation and its wider project from their first day on the job.

4.3 Settling Down

Once the applicant – now employee – enters the ICC building, the victims' exhibition in the main foyer may remind them of the higher aims powering the institution they now work for. But this encounter will

---

[40] Ibid.

[41] Ibid.

[42] Grey, 'Career as a Project of the Self' 487. According to one official discussing the documentation of performance, 'it is nice to have a trace', ICC Interview 004, 16 August 2018 (on file with author).

be superseded by a more immediate one. The first days will be choreographed by the Human Resources Section and the employee's new colleagues and supervisor in the Gender and Children Unit. Human resources will play an important part in formally introducing the ICC to the new recruit. The employee will by now have received an employment contract to sign and a letter of appointment outlining their work conditions and probationary period.[43] Despite having gotten the position, the employee will thus continue to interact with the organisation, colleagues, and human resources through an extended interview period in order to prove their worth to the court. For their part, the human resources officer the employee meets on their first day will likely have these documents close to hand, beginning to compile an employee file that will capture their professional life.

While the organisation seems to hold much of the power in its relationship with the employee, a considerable burden falls on it, through human resources personnel, to position and portray the court positively. This is particularly so for the ICC, which has been described as a 'hostile working environment' with a 'culture of fear' by independent experts, and which has been embroiled in several scandals over the years concerning sexual harassment and bullying.[44] The face of the organisation for new recruits must therefore be a positive one that resembles the mission and values of the court, and it will be for the employee to determine in the long term whether that portrayal is accurate.

4.3.1 Onboarding

The process of habituating the employee is known as 'onboarding', a now routine procedure dreamt up by management practitioners in the late 1970s to socialise new recruits into organisational aims, values, and professional culture as quickly as possible so as to clarify roles and align individual with institutional expectations.[45] This process is not dissimilar

---

[43] Rule 104.1(b)(iv) and rule 104.2(a)(v) Staff Rules of the International Criminal Court (as amended), ICC/AI/2015/004/Corr.1 (entered into force 27 July 2015).

[44] Independent Expert Review of the International Criminal Court and the Rome Statute System: Final Report, ICC, 30 September 2020, paras. 62, 72, 138 and 209, available at: https://asp.icc-cpi.int/sites/asp/files/asp_docs/ASP19/IER-Final-Report-ENG.pdf.

[45] Onboarding is a more recent term for what has, since the 1970s, been categorised as 'organisational socialisation tactics' by John Van Maanen and Edgar H. Schein, 'Toward a Theory of Organisational Socialisation' (1979) 1 *Research in Organisational Behaviour* 209–264. For a history of organisational socialisation, see Alan Saks and Blake Ashforth,

4.3 SETTLING DOWN   149

to the concept of *habitus*, as read by Bourdieu, had he accounted for the possibility of *habitus* being actively taken up and worn by professionals in a field.[46] At the ICC, as elsewhere, it is completed by human resources personnel.[47] They will remind the employee of the court's mission and values, and the wider contribution made by the organisation.[48] They may also be introduced to the concept of the 'one Court' principle devised during the court's first strategic planning exercise in 2006 and intended to create a sense that all employees, regardless of organ or perspective, 'work together as one court' and 'share a common mission'.[49] Despite some initial pushback, employees reported that the principle soon 'became part of our identity'.[50] Our new recruit will likely have the same experience as the months progress. Through these tools, the employee's work is clearly connected to colleagues, wider aims, and the 'clients' the court engages with.

Onboarding dresses the new employee in the court's mission while also allowing the recruit themselves to link their everyday tasks to something bigger.[51] The fact that the mission accomplishes this sense

---

'Organisational Socialisation: Making Sense of the Past and Present as Prologue for the Future' (1997) 51 *Journal of Vocational Behaviour* 234–279.

[46] Habitus here is 'a subjective but not individualised system of internalised structures, schemes of perception, conception, and action common to all members of the same group or class', Pierre Bourdieu, *Outline of a Theory of Practice* ([1977] Cambridge University Press 2013) 86; Pierre Bourdieu, 'The Force of Law: Towards a Sociology of the Juridical Field' (1987) 38 *Hastings Law Journal* 805–853.

[47] ICC, Job Description for Human Resources Assistant (G-5), International Criminal Court, ID 18427 (posted on 19 July 2018) 2 (on file with author).

[48] One ICC staff member reported that the mission acts more as a 'reminder' to staff, for whom such values 'come naturally anyway', ICC Interview 002, 13 July 2018 (on file with author).

[49] Strategic Plan 2006, para. 15. This unifying principle, according to one former ICC judge, helps foster 'a general atmosphere of mutual trust, confidence and reliability between all elected officials, organs, units and staff [to] contribute to more efficiency and a much better work culture', Address of Hans-Peter Kaul at the 6th Annual International Humanitarian Law Dialogues, 'The ICC of the Future', Robert H. Jackson Centre, 28 August 2012, 4, available at: www.icc-cpi.int/NR/rdonlyres/8572B9B0-B827-466C-B67A-3C9C06A5E46E/284994/30082012_ChautauquaSpeech_THEICCOFTHEFUTURE_provis.pdf.

[50] ICC interview 001, 11 July 2018 (on file with author).

[51] UN scholars have sought to foster a similar identity for UN staff members as 'truly international, specialised, mobile, midcareer, entrepreneurial, and independent', see Dirk Salomons, 'Good Intentions to Naught: The Pathology of Human Resources Management at the United Nations' in Dennis Dijkzeul and Yves Beigbeder (eds.), *Rethinking International Organisations: Pathology and Promise* (Berghahn Books 2003) 111–139, at 115.

150   THE ICC EXPERT: MICRO-MANAGEMENT

of a wider contribution for the employee is an achievement that places the precise nature and ambiguities of that link beyond consideration. The mission, which after all, is the *mission civilastrice* of the court, displaces reflection on its contestations, consequences, and desirability.

This closure around demands of the organisation will intensify once the employee is introduced to their supervisor within the OTP Unit, as day-to-day manager of their work. The supervisor will likely continue the work begun during the onboarding process, making real the management structures the employee had until now only read about in the job advertisement. They may be supplied with an organisational chart to clarify the structure of the organ and the employee's place within it. The most important relationship is not between the employee and the anti-impunity project but between employee and supervisor as one that will permit a fraction of that project to be realised.[52]

These organisational charts or organigrams also serve as the outer limit of the employee's professional consciousness. Whatever is to take place in the realm of gender or child protection will have to pass through their OTP Unit. Such practices of onboarding can thus 'fix meanings in ways that orient action and establish boundaries for acceptable action' in the future, according to Barnett and Finnemore.[53] It is these practices and the institution they support that give the employee's professional life meaning, while the ability and incentive to confront the complexities and distributions in which the court is entangled is greatly reduced by the project of becoming a well-managed ICC professional.

4.3.2   Probation

Although it will be easy for our employee to forget the official cues and messages, remembering them will hardly be necessary as they start into their work. They were, after all, selected partly for their fit within the organisation and can largely be relied upon to monitor and adjust themselves to keep this fit as the weeks and months progress.[54]

---

[52] Stanley Deetz, *Democracy in an Age of Corporate Colonisation: Developments in Communication and the Politics of Everyday Life* (State University of New York Press 1992) 240.

[53] Michael Barnett and Martha Finnemore, *Rules for the World: International Organisations in Global Politics* (Cornell University Press 2004) 32.

[54] While some may dispute this point by claiming that it is precisely the failure to do this and other self-monitoring activities that result in individual and court-wide

4.3 SETTLING DOWN

Nevertheless, the court has instituted a set of procedures designed to track early performance and determine whether the recruitment panel's initial apprehension about the candidate was correct with hindsight. This is the probationary period familiar to many employment sectors, not least international organisations and higher education. At the ICC, the probationary period is defined in the Staff Rules and elaborated in an Administrative Instruction.[55]

According to the Administrative Instruction, the probationary process 'provide[s] the court with an opportunity to assess the staff member's performance and suitability for his or her work with the court'.[56] According to rule 4.1 of the Staff Rules, the probationary process is normally conducted by the employee's 'immediate supervisor' and 'confirmed by the immediate supervisor's reviewer'. The period commences as soon as the employee begins their contract and lasts for six months. During that time, the employee and their supervisor should meet at least twice to formally discuss the former's performance, with the supervisor recording results in a 'probationary performance report'.[57] Based on this report, the supervisor and reviewer will either confirm the employee's appointment after six months, or, in case of an 'unsatisfactory' finding by the supervisor, extend the probationary period for another six months.[58]

The probationary process is an important first step in the court's performance management regime. It features performance meetings, competency assessments, and official reports. If confirmed in post after probation has ended, the employee will engage with similar practices as part of the performance appraisal cycle. I thus deal with these practices in this section on probation, recognising that these (self-)disciplining processes do not end once probation is complete.

---

underperformance, I fix on the 'ideal worker' here in order to problematise the idea that more and better (self-)management would solve the problem.

[55] The AI to which this employee would be subjected is the 2013 version, see Probationary Period and Performance Appraisal, ICC/AI/2013/004, 5 April 2013. This remains the applicable procedure for the probationary period. However, the rules on the post-probationary performance appraisal system were updated in 2019, see Performance Appraisal System, ICC/AI/2019/003, 22 February 2019. Accordingly, the 2013 version remains authoritative for probationary period procedures and is used for this section while the following section relies on the 2019 version.

[56] AI on Probationary Period, para. 1.1.

[57] Ibid., paras. 4.2–4.3.

[58] Ibid., para. 5.1.

4.3.3 Performance Meetings

Bilateral meetings between the employee and their supervisor – or 'appraisee' and 'appraiser' – are seen as moments for two-way engagement or dialogue geared towards understanding and, if necessary, alteration of the appraisee's performance in post. Such meetings are a crucial moment in the probation and wider performance appraisal cycle which brings the appraisee and appraiser together formally and allows information to be collected. According to the 2013 Administrative Instruction, the performance meeting should 'establish the objectives against which performance will be assessed during the probationary period', identify the staff member's performance thus far, and signal any necessary training or 'guidance on the implementation of his/her performance objectives'.[59] More generally, the appraisee will be asked how they are settling in and whether they are having any problems in their new role. The performance meeting is thus read as a neutral and mutually beneficial point of contact between professional and manager.[60]

Despite this portrayal, the performance meeting produces a web of power relations both between the appraisee and appraiser, and beyond them. The appraiser must adequately perform their end of the bargain by recording results and addressing any issues that might arise. They, along with the reviewer as the other appraiser, would be held responsible for any major oversights or failure to notice or resolve underperformance at the outset of the appraisee's employment contract. Such failures may not cause problems for the appraiser but may result in much greater state oversight in the event that performance failed to be adequately monitored across the court (a problem which caused the introduction of a more systematic performance appraisal system in 2013). Here, the dynamic between appraiser and appraisee is extrapolated up to a tension between the court and its states parties in the Assembly of States Parties (ASP).

Nevertheless, much of the power seems to lie with the appraiser/supervisor as one of the final arbiters on whether the appraisee has performed adequately enough to be confirmed in their post. The benevolent dynamic of helping employees to help themselves also

---

[59] Ibid., para. 8.2.
[60] Townley, 'Reframing Human Resources Management' 203.

4.3 SETTLING DOWN 153

opens the appraisee up to examination and subjects them to the 'normalising gaze' of the institution.[61] Based on that imbalance, the meeting becomes a motivating force for the appraisee to prove themselves in front of the manager as the court's embodiment. There are clear professional incentives, therefore, for the appraisee to continue to portray themselves as a competent professional with the same commitments and values as the organisation, and thus a good 'fit'. While the disparity in the position of the appraiser and appraisee is visible, then, power nonetheless operates at a level beneath mere coercion as discipline or self-discipline.[62]

A dynamic of self-discipline emerges in the appraisee's chance for individual confession.[63] This is not how the court defines the meeting but as an opportunity to reveal ambiguities, hesitations, and vulnerabilities that might be ironed out at an early stage. Perhaps they are 'not working as hard as they might' because of 'their workmates, their managers, their home life, their anxieties and aspirations'.[64] By 'accessing their feelings' about all these things and more, the appraiser frames and makes sense of the appraisee's experiences through the lens of professional competence, productivity, and organisational commitment.[65] The appraisee will mostly do the same, knowing there is likely to be an unsaid threshold for tolerating mediocre performance. The confessional nature of the performance meeting is not therefore designed to extract correct information as a means to

---

[61] Michel Foucault, *Discipline and Punish: The Birth of the Modern Prison* (Penguin 1991 [1977]) 184.

[62] These two effects broadly correspond to 'technologies of power' and 'technologies of the self' as discussed in Michel Foucault, 'Technologies of the Self' in Patrick Hutton, Huck Gutman, and Luther Martin (eds.), *Technologies of the Self: A Seminar with Michel Foucault* (University of Massachusetts Press 1988) 16–49.

[63] Townley makes the distinction between the dual examination and confessional functions of meetings in Barbara Townley, 'Foucault, Power/Knowledge, and its Relevance for Human Resource Management' (1993) 18 *Academy of Management Review* 518–545, at 533. Foucault also made the connection between the Catholic confessional and the 'secular' confessional as manifested in the modern discipline of psychiatry, Michel Foucault, *The Will to Knowledge: The History of Sexuality Volume 1* [1976] (Penguin 1998) 59–60. See also Patricia Findlay and Tim Newton, 'Re-framing Foucault: The Case of Performance Appraisal' in McKinlay and Starkey, 'Foucault, Management and Organisation Theory' 211, at 214–215.

[64] Findley and Newton, 'Re-Framing Foucault' 215; Townley, 'Reframing Human Resource Management' 109–111.

[65] Ibid.

154 THE ICC EXPERT: MICRO-MANAGEMENT

controlling future behaviour but to permit the appraisee to calibrate their sense of professional self along organisational lines.[66]

4.3.4 Core Competencies Model

The performance meeting bears out relations of power not only in form but in substance. To collect relevant information, both the appraiser and appraisee must be guided by relevant criteria and know the standards to which employees are held. This will ultimately determine the content of the probationary report when the appraiser comes to complete it. The core competencies model, which the appraisee was given a taste of in the job advertisement, now acts as the set of criteria against which they are to be assessed. Similar to the onboarding process of a few months prior, the core competencies model also refines the professional sensibility of those working within the ICC by connecting individual performance to the court's strategic goals and to the wider aims of global justice.

The core competencies model first appeared in an annex to another 2013 Administrative Instruction. Over sixteen pages, it listed seven core competencies against which staff performance was assessed and recorded, and these remain in place in the 2019 and 2021 updated versions. The same criteria as in the job advertisement are again listed, including 'dedication to the mission and values', 'professionalism', 'teamwork', 'learning and development', 'handling uncertain situations', 'interaction', and the ability to 'realis[e] objectives'.[67] Under these headings, each competency is defined and summarised, before being described in 'behavioural terms' to demonstrate its application in concrete situations. The competency is then adapted depending on the appraisee's level of seniority before finally offering positive and negative 'behavioural indicators' to help decide whether the appraisee has met the competency in practice.

All three versions of the model envisage a particular professional attitude. By way of example, the 2021 model (see Appendix 1) summar-

---

[66] Townley, 'Reframing Human Resource Management' 200–201; Townley, 'Foucault, Power/Knowledge' 536. This is in keeping with one official's observation that within the organisation 'there is no big brother' and that performance and expectations must be self-directed, ICC Interview 005, 27 August 2018 (on file with author).

[67] Performance Appraisal System, ICC/AI/2013/003, 6 March 2013, Annex: The Core Competencies of the ICC, 13 (Competencies Model 2013).

ises the 'learning and developing' competency in the following way: 'To continuously enhance the effectiveness of the Court, the employees of the ICC have to learn from their own and others' successes and failures. Developing yourself, others, the organisation and the profession is the central theme.'[68] In 'behavioural terms' this means that the ideal employee 'identifies development strategies needed to achieve work and career goals and makes use of developmental or training opportunities', 'seeks feedback', and 'has an open mind and contributes to innovation'.[69] This overlaps with the positive behavioural indicators expected for the competency while 'disregard[ing] new ideas' and failing to ask for feedback or seek improvement qualify as negative indicators.[70] This is only one of seven competencies applied during the probationary and performance appraisal cycles.

Without discussing each competency at length, the core competencies model hints at the kind of professional the court desires. This turns out to be quite similar to the way the organisation understands itself: as a perpetually deficient but always optimisable set of functions and traits. The connection, implicit though it may be, is that if the employee becomes a 'piecemeal engineer' of the self and the institution, then the institution will also more easily construct a more just world in a piecemeal fashion.[71] Moreover, the core competencies model sets a high premium on organisational loyalty. According to the 'dedication to the mission and values' competency, '[t]he foundation of the ICC competency model is dedication to the Court as a whole'.[72] 'The mission is what drives people to work for the ICC' while '[a]ll ICC employees understand the mission and values and are committed to it'.[73] When interacting outside the institution, the ideal professional 'portrays and promotes a positive image of the Court to the public', 'shows organisational commitment and loyalty', and 'speaks positively about the ICC'.[74] They will

---

[68] Performance Appraisal System, ICC/AI/2021/001, 26 February 2021, Annex 1: The Core Competencies of the ICC (Competencies Model 2021), 7.
[69] Ibid.
[70] Ibid.
[71] Thomas Skouteris, 'The New Tribunalism: Strategies of (De)Legitimation in the Era of International Adjudication' (1999) 17 *Finnish Yearbook of International Law* 307–356, at 345 quoting Karl Popper.
[72] Competencies Model 2021, 4.
[73] Ibid.
[74] Ibid.

'continuously build and maintain [the court's] credibility' among external groups.[75]

Beyond these broad themes, the specific terms and indicators of the various competencies reveal a series of narrowings at the level of individual tasks similar to those witnessed in relation to the more macrostructure of strategic planning and risk. This is visible in the 'dedication to the mission and values competency', which not only fails to mention the content of those values in the document but which also caps employees' contribution to such values by limiting them to what can be done institutionally, that is, 'show[ing] organisational commitment' or its opposite, 'talk[ing] about the organisation in a negative way'.[76] It is not contemplated that to dedicate oneself to certain values might demand critique of the court, never mind that speaking ill of the court may rank quite lowly as a problem of global justice.

The competency of 'handling uncertain situations' is included apparently in ignorance of the uncertain milieu, actors, and concepts with which the court engages on a daily basis. The uncertainty of how to confront indirect, structural violence through criminal proceedings is not the kind of uncertainty the model means. Rather, this is uncertainty at the quotidian level, where the court's aims and concepts are treated as solid and where unpredictable spaces are as stable as possible. Uncertainty then devolves to unforeseen aspects of an organisational plan or project that can be rectified internally through employees' proper storing of information, good communication, prioritisation, and flexibility. Once again, these controllable variables are seen as the primary variables for resolving uncertainty, with others the court is caught up in – including uncertainties the court relies upon and contributes to – being left to one side.

The idea of the institution as means and end is reinforced by some material aspects of the model itself. It relies upon tables, lists, and bullet points, which invite the reader to immediately interact with the model from their own professional position. In each of the competencies, the appraisee (or the appraiser if they will do this for them) will have to figure out if they are being held to levels A (general service), B (professional), or C (managers and supervisors). The higher the level, the more will be expected of them, and the higher standard the employee will hold themselves to. Bullet points, as discussed in Chapter 3, also

[75] Ibid., 9.
[76] Ibid., 4.

4.3 SETTLING DOWN

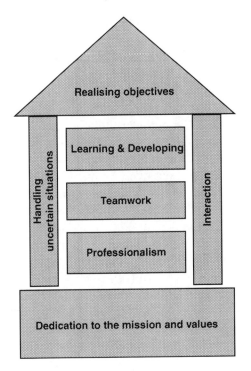

Figure 4.4 Core competencies diagram
© ICC-CPI

present traits or indicators as givens, cut off from context or history. As Strathern has observed of bullet points, 'not only is there no narrative and no plot, there is no record of the process of compilation, no internal monitoring of discourse, no authorial self-scrutiny'.[77] Bullet points are thus inscrutable: '[t]hey appear to be text (form) but they are not to be analysed (content)'.[78]

Interestingly, the updated model from 2019 omits part of the old version, namely a diagram of the core competencies and how they interact (see Figure 4.4). There is no available explanation for this. Yet

---

[77] Marilyn Strathern, 'Bullet-Proofing: A Tale from the United Kingdom' in Annelise Riles (ed.), *Documents: Artifacts of Modern Knowledge* (University of Michigan Press 2006) 181–205, at 196.
[78] Ibid., 198.

depicted as a diagram, the competencies also appear as isolated categories for professional assessment. Their shape portends to the organisation's own aspirations for its employees. The diagram is at once an arrow and a building-like structure. As an arrow, they represent the direction or means by which employees will move as they fulfil the core competencies; as a structure, the competencies are the building blocks of the institution itself, with 'dedication to the mission and values' acting as foundations and 'realising objectives' as the roof. Symbolically, then, the competencies are the extent of the institution, and the direction in which the arrow is pointing employees appears to be the court itself.

Finally, these features are bolstered by an authoritative institutional voice. Klikauer has pointed out that '[i]n managerially distorted communication, nouns govern sentences in an authoritarian and totalitarian fashion'.[79] The competencies model assumes this style. It deploys phrases such as 'client need', 'multicultural context', 'clear vision', or 'the right conclusions' as apparently agreed-upon and indisputable facts. Verbs are no different: by asserting that the optimal employee 'acts', 'clarifies', and 'seeks' while the sub-optimal employee 'fails' and 'does not act', the model's timeless present tense expresses transient personal opinion as institutional fact. It would be easy to forget that someone sat down to write these facts and that they accordingly seek to convey a set of universal truths.[80] In this way, seemingly self-evident language purges the model of traces of personal authorship or politics and reduces the possibility of experiencing the model as simply opinion.

4.3.5   Probationary Performance Report

Having met the appraisee and relied upon the core competencies model, the supervisor/appraiser will 'complete the performance report and submit it to the reviewer'.[81] According to the Administrative Instruction, the probationary performance report (PPR) is the repository for all appraisal information as a 'record of the immediate supervisor's

---

[79] Thomas Klikauer, *Managerialism: Critique of an Ideology* (Palgrave 2013) 122. See Don Brenneis, 'Reforming Promise' in Annelise Riles (ed.), *Documents: Artifacts of Modern Knowledge* (University of Michigan Press 2006) 41–70, at 64.

[80] On similar linguistic dynamics, see Bourdieu, 'The Force of Law' 820. The 'violence' of management-speak is discussed in the context of the IMF in Franco Moretti and Dominique Pestre, 'Bankspeak: The Language of World Bank Reports' (2015) 92 *New Left Review* 75–100, at 80.

[81] AI on Probationary Period, para. 8.2(g).

4.3 SETTLING DOWN

assessment of the ability of the staff member to perform his or her duties, as well as of his or her suitability to work with the Court'.[82] Once the PPR is complete, the employee will have a chance to add their comments before the document is submitted to the reviewer for signature and final appointment (subject to confirmation by the organ head, here the prosecutor).

In the event that the supervisor is unsatisfied with the lawyer's performance after the first appraisal, the supervisor 'shall record in the [PPR] the ways and means suggested for the improvement of the staff member's performance'.[83] If there is no improvement by the end of the probationary period, the supervisor may decide either not to confirm the appointment or, if the employee 'has the potential to perform adequately if given more time in the job', the supervisor may request the prosecutor for an extension of the probationary period for up to six months.[84] At the end of that extension, the only options are confirmation or termination of the employment contract.

It would be a heady experience to confront the probationary period and PPR, no matter how long or how satisfactorily the employee has performed in their first few months. The risk of termination (or even the ire or disappointment of one's colleagues) may loom large enough to instil in the employee the desire to become whatever the organisation wants them to be. And yet, the coercive power of termination offers an incomplete picture. Judging by the late and patchy implementation of the probationary system throughout the court's organs, the power of the probationary process to remove inefficient individuals is not borne out statistically.[85] Its power lies instead in bringing employees into a dialogic relationship with the organisation to allow both to record, classify, rate, and improve the professional. This more subterranean mode of power is visible in the standard four-page PPR form.

In addition to recording all relevant employee details, including functional title, supervisor, and appraisal dates, the PPR is divided into 'performance objectives', 'core competencies appraisal', 'summary performance rating', 'comments', 'recommendation', and finally 'decision'.

---

[82] Ibid., para. 4.2.

[83] Ibid., para. 8.2(g).

[84] Ibid., para. 5.1.

[85] In 2016/2017, the most recent cycle for which figures are available, the completion rate for the performance appraisal system was 92 per cent. Report of the Court on Human Resources Management, ICC-ASP/17/6, 11 May 2018, para. 95.

160 THE ICC EXPERT: MICRO-MANAGEMENT

These are all accompanied by large boxes of blank space, tick-boxes, and signature lines intended to be completed by the appraiser. At least officially, once these are complete, they articulate the employee's professional condition as either fit or unfit to work at the ICC.

The first section details 'performance objectives' agreed between appraiser and appraisee at the beginning of the probationary period and monitored thereafter (see Appendix 2). Up to five objectives comprise the appraisee's work plan for the period, and the appraiser must confirm in the first and then final appraisal whether the employee has displayed 'satisfactory' or 'unsatisfactory' progress or achievement. If progress is unsatisfactory, a footnote asks the appraiser to 'give full particulars' in an annex to the form.[86]

The subsequent part is for appraising the employee's competencies in line with the substantive competencies discussed previously. Not all competencies need to be selected, only those 'most relevant' for the position, and at least three. Whichever are selected, achievement is ranked as 'satisfactory' or 'unsatisfactory' in both probation appraisal moments. A 'summary performance rating' of satisfactory or unsatisfactory must then be ticked, dated, and signed by the appraiser (and later the reviewer). Additional comments can be offered before a formal recommendation either that appointment be confirmed, not confirmed, or probation extended for a selected number of months. A section is left open for the final decision of the prosecutor.

Given the various pressures on both the appraisee and the appraiser's time, not least to complete the duties for which they were recruited, the probation process comprises only a fraction of one's professional attention. Nonetheless, the point is to show that such limited engagement suffices to reframe many of the more elaborate substantive engagements in which court experts partake even when not thinking about probation or appraisal.

First, the probation process demands sustained and thoughtful engagement from employees across the court, arranged into clusters of appraisee and appraiser. The form cannot be forged or completed haphazardly. Second, the form's orientation, which is to assess individual performance through competencies and ratings, enacts a particular kind of court professional. The frame of reference for professionals on a day-to-day basis, and the marker for the success of their work within the

---

[86] Particulars include staff comments, recommendations, the organ head's decision, and space for a 'description of unsatisfactory performance'.

4.3 SETTLING DOWN 161

court, stays at the level of 'minute organisational procedures'.[87] In its purest form, the work of our employee is done (at least for the current appraisal cycle) once performance objectives are complete and competencies achieved. While going beyond these standards is encouraged, even 'outside the box' thinking remains to be judged against the parameters of institutionally ordained 'innovation'. There appears to be no outside-form, to paraphrase Derrida, rather the documentary form and the institutional form of global justice-seeking become synonymous.

The PPR also bears subtle indicators of form, format, and tone which fix the employee's imaginary of global justice within the institution.[88] The form is not a timeless and static document but seeks to constantly recreate a timeless and boundless present. Yet its raison d'être is that it should be completed; forms are 'created in anticipation of being filled in'.[89] It is therefore an interactive medium which creates the categories of appraisee, appraiser, and reviewer, arranging and disposing of these actors over a period of months.[90] The options for recommendation are very limited, but the techniques and methods for self-optimisation are virtually limitless. Even the prospect of future improvement where an employee is currently underperforming suffices to extend the probation period, and the appraiser is often requested to include details as to how this might be realised.

Yet despite such unbounded possibility, the many lines on the form evince – literally and epistemologically – the tight space within which the appraiser and appraisee must operate when evaluating performance. The many pre-set phrases and tick-boxes require very little engagement from the form filler.[91] The blank form dominates the page: even when incomplete, the page is almost entirely blackened by lines and text. Once the form is complete, the page looks only slightly different. The PPR's form, as well as its content, offers an enclosed site for inscribing the appraisee

---

[87] Barbara Townley, 'Performance Appraisal and the Emergence of Management' (1993) 30 *Journal of Management Studies* 221–238, at 226.

[88] Matthew Hull, 'Documents and Bureaucracy' (2012) 41 *Annual Review of Anthropology* 251–267, at 253.

[89] David Frohlich, 'On the Organisation of Form-Filling Behaviour in an Electronic Medium' (1987) 5 *Information Design Journal* 111–128, at 111.

[90] Matthew Hull, *Government of Paper: The Materiality of Bureaucracy in Urban Pakistan* (University of California Press 2012) 134; Riles, 'Introduction: A Response' in Riles, 'Documents' 19. See also Laura Lowenkron and Letícia Ferreira, 'Anthropological Perspectives on Documents: Ethnographic Dialogues on the Trail of Police Papers' (2014) 11 *Vibrant: Virtual Brazilian Anthropology* 76–112, at 83.

[91] Brenneis, 'Reforming Promise' 47–48.

in official terms (the organisational crest at the top of the form affirms this). There is little to no opportunity for reflection by either appraiser or appraisee of whether values, objectives, or competencies are appropriate for thinking through global injustice, even less so what global justice might require beyond an institutional space.

Notably, though, even the PPR cannot overwrite or overcome such complexity entirely. If one of the employee's relevant competencies was 'professionalism' – which demands, inter alia, that they collect evidence expeditiously and reach 'the right conclusions' – the appraiser is left to wonder what those conclusions are and according to whom.[92] If assessed under dedication, which demands organisational loyalty, the appraiser is left to ponder how organisational disloyalty today may be justified or necessary in order to admit to the dilemmas and contradictions the court faces. Beyond this, the form demands attention as an objective tool but has little meaning until it is completed and signed, a process that partly demonstrates its reliance on personal, subjective, contextual engagement.

In the meantime, the professional has had their appointment confirmed. They have passed through and sustained a network of meetings, models, reports, and forms, and emerge at the other end with a sense of institutional expectation now inscribed upon them in their PPR.[93] This identity is a feeling and an officially authorised subjectivity contained in the court's managerial documents as a persuasive account of the professional self.

4.4 Keeping On

The probationary period will be only the first of many of our professional's encounters with the ICC's performance management framework. The 2013 Administrative Instruction specifies that '[o]nce the staff member's appointment is confirmed, the performance appraisal shall be done in line with the established performance appraisal system' and the '[PPR] shall no longer be used'.[94] A 2019 Administrative Instruction on the 'Performance Appraisal System' (PAS) outlines its procedures, which build on the identity work of the probationary process.

---

[92] Competencies Model 2021, 5.

[93] One ICC official stated that 'performance management is part of our culture now'. ICC Interview 001, 11 July 2018 (on file with author).

[94] AI on Probationary Period, para. 9.1.

4.4 KEEPING ON

The PAS is a continuous process for evaluating the performance of all ICC staff through the now-familiar mechanisms of performance objectives, competencies, appraisal meetings, reports, and forms. Like the probationary process, PAS intends to 'ensure the effectiveness of the court by optimising performance at all levels and contributing to a positive work environment'.[95] Unlike the probationary process, PAS is not conducted with a view to confirming appointment but for the long-term benefit of the organisation. It aims to enhance organisational effectiveness by 'promoting a culture of high performance', 'empowering managers and holding them responsible', 'encouraging a high level of staff participation in the planning, delivery and evaluation of work', and 'recognising satisfactory performance and addressing underperformance in a fair and objective manner'.[96]

PAS follows an annual cycle beginning with the setting of the professional's performance objectives for the year and ending with the final storage of the performance appraisal report in their official employee file. At the beginning of the cycle, the professional as appraisee and their supervisor as appraiser meet to discuss an 'individual performance plan'.[97] The plan, informed by the OTP and court-wide strategic plan and goals, includes individual performance objectives, competencies, and 'staff development needs'.[98] Like the probationary process, PAS establishes a frame for assessing performance, prompting a wealth of managerial data designed to assess efficiency and productivity. In addition to those practices of meetings, reports, and forms discussed previously, two new practices are bolted on at this stage as additional points of professional production.[99]

4.4.1 Mid-term Progress Monitoring Worksheet

Like the probation process, the PAS recruits ICC staff including appraisee, appraiser, reviewer, and human resources officer into the project of identity-making, and the relevant Administrative Instruction

---

[95] AI on PAS, para. 2.1.
[96] Ibid., para. 2.2.
[97] Ibid., para. 5.2.
[98] Ibid., para. 5.3.
[99] Riles, '[Deadlines]: Removing the Brackets on Politics in Bureaucratic and Anthropological Analysis' in Riles, 'Documents' 71–94, at 71.

164 THE ICC EXPERT: MICRO-MANAGEMENT

ICC Performance Appraisal Mid-Term Progress Monitoring Worksheet

Name of the staff member: _____ Name of the appraiser (immediate supervisor): _____

PROGRESS ON PERFORMANCE OBJECTIVES			
Performance objective	On track? What has been achieved so far?	Adjustment needed?	Support needed? How to overcome obstacles?

PROGRESS ON DEVELOPMENT OBJECTIVES		
Development objective	On track? What has been achieved so far?	Support needed? How to overcome obstacles?

Other Comments (Optional)

Appraising Officer's signature: Staff Member's signature:

Date: Date:

Figure 4.5 Mid-term progress monitoring worksheet
© ICC-CPI

makes clear each of these actors' responsibilities as part of the cycle. The dynamic between appraiser and appraisee is similar to that of probation, with an individual performance plan, objectives, and competencies motivating the professional's work during the cycle, and being used as a reference for performance at its end. The updated Administrative Instruction on the PAS from 2019 emphasises 'progress monitoring and performance conversations' throughout the performance cycle, and these may manifest as formal or informal conversations, as well as email exchanges between appraiser and appraisee.[100]

Under the old system, appraisers were required to monitor progress through a 'mid-term progress review' six months into the annual cycle, designed to 'indicate the progress made and justify any updates to the performance objectives and development needs.[101] This process was also recorded via the 'ICC Performance Appraisal Mid-Term Progress Monitoring Worksheet' (see Figure 4.5). The worksheet is a slightly truncated version of the PPR but also accounts for 'what has been

---

[100] AI on PAS, para. 6.1.
[101] Ibid., para. 6.2.

4.4 KEEPING ON

achieved so far' and what 'adjustments' are required so objectives can be met before the cycle ends.

The worksheet required further engagement and evaluation by the appraiser and appraisee, which may explain its demise in the updated PAS. In its place, the 2019 Administrative Instruction envisions several performance conversations between the employee and their supervisor throughout the year, to be recorded via an online performance form.[102] In place of a formalised worksheet, then, the new PAS prefers frequent face-to-face but informal chats which should all be recorded. By such a move, the PAS has become less formalised and more reliant on the self-direction of the appraisee and appraiser. This also reflects the internalisation of performance management with professionals and a move away from top-down imposition as necessary for compliance.

4.4.2 Performance Appraisal Form

Near the end of the appraisal cycle for the employee, their supervisor acting as appraiser will meet to discuss overall performance.[103] Thereafter, the appraiser (in consultation with the reviewer) will use an electronic performance form to 'grade the individual's performance objectives and competencies', 'assess the progress made in relation to the performance development plan', and 'evaluate the staff member's overall performance'.[104] The AI indicates that this should be written up by the appraiser in a narrative style.[105] Once the form is completed, it is signed and sent to the appraisee for signature and comments, before being submitted. An additional procedure, not unlike the extended probation process, is provided in case of 'performance shortcomings and underperformance'.[106]

The PAS form itself differs little in layout, style, and content from the court's other performance forms. Yet the PAS form offers an expanded range of rating options to reflect nuances in employee performance (see Figure 4.6). Performance objectives are no longer rated according to the

---

[102] Ibid.

[103] Ibid., para. 7.1.

[104] Ibid., para. 7.2.

[105] Reflecting Foucault's concept of 'care of the self', 'those intentional and voluntary actions by which men not only set themselves rules of conduct, but also seek to transform themselves, to change themselves in their singular being, and to make their life into an oeuvre'. Michel Foucault, *The Use of Pleasure: The History of Sexuality Volume 2* (Vintage 1985) 10.

[106] AI on PAS, section 8.

THE ICC EXPERT: MICRO-MANAGEMENT

SMART: Specific, Measurable, Achievable, Relevant, Timed

PERFORMANCE OBJECTIVES

Immediate supervisors shall work with staff members under their direct supervision on the development on the staff member's performance objectives and development, which shall constitute the performance expectations. Objectives must follow the SMART approach. Each staff member should have no less than 3 and no more than 6 objectives.

	Immediate supervisor's end-of-cycle-evaluation of performance objectives: Comments and evaluation			
Objective 1				
	Incomplete	Partially completed	Completed	Exceeded
	○	○	◉	○
Objective 2				
	Incomplete	Partially completed	Completed	Exceeded
	○	○	◉	○
Objective 3				
	Incomplete	Partially completed	Completed	Exceeded
	○	◉	○	○
Objective 4				
	Incomplete	Partially completed	Completed	Exceeded
	○	○	◉	○
Objective 5				
	Incomplete	Partially completed	Completed	Exceeded
	○	○	◉	○
Objective 6				
	Incomplete	Partially completed	Completed	Exceeded
	○	◉	○	○

Figure 4.6   Performance report objectives
© ICC-CPI

binary distinction of 'satisfactory' or 'unsatisfactory' performance but along a scale from 'incomplete' to 'exceeded' with 'partially completed' and 'completed' between.[107] Competencies are evaluated as 'strength',

---

[107] Performance Appraisal System, ICC/AI/2019/003, 22 February 2019, Annex II: Performance Appraisal Form, 3.

4.4 KEEPING ON

'capable', 'learner', or 'weakness'.[108] At the end, performance remains subject to either a 'satisfactory' or 'unsatisfactory' rating while a large box now exists for the appraiser to narrate the appraisee in management terms.

The PAS creates a performance-oriented professional through a careful balance of power apparatuses. At one level, the degree of responsibility employees are required to take over their own self-improvement and the informalisation of the process shows how effectively performance management practices operate as technologies of the self. From the outset, the employee has made themselves fit with their idea of the ICC, and these practices merely institutionalise that identity work. Beyond this, however, lie the procedures for non-compliance, which hint at the spectre of coercive power the court may, on rare occasions, wield. The Administrative Instruction states that failure to comply with the PAS, such as the appraiser failing to complete the documents or submit them on time, 'shall be recorded as part of his or her performance evaluation' and, for appraisers or reviewers, future performance forms 'shall include an objective for timely implementation of and compliance with the performance appraisal system'.[109] The completion of the PAS, alongside the appraiser's other duties, becomes part of their own professional goals not only a means to recording them. Hence, while certain behaviour is technically sanctioned, it is not intended to result in termination or other results but to redirect the appraiser towards more managerial behaviour.

Findings of appraisee underperformance have similar functions. Both staff dismissal and staff promotion at the ICC are rare, due to limited financial resources and because of the stability such positions offer for staff.[110] Over- or under-performance does not therefore facilitate promotion or termination.[111] Rather, it encourages 'adjustment' of the

---

[108] Ibid., 4.

[109] AI on PAS, para. 4.8.

[110] In 2014, only fourteen staff members left the court due to non-extension of contracts or dismissal, see Report of the Court on Human Resources Management, ICC-ASP/14/7, 4 May 2015, para. 12. In 2017, this figure dropped to six staff members with the Human Resources Section observing an average staff turnover rate since 2014 of 8 per cent, Report of the Court on Human Resources Management, ICC-ASP/17/6, 11 May 2018, paras. 8–9. Even these statistics do not mention the reason for dismissal and thus may not have concerned underperformance.

[111] Cf. the CBF's recommendation 'that the Court develop proposals to introduce a culture of personal accountability including rewards for good performance and sanctions for

employee. 'Remedial measures' may be put in place to that end, including 'counseling, additional training and/or the establishment of a time-bound performance improvement plan'.[112] The improvement plan has its own micro-processes and is recorded in a separate form. When the court states that performance appraisal is not a punitive system, it is thus doing so sincerely and is more interested in aligning individuals with institutional expectations. This is true even for the appeals procedure, which, by its existence, suggests a potentially damaging set of consequences arising from a poor performance rating. Yet the employee is unlikely to engage with the appeals procedure for fear of missing out on promotion. Conversely, the appeals procedure is framed as a means to garner how closely the employee lies to the court's professional ideal, and this is also how employees are expected to engage with the procedure.

A 2010 Administrative Instruction on appeals outlines that before the employee can challenge an unsatisfactory performance rating, they must first exhaust other grievance mechanisms, namely by speaking to their supervisor informally or in the presence of an HR officer. Only once this avenue has been unsuccessful can they bring their complaint to a nine-member Rebuttal Panel.[113] The professional must submit a written rebuttal statement to the Human Resources Section 'setting forth briefly the specific reasons why he/she should have received a different assessment or rating'.[114] The panel will consider this and any other documentation submitted by interested staff and may decide to hold a hearing. The panel will then issue a report on the validity of the original rating, either upholding the supervisor's original assessment or substituting its own if they find the original assessment is not 'fair, objective and consistent with the underlying arguments and facts'.[115]

The PAS appeals procedure reveals the vast expenditure of institutional time, resources, and personnel in the project of making the global justice professional. The procedure requires the complainant to justify themselves in terms of performance objectives and competencies. Given that the entire rebuttal process is geared towards the 'correct' designation of the professional's competency levels, it offers them an opportunity to

---

poor performance', Report of the Committee on Budget and Finance on the Work of its 18th Session, ICC-ASP/11/5, 9 August 2012, para. 49.

[112] AI on PAS, para. 9.1.

[113] Performance Appraisal Rebuttals and Procedures, ICC/AI/2010/002, 22 December 2010, para. 2.1. ('AI on Rebuttal').

[114] Ibid., para. 3.1.

[115] Ibid., para. 3.4.

4.5 MOVING UP

publicise their managerial credentials. Once the process has ended, the procedure's paper trail will be added to the official record to update the story of their refinement as an efficient professional.[116]

Through its annual performance appraisal cycles, the court and staff members co-operate to imbue a professional, court-driven employee. Once probation is passed, the employee takes more responsibility over their own professional mindset, work, and motivations. The various practices involved in self-identification also shorten the employee's horizon from global injustice, domination, and contradiction to institutional sustainability. A final series of encounters shows how this evolves should the employee move up the court's management ladder.

4.5 Moving Up

Practices of recruitment, probation, and performance appraisal habituate the court employee as an efficient cog in the global justice machine. As months at the court turn into years, employees may find themselves sometimes more, sometimes less in alignment with this professional ideal, and the constant process of (self-)evaluation will ensure they do not deviate too far from the court's own idea of itself as a modern, efficient, well-run organisation. Although promotion is rare, it may happen that the employee has an opportunity to move up the organisational hierarchy, perhaps by taking over as Legal Adviser at P-4 or above, or as head of the OTP Gender and Children Unit, where they began their ICC career. Such a move, while allowing the employee to continue proving their professional credentials to the court, also permits a resetting of their relationship with the court and others in a new managerial guise.[117] This section considers those management practices that will increasingly feature within the professional's orbit as they take on the mindset of 'manager'.

4.5.1 Managerial Responsibilities

The employee's elevation to a management role comes with many benefits, not only financial but also in their capacity to influence more long-

---

[116] Ibid., paras. 3.2–3.6.

[117] Current and former senior court staff interviewed described their own roles as 'managerial' and identified themselves as 'managers', ICC Interview 003, 31 July 2018 (on file with author); NGO Interview 002, 16 August 2019 (on file with author).

term strategic and policy choices within their area of work. For the professional in the Gender and Children Unit, this may be an opportunity to experiment with or implement ideas that have surfaced during their time as a legal officer but which they then had no mandate to broach. In this new role, they will be involved in producing and negotiating strategic documents, policies, and guidelines of organisational best practice. They may also engage more widely with other OTP bodies such as the Executive Committee. The employee will likely enter this role with the same sense of professional commitment as when they began at the court some years prior, as well as a better appreciation of the institutional contexts and constraints that shape their work.

Yet the employee's new post will not shield them from the same set of management techniques they became acquainted with in previous appraisal cycles. They will continue to engage with that system as an appraisee, with the Division head or other supervisor acting as their new appraiser. This I discuss further in the following section. In addition, the professional turned manager may also take on the role of appraiser themselves over a team within their Unit. Not only are they responsible for self-improvement but now also the improvement of others. As they encounter new tasks and colleagues within and across the OTP's Units, their identity as manager of global justice solidifies through performance appraisal, as well as encounters with auditors and, potentially, the court's Independent Oversight Mechanism (IOM).

4.5.2 Performance Appraisal Revisited

As in their previous role, the employee is responsible for meeting agreed-upon performance objectives and evaluating their progress alongside an immediate supervisor or appraiser. They are still a staff member and therefore understand the court's goals and how, through their own work, they can help realise them. They will also report on and improve such objectives through the yearly appraisal cycle as before.[118] Their employee file (digital or otherwise) will now have ripened considerably with possible probation reports, mid-term worksheets, appraisal forms, and other important materials defining their professional life within the court.[119]

---

[118] AI on PAS, para. 4.2.

[119] According to one ICC official, 'the file gives a sense of how the professional has progressed', ICC Interview 004, 16 August 2018 (on file with author). For a vivid account

4.5 MOVING UP

Having assumed the role of manager, though, our professional now finds themselves held to higher professional standards. These standards are reflected in the core competencies model, which includes an additional set of 'leadership competencies', namely 'purpose', 'collaboration', 'people', and 'results'. These were published in 2021 as a clear and recent embrace of management talk. Managers ranging from 'executives' (i.e. Heads of Organs) down to 'Team Leaders' (our professional-manager as Unit head) are charged to 'know who you are, what your values are, and be clear on your purpose as a leader'.[120] For the professional-manager, this means 'articulat[ing] how [the] team's work contributes to the organisation's vision and outcomes, and personally bring[ing] the team on board'.[121] As a leader, they must also focus on people: 'know your business, know your people' the model says.[122] As a bringer of results, they will 'lead and empower [their] teams and hold them accountable to deliver results'.[123] This means giving staff ownership over their work, learning from mistakes, being able to say 'no', and 'appraise performance fairly'.[124] From these competencies, the professional-manager not only comes into even closer relation with the organisation but personifies it before appraisees and other colleagues in different units.

When engaging with their appraisee, the professional-manager will, in accordance with the Administrative Instruction, be responsible for developing performance objectives with the appraisee, conducting performance conversations, providing feedback, addressing shortcomings, and completing all relevant paperwork.[125] From this position, the professional now looks at management from both sides of the desk, albeit still within a much wider network of personnel and oversight that continues to render them a component in the institutional machine. Assuming the role of manager, the employee not only takes on additional management tasks but further refines the orientation of those under their supervision towards the efficient and effective functioning of the organisation. As employees become more deeply embedded in the performance management infrastructure, they also take on the court's own sense

---

of the agentic life of legal files, see Bruno Latour, *The Making of Law: An Ethnography of the Conseil d'État* (Wiley 2010) 70.

[120] Competencies Model 2021, 11.
[121] Ibid.
[122] Ibid., 13.
[123] Ibid., 14.
[124] Ibid.
[125] AI on PAS, para. 4.4.

of vision, values, and aspirations for tackling global injustice. By the time our professional is a manager, reinforcing the court's vision and the professional ideal among supervisees equates to commitment to the wider global justice project.

4.5.3 Audit

The professional-manager's new responsibilities in the Gender and Children Unit (or elsewhere) are likely to bring them into contact with the court's oversight apparatus. These are not the individualised processes of staff appraisal but the organ and court-wide frameworks of audit and the court's IOM. As discussed in Chapter 3, the court's audit infrastructure is extensive, having expanded to encompass risk assessment and periodic and ad hoc, internal and external audits. These may relate to the court's finances but also the 'administration and management' of the court's organs, procedures, or specific projects. In conducting such audits, auditors will collaborate with court staff to complete their work. They may access institutional accounts and records to 'make observations with respect to ... the administration and management of the Court'.[126]

Divisions and units (such as the Gender and Children Unit) have been audited in the past to 'assess the extent to which [its] priority objectives ... are achieved or are in the process of being achieved'.[127] Unit-specific audits therefore function as collective versions of the individualised performance appraisal system. During the audit, auditors may decide to conduct 'on-site checks' as part of their enquiries.[128] They may co-ordinate these enquiries through our professional-manager as Unit head in conjunction with the organ's senior management such as the Division head or Head of Organ (i.e. Prosecutor). The employee may therefore be required to answer specific questions posed by the auditors and to back up their answers with supporting documents and statistics. One ICC official described this process as 'a bit like litigation', which suggests not only the possible tensions involved but also the parity of

---

[126] Regulation 12.3, Financial Regulations and Rules, ICC-ASP/1/3, adopted 9 September 2002.

[127] Final Audit Report on the Implementation of a Division of External Operations, ICC-ASP/16/27, 10 October 2017, para. 4 (DEO Audit Report).

[128] Ibid., para. 7.

4.5 MOVING UP

esteem that such experts are given by court staff.[129] As with previous audit exercises at the court, the professional may have sight of a first draft of the auditors' report and be given an opportunity to provide comments, clarify points, and suggest amendments.[130]

As with the court's regime for non-compliance with performance appraisal, encounters with the audit framework will be rare and fleeting. Moreover, unless the professional assumes a managerial role, or is otherwise asked to assist the auditors in their enquiries, they may never meet the court's auditors. However, much like accreditation practices at modern universities, the rarity of such encounters does not render auditing a marginal pursuit. In fact, much of their tasks and how they organise staff and activities in the Unit will be conducted in the shadow of audit. Audit's power is not only the spontaneity of audit processes but its capacity to work on the professional and offices 'without noise' in their drive to make spheres of activity efficient and effective.[131] Records will have to be diligently maintained and procedures vetted internally. At its most optimal, auditors can embed a risk approach to the project of global justice among professionals and offices without ever having to intervene.[132]

When an audit does take place, the professional-manager is integral to the auditor's rituals. One court official noted that internal staff regarded auditors with some suspicion because of their lack of legal and specifically ICL knowledge.[133] Auditors saw fixed rules of procedure and principles of organisational independence too flexibly and did not appreciate the difficulty of enacting institutional change through legal channels. Yet despite this deficiency, the context, problems, and solutions proffered by auditors continue to frame professional work. The professional-manager therefore becomes pivotal to the application of audit expertise by reporting and translating the Unit's legal and other activities into a vocabulary legible to auditors and auditing. Employees provide evidence of the optimal or suboptimal performance of the Unit's objectives and how these fit into wider court aims. Later, the professional may be asked to review a draft of the audit report and suggest amendments, again because auditors may have

---

[129] ICC Interview 002, 13 July 2018.
[130] DEO Audit Report, para. 10; ICC Interview 002, 13 July 2018.
[131] Foucault, 'Discipline and Punish,' 206.
[132] Ibid.
[133] NGO Interview 002, 16 July 2019.

174   THE ICC EXPERT: MICRO-MANAGEMENT

misunderstood the court's procedures.[134] The professional here acts as a knowledge conduit between the institution and the auditors. Along that conduit, they convey an institutional truth about the unit as an 'auditable' body, to which managerial problems and solutions can be applied even despite the supposed primacy of legal knowledge.[135]

4.5.4   Independent Oversight Mechanism

A final process in which the professional-manager may find themselves embroiled is the IOM. Under article 112(4) of the Statute, the ASP is mandated to 'establish such subsidiary bodies as may be necessary, including an independent oversight mechanism for inspection, evaluation and investigation of the court, in order to enhance efficiency and economy'. The IOM was established in 2009 and gradually assumed these three functions by 2017. Operationally independent of the court's organs, the IOM has a broad remit to investigate allegations of misconduct and complaints against elected officials on request of the ASP Bureau or on a *proprio motu* basis. It may 'provide evaluations of any programme, project or policy'[136] and 'conduct unscheduled/ad hoc inspections of any premises or processes'.[137]

Unlike many other management processes, the IOM has attracted the attention of ICL scholars, many of whom have welcomed its establishment as a trend towards greater accountability, transparency and 'good governance'.[138] Some have also taken the creation of the IOM as a sign of the court's maturation as a justice mechanism.[139] Yet the IOM's work suggests that, like audit, its power lies beyond the statutory functions

---

[134]   ICC Interview 002, 13 July 2018.

[135]   Michael Power, *The Audit Society: Rituals of Verification* (Oxford University Press 1997) 91.

[136]   ASP Res 12/6 (27 November 2013) Annex: Operational Mandate of the Independent Oversight Mechanism, para. 16 (IOM Operational Mandate).

[137]   IOM Operational Mandate, para. 6.

[138]   José Alvarez, 'The Proposed Independent Oversight Mechanism for the International Criminal Court' in Richard Steinberg (ed.), *Contemporary Issues Facing the International Criminal Court* (Brill Nijhoff 2016) 143–153; Coalition for the International Criminal Court, 'Independent Oversight Mechanism Team: Comments and Recommendations to the Ninth Session of the Assembly of States Parties', 26 November 2010, available at: www.iccnow.org/documents/CICC_IOM_Team_Paper.pdf.

[139]   Emily Tsui, 'Towards Mature Justice: Expanding the ICC's Independent Oversight Mechanism', *E-International Relations*, 11 October 2015, available at: www.e-ir.info/2015/10/11/towards-mature-justice-expanding-the-iccs-independent-oversight-mechanism/.

4.5 MOVING UP

ascribed to it. Since it began operating, the IOM has investigated a handful of cases annually, some of which deal with matters of professional misconduct, harassment, and fraud.[140] The IOM also receives requests for inspection, such as a 2017 request to inspect the operation of the ICC field offices.[141]

The IOM operates to shape the court and our professional-manager 'from a distance', to quote Rose and Miller. The criteria by which the IOM evaluates the court's programmes and policies are 'relevance, appropriateness, effectiveness, efficiency, impact and sustainability'.[142] Employees, particularly managers, will wish to emulate this focus to align their Unit's operations with institutional expectations. When the IOM becomes involved, this desire to align is intensified. The IOM's inspection mandate allows it to conduct 'special, unscheduled, on-the-spot verifications' of any court activity,[143] while evaluations involve 'a rigorous, systematic and objective process in the design, analysis and interpretation of information'.[144] In discharging its functions, the IOM 'shall have the authority to initiate on a reasonable basis, carry out and report on any action which it considers necessary to fulfil its responsibilities with regard to its functions without any hindrance or need for prior clearance'.[145] Because IOM staff 'shall have access to all (electronic or otherwise) court records, files, documents, books or other materials, assets and premises, and shall have the right to obtain such information and explanations as they consider necessary to fulfil their responsibilities', the professional-manager will find themselves facilitating such work.[146]

With these broad powers, the IOM governs organs and projects from a distance as it instils standards among staff. Through its power to conduct unscheduled visits, the IOM ensures that staff self-regulate periodically to ensure they are performing efficiently even when IOM experts are absent. When the IOM does appear, its ability to access documents and records

---

[140] Annual Report of the Head of the Independent Oversight Mechanism, ICC-ASP/20/16, 17 November 2021, para. 23.

[141] Annual Report of the Head of the Independent Oversight Mechanism, ASP-ICC/17/8, 8 November 2018, para. 23. One exception was an IOM inspection of the 'administrative arrangements' of the ICC field offices, see Annual Report of the Head of the Independent Oversight Mechanism, ICC-ASP/16/8, 17 October 2017, para. 26.

[142] IOM Operational Mandate, para. 6.

[143] Ibid.

[144] Ibid., para. 16.

[145] Ibid., para. 4.

[146] Ibid., para. 43.

means that such papers will be assessed according to the standards of efficiency and effectiveness. As Foucault noted of the disciplinary institution, '[a]n inspector arriving unexpectedly ... will be able to judge at a glance, without anything being concealed from him, how the entire establishment is functioning'.[147] As with audit, the professional-manager ensures staff and documents are ripe for such analysis. They will have to translate structures and policies into a language amenable to IOM inspection or evaluation based on the criteria of effectiveness, efficiency, and impact. After their enquiries have finished, the IOM will leave an exclusively managerial account of the Unit's structures or policies in a documentary report and make recommendations based on that reading.

Finally, the IOM governs professionals through other, more individualised, measures. This is particularly visible in its whistleblowing mandate. The ICC's Whistleblowing Policy, promulgated in a 2014 Presidential Directive, provides staff with an avenue to report, anonymously and in good faith, suspected instances of wrongdoing or misconduct.[148] Whistleblowing allegations – as well as any potential retaliation by staff in response to such allegations – must be reported to the IOM. Only rarely has the IOM considered such cases.[149]

The IOM has been more active in rolling out oversight guidelines and in informing staff of the availability and workings of its whistleblowing function than in investigating instances of misconduct. Despite its rare application, the whistleblowing mechanism is an important route for reporting misconduct without fear of individual reprisal. Yet through this mechanism, the IOM also extends the managerial gaze into individual staff. One ground of misconduct which professionals may report on is 'serious alleged inefficiencies or poor use of resources in court processes or procedures'.[150] This ground exists to 'reinforce the "economy" objective of [the IOM's] oversight mandate'.[151] It also establishes a system of internal and individualised discipline by recruiting staff into their and their colleagues' management. As with the many other managerial techniques and tools which our professional will have encountered, the IOM's whistleblowing policy promotes efficiency as the main vector through which professionals and professional-managers engage with this global justice institution.

---

[147] Foucault, 'Discipline and Punish,' 204.

[148] International Criminal Court Whistleblowing and Whistleblower Protection Policy, ICC/PRESD/G/2014/003, 8 October 2014, para. 1.1.

[149] In 2018, the IOM devoted only 1 per cent of its time to whistleblowing-related activities, see IOM Report 2018, para. 31.

[150] IOM Report 2017, para. 13.

[151] Ibid.

4.6 Conclusion

The account offered in this chapter complements, at the micro level, the account of the ICC organisation provided previously. As noted in that chapter, managerial practices produce knowledge about the court as an efficient, cost-effective institution, narrowing the co-ordinates of global justice down to the institutionally palatable. Similarly, this chapter's narrative of one employee's professional journey through the court demonstrates the pervasiveness of management at every turn, from the applicant's first engagements with the court at recruitment until the point at which they move into a managerial post. These stages comprise a series of quotidian practices that also help frame and constrain expert imagination within an institution dealing with complex matters of mass atrocity and global injustice.

Dynamics of micro-management transpire both internally as with probation and performance appraisal, and externally as in the case of recruitment and audit. These practices are often individualised and require constant engagement. Performance appraisal is the most intensive of these. But such practices may also be collective, as with organ-wide audit inspections. Bodies of experts and professional staff enact and are enacted by this 'massive and invisible' managerial apparatus.[152] This apparatus is an archive of documents, models, reports, and forms, and together, the court's recruitment materials and processes, onboarding, probationary and performance appraisal, audit, and independent oversight record and frame the employee's encounters with this global justice institution in terms of optimal performance. What is lost is the connection to the competing and ever-unstable contexts, goals, and politics the court operates within. From such tools, 'alternative institutions or social arrangements are pushed beyond our line of sight or even our imagination' as we – former, current, or future ICC professionals – engage in the business of micro-management, whether of ourselves or others.[153] In Chapter 5, I turn from analysing the organisation and its professionals to the legal framework and argumentative dilemmas that management ideas and practices get applied to.

---

[152] Stanley Deetz, 'Disciplinary Power in Modern Corporations' in Mats Alvesson and Hugh Willmott (eds.), *Critical Management Studies* (SAGE Publishing 1992) 21–52, at 37.

[153] Tor Krever, 'Quantifying Law: Legal Indicator Projects and the Reproduction of Neoliberal Common Sense' (2013) 34 *Third World Quarterly* 131–150, at 144.

5

ICC Legal Argumentation

Meso-management

5.1 An Appalling Decision

In April 2019, ICC Pre-Trial Chamber II decided not to authorise an investigation into potential Taliban, Afghan, and US crimes in the situation in Afghanistan. The decision, specifically its legal reasoning, prompted considerable outcry among victims' groups, scholars, and court supporters. The judges had concluded that pursuant to article 53 (1)(c) of the Rome Statute, for the Office of the Prosecutor (OTP) to be authorised to investigate alleged crimes in Afghanistan would not be in the 'interests of justice'. In deploying this term, the court looked beyond the narrow criteria previously outlined by the OTP itself, which had focused on gravity and victims' interests. It instead extended its analysis to 'the likelihood that investigation be feasible and meaningful under the relevant circumstances'.[1] According to the judges, these wider considerations were impossible to ignore, given that an incorrect authorisation might adversely affect the 'paramount objectives of the Statute and hence the overall credibility of the Court, as well as its organisational and financial sustainability'.[2]

The 'relevant circumstances' to which the court alluded were not far beneath the surface. The prosecutor's examination of various sides of the Afghanistan situation, notably the US military and CIA, had drawn lukewarm reception from the United States during the Obama administration. After the 2016 Presidential election, however, that response had escalated into outright hostility towards the OTP and the court, led by Donald Trump and his national security adviser, John

[1] *Situation in Islamic Republic of Afghanistan* (Decision Pursuant to Article 15 of the Rome Statute on the Authorisation of an Investigation into the Situation in the Islamic Republic of Afghanistan) ICC-02/17-33 (12 April 2019) para. 35.
[2] Ibid., para. 88.

178

5.1 AN APPALLING DECISION   179

Bolton. To the Pre-Trial Chamber, the consequences of such protracted opposition were plain: low likelihood of co-operation with and support from US authorities, possible hampering of investigative efforts, not to mention ageing testimony, and the potential loss of evidence as the years progressed.

Read generously, the court's decision not to authorise an investigation thus reflected a genuine effort to deal with the tensions erupting from such 'relevant circumstances'. To that end, the judges indicated the 'significant amount of resources' that would be required by the prosecutor to successfully complete the investigation.[3] In his separate and concurring opinion, Judge Mindua also raised the current zero-growth policy for the court's budget (effectively a real-term decrease in the court's annual budget), noting that opening an investigation would 'be a mismanagement of public funds'.[4] Such mismanagement would, in turn, not only reduce states' confidence in the court's capabilities but risked detracting from other scenarios with a more 'realistic prospect' of success.[5] These were the constraints the judges had in mind.

Victims' groups and commentators reacted strongly against the decision. Not only were the judges appearing to reward states for non-cooperation, they had also concluded that opening an investigation into potential crimes suffered by thousands of Afghan victims would not be in the interests of justice, but would raise their expectations only for these to be dashed once the investigation inevitably faltered.[6] Such reasoning was labelled 'appalling', while some scholars predicted the court's demise for having so blatantly welded judicial decision-making with realpolitik.[7] Still others argued that the decision 'conflates and supplants the "interests of justice" with the narrow institutional "interests of the Court"', an

---

[3] Ibid., para. 95.

[4] *Situation in the Islamic Republic of Afghanistan* (Concurring and Separate Opinion of Judge Antoine Kesia-Mbe Mindua) ICC-02/17-33-Anx-Corr, 7 June 2019, para. 48.

[5] Ibid., paras. 95–96.

[6] Gabor Rona, 'More on What's Wrong with the ICC's Decision on Afghanistan', Opinio Juris blog, 15 April 2019, available at: http://opiniojuris.org/2019/04/15/more-on-whats-wrong-with-the-iccs-decision-on-afghanistan/; Kevin Jon Heller, 'One Word for the PTC on the Interests of Justice: Taliban', Opinio Juris blog, 13 April 2019, available at: http://opiniojuris.org/2019/04/13/one-word-for-the-ptc-on-the-interests-of-justice-taliban/.

[7] Heller, 'One World for the PTC'; Sergey Vasiliev, 'Not Just Another "Crisis": Could the Blocking of the Afghanistan Investigation Spell the End of the ICC? (Part 1)', EJIL Talk! Blog, 19 April 2019, available at: www.ejiltalk.org/not-just-another-crisis-could-the-blocking-of-the-afghanistan-investigation-spell-the-end-of-the-icc-part-i/.

180 ICC LEGAL ARGUMENTATION: MESO-MANAGEMENT

effect which has already been traced throughout Chapters 3 and 4 of this book.

Yet the scholarly response to the court's budgetary and management constraints fell short of outright condemnation. Jacobs suggested that the judges had 'transformed themselves into the financial comptrollers of the budget of the OTP' by balancing valid legal reasoning with 'extra-legal, management considerations' and 'confus[ing] their role as managers of the legal proceedings with a role of managers of the funds of the Court'.[8] The animus for such criticism, though, was less the reliance on budgeting and management as such, and more the improper context in which it had surfaced, namely the decision to authorise or deny an investigation under article 15 of the Statute. In fact, beyond this and similar proceedings, practitioners and scholars alike continued to welcome the court's preoccupation with effectiveness and optimal performance, as also seen in previous chapters.

Most commentators agreed that even if judges should not take account of such factors, 'there is no reason why cooperation or budgetary constraints should not be additional factors in the Prosecutor's consideration'.[9] The OTP confirmed as much in its 2019–2021 Strategic Plan, which states that 'while the Office acts in full independence and impartiality and strictly within the legal parameters of the Rome Statute, its operating environment is impacted by the surrounding political reality'.[10] Judges, too, may take account of wider political and economic factors in other areas of their work, both judicial and administrative, as when authorising the participation of victims in court proceedings or devising judicial best practices.[11] Moreover, few scholars rejected outright the

[8] Dov Jacobs, 'ICC Pre-Trial Chamber rejects OTP request to open an investigation in Afghanistan: Some preliminary thoughts on an ultra vires decision', Spreading the Jam blog, 12 April 2019, available at: https://dovjacobs.com/2019/04/12/icc-pre-trial-chamber-rejects-otp-request-to-open-an-investigation-in-afghanistan-some-preliminary-thoughts-on-an-ultra-vires-decision/.

[9] Dapo Akande and Talita de Souza Dias, 'The ICC Pre-Trial Chamber Decision on the Situation in Afghanistan: A Few Thoughts on the Interests of Justice', EJIL Talk! Blog, 18 April 2019, available at: www.ejiltalk.org/the-icc-pre-trial-chamber-decision-on-the-situation-in-afghanistan-a-few-thoughts-on-the-interests-of-justice/. See also Christian de Vos, 'No ICC Investigation in Afghanistan: A Bad Decision with Big Implications', International Justice Monitor, 15 April 2019, available at: www.ijmonitor.org/2019/04/no-icc-investigation-in-afghanistan-a-bad-decision-with-big-implications/.

[10] Strategic Plan 2019–2021, Office of the Prosecutor, 17 July 2019, para. 8b.

[11] Such reasoning was on display in the Ntaganda case, where, in deciding how many common legal representatives to appoint to represent victims, Pre-Trial Chamber II rejected the request to appoint six for reasons including victims' diverging views on the

5.1 AN APPALLING DECISION

dilemma the court confronted: the judges had attempted, if unsuccessfully, to contemplate the 'hard choices that the ICC must start to make about efficiency and resource allocation'.[12] Hence, to reject the Afghanistan decision was by no means to reject the seemingly valid and urgent managerial concerns underpinning it.

This vignette illustrates several important dynamics informing this chapter. In the Afghanistan decision, the court pointed to what scholars have called extra-legal or non-legal factors but also to managerial ones: a concern for the proper allocation of the court's financial and human resources, organisational sustainability, and potential mismanagement. They also acknowledged the difficulties and tensions confronting the court as it sought to make its effects known in the world. The judges admitted to being caught within certain dilemmas: the difficulty of reconciling the court's legal mandate with the complex political environment in which such legal mandate is to be carried out, or the problem of relying upon victims' interests to authorise an investigation, only for that same justification to later undermine the effort to realise those interests. The PTC's reliance upon managerial rationales came also as a response to such intractable issues, and was for the judges (even if for no one else) the most appropriate means of overcoming a difficult situation. It may also have been the managerial hens of the preceding two decades finally coming home to roost.

This chapter looks to these dynamics both inside and outside the courtroom of the International Criminal Court (ICC) to examine the role that management rationales and practices play in responding to the kinds of legal dilemmas raised in the Afghanistan decision and elsewhere. In previous chapters, I showed how management does not only exist as an *ex post* set of ideas, tools, and processes to respond to the court's external and internal challenges in problem-solving mode. It also produces that which it names – the challenges of co-operation, outreach, workload, and performance. In this chapter, I move from the expert's general professional engagement with management to their engagements with management during legal argumentation, or when attempting to deal with certain argumentative dilemmas. At the operational level, these

---

point and the 'financial implications of having up to six legal representatives ... who would be paid from the Court's legal aid budget', *The Prosecutor v. Ntaganda* (Decision Concerning the Organisation of Common Legal Representation of Victims) ICC-01/04-02/06-160 (2 December 2013) para. 24.

[12] De Vos, 'No ICC Investigation in Afghanistan'.

182   ICC LEGAL ARGUMENTATION: MESO-MANAGEMENT

dilemmas are established patterns of justification familiar to the ICC expert, such as the tensions between law and politics, dependence and independence, and suspects and victims, to name a few. Since such patterns structure the ICC expert's engagements, management rationales and tools are always already invoked within these argumentative milieux. This chapter considers the work management does within such milieux.

I begin first by mapping the various patterns of justification or dyads that frame argumentation within international criminal law (ICL) in broad terms. These patterns have been well traced by Koskenniemi in the context of international law, and by Simpson, Robinson, and others in ICL specifically. After this summary, I then consider the work done by management rationales and tools to confront, respond to, and displace the seemingly intractable argumentative moves that make up ICL. Indeed, it is the last of these dynamics – displacement – that most accurately captures the work of management vis-à-vis such dilemmas. Management frequently works as a professional response to displace or escape from the ICC's recurring dilemmas. The *deployment of* management more accurately reads as a *flight to* management, appealing both because of its constraining and liberating effects on the expert who engages it. Constraining because the expert can point to the seemingly inherent 'realities' of resources, planning, and accountability as justification for their actions and decisions; liberatory because it momentarily frees the expert from judgments arising from the court's irresolvable tensions.[13] The chapter therefore reveals the professional invocation of management within the ICC's argumentative dilemmas and why it has proven so resilient and attractive.

5.2   The ICC's Argumentative Dilemmas

Management is not deployed in a vacuum. As seen in the previous chapters, there are various historical and institutional forces and factors informing the turn to management as a response to institutional 'challenges'. But the situatedness of management also extends to the points at which management is invoked within ongoing legal debates. This is no simple task. Ongoing debates about the politicisation of the court or the difficulties of state co-operation are seemingly intractable. They also form

---

[13] These effects have already been acknowledged by the Co-Investigating Judges at the Extraordinary Chambers in the Courts of Cambodia, see Introduction, Axiom 2.

5.2 THE ICC'S ARGUMENTATIVE DILEMMAS   183

the basis of the argumentative dilemmas that experts struggle over.[14] How best to deal with the problems of politicisation or non-cooperation is a debate that will be framed according to well-worn trenches of legal argument. How to set the appropriate scope for an investigation, that is, who to include and who to exclude, becomes a pattern of arguments around law and politicisation. How to ensure a complementary system of international criminal justice entails a setting of the appropriate balance between the authority of the international community and state sovereignty. Even what kind of justice is meted out by the court becomes a debate about the more or less defence-oriented, more or less victim-focused basis for ICC-style justice. These well-trodden paths of legal argument are briefly examined in this section to distinguish the specific background tensions against which management is invoked and deployed.

Martti Koskenniemi posited a way of conceiving of international law's substantive indeterminacy under conditions of formal determinacy. International law's unsteady location between politics on one side and morality on the other has left it susceptible to arguments flowing from each of these two poles. On one side, law's concreteness is affirmed as against its more utopian, moral claims. On the other, law's normative value is affirmed as against the apology of mere state power. The result is that any given position or legal doctrine is simultaneously susceptible to the critique that it is both apology for state power and therefore not constraining on state action in any meaningful way, as well as utopian and therefore not sufficiently grounded in the concrete behaviour of states.

As Koskenniemi explains through his detailed elaboration of international legal doctrines (sovereignty, sources, custom, and so on), neither apologetic nor utopian justifications are capable of truly winning out over the other since one always contains its opposite. Likewise, '[r]-econciliation is impossible' as any such doctrine which purports to strike a balance between these poles 'will reveal themselves as either incoherent or making a silent preference'.[15] The upshot is that 'doctrine is forced to

---

[14] I refrain from calling this structural indeterminacy but understand it as an indeterminacy resulting from consistent international legal work both informed by and informing dyadic patterns of argument, see Duncan Kennedy, 'A Left Phenomenological Alternative to the Hart/Kelsen Theory of Legal Interpretation' in Duncan Kennedy, *Legal Reasoning: Collected Essays* (Davies Group Publishers 2008) 157.

[15] Martti Koskenniemi, *From Apology to Utopia: The Structure of International Legal Argument* (Reissued with a new epilogue, Cambridge University Press 2005) 65. See

maintain itself in constant movement from emphasising concreteness to emphasising normativity and vice-versa without being able to establish itself permanently in either position'.[16]

Koskenniemi's analysis or mechanism has been taken up in various areas of international law to help shed light on different patterns of justification.[17] In international criminal law, a comparable exercise was conducted by Darryl Robinson in his map of the field's 'inescapable dyads'.[18] Robinson posits a similar set of dynamics in the institutional setting of the ICC to those traced by Koskenniemi. These dyads revolve around the familiar dialectic of apologist and utopian arguments. Utopian arguments at the ICC resemble those posited by Koskenniemi as unmoored from the everyday behaviour of states. But they also extend to the arguments that claim the ICC as an independent institution on the international plane, a body whose authority derives from the 'international community'. Apologist arguments are those which appear to offer little in the way of normative constraint on state power but also those which position the ICC as dependent upon states for its existence and functioning, and whose authority derives from the will of states parties.

These and related dilemmas seem to structure ICC expert engagements, making the dilemmas paradoxically predictable and unending.[19] As noted by Kendall, 'scholarship on international criminal law and human rights continues to inhabit a spectrum between these poles of triumph and scepticism, moving between a "utopian" cosmopolitan vision of law and an "apologist" deference to state sovereignty'.[20] Hence, despite significant efforts towards overcoming these perceived

---

similarly, David Kennedy, *International Legal Structures* (Nomos Verlagsgesellchaft 1987).

[16] Koskenniemi, 'From Apology to Utopia' 65.

[17] See recently, Ntina Tzouvala, *Capitalism as Civilisation: A History of International Law* (Cambridge University Press 2020).

[18] Darryl Robinson, 'Inescapable Dyads: Why the International Criminal Court Cannot Win' (2015) 28 *Leiden Journal of International Law* 323–347.

[19] Simpson offers an alternative set of structuring tensions that power ICL, including law/politics, cosmopolitan/local, individual responsibility/collective guilt, history/justice, and justice/show trials, see Gerry Simpson, *Law, War and Crime: War Crimes, Trials and the Reinvention of International Law* (Wiley 2007), 1.

[20] Sara Kendall, 'Beyond the Restorative Turn: The Limits of Legal Humanitarianism' in Christian De Vos, Sara Kendall and Carsten Stahn (eds.), *Contested Justice: The Politics and Practice of International Criminal Court Interventions* (Cambridge University Press 2017) 352–376, at 355.

5.3 MANAGEMENT AND THE ARGUMENTATIVE DILEMMAS 185

tensions, often through legal or policy innovations, '[t]he main points of contention have remained more or less the same'.[21]

An example of one such effort at reconciliation is to find, as Stahn does, a balance of idealism and realism in the 'interplay between "international", "domestic", and "local" responses to conflict'.[22] Yet this only reiterates or restates the apology/utopia dialectic in different terms, one which would still require a confrontation with dyads of authority and sovereignty, cosmopolitanism and localism. As Simpson reminds us, '[w]ar crimes law is a field of repetition and recurrence. What repeats and recurs are unresolved arguments about the shape and fate of retributive justice in the international order'.[23] The following section orients management in relation to these argumentative dilemmas.

5.3 ... Always Already: Management and the Argumentative Dilemmas

From the previous discussion, it follows that management can only ever be invoked in context (a context which, as we have seen, management also helps produce). The context within which management is invoked are the parameters of ICC discourse which frame expert interpretation and decision-making. Management may be reached to in an open field when it comes to its deployment as an organisational response, as seen in Chapter 4. But in the context of legal debates, the terrain of argument is much more settled, and management gets invoked in the context of the ICC's argumentative dilemmas.

Scholars have yet to broach the phenomenon of management as it appears in such dilemmas. Yet there are some hints as to its possible function, not least for the professional consciousness of the ICC expert who must daily engage with these dilemmas. Robinson ends his foundational article by listing the various strategies which can and have been proffered by ICC experts to overcome its argumentative dilemmas. These include efforts to find the 'just right' balance between two poles, improve transparency and deliberation, and allow the 'right' argument to win

---

[21] Kendall, 'Beyond the Restorative Turn' 355; See also Caroline Fehl, 'Explaining the International Criminal Court: A Practice Test for Rationalist and Constructivist Approaches' (2004) 10 *European Journal of International Relations* 357–394.

[22] Carsten Stahn, 'Between "Faith" and "Facts": By What Standards Should We Assess International Criminal Justice?' (2012) 25 *Leiden Journal of International Law* 251–282, at 251.

[23] Simpson, 'Law, War and Crime' 4.

186   ICC LEGAL ARGUMENTATION: MESO-MANAGEMENT

out.[24] Among these strategies is the attempt to come up with a new 'framework of evaluation' that could somehow balance certain values.[25] Robinson is not optimistic that such a general formula would be capable of offering the right 'vocabulary and methods of measurement' to so fundamentally recalibrate the court's dilemmas.[26]

Nevertheless, Robinson's notion of an alternative evaluative framework is salient for thinking about the role of management. Without offering any neat corollary, the management rationales and practices which have erupted during the court's attempts to deal with problems of politicisation, complementarity, non-cooperation, and victim participation have offered ICC experts just such a vocabulary. They have deferred critiques flowing from the court's inability to resolve such dilemmas and often displaced them entirely. From the perspective of the ICC expert, management offers a sense of resolution, both by attributing solutions to seemingly inherent realities and by delaying critique to an unspecified future point in time. These dynamics of escape, constraint, and liberation are traced in the following sections detailing various argumentative dilemmas that management has often been applied to.

Before considering these dilemmas in detail, it is worth clarifying that whatever role management plays in offering a sense of resolution for the ICC expert, this in no way corresponds to management's actual resolution thereof. In fact, whether management rationales and practices can overcome the ICC's argumentative dilemmas is highly debatable. As Robinson forewarns, any new framework of evaluation would be just as 'amenable to apologia-utopia critiques' as the last.[27] Yet as this chapter reveals, management's power rarely lies in doing what it promises, and the following sections are not designed to empirically prove or disprove management's success or failure in this regard.

Another counter to the interpretation offered in this chapter is that ICC experts are savvy enough not to think management could ever resolve the court's problems outright. This is implicit in the mechanics of a dyad, which sees any argument as susceptible to its opposite. Davis offers this point directly when arguing that 'attempts to provide normative guidance to prosecutors on how to navigate [prosecutorial] discretion', themselves susceptible to critiques of politicisation, 'have inevitably

---

[24] Robinson, 'Inescapable Dyads' 344.
[25] Ibid., 331.
[26] Ibid., 344.
[27] Ibid., 331.

5.3 MANAGEMENT AND THE ARGUMENTATIVE DILEMMAS   187

failed to placate critics', referring explicitly to the inadequate solutions of the OTP's numerous policy papers and strategic plans.[28] Yet management's power is not that it provides a permanent stop to all criticism. Rather, it offers a set of rationales and tools with which to confront the court's dilemmas, as a new plane of critique, one that temporarily sidelines the dilemma. Davis himself engages in such displacement when arguing about 'macro managerial considerations' and the 'budgetary and resource limitations' as realities the prosecutor must necessarily 'work within'.[29]

In response to these positions, the following sections intend to show that management's power lies in its ability to defer consideration of the argumentative dilemmas that make up ICC legal argumentation. This is no minor achievement. The flight to management not only momentarily halts the argumentative dilemma by seeming to resolve it, it also allows the machinery to remain intact and go partially unchallenged under the promise of future improvement and optimisation. Its promise is captured in the reformist sensibility that 'its never too late ... it might take time ... its just a matter of chipping away, chipping away'.[30] This is a somewhat irresistible professional stance at a time when the ICC appears to be under attack from all sides.[31] In the last instance, it is a stance that many more ICC experts than the pre-trial judges in the Afghanistan decision have adopted, including those who led the critique of that same decision. I now trace these dynamics to show the power of the flight to management as an escape from the problems of doing global justice.

5.3.1 The Authority of Sources: Voluntarism versus Idealism

A first area of argumentation in which management rationales and tools feature is in relation to the range of source materials relied upon by ICC

---

[28] Cale Davis, 'Challenges in Charge Selection: Considerations Informing the Number of Charges and Cumulative Charging Practices' in Xabier Agirre Aranburu et al. (eds.), *Quality Control in Criminal Investigation* (Torkel Opsahl Academic EPublisher 2020) 703–734, at 704.

[29] Ibid., 726.

[30] Samaria Muhammad, 'Reimagining the ICC: Exploring Practitioners' Perspectives on the Effectiveness of the International Criminal Court' (2021) 21 *International Criminal Law Review* 126–153, at 149.

[31] This desire to become unstuck from the argumentative dilemmas is partly explained by a professional faith in the project, see David Koller, 'The Faith of the International Criminal Lawyer' (2013) 40 *NYU Journal of International Law & Policy* 1019–1069.

experts. The debate over which materials are to be regarded as authoritative, and where those materials derive their authority from within the ICC, is a significant one. When determining whether a particular rule exists for the court to apply, judges are instructed to follow its applicable law as laid down in article 21 of the Statute. Article 21 identifies, 'in the first place' the Statute and the court's core legal texts, namely the Elements of Crimes and Rules of Procedure and Evidence (RPE). Other applicable treaties, principles, and rules of international law and international humanitarian law are treated as secondary sources, while general principles of law from national legal systems offer a third layer of materials 'failing that'. Customary law has also proven a vital source for establishing the existence of rules of international criminal law, both at the ICC and previously in the jurisprudence of the ad hoc tribunals.

Although these sources largely reflect those relied upon in other international criminal tribunals, they nonetheless bear marks of structural ambiguity around the basis for their authority. To simplify, this ambiguity is frequently represented as a division between those who locate the authority of such sources in the voluntary will of states, and those ascribing their authority to certain values in the name of the international community. Article 21 of the Statute exhibits both sides of this dyad: it refers to the Statute and other treaties and principles of international law as consented to by states, while also signalling to the importance of human rights in the application and interpretation of these sources in article 21(3). Indeed, despite dogged attempts to ground the existence of certain norms in the will of states in keeping with the voluntarist argument, the court has frequently looked to non-voluntarist or normative arguments in seeking to identify and interpret norms of international criminal law. In the Gaddafi admissibility decision, Pre-Trial Chamber X considered a challenge to its admissibility by Saif Gaddafi on the grounds that, inter alia, a 2015 amnesty law had been applied to him for potential crimes committed in Libya. In determining that such a law (and related amnesty laws) would not be in accordance with international law, the court cited article 21(3) of the Statute, pointing to the 'strong, growing, universal tendency that grave and systematic human rights violations ... are not subject to amnesties or pardons under international law'.[32]

---

[32] *The Prosecutor v. Saif Al-Islam Gaddafi* (Decision on the 'Admissibility Challenge by Dr. Saif Al-Islam Gadafi pursuant to Articles 17(1)(c), 19 and 20(3) of the Rome Statute') ICC-01/11-01/11-662 (5 April 2019) para. 61.

5.3 MANAGEMENT AND THE ARGUMENTATIVE DILEMMAS 189

In a more recent case, the ICC Appeals Chamber considered whether Jordan's failure to arrest and surrender then-president of Sudan, Omar Al Bashir, when on Jordanian territory, constituted non-compliance with Jordan's statutory obligations, given Sudan's status as a non-party to the Rome Statute. Among other arguments, the court found that an 'international tribunal' acting in the name of 'the international community as a whole' is capable of removing the immunity of heads of states not party to the Statute.[33] The court argued that the non-existence of Bashir's immunity sufficed to remove any conflict between the provisions of the Statute and wider international law that might have prevented Jordan from complying with its co-operation obligations with the court. Yet that argument, too, relied upon the status of the international community, rather than state consent. In such examples, consent is never the sole basis for legal authority.

Nonetheless, and in keeping with the instability of the dyad, such arguments have been challenged as too normatively detached from the behaviour of states, and therefore 'utopian'. The court's reasoning in the Jordan appeals decision has been critiqued on such grounds, with scholars asking how the 'international community' is capable of removing immunities via an international tribunal when states themselves do not possess such power.[34] Such a counter-argument again reverts to the will of states as the basis for international law's authority. Without proceeding along such lines of argument ad infintum, these debates over the authoritative basis of ICL portend to the same dynamics of apology and utopia identified by Koskenniemi.

It is often within the context of identifying and interpreting sources that management rationales and practices are invoked by ICC experts. This takes place both at the level of sources themselves and at the level of arguing about the authoritative basis of such sources. Evidently, management practices are not part of the ICC's applicable law. Nevertheless,

---

[33] *The Prosecutor v. Omar Hassan Ahmad Al-Bashir* (Judgment in the Jordan Referral re Al-Bashir Appeal) ICC-02/05-01/09-397 (6 May 2019) para. 115. See Dov Jacobs, 'You have just entered Narnia: ICC Appeals Chamber adopts the worst possible solution on immunities in the Bashir case', Spreading the Jam blog, 6 May 2019.

[34] Paola Gaeta, 'Does President Al Bashir Enjoy Immunity from Arrest?' (2009) 7 *Journal of International Criminal Justice* 315–322. Nouwen raised a similar argument against the Special Court for Sierra Leone when it relied on the distinction between national and international courts to justify the removal of Charles Taylor's immunity, see Sarah M.H. Nouwen, 'The Special Court for Sierra Leone and the Immunity of Taylor: The *Arrest Warrant* Case Continued' (2005) 18 *Leiden Journal of International Law* 645–669, at 651.

190 ICC LEGAL ARGUMENTATION: MESO-MANAGEMENT

strategic plans, audits, performance indicators, and best practice manuals have all been cited to interpret the court's legal framework or persuade judges as to a certain course of action. In 2010, in *Prosecutor v. Bemba*, the Registry was asked to provide courtroom technology enabling the use of a case map in the presentation of evidence. The Registry agreed to do so via a prosecutor's laptop but cautioned that while 'today it is the installation of a case map that is requested, tomorrow it may be yet another case preparation tool', which might overburden the Registry's resources.[35] The Registry then cites the 'detailed audit of its *eCourt* systems' to argue against offering further technology support, given the auditor's findings that the court's technology was complex and 'supporting resources [were] already extremely stretched'.[36]

Management practices have also been used as arguments against other parties, including their authors. In the Kenya situation, the legal representative of victims (LRVs) requested that the court review the prosecutor's decision to cease active investigations into the situation after the cases against Uhuru Kenyatta and William Ruto collapsed. While largely placing the blame for the collapsed cases on the Kenyan government, the LRV also describes how the OTP raised expectations among victims which it was unable to fulfil. They cite to the OTP's 2012–2015 Strategic Plan and the strategic goal of increasing opportunities for consulting with victims and to thoroughly investigating sexual and gender-based crimes before demonstrating the 'vast gap' between such goals and the OTP's practices in the Kenya situation.[37] As early as 2008, the prosecutor was also relying on risk-based arguments and its risk-related strategic goals, to argue for an extension of non-disclosure relating to victim and witness information.[38]

Judges have also relied on management ideas and practices in their reasoning, in a prelude to their more explicit appearance in the Afghanistan decision. In *Prosecutor v. Gbagbo and Blé Goudé*, the Appeals Chamber relied on 'the need for more efficient and expeditious

---

[35] *The Prosecutor v. Jean-Pierre Bemba Gombo* (Registry Submission on the Installation of Additional Software in the Courtrooms and Certain Modalities of Evidence Presentation) ICC-01/05-01/08-920 (1 October 2010) para. 5.

[36] Ibid.

[37] *Situation in the Republic of Kenya* (Victims' Request for Review of Prosecution's Decision to Cease Active Investigation) ICC-01/09-154 (3 August 2015) paras. 102 and 174.

[38] *The Prosecutor v. Jean-Pierre Bemba Gombo* (Prosecutor's Submission of Additional Information Demonstrating the Existence of an Objectively Identifiable Risk) ICC-01/05-01/08-122-Redacted (26 September 2008) para. 11.

5.3 MANAGEMENT AND THE ARGUMENTATIVE DILEMMAS 191

proceedings' as the context for interpreting rule 68 of the RPE on the admission of prior-recorded testimony.[39] It cited relevant reports of the ICC's Study Group on Governance, an OTP Strategic Plan, the court's performance indicators, and the Chambers Practice Manual in support of this interpretation. The court also explicitly notes that such an interpretation is in keeping with the Statute and the RPE's 'object and purpose' in accordance with the Vienna Convention on the Law of Treaties.[40]

Finally, as McDermott shows, judges have also consistently relied upon their own best practices, collated in a Chambers Practice Manual, to guide their decisions. While discussed in more detail later, the manual was expressly developed 'as an alternative to the Court's formal processes for the amendment of RPE' and implicitly as an alternative to the politicisation of such amendments.[41] Although judges have accepted its non-binding status, successive benches have stuck closely to its guidance, as when deciding upon appropriate victim participation procedures.[42] More consequentially, the manual has served as the basis for many decisions relating to confirmation of charges such as the non-necessity of live witnesses appearing at confirmation proceedings. Given the efficiency rationale underpinning the manual, it becomes less surprising that a later judicial bench would seek to rely on a similar set of rationales to interpret the 'interests of justice' criteria in the Afghanistan decision. Indeed, scholars largely welcomed these judicial turns for their pragmatism.[43]

In these examples, management is relied upon as an alternative set of sources to those in the ICC's applicable law. Moreover, the authoritative basis for their invocation seeks to strike a balance between a purely

---

[39] *The Prosecutor v. Laurent Gbagbo and Charles Blé Goudé* (Consolidated Response to Laurent Gbagbo's and Charles Blé Goudé's Appeals Against the 'Decision on the Prosecutor's Application to Introduce Prior Recorded Testimony under Rules 68(2)(b) and 68(3)') ICC-02/11-01/15-644 (1 August 2016) para. 14.

[40] Ibid.

[41] Yvonne McDermott, 'The International Criminal Court's Chambers Practice Manual: Towards a Return to Judicial Law Making in International Criminal Procedure?' (2017) 15 *Journal of International Criminal Justice* 873–904, at 886 and 904.

[42] *The Prosecutor v. Al Hassan Ag Abdoul Aziz Ag Mohamed Ag Mahmoud* (Decision on the Procedure for the Admission of Victims to Participate in Proceedings for the Purposes of Trial) ICC-01/12-01/18-661 (12 March 2020) para. 21.

[43] Kai Ambos, *Treatise on International Criminal Law, Volume III: International Criminal Procedure* (Oxford University Press 2016) 661; Philipp Ambach, 'A Look Towards the Future – The ICC and "Lessons Learnt"' in Carsten Stahn (ed.), *The Law and Practice of the International Criminal Court* (Oxford University Press 2015) 1277–1295, at 1285–1287.

192   ICC LEGAL ARGUMENTATION: MESO-MANAGEMENT

voluntarist and purely normative rationale. Management's authority rests upon the importance of values such as judicial efficiency and court effectiveness, and the posture of pragmatism adopted across various international institutions. In this regard, it need not find its authority in state will, nor need states have explicitly consented to the introduction of certain management practices. Nonetheless, such values largely represent the desire of some states parties that the court be cost-effective and accountable to its donors, and many practices, including performance indicators and strategic plans, have received the explicit approval of states through the Assembly of States Parties. Yet the combination of both bases of authority nonetheless leaves management sources open to attack as either utopian – from where do these values of efficiency and pragmatism derive? – or apologist, as representative of state interests and merely a new vector for state power.

Despite this inability to overcome the sources dilemma, management is nonetheless deployed by scholars, practitioners, and judges to identify norms, interpret legal sources, and advance judicial outcomes. By appearing to overcome some of the limits of voluntarism and idealism, management temporarily closes off discussions about the instability of the ICC's sources and their authority. As seen in previous chapters, but reiterated here at the level of legal argument, management's seemingly apolitical and pragmatic quality gives ICC experts the freedom to bracket and deflate attacks from both a voluntarist and utopian standpoint. This is a first example of the flight to management.

5.3.2 Situation/Case Selection: Law versus Politics

The second dyad to which management is introduced concerns the binary of law and politics. I illustrate this binary through the controversial topic of situation and case selection. It is commonplace, particularly among ICC prosecutors, to assert that the International Criminal Court is 'a court of law not of politics'.[44] Nonetheless, such a separation cannot

---

[44] 'Building a Future on Peace and Justice', Address by Mr Luis Moreno-Ocampo, Nuremberg, 24–25 June 2007, 6, available at: www.icc-cpi.int/sites/default/files/NR/rdon lyres/4E466EDB-2B38-4BAF-AF5F-005461711149/143825/LMO_nuremberg_ 20070625_English.pdf. Ocampo's successor, Fatou Bensouda, echoed the law-not-politics argument repeatedly. See Statement of the Prosecutor of the International Criminal Court, Fatou Bensouda: 'The Public Deserves to know the Truth about the ICC's Jurisdiction over Palestine', 2 September 2014, available at: www.icc-cpi.int/news/state ment-prosecutor-international-criminal-court-fatou-bensouda-public-deserves-know-

5.3 MANAGEMENT AND THE ARGUMENTATIVE DILEMMAS 193

only be asserted but must be upheld, reiterated, and managed at an everyday institutional level. In efforts to uphold such a separation, politics is routinely equated with a crude realism characterised by self-interested states bumping into one another, as if on a billiard table.[45] According to this image, politics is an inherent condition of the world in which the ICC finds itself, and thus frequently risks impinging upon court activity, whether in displays of state non-cooperation or efforts to instrumentalise the court for state gain. Indeed, the court's Afghanistan decision was read by some as an example of politicisation in the form of state-driven reasoning.[46] Politics is here an 'abnormality or defect' of a liberal ideology that otherwise ascribes paramount importance to the rule of law.[47] The only way to establish a 'just and meaningful international criminal order', then, is 'by cleansing that system of political influence'.[48] Hence, being an ICC prosecutor, who is guided only by legal considerations when deciding where to investigate and to what extent, is the fullest expression of liberal legalism.

And yet law itself turns out to be insufficient as an explanation or justification of investigations, notably practices of situation and case selection. As Davis acknowledges, the OTP 'finds itself – remarkably – unable to use legal explanations to satisfactorily explain its selection of cases'.[49] Pues has also stated that 'the legality of decisions is crucial but not sufficient'.[50] Years of deploying the court's objective legal frameworks in deciding where and who to investigate has not dampened the critique that most of these investigations concern Africa and Africans.[51] Claiming to be a 'court of law' appears not to have dented allegations of an anti-African bias and has even reinforced the suspicion that the legal

---

truth; David Pilling, 'Fatou Bensouda: "It's about the Law. It's not about Power"', *Financial Times*, 25 September 2020, available at: www.ft.com/content/beeb8dba-ce3c-4a33-b319-3fcff0916736.

[45] Hedley Bull, *The Anarchical Society: A Study of Order in World Politics* (Springer 1977).

[46] Vasiliev, 'Not Just Another "Crisis"'.

[47] Simpson, 'War, Law and Crime' 11.

[48] Ibid., 20.

[49] Cale Davis, 'Political Considerations in Prosecutorial Discretion at the International Criminal Court' (2015) 15 *International Criminal Law Review* 170–189, at 178.

[50] Anni Pues, *Prosecutorial Discretion at the International Criminal Court* (Hart Publishing 2020) 20.

[51] Christopher Gevers, 'Africa and International Criminal Law' in Kevin Jon Heller et al. (eds.), *Oxford Handbook of International Criminal Law* (Oxford University Press 2020) 154–194.

194   ICC LEGAL ARGUMENTATION: MESO-MANAGEMENT

infrastructure is itself a mere fig leaf for neo-colonialism. Hence, as Pues elaborates, legality has been supplemented by legitimacy as a wider standard, meaning purely 'legal' decisions may nonetheless remain illegitimate in the eyes of interested parties, including victims, practitioners, and NGOs.[52]

Consequently, determining the scope of an investigation on the basis of law alone, without considering wider political forces, is a potentially utopian move, in which claims are too unmoored from the reality of state power. Other factors besides the scope of charges or parties targeted, including resources, planning, and political relations with the situation country must also be taken into account. To ignore these factors would be to engage in 'legalism', a negative term recently used to critique the OTP's selection practices. Clark sees legalism, or the effort to remain above politics, as largely responsible for the court's 'political and philosophical separateness' from domestic situations.[53] Such distant modalities of justice have led to significant problems including a failure to understand domestic interests and struggles, and the obstruction of peace efforts and alternative justice mechanisms.

The response to legalism for Clark and others is clear, also when placed within the law/politics argumentative frame. For Clark, legalism in the form of distant justice should be countered by a policy of being 'politically savvier' and engaging in a more 'prudent politics'.[54] This may require, in his analysis, greater reliance upon context-specific expertise, and the input and direction of local actors including civil society. A politically savvy OTP would be aware of the domestic interests, motivations, and constraints that inform states' interactions with the court, in order to prevent the court from being used or abused for political ends, and to ensure the most appropriate justice-seeking efforts are fostered by both national and international actors. As De Vos summarises it, the court must adopt an approach that 'underscores the primacy of process, and of political context'.[55]

---

[52] Pues, 'Prosecutorial Discretion' 20.

[53] Phil Clark, Distant Justice: The Impact of the International Criminal Court on African Politics (Cambridge University Press 2018) 34.

[54] Ibid., 99 and 309–312.

[55] Christian de Vos, Complementarity, Catalysts, Compliance: The International Criminal Court in Uganda, Kenya, and the Democratic Republic of Congo (Cambridge University Press 2020) 12.

5.3 MANAGEMENT AND THE ARGUMENTATIVE DILEMMAS   195

Within this 'prudent' approach, however, lies the kernel of justification that prompted the turn to legalism in the first place. To take account of political forces and factors in the selection of situations and cases would arguably reinscribe the political. These criticisms are very familiar, not only in the ICC but also throughout the history of war crimes trials.[56] It was immediate post-war political alliances that may have precipitated the prosecution of high-ranking Nazi officials like Goring and Ribbentrop at the International Military Tribunal at Nuremberg. But it was that same politics that gave rise to 'victor's justice', with all the critiques of selectivity and double standards that followed.[57] The 'new tribunalism' of the post-Cold War era raised similar critiques when Carla del Ponte, then ICTY chief prosecutor, stated that the tribunal was not intended for prosecuting events such as the NATO bombing of Serbia in 1999 but only the various internal parties to the Yugoslavia conflict.[58]

The ICC is susceptible to the same critiques, despite its potentially universal reach. When identifying its first situation countries, the OTP worked closely with the Ugandan government to arrange a self-referral of the conflict between the government and rebel forces, including the Lord's Resistance Army (LRA). However, the self-referral was limited to investigating only alleged LRA crimes, excluding any scrutiny of similar government acts. The self-referral lodged by the Democratic Republic of the Congo (DRC) in the same year was criticised for similar reasons. In such instrumental uses of the self-referral mechanism, 'the referring state is motivated by its own political interests and thus the court is being used as a tool'.[59] Accordingly, and despite calls for the court to 'get closer' to situation countries, thereby counteracting overt legalism, the OTP has already been criticised for being 'too close' to the territorial state out of both domestic and institutional self-interest.[60] It seems hardly constraining on Ugandan or Congolese state forces for

---

[56] Simpson, 'War, Law and Crime'; Barrie Sander, *Doing Justice to History: Confronting the Past in International Criminal Courts* (Oxford University Press 2021).

[57] Kevin Jon Heller and Gerry Simpson (eds.), *The Hidden Histories of War Crimes Trials* (Oxford University Press 2013).

[58] Thomas Skouteris, 'The New Tribunalism: Strategies of (De)Legitimation in the Era of International Adjudication' (1999) 17 *Finnish Yearbook of International Law* 307–356.

[59] Robinson, 'Inescapable Dyads' 327.

[60] William Schabas, 'Victor's Justice: Selecting "Situations" at the International Criminal Court' (2010) 32 *John Marshall Law Review* 535–552. See also Richard Clements, 'Near, Far, Wherever You Are: Distance and Proximity in International Criminal Law' (2021) 32 *European Journal of International Law* 327–350.

196 ICC LEGAL ARGUMENTATION: MESO-MANAGEMENT

the court to investigate only rebel atrocities, thereby leaving such efforts open to the charge of politicisation.[61]

Nonetheless, legalism is no less free from politicisation. To remain detached from domestic situations may equally leave it susceptible to the charge of imposing its own frames and narratives, as well as assumptions and interests, upon situation countries in ways that resemble the neo-colonial dynamics alleged by some African states parties and several critical scholars. As this counterpoint makes clear, '[e]ach choice is open to controversy and claims of politicisation'.[62] Seeking to avoid this risk by relying on actors other than the OTP for situation selection, notably the UN Security Council under its referral powers, has not mitigated claims of politicisation, given the position of its five permanent members and the experience of referring both Libya and Sudan.[63]

In each trigger mechanism, the argumentative dilemma over law and politics is reproduced, as well as in the preliminary stages of situation and case selection/prioritisation by the OTP. How do management rationales and practices get invoked to manage or ostensibly resolve debates around politicisation arising in such instances? This takes place at various stages, during case selection and in the OTP's long-term planning. The OTP's sensitivity to claims of acting either too legalistically or too politically has led it to deem certain realities or constraints as 'inherent' to its activities, thereby diminishing its own responsibility for decisions on situation/case selection and prioritisation. This is visible in the Office's 2019 Policy Paper on Case Selection and Prioritisation. The policy paper acknowledges that despite operating under the court's legal framework and within political settings, there is a need to prioritise situations and cases in order 'to manage the overall workload of the Office in the light of its overall basic size and capacity constraints'.[64] This reliance on organisational and resourcing limits partly externalises responsibility by turning such arguments into external 'fact' and placing them beyond contention as either legalistic or political arguments. These facts become relevant at several stages of the selection process, as noted in the policy paper:

---

[61] William Burke-White, 'Complementarity in Practice: The International Criminal Court as Part of a System of Multi-Level Global Governance in the Democratic Republic of Congo' (2005) 18 *Leiden Journal of International Law* 557–590, at 567.

[62] Robinson, 'Inescapable Dyads' 333.

[63] Gabriel Lentner, *The UN Security Council and the International Criminal Court: The Referral Mechanism in Theory and Practice* (Edward Elgar 2018).

[64] Policy Paper on Case Selection and Prioritisation, Office of the Prosecutor, 15 September 2016, paras. 11–12.

5.3 MANAGEMENT AND THE ARGUMENTATIVE DILEMMAS   197

> Given that the resources available to the Office limit the number of cases it can investigate and prosecute at any one time, the Case Selection Document will also inform decisions on the appropriate number of cases to be pursued within any given situation, whether to proceed with further cases, or whether to end its involvement in a situation.[65]

Decisions are determined by neither law nor politics but a reality lying beyond prosecutorial control. However real those constraints may be, such a displacement of responsibility requires a considerable legal, policy, and managerial infrastructure to sustain. Much of this work is conducted via the OTP sections, notably the Situation Analysis Section and Strategic Analysis Section within the Jurisdiction, Cooperation and Complementarity Division. During preliminary examinations, the Situation Analysis Section 'carries out all preliminary examinations and provides advice on complex matters of fact and law regarding jurisdiction, admissibility, and the interests of justice'.[66] This work is intended to 'lay the foundation for cooperation' and contribute to situation analysis for 'successful investigations' once officially opened by the prosecutor.[67] The OTP Basic Size model illustrates this section's role in rendering management concerns as fact.

The Basic Size model was compiled by the OTP and submitted to the ASP in 2015. The model is designed to map and allocate the resources available to the OTP in order to adequately account for fluctuating workload and other variables over the course of several years. It relies upon calculations of budgetary changes but also increasing levels of court activity to produce a 'basic size' for the Office and its sections to operate. For preliminary examination activities, in which the Situation Analysis Section has a central role, this translates to five legal analysts, five context analysts, and five crime analysts.[68] With the plotting of these resource needs along a 'projected timeline', the framework of evaluation shifts from whether decisions are sufficiently legal or politically savvy to pragmatic calculations intended to balance supply and demand. This is made possible by the reification of 'overall workload' and 'capacity constraints' which cannot be contested at the level of everyday decision-making. Claims of legalism or politicisation are displaced by the need to optimally

---

[65] Ibid.

[66] Report of the Court on the Basic Size of the Office of the Prosecutor, International Criminal Court, ICC-ASP/14/21, 17 September 2015, Annex 2, para. 7.

[67] Ibid.

[68] Ibid., para. 6.

198   ICC LEGAL ARGUMENTATION: MESO-MANAGEMENT

allocate financial and human capital within a situation of resource scarcity.[69]

These managerial concerns about resource allocation and long-term planning also rearrange the framework and temporality of evaluation. International Criminal Court experts not only concern themselves with the procedures, practicalities, and risks of engaging with the territorial state but also with devising techniques to match institutional supply with 'external' demand. These include developing 'standard template responses to communications' to save time, and introducing software to streamline the management of disclosed evidence. These efforts are not only seen as peripheral but as crucial to the functioning of the court's core mandate.[70] Likewise, as the language of projections and hypotheses suggests, the model defers judgment of its consequences to the future as officials take stock. Criticism can (and should) be deferred until personnel, structural, and planning improvements have been realised.

This does not mean that the problem goes away. In fact, the OTP's early adoption of a 'focused approach' to investigations created new problems which had to be dealt with and which, ultimately, were used as the prompt for updating the prosecutor's approach. After a decade of activity, the emphasis shifted towards conducting 'open-ended and in-depth investigations with the aim of being trial-ready as early as possible in the judicial proceedings'.[71] This open-ended approach may have sought to temper some of the more trenchant criticisms that the OTP was taking too narrow a position too early in their investigations, potentially foreclosing alternative narratives and charging priorities. Nonetheless, the shift from focused to open-ended investigations did not resolve the law/politics dilemma for the OTP.

Beyond the preliminary stages, management also deflects law/politics arguments later in the prosecution cycle. The OTP Strategic Plan for 2012–2015 explicitly mentions organisational constraints as the basis for

---

[69] On scarcity as a socially constructed mode of governance, see Michel Foucault, '18 January 1978', in *Security, Territory, Population: Lectures at the Collège de France 1977–1978* (Michel Snellart ed., Palgrave Macmillan 2009) 29–53. On scarcity as 'regulatory device' see Ute Tellmann, 'Catastrophic Populations and the Fear of the Future: Malthus and the Genealogy of Liberal Economy' (2013) 30 *Theory, Culture and Society* 135–155.

[70] Report on Programme Performance of the International Criminal Court for the Year 2004, ICC-ASP/4/13, 6 September 2005, para. 20, available at: https://asp.icc-cpi.int/iccdocs/asp_docs/library/asp/ICC-ASP-4-13_English.pdf.

[71] Office of the Prosecutor Strategic Plan June 2012–2015, 11 October 2013, para. 4.

5.3 MANAGEMENT AND THE ARGUMENTATIVE DILEMMAS   199

rearranging the OTP infrastructure for investigations. This primarily consisted of restructuring the Jurisdiction, Cooperation, and Complementarity Division and introducing a 'revised cooperation model' to manage global partners.[72] The Office also adopted 'multiple case hypotheses throughout the investigation' to 'further strengthen decision-making'.[73] Since the evaluative frame was no longer whether the OTP was overly legalistic or political in its decision-making, it could focus on matching resources to needs. This entailed 'strengthening information management systems', implementing 'lessons learnt', working more closely with the Office of Internal Audit, and building the skill level and efficiency of the Joint Teams who decided the scope and narratives of investigation.[74] This last measure later evolved into the concept of Integrated Teams headed by a senior trial lawyer and based on a horizontal arrangement of both operational and managerial staff.[75] Such measures ostensibly operated beyond the law/politics dyad, while also offsetting critique to a distant yet optimised future.

Lastly, for many ICC experts, the law/politics dilemma is captured by dynamics of prosecutorial discretion. As Pues states, 'in the exercise of prosecutorial discretion at the ICC, the demands of the rule of law, and of a neutral, impartial and independent institution, meet with the task of managing highly politicised cases and practical constraints'.[76] Managing here becomes the operative word in an attempted reconciliation of the law/politics dilemma. In advocating a 'principled and purposeful exercise of the Prosecutor's power', Pues locates the solution partly in 'accountability mechanisms for prosecutorial discretion' and greater transparency based on 'accessibility, self-justification and encouragement'.[77] Again, greater management, including enhanced self-management of prosecutorial staff, offers an escape from the limits of legalism and the intractability of politics. Kotecha reaches a similar conclusion in proposing

---

[72] Ibid., para. 4(c).
[73] Ibid., para. 4(a).
[74] Ibid., para. 26.
[75] War Crimes Research Office, Investigative Management, Strategies, and Techniques of the International Criminal Court's Office of the Prosecutor, Washington College of Law, American University, October 2012, 19; Response of the ICC Office of the Prosecutor to an Outcome Report and Recommendations from Open Society Justice Initiative and Amsterdam Law School, 8 May 2020, 6, available at: www.icc-cpi.int/itemsDocuments/200508-OTP-response-to-OSJI-UoA-report.pdf.
[76] Pues, 'Prosecutorial Discretion' 21.
[77] Ibid., 23 and 28.

200 ICC LEGAL ARGUMENTATION: MESO-MANAGEMENT

benchmarking and indicators as techniques for regulating the OTP's selection practices. Indicators relating to the timing of investigations, as well as to their perceived fairness, would, in Kotecha's view, allow 'the progress of all preliminary examinations [to] be readily compared, contrasted and ultimately judged'.[78] Performance indicators at the preliminary examination stage would also enhance transparency and allow performance to be more visibly assessed by a range of interested parties, from states to victim groups.

More than Pues, Kotecha's invocation of indicators points to the temporal attractions of management. It permits 'a way forward' that 'would improve' the consistency of OTP activities. This set of proposals implies a stay of the ongoing dilemma between law/politics in prosecutorial decision-making until the point at which the results of such indicators and the data they have collected can be parsed. Only then would such results 'ultimately' permit judgment.[79] Without intending to foreclose critique, Kotecha and Pues separately rebuild a faith in the ICC's ability to overcome law/politics critiques by delaying judgment of those aspects of the court's mandate most susceptible to it.

To close this section, various aspects of ICC practice and scholarship display a flight to management as a promised escape from the intractable problems of legalism and politics. For their parts, the OTP Strategic Plan and Basic Size model attempt to escape the dilemma through the language of court capacity, human resource allocation, and management structures. For scholars, the answer to the dilemma lies in greater oversight and measurement of prosecutorial discretion to ostensibly minimise the possibility of legalism and politics. Yet the problem is not entirely overcome. Rather, concerns about legalism and politicisation are merely delayed. This is achieved by both the constraining force of arguments about the inherent reality of workload and capacity constraints, and the liberating experience of having apparently closed the argument until some future point.

5.3.3 Complementarity: National versus International

Another animating dilemma for the ICC is the tension between the international and the national, particularly in the context of debates

---

[78] Birju Kotecha, 'The International Criminal Court's Selectivity and Procedural Justice' (2020) 18 *Journal of International Criminal Justice* 107–139, at 137.
[79] Ibid., 137.

5.3 MANAGEMENT AND THE ARGUMENTATIVE DILEMMAS 201

about complementarity.[80] The national/international dilemma is not specific to international criminal justice and offers a backdrop to debates in other sub-fields of international law.[81] In international criminal law, however, the tension runs throughout not only the legal frameworks but also the field's institutions. Institutions such as the ICC are routinely established to administer *international* justice in predominantly *national* settings. Simpson sums up the 'history of war crimes law . . . as a series of undulations between recourse to the administration of local justice and grand gestures towards the international rule of law'.[82]

Within this dyad, the international stands in for the authority of a universal, cosmopolitan community of states, while the domestic offers a local, parochial space grounded in the authority of state sovereignty. These representations of the international and the domestic are the basis for an argumentative tension that the ICC has had to deal with since its early jurisprudence. Much like the law/politics dyad, the national/international dyad posits not only a binary but an implicit hierarchy. The cosmopolitan vision of the ICC is often represented as a 'high point' and 'end-point' of international criminal justice where the domestic finally cedes to the international.[83] The court emerges as the embodiment of an 'international community' driven by the values of peace, justice, and the rule of law, as opposed to the local authority of state sovereignty. As Simpson states, '[w]hat we might expect from all of this is a highly robust piece of international justice machinery, reaching its tentacles into states and prising war criminals away to The Hague to face exemplary international justice, alongside an absolute commitment to the international over the parochial'.[84]

However, the domestic or the parochial can never be entirely expunged. The sovereignty of the nation state remains a basis for international law's authority, and even the ICC cannot deny that its cosmopolitanism 'remain[s] largely reliant on particular instantiations of [sovereignty]', including the existence of functional national criminal justice systems and co-operative governments.[85] Moreover, in practice, the international and the domestic were never so easily separated. The

---

[80] This dilemma overlaps with the dependence/independence dyad in the following section.
[81] For further details, see Koskenniemi, 'From Apology to Utopia' 300.
[82] Simpson, 'War, Law and Crime' 33.
[83] Ibid., 34.
[84] Ibid.
[85] Ibid., 46.

preamble to the Rome Statute captures the tension in affirming that 'the most serious crimes of concern to the international community as a whole must not go unpunished and that their effective prosecution must be ensured by taking measures at the national level and by enhancing international cooperation'. The international was less the renunciation of the domestic than its reiteration on a different plane. The Obama State Department lawyer Harold Koh captures that reiteration when asserting that 'international criminal justice, and accountability for those responsible for atrocities, is in our [US] national security interests as well as in our humanitarian interests'.[86] Cosmopolitan and parochial interests cannot be so easily disentangled, meaning that despite their allure, invocations of the international remain susceptible to the critique of utopianism, which sees international authority as too detached from the behaviour of states.

Nonetheless, as Koh's statement also reveals, the alternative move which sees greater reliance upon domestic settings to further the cause of anti-impunity may also deflate the normatively constraining force of international criminal law. For international law to mean something, it has to signify more than the sum of state interests. For Koh, this becomes humanitarian interests, but this appears a somewhat unstable reconciliation of international utopianism and national apologism. If the humanitarian is the operative part, then this set of values may be insufficiently connected to the reality of state will – a set of particular moral values; if interests are the focus, then these may be too connected to particular sovereign agendas to constrain the state in any meaningful way. The ICC 'style of justice' thus 'represent[s] a perpetual accommodation of the hopes for cosmopolitan justice and the requirements of sovereignty and particularity'.[87]

The ICC's complementarity regime foregrounds the argumentative patterns about the international and the domestic. The ICC is defined as a court of last resort, meaning that the lion's share of responsibility for prosecuting international crimes lies with national jurisdictions. Article 17 of the Statute confirms this position in stating that 'the court shall determine that a case is inadmissible where ... the case is being investigated or prosecuted by a State which has jurisdiction over it'. Yet

---

[86] Harold Hongju Koh, 'International Criminal Justice 5.0', Remarks at the Vera Institute of Justice, New York City, 8 November 2012, available at: www.state.gov/s/l/releases/remarks/200957.htm.

[87] Simpson, 'War, Law and Crime' 44.

5.3 MANAGEMENT AND THE ARGUMENTATIVE DILEMMAS 203

competence is not entirely removed to the domestic, rather the court has complementary jurisdiction over such crimes. This is captured in the remainder of the provision, which states that such a case will be inadmissible before the court 'unless the State is unwilling or unable genuinely to carry out the investigation or prosecution'. The court may rule cases admissible before the ICC due to the reluctance or inability of states to prosecute. This complementarity regime has been described as a 'cornerstone' of the Rome Statute system.[88]

Article 17 appears to strike a balance between the international and the domestic, providing a division of labour between the ICC and national courts. Newton captures this balancing act:

> The creation of a vertical level of prosecutorial authority that operates as a permanent backdrop to the horizontal relations between sovereign states in large part depended on a delineated mechanism for prioritising jurisdiction while simultaneously preserving sovereign rights and serving the ends of justice.[89]

Yet questions proving the difficulty of such a balance began to emerge early in the court's jurisprudence. Article 17 did not offer guidance on the scope of the cases that would have to be compared. In response, Pre-Trial Chamber I offered a strict reading by delimiting domestic proceedings according to 'both the person and the conduct which is the subject of the case before the court'.[90] Although narrow in scope, this had the effect of respecting the charging decisions of national investigators rather than judging these against those of the ICC prosecutor. Arguably, the domestic was given greater leeway in relation to international authority.

Yet the domestic could not be given complete freedom lest the court's international character be undermined. The same jurisprudence therefore also confirmed the ultimate authority of the international over the domestic. Hence, despite the leeway given to domestic courts, the ICC remains the final arbiter of what constitutes 'same conduct' in assessing admissibility. It is also able to decide whether a state is unwilling or unable genuinely to investigate or prosecute. Consequently, the international here is given preference over the domestic in ways that do not

---

[88] *The Prosecutor v. Joseph Kony* (Decision on the Admissibility of the Case under Article 19 (1) of the Statute) ICC-02/04-01/05-377 (10 March 2009) para. 34.

[89] Michael Newton, 'A Synthesis of Community-Based Justice and Complementarity' in De Vos, Kendall and Stahn, 'Contested Justice' 122–144, at 125.

[90] *The Prosecutor v. Thomas Lubanga Dyilo* (Decision on the Prosecutor's Application for a Warrant of Arrest, Article 58) ICC-01/04-01/06-1 (10 February 2006) para. 31.

204   ICC LEGAL ARGUMENTATION: MESO-MANAGEMENT

resolve the tension between international authority and national sovereignty. Nouwen demonstrates the growth of the implicit hierarchy of international over domestic in the court's complementarity jurisprudence. The extent of the court's authority to determine unwillingness and inability has, in her words, 'weakened the idea that states have a domestic responsibility' and given rise to a 'pro-ICC ideology' that 'international courts mete out better justice than domestic systems'.[91] Even within a system of 'last resort', then, the court continues to confront the tensions of enacting the international even as it continues to rely upon the domestic in various ways.

Efforts to overcome the national/international dilemma have frequently relied on management. The most prominent of these appears in the ICC's development of the concept of 'positive complementarity'. Whereas 'negative' complementarity entails a division of labour to confer exclusive responsibility on either the ICC or domestic courts, positive complementarity conceives of the relationship between the international and the domestic differently. According to Burke-White, it is founded upon a notion of 'multi-level global governance', wherein

> international and domestic governance structures (such as courts) are engaged in deeply interconnected governance efforts where each level of authority continuously cross-influences, reshapes, and ideally reinforces activities at other levels of governance.[92]

Blurring the boundaries of the international and the domestic, positive complementarity involves fostering connections between their respective institutions in order to 'catalyze change at the national level' and allow domestic institutions to take on greater responsibility for anti-impunity efforts.[93] An OTP Policy Paper captures the scope of activities made possible by a positive approach to complementarity:

> the Office can report on its monitoring activities, send in-country missions, request information on [national] proceedings, hold consultations with national authorities as well as with intergovernmental and non-governmental organisations, participate in awareness-raising activities

---

[91] Sarah Nouwen, *Complementarity in the Line of Fire: The Catalysing Effect of the International Criminal Court in Uganda and Sudan* (Cambridge University Press 2013) 13.

[92] Burke-White, 'Complementarity in Practice' 558.

[93] Ibid; William Burke-White, 'Proactive Complementarity: The International Criminal Court and National Courts in the Rome System of International Justice' (2008) 49 *Harvard International Law Journal* 53–108.

5.3 MANAGEMENT AND THE ARGUMENTATIVE DILEMMAS 205

on the ICC, exchange lessons learned and best practices to support domestic investigative and prosecutorial strategies, and assist relevant stakeholders to identify pending impunity gaps and the scope for possible remedial measures.

The policy was hailed as a positive development for the court, particularly in light of its low number of ongoing cases. For Burke-White, 'a policy of proactive complementarity offers the potential to transform the Court's statutory limitations into advantages that would allow it to maximise its impact on impunity'.[94] The concept thus appeared to reconcile the international and the domestic by rendering international justice more sustainable through domestic action.[95] Burke-White's justification for a more 'proactive' policy of complementarity, however, also drew upon the wider context of organisational and budgetary constraints. He claimed that the policy 'ha[d] the potential to make a considerable contribution toward ending impunity without the need for a substantial expansion of the Court's resources and capacity'.[96] This cost-effective measure would help 'shift burdens back to states' and rebalance the international and domestic.[97]

Burke-White's budgetary justification is consistent with the history of complementarity itself. Complementarity was understood by Stahn and others as a 'forum for managerial interaction' in which various international and local actors are bound together.[98] Sekhon describes complementarity as 'a bureaucratic mechanism for managing international relations between the ICC and national criminal justice bureaucracies'.[99] It has therefore acquired significance, first and foremost, as a resource allocation tool. By the time positive complementarity was enshrined in official court policy, it was thus being described as both a legal and a managerial achievement. It began life in the 2009 Prosecutorial Strategy, and later morphed into a strategic goal in the OTP's 2016–2018 Strategic Plan. The aim was 'to develop with partners a coordinated investigative and prosecutorial strategy to close the impunity gap'[100] to ensure 'the most efficient sharing of competencies between the national and

---

[94] Burke-White, 'Proactive Complementarity' 67–68.
[95] Stahn, 'Between Faith and Facts' 275.
[96] Burke-White, 'Proactive Complementarity' 67.
[97] Ibid., 67.
[98] Nouwen, 'Line of Fire' 17 (footnote 21).
[99] Nirej Sekhon, 'Complementarity and Post-Coloniality' (2013) 27 *Emory International Law Review* 799–828, at 826.
[100] OTP Strategic Plan 2019, para. 5(d).

206   ICC LEGAL ARGUMENTATION: MESO-MANAGEMENT

international level'.[101] Burke-White explicitly adopted the same rationale, arguing that 'by mobilising such external resource networks, the Court may be able to leverage its own limited resources in an efficient manner to support broader judicial development by other actors in the international system'.[102] Already the constrained context within which the court operated was being used as a blueprint to efficiently resolve the tensions between the international and the domestic.

Positive complementarity sought to overcome this dilemma through resource allocation techniques. Like previous attempts at international administration, techniques of capacity-building, technical assistance, and domestic reform were not intended to overcome the domestic but to extend the international gaze into 'the interior life of the state'.[103] As with the rationale for the administration of the mandate territories after World War I, positive complementarity allowed a more robust domestic infrastructure to come into being, affirming rather than negating state sovereignty.[104] The ICC's first prosecutor, Luis Moreno-Ocampo, promoted '[n]ational efforts to build expertise and capacities' and later a Justice Rapid Response Mechanism was established to allow criminal justice professionals to be deployed domestically to 'support compliance with and effective enforcement of international criminal justice'.[105]

In addition to this allocation of human resources, a restructuring of state authorities would also help optimise relations between the court and domestic systems. The 2009–2012 Prosecutorial Strategy foregrounded the training of 'politicians, negotiators, the police, the military and finance departments alike' in the 'role and decisions' of the court.[106] A focal point of managerial restructuring was the reform of domestic justice sectors in order to institutionalise state-donor funding networks. One of these was the 2007 Priority Action Plan, which entrenched

---

[101] De Vos, 'Complementarity, Catalysts, Compliance' 45.

[102] Burke-White, 'Proactive Complementarity' 95.

[103] Antony Anghie, 'Colonialism and the Birth of International Institutions: Sovereignty, Economy, and the Mandate System of the League of Nations' (2002) 34 *NYU Journal of International Law & Policy* 513–634, at 546. See chapter 2.3.2.

[104] Ibid., 548.

[105] High Representative of the European Union for Foreign Affairs and Security Policy, Joint Staff Working Document on Advancing the Principle of Complementarity, 31 March 2013, SWD(2013)26 final, 16.

[106] Prosecutorial Strategy 2009–2012, Office of the Prosecutor, 1 February 2010, para. 72.

5.3 MANAGEMENT AND THE ARGUMENTATIVE DILEMMAS   207

existing funding streams for rule-of-law programming in the DRC by prioritising funding for joint government and external donor projects.[107] A similar mechanism was established in Uganda.[108] Whatever their achievements, these efforts demonstrate the court's willingness to apply techniques for the efficient allocation of resources in an effort to resolve the international/national dilemma.

Positive complementarity tools have achieved the support of NGOs and commentators. One palpable reason for this lies in its capacity to replace the somewhat intractable discussions of the international/domestic divide with more technical and narrow discussions about where to best allocate resources. The discussion has now taken on a technical quality by focusing on 'a careful balancing of resource allocation to maximise the Court's impact' and employing the most 'cost-effective means of encouraging national prosecutions'.[109] How far to intervene at a domestic level is thus influenced by court resources. Burke-White promoted such thinking in arguing that '[e]ven if more resource-intensive efforts, such as the provision of considerable national judiciaries, were to enable domestic prosecution, they would likely divert sufficient resources away from the court's core mission to make them inadvisable'.[110]

Discussions about the efficient allocation of financial and human resources have dampened judgment of the court's inability to resolve the international/domestic tension by taking these resources as part of an objective reality to be baked into institutional calculations. Already the complementarity principle held the possibility of shifting the discussion from who has competence over cases to where institutional resources should be allocated. The positive approach to complementarity operationalised this discursive shift through its focus on techniques of resource allocation between the international and the domestic. Management again proves attractive for appearing to settle the debate between international and domestic authority, even as it reinscribes those debates at the level of institutional governance.

---

[107] Open Society Foundation, 'Putting Complementarity into Practice: Domestic Justice for International Crimes in DRC, Uganda, and Kenya' (2011) 45; Milli Lake, 'Organising Hypocrisy: Providing Legal Accountability for Human Rights Violations in Areas of Limited Statehood' (2014) 58 *International Studies Quarterly* 515–526, at 520.

[108] Open Society Foundation, 'Putting Complementarity into Practice' 10.

[109] Burke-White, 'Proactive Complementarity' 85.

[110] Ibid., 85.

5.3.4 Co-operation: Dependence versus Independence

As well as positing its cosmopolitanism as against national parochialism, the ICC also lays claim to a certain independence from states despite its reliance upon them. This gives rise to a further dilemma over the independence of the court under conditions of state dependence. The ICC is an international organisation upon which legal personality is conferred by article 4 of its Statute. The court is independent from the will of its members, and the independence and impartiality of ICC judges and prosecutors both reflect and reinforce this principle. However, the dependence/independence dilemma emerges from the fact that the court does not operate in a vacuum and must depend upon states parties and others to function. Aside from its status as a treaty-based organisation funded by states, the court is, paradoxically, only independent under conditions of dependence. Only as a result of state co-operation with court requests to arrest and surrender suspects will the OTP be able to pursue its independent investigative mandate, and the judges their impartial judicial function.

Simpson frames the problem of an independent court depending on states as characteristic of international criminal law as a field. Since ICL 'seeks to create a vertical regime on a horizontal plane', the apparatus with which the Rome Statute system is furnished rubs up against its establishment by states.[111] The result, as Antonio Cassese famously described it, is a 'giant with no arms and legs'.[112] The dilemma becomes intractable since any move towards a more independent regime will be susceptible to the critique that it does not sufficiently account for the consent-based, horizontal system within which the ICC is established, while any effort to enshrine a more consensual system will defy the vertical, normative mandate that the ICC sought to establish in the first place.

The Statute's state co-operation regime captures the binary. The very terms of Part 9 of the Statute on international co-operation indicate the presence of such a dilemma. Article 86 notes that 'states parties shall, in accordance with the provisions of this Statute, co-operate fully with the Court in its investigation and prosecution of crimes within the jurisdiction of the Court'. The interdiction 'shall', reflective of the ICC's vertical aspirations, comes into conflict with the reliance upon co-operation,

---

[111] Robinson, 'Inescapable Dyads' 332.
[112] Quoted ibid., 338.

5.3 MANAGEMENT AND THE ARGUMENTATIVE DILEMMAS 209

rather than the more coercive means associated with a purely vertical system. The tension is even more acute when considering co-operation requests under article 89. As article 89(1) demonstrates, the tension remains palpable, given the expectation that 'States Parties, shall, in accordance with the provisions of this Part and the procedure under their national law, comply with requests for arrest and surrender'. The OTP has also sought a balance in this regard, recognising that it is 'dependent on other actors for co-operation to carry out its work' and should therefore 'enter into arrangements or agreements to facilitate cooperation'.[113]

The dilemma has been confronted directly in a string of cases dealing with the co-operation obligations of states parties in relation to the surrender of nationals of non-states parties. These hinged upon the multiple instances over many years of state party non-compliance with co-operation requests issued by the court in relation to the surrender of former Sudanese president, Omar Al Bashir. One act in that saga is used to demonstrate the difficulty of escaping the dependence/independence dichotomy, namely the DRC's failure to arrest Al Bashir in 2014.

The ICC's jurisdiction over atrocities in Sudan was triggered in 2005 after a referral by the UN Security Council (UNSC). By UNSC resolution 1593, the Security Council referred the situation in Sudan and decided that 'the Government of Sudan and all the parties to the conflict in Darfur, shall cooperate fully' with the court.[114] After the ICC prosecutor opened an investigation into the situation, an arrest warrant was requested against Al Bashir and granted soon after by the Pre-Trial Chamber. The Registry issued requests for co-operation to all ICC states parties in 2009 and 2010.

Despite the Security Council referral and the court's granting of an arrest warrant, Al Bashir travelled to several ICC states parties, which in turn refused to arrest and surrender him to the court. These states, which were also members of the African Union, were developing their own position on the question of whether a head of state should be immune

---

[113] Davis, 'Political Considerations' 173. Some efforts take this tension to its limit. Errol Mendes' proposal to 'make the burgeoning debt of Sudan a lever against crimes against humanity' drew on a 'financial carrot strategy to exert effective pressure on the Khartoum government', Errol Mendes, 'The Important Role of the IMF and External Creditors in Case of Arrest Warrants from the ICC – The Case of Sudan', OTP Guest Lecture Series (2009) 2–4.

[114] UNSC Res 1593 (31 March 2005) para. 2.

210 ICC LEGAL ARGUMENTATION: MESO-MANAGEMENT

from prosecution at the international level.[115] This ostensibly brought states' obligations into conflict – on one side their obligations to comply with ICC co-operation requests and arrest Al Bashir and on the other the potential obligation towards Sudan to uphold head-of-state immunity under international law. In such situations, article 98 permitted non-compliance with the co-operation request. The conflict came to a head in several cases requesting that such states be found non-compliant with their statutory obligations to arrest Al Bashir.

Proceedings were brought against non-complying states, including Malawi, Chad, South Africa, and Jordan. However, the arguments raised during proceedings against the DRC reveal most clearly the difficulty of escaping the dependence/independence dilemma. In the decision against Malawi in 2011, the Pre-Trial Chamber had found that it was required to comply with the co-operation request. This was despite Malawi's assertion that Al Bashir was entitled to head-of-state immunity under international law and that any request for co-operation would contravene article 98 of the Statute. The conflict posited by Malawi was resolved by the PTC's finding that a 'critical mass' had been reached for an exception to this customary rule of head-of-state immunity when sought by an international court, meaning that there was no longer a conflict for the purposes of article 98.[116]

In hearing a similar claim against the DRC in 2014, the PTC took a different route to the same conclusion that article 98 did not apply and that the DRC had to comply. Instead of looking to customary law, the PTC instead considered the status of the Security Council resolution referring Sudan to the court. Interpreting its terms in the context of the UN Charter, the PTC found that resolution 1593 implicitly waived any immunity Al Bashir enjoyed as head of state. According to the court,

---

[115] African Union Assembly Decision 264(XIII), Decision on the Abuse of the Principle of Universal Jurisdiction, Doc. Assembly/AU/11(XIII), Thirteenth Ordinary Session of the Assembly of the Union, 1–3 July 2009, para. 6, available at: https://au.int/sites/default/files/decisions/9560-assembly_en_1_3_july_2009_auc_thirteenth_ordinary_session_decisions_declarations_message_congratulations_motion_0.pdf. On the ICC-AU relationship, see Gino Naldi and Konstantinos Magliveras, 'The International Criminal Court and the African Union: A Problematic Relationship' in Charles Chernor Jalloh and Ilias Bantekas (eds.), *The International Criminal Court and Africa* (Oxford University Press 2017) 111–137.

[116] *The Prosecutor v. Omar Hassan Ahmad Al Bashir* (Decision Pursuant to Article 87(7) of the Rome Statute on the Failure by the Republic of Malawi to Comply with the Cooperation Requests Issued by the Court with respect to the Arrest and Surrender of Omar Hassan Ahmad Al Bashir) ICC-02/05-01/09-139 (12 December 2011) para. 42.

5.3 MANAGEMENT AND THE ARGUMENTATIVE DILEMMAS 211

'since immunities attached to Al Bashir are a procedural bar from prosecution before the Court, the co-operation envisaged in the Security Council resolution was meant to eliminate any impediment to the proceedings before the Court, including the lifting of immunities'.[117] This implicit waiver of consent thereby removed any conflict at the horizontal level between the DRC and Sudan. The real conflict therefore lay between the UN Security Council resolution and the African Union resolution confirming head-of-state immunity. The court resolved this tension by reaffirming the primacy of the UN Charter under international law and, thereby, the independence of the ICC framework as against states.

Despite this reasoning, it was still possible to question the basis of the authority under which the UN Security Council acted when referring Sudan to the ICC. Was it acting under the UN Charter, or article 13(b) of the Statute? If the Security Council was acting on the basis of article 13 (b), then it was again operating under the Statute's consent-based system. The argument was that if states cannot relinquish immunities of non-states parties on their own in line with the horizontal nature of the international legal order, then how could the Security Council do so when acting under the same authority?[118] After all, the independence of the court derives from, and thus depends upon, what states have bequeathed to it via the Statute. The implicit waiver argument, which asserts a vertical relationship vis-à-vis states, relies upon a rationale that can be challenged by reference to the horizontal system of states.

The DRC decision illustrates the difficulty of establishing the court's vertical relationship to states parties even while remaining constrained by a system that does not entirely allow for such a possibility.[119] Where the independence of the ICC (and the UN Security Council) is asserted to such a degree, it is susceptible to the criticism that it defies the consensual nature of the system, while relying only upon consent as a basis for action would undermine the independent status of the international system. The OTP has acknowledged as much in its 2006 Strategic Plan. Here, it recognises that 'while independent, the Court also has an *interdependent*

---

[117] *The Prosecutor v. Omar Hassan Ahmad Al Bashir* (Decision on the Cooperation of the Democratic Republic of the Congo regarding Omar Al Bashir's Arrest and Surrender to the Court) ICC-02/05-01/09-195 (9 April 2014) para. 29.

[118] Paola Gaeta, 'Does President Al Bashir Enjoy Immunity from Arrest?' (2009) 7 *Journal of International Criminal Justice* 315–322.

[119] *The Prosecutor v. Omar Hassan Ahmad Al-Bashir* (Judgment in the Jordan Referral re Al Bashir Appeal) ICC-02/05-01/09-397 (6 May 2019).

relationship with States, international organisations and civil society'.[120] Arrest and surrender is a 'particularly pressing issue of cooperation as without the support of States and international organisations in making arrests, there can be no trials'.[121]

Through such notions of interdependence, both the OTP and Registry have sought to minimise the dependence/independence dyad through a more managerial approach to state co-operation. While judges continue to issue decisions of non-compliance with its co-operation requests, other organs are engaged in network-building among domestic and international authorities, information-sharing, and the provision of technical expertise and best practices on arrest and surrender procedures. This includes the Registry, which has issued model surrender procedures and checklists for logistical tasks associated with successful arrests to increase the arrest and surrender rate.[122] The basis for these activities is the court's desire to promote understanding of its mandate and functions by 'reaching new audiences, while also ensuring sustained dialogue with States Parties and other stakeholders'.[123]

The shift occasioned by these additional activities is consistent with other efforts to escape engrained argumentative tensions. By redescribing the problem of dependence as a problem of deficient domestic understanding and expertise, the court once again rearranges the framework for evaluation. The inherent problem of state dependence is supplanted by a problem of how to improve information-sharing, provision of training, and best practices. These measures can be taken regardless of states' willingness to co-operate with arrests and thereby shifts the markers for court success. The question is no longer how many arrests are successfully made but how many networks for co-operation the court has established, or with how many domestic authorities the court has shared its information and expertise. In such efforts, ICC experts rely heavily on management to manage collected data, chart progress through indicators, and establish strategies for co-operation.

In this discursive shift, judgment is both deferred and diffused. Goals instantiate a new process of data collection on the extent of information-

---

[120] Strategic Plan of the International Criminal Court, ICC-ASP/5/6, 4 August 2006, para. 8.
[121] Ibid.
[122] 'Arresting ICC Suspects at Large: Why It Matters, What the Court Does, What States Can Do', International Criminal Court, January 2019, 16, available at: www.icc-cpi.int/news/seminarBooks/bookletArrestsENG.pdf.
[123] Strategic Plan 2006, para. 10.

5.3 MANAGEMENT AND THE ARGUMENTATIVE DILEMMAS 213

sharing, training, and outreach. These will all require several rounds of statistical analysis and building of networks in order to permit further evaluation. Only after a picture emerges can the court's efforts towards managing state co-operation networks be assessed. Similarly, judgment is diffused. While the court remains responsible for improving co-operation, it is less susceptible to judgment for failure to secure arrests, which is a responsibility (and criticism) increasingly placed on states. The court is then left to focus on fostering the conditions for successful co-operation.

5.3.5 Victim Participation: Victims versus Suspects

Until now, many of the dilemmas comprising the court's argumentative terrain have centred on its relationship with states parties, whether as states on whose territory atrocities are committed or on whom the court must rely to arrest suspects. Yet argumentative dilemmas have also emerged between key players in the judicial process. The clearest of these is the relationship between suspects accused of international crimes on the one hand and victims of alleged atrocities on the other. Despite being hailed as a uniquely victim-centred institution, the ICC nonetheless remains a criminal tribunal dedicated to determining individual responsibility. This confrontation of parties emerges from the dyadic character of the court as both a victim-centred *and* a criminal tribunal. I map this final argumentative dilemma between victims and suspects before tracing management's part in that debate through the discourse of judicial expediency.

As with any criminal court, the ICC provides rights to those accused of international crimes, including the right to legal representation, a fair trial, and the presumption of innocence. Moreover, the Rome Statute enshrines principles of criminal law, including the *ne bis in idem* rule and the principle of *nullum crimen sine lege* (principle of legality), which also act as safeguards against double jeopardy and retroactivity of the law. The importance of upholding the rights of the accused is exemplified by article 22(2) of the Statute, which states that the definition of a crime 'shall be strictly construed' and that 'in case of ambiguity, the definition shall be interpreted in favour of the person being investigated, prosecuted, or convicted'. This presumption in favour of the defendant, alongside other protections, exhibits the suspect-oriented nature of ICC-style justice.

Despite these safeguards, the ICC is also the first permanent international court to enshrine victim participation and reparation awards in its statutory framework. Since its creation, this has been deemed a major institutional innovation and a considerable step towards international justice. Certain provisions lay out the contours of victims' status during proceedings. Under rule 85, victims are any 'natural persons who have suffered harm as a result of the commission of any crime within the jurisdiction of the Court'. Article 68(3) permits such victims' 'views and concerns' to be considered during the proceedings where their interests are affected. Beyond participation, article 75 establishes a regime for awarding reparations to victims 'including restitution, compensation and rehabilitation' and may 'determine the scope and extent of damage, loss and injury' suffered by victims in deciding to award reparations. A large body of jurisprudence and academic scholarship has arisen on the ICC's innovative victims regime.

The debate over how far to extend victim participation is a key site of this victim/suspect dilemma. From an expansive reading of victim participation, it is always possible to argue that however many victims are allowed to participate in proceedings, or however many are included in awards for reparations, others remain excluded. This is a point implied by Kendall and Nouwen as they seek to show how the ICC 'narrow[s] the pyramid' of victimhood.[124] Victimhood theoretically extends far beyond the parameters of international criminal justice to 'millions if not billions of people [who] have reason to consider themselves victims, individually or as part of a group'.[125] Yet ICC-designated victimhood, what Kendall and Nouwen call 'juridified victimhood ... is much narrower than that massive base'.[126] Narrowing ensues through multiple parameters, whether in excluding those not victims of the court's core crimes, those victims of core crimes outside the temporal, personal, or territorial scope of an investigation, or those victims of core crimes within the scope of an investigation who nonetheless may be unaware of the ICC or lacking in representation or resources.[127] From this perspective, it is always possible to argue that the range of victim participants, and indeed the category of victimhood itself, could always be more inclusive in line with a victim-oriented court.

---

[124] Sara Kendall and Sarah Nouwen, 'Representational Practices at the International Criminal Court: The Gap between Juridified and Abstract Victimhood' (2013) 76 *Law & Contemporary Problems* 235–262, at 241.

[125] Ibid.

[126] Ibid.

[127] Ibid., 244–246.

5.3 MANAGEMENT AND THE ARGUMENTATIVE DILEMMAS 215

Nevertheless, the victim-oriented approach is susceptible to the argument that such inclusion of victims may itself undermine the pursuit of justice, disadvantaging victims themselves in the long term. Moreover, it may undermine the accused's right to equality of arms.[128] It has been a long-standing critique of the court, primarily from defence counsel, that the court fails to uphold an equality of arms between the suspect and the prosecution, not least because victims' legal representatives frequently equate to a second prosecutor. Despite this failure, the suspect-oriented position continues to act as the opposing side of this argumentative tension surrounding the limits of victim inclusion. However heavily the court regulates victim participation, and however much the court provides guidance to prevent victims and victims counsel from creating an inequality of arms, victim participation is always susceptible to the argument that it does not sufficiently account for the rights of the accused within a criminal court setting. Yet, as we have seen, the opposite remains true at the same moment: were the rights of victims to participate and receive reparations to be limited, the victim-centrism of the court would be undermined.

Judges and scholars have sought to resolve the tension through alternative discourses. The most prominent of these is the discourse of fairness. The risk to fairness of including victims in the judicial process has been clearly laid out in an International Bar Association report of 2011. The report finds that 'there is a very real risk that, if not correctly managed, the participation of victims in the proceedings could negatively impact its fairness'.[129] The risk to fairness of including victims has often been discussed in these terms. However, fairness may also be open to the opposing argument, namely that there is a risk to the fairness of proceedings by *not* sufficiently giving voice to the victims and leaving the court to piece together an incomplete narrative of events. On its own, fairness is unable to resolve the tension between victims and suspects.

Interestingly, the flight to management that occurs within the victim participation debate emerged from ideas of judicial expediency. Judicial expediency arguments concern the need to uphold the administration of

---

[128] Haslam and Edmunds acknowledge a similar balancing act in relation to victims' legal representation, see Emily Haslam and Rod Edmunds, 'Whose Number Is It Anyway?: Common Legal Representation, Consultations and the "Statistical Victim"' (2017) 15 *Journal of International Criminal Justice* 931–952, at 934.

[129] International Bar Association, 'Enhancing Efficiency and Effectiveness of ICC Proceedings: A Work in Progress', January 2011, Executive Summary, 10.

216 ICC LEGAL ARGUMENTATION: MESO-MANAGEMENT

justice, not only its speed and expeditiousness but also court capacity. The discourse on expediency began to shift the ICC expert away from the victim/suspect dyad by contextualising it as an institutional problem. Whilst the tension between victims and suspects over participation could be conducted on the basis of principles such as justice, fairness, and so on, positioning judicial expediency as the context of the debate situated that tension within the confines of the court's procedural and institutional capabilities. Victim-oriented and suspect-oriented arguments could continue to be made but would have to account for the limitations of international trials.

Some ICC experts reinforced this discourse of expediency. Philipp Ambach, a senior ICC official, noted that '[t]rials in international criminal courts and tribunals for international crimes are inherently slow compared to national proceedings for ordinary crimes'.[130] Other limitations include the 'multiple crime sites ... amounts of witnesses per case ... thousands of pages of documentation ... [and] the high legal complexity of these proceedings', which mix adversarial and inquisitorial models of domestic criminal justice.[131] Ambach thus relies upon the court's constraints to describe judicial expediency as a necessary fact of institutional life.

These arguments have been increasingly relied upon as backdrop to the debate on victim participation. A 2014 expert panel posed a range of measures to 'save time and resources', including further regulating victim filings, 'the scope of questioning by their representatives', and the extent of their written submissions.[132] The panel recommended that the court adopt 'a realistic and economical view of the manner and scope of victims' participation' by upholding standards on knowledge of international criminal law and by merging offices relating to witness protection, victim participation, and reparations into a consolidated 'Victims Office'.[133] This preference for regulating and possibly limiting victim participation nonetheless remains subject to challenge.

---

[130] Philipp Ambach, 'The "Lessons Learnt" Process at the International Criminal Court – A Suitable Vehicle for Procedural Improvements?' (2016) 12 *Zeitschrift für Internationale Srafrechtsdogmatik* 854–867, at 854.

[131] Ibid.

[132] Expert Initiative on Promoting Effectiveness at the International Criminal Court, December 2014, para. 21, available at: https://asp.icc-cpi.int/sites/asp/files/asp_docs/ASP19/Ind_Exp_Initiative.pdf.

[133] Ibid., paras. 54 and 118.

5.3 MANAGEMENT AND THE ARGUMENTATIVE DILEMMAS 217

This is clear from the perspective of the accused but also from a more victim-oriented position. In its 2010 policy paper on victim participation, the OTP rejected 'resource-related arguments, such as the high number of victims, the costs involved or any other organisational problems' as a basis for limiting victim participation.[134] Such issues demanded 'practical solutions' and should 'never [constitute] a basis to oppose participation per se once the legal requirements for participation are met'.[135] Yet even this victim-oriented position slips into the same argumentative dilemma as before, revealing how judicial expediency itself was not enough to escape the dyad. Although the OTP rejects 'bureaucratic or resource-related arguments' as the basis for denying victim participation, it nonetheless acknowledges the need to analyse the 'requirements, timing and modalities' of victims' participation based on the Statute and relevant jurisprudence. Rather than rejecting expediency outright, the OTP deploys it in victims' favour, noting that victims can contribute to 'fair and efficient trials' and that 'the overall modalities [of victim engagement] should be consolidated to the largest extent possible in order to ensure certainty and consistency for victims themselves'.[136] Admission to victim status at least presupposes the streamlining of the process, even if this is justified as being in the interests of victims.[137]

If, like fairness, expediency has not offered an escape from the victim/suspect tension, then how have subsequent but similar ideas and tools of effectiveness, efficiency, and results-based reasoning been more effective? This transpired through an expanded managerial infrastructure within both the Registry and Chambers. As the primary administrative organ of the court, the Registry was tasked with responsibility for all 'non-judicial aspects of the administration and servicing of the Court'.[138] The Registry is charged with managing courtroom logistics, translation services, and the dissemination of court filings between parties.[139] Article 43(6) of the Statute also mandates the Registry to establish a Victims & Witnesses Unit, giving it an important role in the protection of victims and witnesses, and in processing victim applications to participate in proceedings. Under this last set of functions, the Registry infrastructure around

---

[134] Policy Paper on Victims' Participation, Office of the Prosecutor, April 2010, 5.
[135] Ibid., 5.
[136] Ibid., Executive Summary, 1.
[137] OTP Strategic Plan 2012, para. 21.
[138] Article 43(1) Rome Statute.
[139] Clements, 'Near, Far, Wherever You Are' 262.

218   ICC LEGAL ARGUMENTATION: MESO-MANAGEMENT

victims and witnesses has been shaped according to rationales of efficient management, court planning, and operational capacity.

In 2004, the Victims & Witnesses Unit created under the auspices of article 43 'established operational capacity to receive witnesses in The Hague' as well as other support networks including medical support.[140] In the same year, the court established a Victims Participation and Reparations Section (VPRS) to be housed within the Registry after a divisional restructuring exercise. Its tasks included establishing databases and forms to process victims' applications and establish links with NGOs, international organisations, and states to foster victims' access to court.[141] These structural achievements were rationalised as part of a 'detailed review of programme performance' with a focus on 'expected results'.[142] They were also analysed in light of the annual programme budget. These were the conditions under which the court's early victim architecture was created and subsequently evaluated.

A later example of the same phenomenon came after several years in operation. By then, the volume of victim applicants had increased dramatically, with the cases in the DRC and Uganda well underway. In 2008, in the *Kony et al.* case, the Registry filed 176 documents 'on issues pertaining, inter alia, to witness protection, victim participation and detention'.[143] Two hundred and seventy-two victim applications were processed in the case during the same period.[144] These statistics were interpreted as 'significant achievements', and the Registry emphasised their potential to increase through improved data collection and internal management.[145] In some cases, judges reached to resourcing rationales in order to engage directly with the victim/suspect dilemma over victim participation. In the *Mbarishumana* case, for example, judges decided not to allow 470 additional victims to participate in the proceedings due to a lack of resources.[146] This came after recognition of 'the need to

---

[140] Report on Programme Performance of the International Criminal Court for the Year 2004, ICC-ASP/4/13, 6 September 2005, para. 50.

[141] Ibid., para. 58.

[142] Ibid., para. 2.

[143] Report on Programme Performance of the International Criminal Court for the Year 2008, ICC-ASP/8/7, 6 May 2009, para. B(d)(i), available at: https://asp.icc-cpi.int/sites/asp/files/asp_docs/ASP8/ICC-ASP-8-7-ENG.pdf.

[144] Ibid., para. B(d)(iii).

[145] Ibid., para. 1.

[146] Kendall and Nouwen, 'Representational Practices' 246.

5.3 MANAGEMENT AND THE ARGUMENTATIVE DILEMMAS 219

maintain the balance between the rights and interests of victims on the one hand and the rights of the Defence on the other'.[147]

Beyond judicial expediency, concerns for efficient management of resources, personnel workflows, and data management permeated the wider institution. In the *Bemba* case, judges received over 1,300 applications to participate. '[C]reative procedural solutions' were deployed to ensure all applications were processed before November 2010, including use of a 'batch system' for assessing applications and enforcing deadlines.[148] Judicial methods were also supplemented with administrative adjustments, including a 'shorter application form' designed to 'minimise delay in judicial rulings'.[149] The form shrunk in size from seventeen to seven pages, and since then to one page.[150] The Chambers Practice Manual has formalised this one-page 'simplified standard form' to reduce the length of time that needs to be spent assessing victims' claims.[151] Application forms consisted of tick boxes to aid 'fluid data and statistical generation', and to allow algorithms to 'automatically assess application forms for admission'.[152] Staff were also rearranged to avoid the 'unsustainable' practice of 'redeploying interns and staff from other sections of the Registry'.[153] Expediency at the judicial level demanded that the dilemma over victim participation be assessed as an operational and workflow problem rather than one of inclusion and fairness.

Such an approach identified poor management as the problem, and better management as the solution. 'Varying types of application form and application process' are deemed responsible for a growing judicial workload.[154] A consolidated reporting system and database would resolve the issue. The focus on high numbers led the court to discourage the submission of participation forms despite the fact that it 'was technically still required to accept new participant applications'.[155] The

---

[147] *The Prosecutor v. Callixte Mbarushimana* (Decision Requesting the Parties to Submit Observations on 124 Applications for Victims' Participation in the Proceedings) ICC-01/04-01/10-265 (4 July 2011) 5.

[148] International Bar Association Report, 23.

[149] Ibid.

[150] Mikel Delagrange, 'The Path towards Greater Efficiency and Effectiveness in the Victim Application Processes of the International Criminal Court' (2018) 18 *International Criminal Law Review* 540–562, at 558.

[151] Chambers Practice Manual, Third Edition, International Criminal Court, May 2017, 25.

[152] Delagrange, 'Path towards Greater Efficiency' 559.

[153] International Bar Association Report, 23.

[154] Kendall, 'Beyond the Restorative Turn' 367.

[155] Ibid., 368.

Mbarushimana example also reveals the resourcing limitations of the victim participation regime. These management problems are partly a *mea culpa* for institutional failure, but they also look to data collection and improved staffing arrangements as a distraction from unresolved tensions.

For the judges who must assess victim applications, the tension is translated into a challenge of court management. These challenges are captured in the Chambers Practice Manual, a document designed to instil best practices for judicial management. The manual began life as a pre-trial chamber compendium of best practices designed to 'identify solutions to challenges faced in the first years of the court and build on the experiences acquired so far'.[156] Rather than taking a stance on the difficult balance between victims and suspects, the manual's 'final goal' is to 'contribute to the overall effectiveness and efficiency of the proceedings before the court'.[157] Updated editions of the manual also characterise it as a 'living document' which can be 'updated, integrated [and] amended as warranted by any relevant development'.[158]

The manual largely deals with judicial timeframes, flexible communication arrangements between the parties, and clarification of Chambers' functions. These efforts are intended to be backed up by other organs, such as the Registry in its Judicial Workflow Platform for disclosing and processing case materials.[159] The 2017 edition of the manual is particularly relevant for the victim/suspect dilemma since it added a section on the admission of victim participants. This section outlines the stages for processing such applications, proposing a suitable timeframe for judges to assess them, the appointment of victims' legal representatives, and the adjustment of victims' lists. By framing the question of victim participation through such concerns, questions about a victim- or suspect-centred institution are replaced with questions about who should do what institutionally, and when.

The manual both externalises and internalises decision-making through such a flight to judicial management. On one hand, because such measures are deemed 'best practices', decisions about the admission

---

[156] Third Chambers Practice Manual, 5.
[157] Ibid.
[158] Chambers Practice Manual, Second Edition, International Criminal Court, February 2016, 5.
[159] Registry Strategic Plan 2019–2021, International Criminal Court, 17 July 2019, para. 22, available at: www.icc-cpi.int/sites/default/files/itemsDocuments/190717-reg-strategic-plan-eng.pdf.

5.3 MANAGEMENT AND THE ARGUMENTATIVE DILEMMAS   221

of victims, setting of time limits, and transmission to the Trial Chamber are judged to have been successful in the past. They offer a precedent of relevant expertise, which allows the manual's user to attribute the decision (and its consequences) to 'best practices' rather than their own reasoning.[160] On the other hand, the manual is followed by the judge who may claim its knowledge as a valid and authoritative tool for justifying their decisions. It allows some decisions to be internalised and controlled by the judges while supplanting debates about who benefits more, victims or suspects.

Performance indicators and 'lessons learnt' exercises complete the set of management tools relied upon by judges. Performance indicators were introduced to measure criteria such as the 'expeditious, fair and transparent' nature of ICC proceedings. This terminology already reflects some of the tensions inherent to the victim/suspect dilemma, with its signal to both fairness and expediency. Yet the dilemma was undercut by the fact that performance indicators were expected not just to measure existing workload statistics but to 'become qualitatively meaningful' when combined with 'the components "time" and "resources"'.[161] Through this formula, the indicator for court proceedings enacted a temporal deferral. Orienting court constituencies towards the future collection of relevant statistics, the question of fairness for either victims or suspects was temporally deferred. For its part, the resources variable allowed the problem of slow or unfair proceedings (usually seen as damaging to both victims and suspects) to be reinterpreted as a matter of (in)adequate personnel and funding.

Judicial 'lessons learnt' exercises held a similar promise. After a dialogue between the court and states parties, the ASP launched a lessons learnt exercise in 2011 'to assess the functioning of the ICC's procedural framework and look into possible improvements'.[162] The vocabulary of 'lessons' performs an important reimagination of past deficiencies. It does not deny the deficient nature of past court activities but admits to such failure in order to reinscribe it as productive material for future

---

[160] David Kennedy, *A World of Struggle: How Power, Law, and Expertise Shape Global Political Economy* (Princeton University Press 2016).

[161] Philipp Ambach, 'Performance Indicators for International(ised) Criminal Courts – Potential for Increase of an Institution's Legacy or "Just" a Means of Budgetary Control?' (2018) 18 *International Criminal Law Review* 426–460, at 435.

[162] Ambach, 'The "Lessons Learnt" Process at the International Criminal Court' 854. See Study Group on Governance, Lessons Learnt: First Report of the Court to the Assembly of States Parties, ICC-ASP/31/Add.1, 23 October 2012.

222   ICC LEGAL ARGUMENTATION: MESO-MANAGEMENT

action. As well as quelling a sense of past disappointment, this also creates a re-opening or renewed possibility from what would otherwise have remained the uncomfortable traces of past failure.

Once the lessons learnt exercise was established, it focused on rule amendments and the standardisation of best practices that later bore fruit in the Chambers Practice Manual. Some of the proposals arising from the 'Roadmap' included a uniform disclosure system and e-Court protocol, improvement of victim application management systems, and streamlining of victim application processes.[163] The Roadmap also established a Working Group on Lessons Learnt (WGLL) as a forum for directing professional energy towards the improvement of past deficiencies. Like the manual, the Roadmap was kept under review.[164]

The WGLL's main topics for discussion were the relationship between the pre-trial and trial chambers, and victim participation. Its primary weapon was the proposal of rule amendments to clarify and optimise the court's role in these areas. Following a 'state-driven quota of rule amendment proposals per year', the WGLL was to submit these annually to the ASP's Study Group on Governance.[165] Few of these proposals passed, however, so the ASP instead 'encouraged the court to continue exploring a more "informal" avenue of streamlining of processes and procedures through practice changes'.[166] Seeking 'practice-based solutions' was preferred since it would 'vest the institution with the necessary tools to master these challenges and improve its efficiency as it moves along'.[167]

By 2016, the Roadmap was being criticised for failing to deliver results while states were also being blamed for placing too much emphasis on efficiency savings. Despite its failures, the Roadmap and lessons learnt exercise 'was maintained in principle and supported as a vehicle for rule changes',[168] while also being lauded for 'provid[ing] the Court with the necessary impetus to bring forward efficiency gains through practice changes'.[169] This hints at the more subtle function of lessons learnt exercises. Beyond rule or practice changes, such exercises redirected the professional energy and commitment of ICC experts towards technical adjustments. This narrowed the focus to what could be controlled – at

---

[163] Ibid., 859.
[164] Ibid.
[165] Ibid., 861.
[166] Ibid., 862.
[167] Ibid., 863.
[168] Ibid.
[169] Ibid., 864.

least in the minds of the experts – and thereby opened new technocratic possibilities. Such a move was possible not because it resolved argumentative tensions but because it managed to bracket them.

This sense of possibility is captured in one insider's commentary on the lessons learnt exercise after several years. 'The Lessons Learnt initiative', stated Ambach, 'is an ongoing process and has proven to be increasingly effective'.[170] It has 'gained momentum' and 'has proven both stamina and innovativeness'.[171] These qualities occasion a reinvigorated expert, like Ambach, who, looking backwards at the court's mounting institutional failures, sees only future possibility. This is a powerful shift which, together with workflow improvements, personnel changes, performance indicators, and best practices, collectively redirects expert energy and faith in the court's ability to overcome its problems.

5.4 The Flight to Management

This chapter makes several observations about the relationship between management and the legal terrain upon which ICC experts frequently meet and argue. Management rationales about efficient allocation of resources, planning, capacity, and optimisation, and techniques from basic size models to lessons learnt exercises are commonly invoked by a range of ICC experts. The first observation of this chapter was that management's invocation does not take place in a vacuum. Consequently, management is not deployed to resolve every conceivable problem the ICC confronts. In the diverse areas of court activity surveyed in this chapter, management is invoked by experts within well-worn trenches of argumentation, or argumentative dilemmas. While the previous chapters showed the macro and micro levels within which management operates, this chapter considers the mid-level invocations of management by ICC experts as they attempt to grapple with difficult problems, such as the politics of ICC investigations or the court's dependence upon states for its continued independence.

Having elaborated upon some of these argumentative dilemmas, the chapter then revealed the extent to which the institutional and expert response to them has taken place in a remarkably similar key and via similar means. The OTP response to criticisms of legalism on one side and politics on the other has been to reify the budgetary constraints on

---

[170] Ibid., 867.
[171] Ibid.

224 ICC LEGAL ARGUMENTATION: MESO-MANAGEMENT

the court and focus on matching the supply of resources at its disposal to global demands for intervention. When confronting the lack of state co-operation in the arrest and surrender of suspects, court officials have also pointed to the limited resources at its disposal, while also installing a range of techniques to strengthen understanding, engagement, and national expertise around arrest and surrender. And the way in which the court has overcome the problem of over- or under-including victims in court proceedings has been through designating the limits of its own capacity. Registry officials and judges have centred the concerns of standardisation, timing, and measurement in managing victim applications.

Whatever role management plays as it gets applied to these argumentative dilemmas, its capacity to improve the court's functioning is rarely visible. The lessons learnt exercise is the clearest example of this, being said to have delivered meagre results even by advocates. Yet such tools are rarely removed but continue to bear the weight of professional commitment. This may be part of management's attraction among ICC experts as it directs concern away from ingrained dilemmas and towards technical recalibration. When the OTP directs itself towards matching limited institutional supply to global demand, this dampens judgment of its decision-making as either too legalistic or too politicised. Where the complementarity regime fails to resolve the tension between international and national authority, it can be reframed as a 'forum for managerial interaction' and 'positive complementarity' can seek to distribute resources, assistance, and expertise between the international and the domestic. Such arguments do not disappear but, like international law, management turns out to be 'an elaborate framework for deferring substantive resolution elsewhere: into further procedure, interpretation, equity, context, and so on'.[172]

Management arguments are at once constraining and liberating. They inscribe arguments of economic status, budgetary constraint, and value-for-money into the court's everyday reality. This seemed difficult to do in the context of prior legal debates and the necessity of judicial and prosecutorial independence. But such developed sense of 'reality' has constrained the court in terms of what it can legitimately argue. It is no longer possible to put large numbers of analysts into one situation analysis when multiple situations *have to* be analysed at once. Likewise,

---

[172] Martti Koskenniemi, 'The Politics of International Law' (1990) 1 *European Journal of International Law* 4–32, at 28.

5.4 THE FLIGHT TO MANAGEMENT 225

the number of victims admitted to participate in proceedings *must*, due to budget constraints, have an upper limit. These 'facts' have shaped the range of options the ICC expert has posited in attempting to resolve the court's underlying tensions.

Yet such constraint is simultaneously a liberation from responsibility. To cite capacity or timing as fixed, almost agentic forces playing on professional activity, distances the expert from the consequences of their choices. The judge who follows the Chambers Practice Manual may rely upon it to prevent further victim applications from being reviewed, citing time and expediency concerns. This also works not only as an apology for underperformance but a positive achievement. The ability to cite statistics gathered on the reach of court communications on arrest procedures supplants discussion of the relationship between the court and domestic authorities. Ultimately, it was management's constraining yet freeing quality that permitted the pre-trial judges to argue, not unreasonably, that the prospects for a successful investigation in the Afghanistan situation were too low to warrant authorising one. Regardless of the court's flawed reasoning or competence, this feeling of being constrained by 'hard choices' now characterises ICC expertise in general despite scholarly efforts to distance themselves from such reasoning.

Management also offers a new plane or framework upon which evaluation may take place, one whose terms can be controlled better than debates on politicisation, complementarity, or co-operation. Here, the discussion centres instead on goals, indicators, results, and lessons learnt. Moreover, this new argumentative plane demands that the critic defer judgment on court activity until such point as optimisation has been completed, workflow improved, and statistics collected. Professional freedom here comes as the power to state 'not yet' in response to criticisms about politicisation, complementarity, lack of co-operation, or victim participation. There is always an indicator that needs to be refined to account for new developments, while mixed results today can always be fashioned into 'lessons' in tomorrow's effort to do it all again. The court manages to elude immediate judgment, even at its most critical moments, thereby offering a stable point from which to continue its activities.

Deferral has proven extremely useful for the court. Those who may have stuck to the problem of politicisation or for whom the court's victim-centrism was an existential challenge to its penal function now propose greater transparency and accountability in prosecutorial discretion or find comfort in the accumulation of best practices to balance victim participation with the rights of the accused. One might think that a set of solutions arising from management rationales would require a serious rethink of the relationship between law and politics, or the court's international authority as against domestic sovereignty. But these dilemmas now seem water under the bridge. The dilemma is refashioned, and for many this may help to salvage a wavering faith in the project.[173] Rather than having to decide whether the court can resolve its tensions or not, a new approach of waiting and seeing has removed the stakes of such a decision. One need not have faith today, and tomorrow it may be upended, but in the meantime, one must 'wait and see'.

As a final note, there is remarkably little discussion of the consequences of turning to management rationales and techniques to justify a whole range of court activities. There also appears to be very little desire to countenance any downsides beyond potentially expanding the judicial function. Ironically, the few experts who sought to confront the heaviness and consequences of the Afghanistan situation were judges of the pretrial chamber. They have come closest to admitting to the impossibility of resolving the law/politics tension in a satisfactory manner. They also did not seek to escape to management as a deferral of judgment but as a way of forcing a decision in a choice between two unsatisfying outcomes. For all its criticisms, the Afghanistan decision illustrates the force of the court's argumentative dilemmas as well as the promise and peril of management as an escape from them.

5.5 Conclusion

In his pathbreaking analysis of the ICC's argumentative patterns, Robinson hints at what acknowledging such patterns might offer the international criminal lawyer. He proposes that 'awareness of the dyadic structure of many issues would lead many to accord the court's officials some "margin of appreciation".[174] While such a margin of appreciation appears not to have been afforded the court since these patterns were outlined, it has arisen instead from an alternative set of rationales, arguments, and techniques taken up by the ICC expert. After many years confronting, challenging, and responding to the court's argumentative dilemmas, ICC experts have constructed a new plane for arguing about, critiquing, and evaluating the success or failure of the court. The

---

[173] Ambach, 'Performance Indicators' 447–448.
[174] Robinson, 'Inescapable Dyads' 345.

5.5 CONCLUSION

Afghanistan decision of 2019 is only one (admittedly extreme) rendition of a move that is being played out across the court every day. Regardless of the Appeals Chamber's choice to overturn the earlier decision, management continues to prove useful in both solidifying new arguments as facts while also deferring final judgment. Indeed, to enact the flight to management, and to experience its constraining and liberating potential, captures much of what it means to be an ICC expert today.

6

'In a Technical and Political View'

A Study of the ICC Registry's *Re*Vision Project

6.1 Introduction

In November 2015, the registrar of the International Criminal Court (ICC), Herman von Hebel, stood before states parties in The Hague to update them on the activities of the Registry. Beginning to trace one of his chief accomplishments – the reorganisation of the Registry – von Hebel struck a reflective tone. 'Two years ago,' he began, 'I presented to you my vision and plan for the reorganisation of the Registry'.[1] At that time, the organ had yet to undergo any large-scale transformation, but it had become clear to von Hebel and many others that the Registry, as the court's largest and most expensive organ, had become 'inadequate to meet the developing needs of a now well-established institution'.[2] Upon taking office, von Hebel 'promised change from within' through a root-and-branch reform effort demanding significant investment of time, resources, and expertise.[3]

The Committee on Budget and Finance (CBF) had described the exercise as an 'ambitious plan',[4] but von Hebel and his co-reformers were confident that 'the new structure will yield significant efficiency and effectiveness gains in the years to come'.[5] Another report, published towards the project's end, found that 'Registry functions will now be

---

[1] Registrar Herman von Hebel Remarks to the 14th Session of the Assembly of States Parties, Herman von Hebel, Assembly of States Parties 14th Session, 21 November 2015, 4, available at: https://asp.icc-cpi.int/iccdocs/asp_docs/ASP14/ASP14-BDGT-REGISTRAR-ST-ENG-FRA.pdf.

[2] Registrar Remarks to the ASP 14th Session, 4.

[3] Ibid., 7.

[4] Report of the Committee on Budget and Finance on the Work of its 21st Session, ICC-ASP/12/15, 4 November 2013, para. 83.

[5] Report on the Review of the Organisational Structure of the Registry, ICC-ASP/13/26, 28 October 2014, para. 16.

6.1 INTRODUCTION 229

organised and structured so that they deliver cost-effective high-quality services in a timely manner'.[6] The Immediate Office of the Registrar would now focus more on strategic, less on operational tasks; a new division had been created to co-ordinate field operations; there were now clearer managerial lines of authority; and the Budget Section now also concerned itself with planning and monitoring. With these and many more reforms, von Hebel informed states parties, 'the Registry has been transformed into a new structure . . . with capability to perform better'.[7]

For all this praise, remarkably few scholars have analysed the effects of this major reorganisation, branded *ReVision* by its architects. Only a handful of interventions address the project, despite many prior and subsequent calls for court reform.[8] What characterises most, if not all, of these accounts is the mode of critique underpinning them, best described by Schwöbel-Patel as 'effectiveness critique', or assessing the project against its self-imposed standards.[9] Yet it is also possible to approach the *ReVision* project as a key site of management or instance of managing at multiple layers. As previous chapters have shown, the ICC's management practices range from the individualised and ad hoc to

---

[6] Report on the Review of the Organisational Structure of the Registry: Outcomes of Phase 4 of the *ReVision* Project, ICC-ASP/14/18, 4 May 2015, para. 2.

[7] Comprehensive Report on the Reorganisation of the Registry of the International Criminal Court, August 2016, Foreword by the Registrar, ix.

[8] Franziska Boehme, 'Exit, Voice and Loyalty: State Rhetoric about the International Criminal Court' (2018) 22 *International Journal of Human Rights* 420–445, at 424; Sam Shoamanesh, 'Institution Building: Perspectives from within the Office of the Prosecutor of the International Criminal Court' (2018) 18 *International Criminal Law Review* 489–516, at 497; Isabel Düsterhöft and Dominic Kennedy, 'How to Manage the Defence – Experiences from the ADC-ICTY' in Mayeul Hiéramente and Patricia Schneider (eds.), *The Defence in International Criminal Trials: Observations on the Role of the Defence at the ICTY, ICTR and ICC* (Nomos 2016) 227–244, at 243. Haslam and Edmunds acknowledge a similar balancing act in relation to victims' legal representation; see Emily Haslam and Rod Edmunds, 'Whose Number Is It Anyway?: Common Legal Representation, Consultations and the "Statistical Victim"' (2017) 15 *Journal of International Criminal Justice* 931–952, at 934; Luc Walleyn, 'Victims' Participation in ICC Proceedings: Challenges Ahead' (2016) 16 *International Criminal Law Review* 995–1017, at 1014. Calls for reform continued unabated after *ReVision* ended; see Zeid Raad Al Hussein et al., 'The International Criminal Court Needs Fixing', *New Atlanticist*, 24 April 2019, available at: www.atlanticcouncil.org/blogs/new-atlanticist/the-international-criminal-court-needs-fixing. This is consistent with certain argumentative patterns within the field itself, see Sergey Vasiliev, 'The Crises and Critiques of International Criminal Justice' in Kevin Jon Heller et al. (eds.), *The Oxford Handbook of International Criminal Law* (Oxford University Press 2020) 626–651.

[9] Christine Schwöbel, 'Introduction', in Christine Schwöbel (ed.), *Critical Approaches to International Criminal Law: An Introduction* (Routledge 2015) 1–14, at 3.

the collective and cyclical. But of the many attempts at organisational reform over the years, the *Re*Vision project ranks as one of the largest carried out by the court to date.[10] The reorganisation officially ran from January 2014 until July 2015, and in keeping with the themes established in previous chapters, those months witnessed both macro-organisational transformations and micro-level adaptations of individual Registry staff. Following on from those observations, this chapter-length study seeks to retell the *Re*Vision exercise from the perspective of the various management ideas and practices that precipitated, shaped, and realised it. This is conducted in the redescriptive mode outlined in the introduction, where to redescribe is 'to make visible precisely what is visible', in Foucault's words.[11]

This entails first situating the Registry in its wider institutional and political milieu. For all its patterns and common anxieties, that milieu is best described as one of 'contention, discourse, and complexity'.[12] The early 2010s were a time of great change for the court, when it moved from a budding experiment into a fully fledged fixture of the global justice project. Having described this wider set of forces, I then turn to the Registry's functions and indeed, its potentialities in the face of such tumult. The Registry, despite being responsible for *only* the 'non-judicial aspects of the administration and servicing of the Court',[13] constantly regulates the court's interaction with key groups, such as suspects, victims, witnesses, and communities experiencing mass violence and oppression. In this sense, the Registry's capacity – although perhaps never its intention – of radically engaging such groups is striking. Yet despite this, *Re*Vision conditioned an escape from such political possibilities and contestations to the immediate comfort of technique. Tracing *Re*Vision as a flight from politics to technique through management is this chapter's first aim.

---

[10] The Independent Expert Review of the court, commissioned by states parties in 2019 and completed in September 2020, now rivals *Re*Vision for this accolade, see Independent Expert Review of the International Criminal Court and the Rome Statute System: Final Report, 30 September 2020.

[11] Translated in Anne Orford, 'In Praise of Description' (2012) 25 *Leiden Journal of International Law* 609–625, at 617.

[12] This is an understanding of ICL first posited in Christine Schwöbel, 'The Comfort of International Criminal Law' (2013) 24 *Law & Critique* 169–191.

[13] Article 34, Rome Statute of the International Criminal Court (signed 17 July 1998, entered into force 1 July 2002) A/CONF.189/9.

6.2 CONTENTION, DISCOURSE, COMPLEXITY

The second aim is to demonstrate the reverse set of dynamics, namely appreciating the exercise as reformers' most radical form of organisational redistribution or, in other words, as the extent of their politics. This elision of the technical and the political came with the refashioning of the organ. It was not just that *Re*Vision improved the Registry but that it created 'a new Registry' altogether.[14] The second argument, then, is that management ideas and practices not only helped deflect and funnel the political into the technical; it also facilitated expert imagination of institutional possibility (in an institution dealing with mass atrocities, no less) in technical terms. The technical becomes the political, in a somewhat discomforting adaptation of the feminist slogan. Indeed, the very discomfort that such a reading of *Re*Vision occasions serves as the starting point for the concluding chapter.

6.2 Contention, Discourse, Complexity

*Re*Vision entailed not only its immediate justifications and processes but the wider debates and contestations comprising the ICC project in the years preceding reform. Appreciating these debates and contestations, one witnesses a major dynamic of management reform exercises such as *Re*Vision, which is to both decontextualise the institution from such contestations, before then recontextualising them in a manner fitting with certain institutional parameters, priorities, and expertise. Throughout this section, I rely on Schwöbel-Patel's reading of the international criminal law (ICL) field as characterised by a 'contemporary desire for certainty over contention, action over discourse, and simplicity over complexity'.[15] The chapter foregrounds contention, discourse, and complexity as it manifested pre-*Re*Vision before offering an account of the Registry and *Re*Vision's relation to such contentions. Specifying further some of the broad dilemmas outlined in Chapter 5, as well as more explicitly political ones, the milieu in which *Re*Vision was launched can be read as a particularly tense, if promising, moment for rethinking the 'givens' of the organ's work.

By 2013, when *Re*Vision was getting underway, the court's activities had increased dramatically from the trickle of cases before it a decade prior. The Office of the Prosecutor (OTP) was investigating alleged crimes in seven different situations and had just opened its eighth after

[14] Comprehensive Report on Reorganisation, Foreword, ix.
[15] Schwöbel, 'Comfort' 169–70.

232 'IN A TECHNICAL AND POLITICAL VIEW'

reports of alleged war crimes in Mali. It was still riding on the completion of its first full case after Thomas Lubanga was sentenced in 2012 to fourteen years in prison. The court had also benefitted from the voluntary surrender of Bosco Ntaganda, the commander of the Patriotic Forces for the Liberation of Congo (FPLC), who made his first court appearance in March 2013. Outside Africa, the new ICC prosecutor, Fatou Bensouda, was continuing her Office's preliminary examination into possible crimes by US and Afghan forces in Afghanistan. While many constraints dogged investigations even at this early stage, including 'security concerns and limited or reluctant cooperation from many partners', the OTP was not yet facing the kind of criticism it would later experience once months of work turned to years.[16] The court was also experiencing a public relations coup, having featured positively in the NGO-led 'Kony 2012' campaign, 'one of the greatest brand awareness campaigns ever'.[17] This hugely increased visibility and support for the ICC's investigations into the Lord's Resistance Army in Uganda.[18] On many accounts, the ICC was experiencing success and high praise in ways that have since been unmatched.

From these achievements, it is perhaps unsurprising that the architects of Registry reform would be concerned to build upon such successes and to ensure the organ could meet increasing demand. Yet cracks in the edifice were already apparent, as were more robust challenges to the court's architecture and aspirations. Despite improved relations between the United States and the court after the election of the Obama administration in 2008, investigations into alleged US army and CIA crimes in Afghanistan progressed slowly. Some observers also raised questions about the selection and prioritisation practices of the OTP. Despite reaching the end of the Lubanga trial with its first conviction, the OTP had partly relied upon a paired-down docket, invisibilising sexual and gender-based crimes, in order to achieve this result.[19] The former

---

[16] Report on the Activities of the Court, ICC-ASP/12/28, 21 October 2013, para. 70.

[17] Christine Schwöbel-Pabel, *Marketing Global Justice: The Political Economy of International Criminal Law* (Cambridge University Press 2021) 154.

[18] Kamari Maxine Clarke, *Affective Justice: The International Criminal Court and the Pan-Africanist Pushback* (Duke University Press 2019) esp. chapter 3.

[19] Lubanga was charged and convicted of the war crime of conscripting and enlisting child soldiers but despite evidence of rape and sexual violence during the DRC conflict, the prosecutor declined to add such charges to the indictment. For a detailed account, see Rosemary Grey, *Prosecuting Sexual and Gender-Based Crimes at the International Criminal Court* (Cambridge University Press 2019) 128–142.

6.2 CONTENTION, DISCOURSE, COMPLEXITY 233

prosecutor, Luis Moreno-Ocampo, had also relied on significant support from the then-president of the Democratic Republic of the Congo (DRC), Joseph Kabila, giving rise to further concerns about the failure to investigate alleged government crimes committed during that conflict.[20] The familiar dilemmas of law versus politics and institutional independence versus state dependence surfaced even as the court celebrated its successes.[21]

The court also confronted a wider critique that both encompassed and extended beyond these argumentative dilemmas. If 2008 was an important year for Registry reformers concerned with the new austerity politics of major funders, then it could equally have represented the starting point for the court's cooling relationship with African states parties. This hostility only increased by the time *ReVision* began, although there was no mention of this during the exercise except at its margins. As demonstrated by the court's work in the DRC, but also Uganda and the Central African Republic, the OTP relied upon the support of African governments in its attempts to populate the court's early docket. A policy of strategic co-operation between Ocampo and several African heads of state characterised this early period. While much of this support remained after 2008, that year saw the court issue an arrest warrant for then-Sudanese president Omar Al Bashir. The African Union (AU) and the Arab League opposed the warrant, fearing it would 'bring even more conflict in Darfur'.[22] The swiftness of the UN Security Council's referral of the situation in Libya in 2011[23] only exacerbated the sense that 'the ICC was being used to fight the wars of the West', this time against 'an old enemy' in the form of Colonel Muammar Gaddafi.[24]

The prospect of a new prosecutor, a Gambian national, prompted some optimism that the court would be able to assert itself against Western influence. But by 2011, the traces of the earlier arrest warrant

---

[20] Phil Clark, *Distant Justice: The Impact of the International Criminal Court on African Politics* (Cambridge University Press 2018) 74.

[21] See Chapter 5.

[22] Michelle Faul, 'ICC Warrant Raises Questions on Leaders Targeted', *San Diego Union-Tribune*, 5 March 2009, available at: www.sandiegouniontribune.com/sdut-af-international-court-africa-fallout-030509-2009mar05-story.html; 'AU Rejects Bashir Darfur Charges', *BBC News*, 21 July 2008, available at: http://news.bbc.co.uk/2/hi/africa/7517393.stm.

[23] UN Security Council Resolution 1970 (26 February 2011) para. 4.

[24] Makau Mutua, 'Africans and the ICC: Hypocrisy, Impunity, and Perversion' in Kamari Maxine Clarke, Abel S. Knotterus, and Eefje de Volder (eds.), *Africa and the ICC: Perceptions of Justice* (Cambridge University Press 2016) 47–60, at 54.

234 'IN A TECHNICAL AND POLITICAL VIEW'

against Al Bashir were beginning to spill into more protracted dissent. That same year, Al Bashir visited several African states parties to the court, including Chad and Malawi. Those visits had precipitated cases against the two states parties for failure to comply with the obligation to arrest and surrender Al Bashir under the Statute. As discussed in Chapter 5, all states, which later included the DRC, South Africa, and Jordan, were found to have failed to comply with these obligations despite the court's differing arguments as to the removal of head-of-state immunity.

In the wake of the court's first non-compliance rulings, the African Union convened in January 2012. It took a strong position against the court's approach to African states parties and their interpretation of head-of-state immunity. The AU also noted that it would 'oppose any ill-considered, self-serving decisions of the ICC as well as any pretentions or double standards that become evident from these investigations, prosecutions and decisions by the ICC relating to situations in Africa'.[25] A year later, the position hardened into a claim that the court was 'hunting Africans because of their race'.[26]

Although the court and its supporters responded to this allegation with their own counter-arguments, the claim itself did much to articulate a new set of concerns and allegiances around the court's relationship to the Global South and its latent neo-colonialism. As a result, it is worth positioning such allegations of an anti-Africa bias alongside other (legal) tools deployed by the same actors at the time. A highly symbolic struggle over the meaning of the court and its actions was also borne out in the key of law, wherein the court and African states parties held opposing views on state obligations towards the court in regard to non-state party nationals. And while the court engaged in such legal debate through its various decisions on non-compliance, it also engaged with more explicit

---

[25] African Union Commission, Press Release No. 002/2012 (9 January 2012).

[26] Aislinn Laing, 'International Criminal Court is "Hunting" Africans', *Daily Telegraph*, 27 May 2013, available at: www.telegraph.co.uk/news/worldnews/africaandindianocean/ 10082819/International-Criminal-Court-is-hunting-Africans.html; Chikeziri Sam Igwe, 'The ICC's Favourite Customer: Africa and International Criminal Law' (2008) 41 *Comparative and International Law Journal of Southern Africa* 294–323. See also Wambui Mwangi and Tiyanjana Mphepo, 'Developments in International Criminal Justice in Africa during 2011' (2012) 12 *African Human Rights Law Journal* 254–282, at 273. For an overview, see Ellis Witcher, 'Doing History to Justice: Theory and Historiography in the History of International Criminal Law', PhD Dissertation, University College Dublin, May 2022, 3–6, available at: https://researchrepository.ucd .ie/bitstream/10197/13169/1/103255081.pdf.

6.2 CONTENTION, DISCOURSE, COMPLEXITY

claims of bias on a political level by alleging blatant instrumentalism on the part of certain African heads of state.[27]

By 2013, then, the court was not only engaged in deliberations over its effective performance but protracted skirmishes that were potentially even more decisive for the court's future activities and reputation. Court officials were keenly aware of the damage this might cause, as suggested by the number of public engagements dealing with the topic that year. One such was the October 2013 retreat on future ICC challenges and opportunities, at which the primary question posed to participants was 'How to maintain and generate support in the African region?'.[28] The fifty states parties represented at the retreat took opposing views on the question and on the wider ICC–AU relationship, showing how fractured court supporters were in dealing with organised dissent.

On one side, many retreat participants took the position that while every effort should be made to engage in 'constructive dialogue' with African states parties, states should be reminded that the court is 'an independent judicial institution' and that any debates should take place between states in the Assembly, not directly with the court. Alongside this position lay the proposal that in order to improve ICC–AU relations, the court should make a more concerted effort towards outreach 'to generate support for its work and to clear up misunderstandings'.[29] Many on this side of the discussion 'emphasised that there was no bias of the ICC against Africa' pointing to the fact that most of the court's situations were referred by African members themselves.

On the other side, many participants noted that 'the concerns of the African Union should be taken seriously'.[30] Public support for the court in Africa was declining, although much of this came from leaders themselves. There was even a proposal that ICC judges 'should take societal developments in Africa into account in their decisions'.[31] Although some of the stronger bias arguments against the court were barely visible at these meetings, the diversity of views on how to address

---

[27] See Arlette Afagbegee, 'The International Criminal Court's Relationship with Africa: An Unfair Bias?', *Pambazuka News*, 4 June 2014, available at: www.pambazuka.org/governance/international-criminal-court%E2%80%99s-relationship-africa-unfair-bias.

[28] Informal Summary of the Retreat: International Criminal Court – The Challenges and Opportunities in Light of the Upcoming November Assembly of States Parties, ICC-ASP/12/INF.2, 12 November 2013.

[29] Ibid.

[30] Ibid.

[31] Ibid.

such questions demonstrates how seriously allegations of bias were being treated by court participants at the time.

Within this climate, the circumstances surrounding the Kenya cases and the Mavi Marmara incident threw the more managerial discussions around court reform into stark relief. When the cases against Uhuru Kenyatta and William Ruto were initiated in 2013, the treatment of not only non-party heads of state but also heads of state from ICC members arose. While proceedings were ongoing against him for alleged crimes against humanity committed during post-election violence in 2007/2008, William Ruto was elected Kenyan vice-president (the Kenyatta-Ruto ticket put its existence and eventual electoral success down to their 'persecution' by the court). Pursuant to this, Ruto requested that he be absented from appearing at trial, given his executive duties.

Although African states parties were able to secure amendments to the Rules of Procedure and Evidence to widen the criteria for excusal, the tenor of the discussion frequently mimicked existing discussions on a wider anti-Africa bias. As Kamari Clarke has shown, both Kenyatta and Ruto were eager to reframe the discussion about their alleged criminality away from matters of individual responsibility and towards ideas of structural violence and capacious victimhood.[32] Indeed, however cynical, Ruto and Kenyatta sought to tell an alternative history of modern Kenyan politics by commencing with its origins as a British-East African Protectorate in 1895.[33] This, too, portends to a different set of historical events and concerns than those the Registry reformers would focus on when contextualising ReVision. The same applied to another situation brought before the court in 2013 relating to the attack by Israeli forces on the Mavi Marmara in the Mediterranean Sea. Although the referral of the case suggested a more active role for the court in relation to Palestine, the pre-trial chamber declined to open an investigation.[34]

This pre-ReVision timeline suggests that there were many more discussions going on at the time beyond organisational fine-tuning. Fundamental questions remained about the court's ability and willingness to respond to postcolonial critiques of its focus on Africa. Although court officials and supporters were eager to associate such critiques only with select African leaders, they were also being raised in other spaces.

---

[32] Clarke, 'Affective Justice' 49–50.

[33] Ibid., 156.

[34] John Dugard, 'Palestine and the International Criminal Court' (2013) 11 *Journal of International Criminal Justice* 563–570, at 563.

6.2 CONTENTION, DISCOURSE, COMPLEXITY

Activists within Greece called for an 'austerity trial' in 2012 over the measures imposed by the Greek government (and European 'Troika' institutions). Organisers of the campaign alleged that the destitution large parts of the Greek population faced as a result had effectively restricted possibilities to marry and have children, prompting arguments of peacetime genocide and crimes against humanity.[35] Similar calls were made in the United Kingdom, where British organisers sought to draw attention to the immiserating effect of social security reform introduced by the Conservative-Liberal Democrat coalition government, and Iain Duncan Smith as Work and Pensions Secretary.[36] The fact that such developments did not feature on the court's radar tells of the difficulty of assuaging the postcolonial critique and the exceptional treatment of alleged crimes in Europe.

These dissenting voices raised many important questions with which the court seemed unwilling to grapple. Ten years into the ICC project, the mood among supporters had understandably shifted from one of optimism to a sense that the court and its activities were coming under pressure. And yet the context of contestation and dissent barely featured in many of the debates on how to proceed. Practitioners and scholars were much more likely to point to the court's paltry conviction rate or its large expenditure than to concerns about its treatment of Africa and Africans.[37] When Africa did appear on the Assembly of States Parties (ASP) agenda, as with the 2013 retreat, it was treated as a problem of miscommunication or failure of outreach which needed to be better managed rather than as structural limitations of the anti-impunity approach *tout court*. The discontent coming from the African continent was treated as a 'setback' or a 'backlash' that could be rectified through better communication, further outreach, and more good faith engagement on the part of detractors. Describing dissent as a communication problem both neutered the structural basis of such critiques and

---

[35] Mark Lowen, 'Greeks Seek Austerity Trial at The Hague', *BBC News*, 24 April 2012, available at: www.bbc.com/news/world-europe-17811153.

[36] Olga Yeritsidou, 'Greek Case for Austerity "Genocide" Creates Hope in UK', *Vox Political Online*, undated, available at: https://voxpoliticalonline.com/tag/olga-yeritsidou/.

[37] David Davenport, 'International Criminal Court: 12 Years, $1 Billion, 2 Convictions', *Forbes*, 12 March 2014, available at: www.forbes.com/sites/daviddavenport/2014/03/12/international-criminal-court-12-years-1-billion-2-convictions-2/?sh=4d2e0b672405;
Florian Jessberger and J. Geneuss, 'Down the Drain or Down to Earth? International Criminal Justice under Pressure' (2013) 11 *Journal of International Criminal Justice* 501–503.

238 'IN A TECHNICAL AND POLITICAL VIEW'

transformed them into fuel for institutional action under status quo assumptions. From here, the utopianism of the court's first decade was replaced with a self-professed pragmatism that warned against 'messianic thinking' as it sought to 'nudge the world political system in the direction of accountability'.[38] As Payam Akhavan, an ICC vanguardist, put it, there was 'a need to creatively confront the challenges the ICC's normative empire face[d]' in order that the international criminal justice project could 'rise again with adjusted expectations'.[39]

The form this creativity would take was already suggested by the court's ongoing approach to its activities. At the ASP, court officials declared that efficiency gains in the previous year had 'enabled an 18% increase in workload' of field operations staff while 'efforts to ensure cost-effective management of field operations resulted in the redeployment of staff and non-staff resources to situation countries with greater operational needs'.[40] The focus thus remained on the dilemma of how to match institutional supply to external demand, and the new strategic plan reflected this desire. Internally, the efficiency drive was written down to the individual: 2013 was the year in which competency-based interviewing was introduced into the court's recruitment procedure for new staff while the court's regime on probation and performance appraisal was inaugurated in an Administrative Instruction. The creative energy lay more in technical matters than in confronting other political dynamics. The following discussions demonstrate the dynamics of depoliticisation and politicisation that characterised the *Re*Vision project.

6.3   *Re*Vision's Flight to Management

To begin to understand the flight towards management and away from contestation and complexity, I consider the early justifications for reorganisation. These justifications came not only in the immediate run-up to *Re*Vision but over several years of expert engagement with the Registry, which sought to escape the complexity posed by the wider

---

[38] David Luban, 'After the Honeymoon: Reflections on the Current State of International Criminal Justice' (2013) 11 *Journal of International Criminal Justice* 505–515, at 508.

[39] Payam Akhavan, 'The Rise, Fall, and Rise of International Criminal Justice' (2013) 11 *Journal of International Criminal Justice* 527–536.

[40] Report on the Activities of the Court 2013, para. 108.

6.3 REVISION'S FLIGHT TO MANAGEMENT

politico-institutional milieu I have just outlined. One of the earliest expert assessments of the Registry was conducted by the Office of Internal Audit (OIA) in May 2010.[41] The internal auditors focused mainly on the organisational structure of field operations. Their findings revealed several 'deficiencies', including 'functional silos and no overall authority in the field structure', 'duplication of administrative tasks', and 'underdeveloped reporting and performance indicators which reduces planning and monitoring controls'.[42] They recommended to 'merge support and substantive field-related Registry functions and consider developing a single organisational unit for field operations'.[43] This would later become a cornerstone reform measure of the *ReVision* exercise. As part of *ReVision*'s pre-history, OIA also set a premium against management deficiencies rather than more intractable political dilemmas around the ICC-Africa encounter or questions of victim voice and positionality.

This managerial voice was complemented by pronouncements of key ICC bodies such as the CBF. A year after the OIA report, the CBF expressed its concern with the 'organisational structure of the Registry, where there appeared to be a proliferation of senior positions that reported directly to the Registrar'.[44] The CBF recommended that the court 'undertake a thorough evaluation/review of its organisational structure with a view to streamlining functions, processes and corresponding structures'.[45] This prompted the court to recruit external management consultants to advise on such issues, which it acknowledged would also 'enhance the credibility of the review's findings and bring objectivity and added value deriving from a broad base of expertise'.[46]

PricewaterhouseCoopers (PwC) won the procurement bid for €90,000. In its diagnosis, PwC echoed the CBF by emphasising the 'rather high degree of internal complexity' and the difficulties with co-operation across the Registry's many sections and units. It was imperative that the court 'modernise its methods to achieve a Court model which meets

---

[41] Audit of the Registry's Field Operations – Organisational Structure, Office of Internal Audit, OIA.08-A09, 31 May 2010.

[42] Comprehensive Report on Reorganisation, para. 9.

[43] Ibid., para. 10.

[44] Report of the Committee on Budget and Finance on the Work of Its 17th Session, ICC-ASP/10/15, 18 November 2011, para. 45.

[45] Ibid., para. 46.

[46] Ibid., para. 16.

the expectations of the community of States Parties'.[47] Administrative complexity and outdated practices became the trauma court experts wished to overcome. Despite the contention brought to the court by African states and others, it was the line of reasoning relating to streamlining, planning, and performance that the ReVision architects took as their starting point. The 2016 Comprehensive Report on ReVision retrospectively relies on OIA and CBF assessments but also the 'unplanned' nature of pre-ReVision reforms to narrate the Registry's history before ReVision as a growing set of managerial deficiencies.[48] This narration turned organ-wide reform into an urgent task.

The course of the ReVision exercise also demonstrates a focus on the technical, to the exclusion of dissenting voices. The aim of the exercise was to 'modernise [the Registry's] methods' and to simplify and streamline what was perceived to be an 'over-complex' organ.[49] These justifications were never framed as tools for avoiding bigger problems but rather for confronting them directly based on a collective desire held by multiple stakeholders. Two months before the exercise began, the registrar noted the 'widespread agreement across the court that change is necessary'.[50] As we will see later, framing quite particular demands from Registry managers, management experts, and selected states parties in consensus terms also helped deflect attention and responsibility for more sensitive issues arising from reform such as the effect on victims and staff welfare. Von Hebel impressed upon all stakeholders the importance of finding an optimal size for the Registry. This was not a question of 'downsizing, but rightsizing'.[51] Redundancies were deemed a necessary sacrifice 'to implement the new structure and to sustain the reorganisation process'.[52] Any damaging consequences arising from ReVision were an unfortunate but justified outcome, having been 'universally' demanded by experts, states, civil society groups, and 'Registry staff members themselves'.[53]

---

[47] Report of the Committee on Budget and Finance on the Work of its 20th Session, ICC-ASP/12/5/Rev.1, 7 June 2013, para. 62, available at: https://asp.icc-cpi.int/iccdocs/asp_docs/ASP12/ICC-ASP-12-5-Rev1-ENG.pdf.

[48] Comprehensive Report on Reorganisation, Executive Summary, 28.

[49] Ibid.

[50] Registrar Remarks to the ASP 14th Session, 6.

[51] Ibid.

[52] Ibid.

[53] Comprehensive Report on Reorganisation, para. 560.

6.3 REVISION'S FLIGHT TO MANAGEMENT 241

Consultations conducted in the early stages of *Re*Vision also diffused responsibility away from the organ. Upon assuming office, the registrar hosted a meeting for all Registry staff to discuss common issues across the organ.[54] According to von Hebel, those discussions 'categorically showed the need for urgent change'.[55] He also presented the reorganisation proposal to the Hague Working Group, a body comprised of state representatives established by the ASP. The proposal was 'positively received' and the registrar promised to keep the group, as well as states and the CBF, constantly updated about the progress of reform.[56] This broad consensus was cited throughout *Re*Vision and subsequently, in *ex post* legitimations of the project. The Comprehensive Report stated that '[f]or a number of years in the lead-up to the reorganisation of the Registry, there was a collective and widespread understanding that organisational change was necessary and long overdue'.[57] Through these different exchanges over several years, court experts constructed a case for reform that eclipsed any deeper contentions and dilemmas. Indeed, such a flight simultaneously responsibilised others for the set of organisational deficiencies reformers were willing to confront.

Nevertheless, *Re*Vision did not manage to resolve the contradictions and complexities underlying the ICC project. One clear instance of this is in the demand for equality of arms in proceedings, particularly raised by defence counsel. This demand appeared to satisfy the requirement that victim-oriented justice does not stray too far away from the criminal nature of proceedings with its attendant concern for the rights of the accused. Dominic Kennedy noted the importance of managing and giving institutional support to the defence within international criminal tribunals, in line with the equality of arms principle. Yet he questioned one of the early *Re*Vision proposals for a separate Defence Office within the Registry.[58] In particular, Kennedy was concerned that any 'Defence Office will cease to be independent and [will] become part of the hierarchy of the Registry both in legal and practical terms'.[59] Philipp Müller commented that the inclusion and centralisation of Office of Public

---

[54] Registrar Presentation of the 2014 Proposed Programme Budget, Assembly of States Parties 12th Session, 23 November 2013, 8.

[55] Report on the Review of the Organisational Structure, para. 10.

[56] Registrar Presentation of the 2014 Proposed Programme Budget, 8.

[57] Comprehensive Report on Reorganisation, Foreword, ix.

[58] Düsterhöft and Kennedy, 'How to Manage the Defence' 243.

[59] Ibid., 243.

Counsel for Defence (OPCD) functions in the Division of Judicial Services would paradoxically 'be seen as a significant downgrading of the status of the [OPCD], and hence the Defence, within the structure of the court'.[60] He also situated this proposal within the wider dilemma of judicial expediency and fairness, stating 'it is a troubling development that current efforts by the registrar to improve on alleged redundancies and inefficiencies disproportionately affect Defence interests and capabilities'.[61]

A similar problematic remained in place in relation to victim representation even with *Re*Vision's many proposals and the reforms it brought forth. The adequate arrangement for victims' legal representation was debated between the registrar in early draft proposals, NGOs, bar associations, and the Office of Public Counsel for Victims (OPCV). Confronting the dilemma of how to adequately represent victims' voices without rubbing up against the essentially criminal nature of the project, reformers proposed centralising both arms within the Registry: a Victims Office and a Defence Office. The Victims Office would merge the Victims Participation and Reparations Section (VPRS) and OPCV to offer 'in-house' counsel to victims instead of external representation. There was a back and forth in which many external groups criticised the move for reducing victims' choice while the OPCV attempted to reassert its own position in any future bureaucratic rearrangement. It was said that such an arrangement would lead to 'competition and tensions' between external counsel and OPCV.[62] With the proposal shelved for potentially infringing the rights of the accused, the underlying dilemma went unresolved. Such a justification offered an escape to the organisational status quo in place of more deep-seated reflection on the status and voice of victims within the court.

Moreover, Haslam and Edmunds expressed concern about the rise of statistical victimhood within the ICC, wherein victims are principally represented by and mediated through numbers and quantified statistics. This development, they say, would 'inadvertently deflect attention from

---

[60] Philipp Müller, 'Promoting Justice between Independence and Institutional Constraints: The Role of the Office of the Public Counsel of the Defence at the ICC' in Hiéramente and Schnieder, 'The Defence in International Criminal Trials' 245–268, at 266.

[61] Ibid.

[62] Basic Outline of Proposals to Establish Defence and Victims Offices (Draft), International Criminal Court, 15 September 2014, available at: http://michaelgkarnavas.net/files/140954-outline-defence-proposals.pdf.

6.4 FROM POLITICS TO TECHNIQUE 243

the substantive challenge of how best to maximise victims' choice in the selection of their legal representation'.[63] They note that statistical victimhood

> contributes to a wider climate of institutional management within the ICC, which seeks to bridge the gap between the formal emphasis on victims' right to choose legal representation, on the one hand, and what the Registry and the Chambers regard as achievable in practice on the other.[64]

However, wider possibilities of victim representation did not make it into the *Re*Vision proposals, with the institutional interests becoming the preferred orienting factor, even before any larger reorganisation of victims and defence sections were shelved. As a result of this, Haslam and Edmunds found that 'the complex issues of policy and practicalities surrounding the appropriate model for victim representation at the ICC look set to remain contentious and in a state of flux for the foreseeable future'.[65] This set of proposals and the dilemmas they failed to resolve demonstrate patterns of argumentation similar to the meso-management discussed in Chapter 5.

6.4 From Politics to Technique: Narrowing through Expert Articulation

*Re*Vision was a moment of institutional renewal and production. *Re*Vision's managerial frame solidified the court's reading of global justice as a largely settled project necessitating only minimal tweaking. To quote Koskenniemi, this reinforced 'the sense that questions of distribution and preference', as well as of justice 'have already been decided elsewhere, so all that remain are technical questions, questions about how to smooth the prince's path'.[66] The following sections document the narrowing of options through contextual articulation and problematisation by experts before discussing the *Re*Vision process and results.

[63] Haslam and Edmunds, 'Whose Number Is It Anyway?' 934.
[64] Ibid., 932.
[65] Ibid., 949.
[66] Martti Koskenniemi, 'The Politics of International Law – Twenty Years Later' (2009) 20 *European Journal of International Law* 7–19, at 16.

6.4.1 Context

'[T]he assertion that something is context and the interpretation of its consequences', notes David Kennedy, 'are the acts of experts'.[67] In this spirit, the context fashioned by court experts differed markedly from the wider and more turbulent discourse at the time. Experts identified two contextual factors as justification for comprehensive Registry reform: an increasing workload and financial restraint. Both of these factors were deemed 'facts' by experts in the run-up to *ReVision*, a move which both occluded their clear political and distributive effects and denied any room for political struggle over the shape and orientation of the future Registry. These contexts I study in turn.

In July 2004, the OTP was seized of only one investigation; exactly ten years later while *ReVision* was underway, the OTP was dealing with eleven preliminary examinations and eight investigations, not to mention the trial and sentencing phases of several cases.[68] This steady growth had a direct effect on the Registry's workload. Between 2009 and 2011, the number of victim participation requests rose from 757 to 5,865, and field offices were opened in several situation countries.[69] From the outset, the Registry sought to adapt to these changes. It produced an Outreach Strategy in 2006 to manage the court's relationship with victim communities. It also sought to deal with the growth in Registry staff by instituting a performance appraisal system. Nonetheless, as Registry officials later concluded, these early efforts developed 'without benefiting from a Registry-wide organisational vision or review'.[70] Such a review was deemed necessary for the Registry to remain 'sustainable in the long term [and] better able to absorb fluctuations in workload'.[71]

The embedding of such a contextual factor in the early narrative of reform foregrounded many elements, with clear political effects. First, reformers traded in ideas of supply and demand that projected a homogeneous international community calling out primarily to this institution to fulfil its needs. Yet here it was clear that demands were often politically

---

[67] David Kennedy, 'Challenging Expert Rule: The Politics of Global Governance' (2005) 27 *Sydney Law Review* 1–24, at 5.

[68] Report on the Activities of the International Criminal Court, ICC-ASP/13/37, 19 November 2014, Part I.C.

[69] Judge Sang-Hyun Song Remarks to the Assembly of States Parties, Assembly of States Parties 10th Session, 12 December 2011, 2.

[70] Comprehensive Report on Reorganisation, Executive Summary, 28.

[71] Report on Phase 4 of the *ReVision* Project, para. 2.

6.4 FROM POLITICS TO TECHNIQUE

filtered, that some demands were not being ascribed the same value, and that the demands of AU members of the ICC were also being ignored. By 2008, the sole focus of the prosecutor's activities had been the African continent. Concerns about selectivity only grew when Ocampo applied for an arrest warrant against President Al Bashir of Sudan despite worries voiced by African states that ICC intervention might derail ongoing peace-building efforts in the country.[72]

Second, reformers promoted business-like growth in which expansion is both the expectation and the hope. This contrasts slightly with an alternative institutional projection offered by Ocampo himself. For him, success lay not in *more* court cases but in *fewer*, as this would signify greater domestic involvement in and ownership over the prosecution of international crimes.[73] Moreover, in several situations, not least in Sudan, it was unclear if court involvement amounted to unwanted interference. Yet in visualising an ever-expanding court docket, officials were concerned with the institutional and managerial challenges likely to arise from that expansion, rather than with bigger questions about the court's role in Africa, the vision of justice it applied to its work, or the appropriateness of expansion as a policy.

Finally, officials relied on ideas of sustainability, which prioritised institutional stability and longevity over the stability of populations most proximate to mass violence. Some NGOs engaging with the *Re*Vision project alluded to the problems inherent in such a stance. Yet references to an increased workload, and to volumes of facts and figures helped to train the institutional gaze inwards, on its own activities and aspirations, even as those aspirations took into account only some concerns and global demands.

The second set of management ideas overlapped with those of the court's budget. Through the reinforcement of these ideas in preceding years, court experts and Registry managers had worked up an appetite for efficiency gains and optimisation in all areas. By the time an organisational review of the Registry was commissioned by the ASP in 2011, the court had already identified yearly efficiency gains and reported to the

---

[72] Max du Plessis and Chris Gevers, 'The Sum of Four Fears: African States and the International Criminal Court in Retrospect – Part I', Opinio Juris blog, 8 July 2019, available at: http://opiniojuris.org/2019/07/08/the-sum-of-four-fears-african-states-and-the-international-criminal-court-in-retrospect-part-i/.

[73] Todd Benjamin, Interview with Luis Moreno Ocampo, International Bar Association, 1 February 2013, available at: www.ibanet.org/Article/NewDetail.aspx?ArticleUid=81213DCF-0911-4141-AD29-A486F9B03D37.

246 'IN A TECHNICAL AND POLITICAL VIEW'

CBF on cost-cutting efforts.[74] On the question of Registry reform, the CBF observed that 'economic constraints and limited self-financing ... needed to be taken into account'.[75]

This austerity mindset not only framed the discussions of experts but created a rationale for any reform exercise. Once elected as registrar, Herman von Hebel was asked by the CBF to 'set a tentative target of 3 per cent savings in his plan' to reorganise the Registry.[76] The Committee further requested that von Hebel report on efficiency measures taken 'together with the realised and anticipated improvements and savings' throughout *ReVision*.[77] During the reorganisation, von Hebel confirmed that '[c]ost-efficiency is both the Registry's day-to-day concern and its ultimate long-term commitment'.[78] Some months later, he was 'happy to say that, as requested by the States Parties ... the Registry has achieved the three per cent savings target in the implementation of the 2014 budget'.[79] Despite asserting that *ReVision*'s aim was 'not to generate significant cost savings', officials were nonetheless guided by an economic climate of budgetary restraint, thereby prompting a sustained focus on resource allocation and internal efficiencies.

Much like ideas of workload and growth, the austerity mindset enacted several political prioritisations and deprioritisations. It entrenched a version of the institution's past in which the global financial crisis served as a historical break that permitted or demanded different thinking, arguments, and factors to be accounted for by court officials and supporters. Yet 2008 could equally have been interpreted as the year in which the court's 'Africa problem' originated, with the arrest warrant issued against Omar Al Bashir. The year 2013 could equally have been a watershed year, with the AU's statements against ICC activity in Sudan, Libya, and Kenya, and a new request to investigate crimes in Gaza by Comoros and others. Beginning its conversation on Registry reform in

---

[74] Seventh Status Report on the Court's Progress Regarding Efficiency Measures, ICC-ASP/11/9, 4 May 2012, para. 3.

[75] Report of the Committee on Budget and Finance on the Work of Its Twentieth Session, ICC-ASP/12/5/Rev.1, 7 June 2013, para. 65.

[76] Report of the Committee on Budget and Finance on the Work of Its Twenty-first Session, ICC-ASP/12/15, 4 November 2013, para. 83.

[77] Report of the CBF, 4 November 2013, para. 83.

[78] Proposed Programme Budget for 2015, ICC-ASP/13/10, 18 September 2014, para. 272.

[79] Registrar Herman von Hebel Remarks to the Thirteenth Session of the Assembly of States Parties, 15 December 2014, 7, available at: https://asp.icc-cpi.int/iccdocs/asp_docs/ASP13/ASP13-BG-Statement-Registrar-ENG.pdf.

6.4 FROM POLITICS TO TECHNIQUE

the shadow of these events, rather than generalised demand and Western-led austerity, many concerns, voices, and priorities were left off the table in an effort to establish the context for reform.

Moreover, such an austerity mindset occluded alternative reasons for the court's financial condition. Aside from reduced budgetary allocations from major financial contributors – themselves the result of similar political decisions at the national level – there was also the issue of financial arrears. By 2014, the ICC had financial arrears amounting to €69 million, or over half the court's annual budget.[80] Many of the court's most indebted members were those who now made calls for a more restrained budget, including Germany, Japan, and the UK. The austerity mindset, however, focused the problem on institutional matters of inefficiency and waste rather than external issues of underinvestment. This is not to say that increasing the court's budget was preferable but rather to highlight the (in)visibilising tendencies of an austerity mindset as the precondition for reform.[81] This, coupled with ideas of expanded workload, fashioned any future reform effort as a response consistent with both particular global demands for justice and Western-backed financial prudence.

6.4.2 Problem

Articulating a context in the background of more public debates about the future direction of the court, Registry experts, PwC, and pro-bono 'high level experts' helped to settle the parameters and expectations of the upcoming reform project.[82] Some of their diagnostic efforts were already being translated into concrete proposals. In 2013, PwC recommended, inter alia,

> (a) Defining a new organisational chart for the various departments and teams; (b) Ensuring the involvement and accountability of management; (c) Maintaining work capabilities at a high level of efficiency; (d) Defining

---

[80] Report of the Committee on Budget and Finance on the Work of its Twenty-second Session, ICC-ASP/13/5, 18 August 2014, Annex 1.

[81] A major point of scholarly contention is the lack of adequate funding for the ICC, and this has only increased with moves towards a zero-growth budget in recent years. Yet such calls assume that the court's full potential will be realised once sufficient resources are placed at its disposal. This assumption is a variation of arguments contested in Chapter 5.

[82] Report of the Committee on Budget and Finance on the Work of Its Nineteenth Session, ICC-ASP/11/15, 29 October 2012, para. 71.

248 'IN A TECHNICAL AND POLITICAL VIEW'

> tasks associated with the strategic plan, and (e) Ensuring that directorates and sections take ownership of the objectives assigned to them.[83]

In addition to having the ear of Registry managers, PwC's proposals resembled those made previously, reaffirming the managerial efforts that senior court leaders had been pursuing for years. They showed that the problem lay within. This applied at the level of the Registry as a whole, necessitating a focus on organisational co-ordination and organ-wide strategic planning. But it also extended more diffusely into individual units and court professionals, whose problems were defined in terms of work capability and ownership of objectives.

This expert analysis was reiterated during *Re*Vision by another management consulting firm, Mannet. Specialising in 'change management', Mannet was recruited to assist in the 'organisational development of the new Registry'.[84] Deploying its expertise, it offered 'procedural input on the *Re*Vision recommendations' and 'support[ed] the Registrar in preparation for an implementation of the reorganisation-related decisions, as well as coaching the Directors and Section Chiefs in the preparation of the reorganisation'.[85] The problem again lay with organ-level mismanagement requiring the channelling of institutional energy and resources towards those issues.

From these interventions, the *Re*Vision team set out to frame the Registry's problems as partly 'structural' and partly 'non-structural'. These left little room for the contentions and complexities that simultaneously flowed through the institution. Structural problems included 'the distribution of functions and reporting lines', while the latter encompassed 'work processes and workflows; systems and databases; communication, cooperation and coordination; regulatory framework; human resources management; and staff morale'.[86] Collectively, the pre-*Re*Vision assessments of context and problems coalesced to render managerial reform the most appropriate and desirable fix to the institutional project. These manoeuvres represented key elements of a managerial worldview, in which the answer to the court's problems was located in the technical solutions of experts.

---

[83] Report of the CBF Report, 7 June 2013, para. 63.

[84] Comprehensive Report on Reorganisation, para. 89.

[85] Ibid., para. 89(b).

[86] Ibid., para. 54. Non-structural issues comprised approximately 70 per cent of the changes made under *Re*Vision; see Comprehensive Report on Reorganisation, para. 115.

6.4 FROM POLITICS TO TECHNIQUE 249

6.4.3 *Phases and Results of ReVision*

*Re*Vision formally commenced in January 2014. However, the foregoing discussion shows the discourse of deliberation and expertise within which that exercise began. While the prologue to *Re*Vision evinced the burial of political contestations confronting the court, the project's commencement signalled a paradoxical politicisation of the technical as the limits of institutional possibility. An audit of *Re*Vision conducted in 2016 tellingly described the election of Herman von Hebel as Registrar in April 2013 as the 'political' justification for launching the reorganisation.[87] Von Hebel had gained considerable administrative experience at several international criminal tribunals, most recently as Registrar of the Special Tribunal for Lebanon (STL) since 2009. In his election campaign before states parties, he extolled his accomplishments in these institutions, including the development of a fundraising strategy at the STL and implementation of a 'downsizing policy' for staff at the Special Court for Sierra Leone.[88] Following this trend, von Hebel made comprehensive reform of the Registry a central pillar of his campaign during the registrar elections.

That von Hebel's appointment should be labelled 'political' is unsurprising, given his elected status and the lengths to which candidates go to gather state support. Yet political here could also be equated to the platform on which von Hebel ran. The CBF recognised that '[t]he appointment of a new Registrar provides an opportunity to drive through reforms of this nature'[89] and his success was put down to this promise of reform.[90] During his swearing-in ceremony, von Hebel promised to 'strengthen and fine-tune the services of the Registry in the coming five years'.[91] By this campaign platform, von Hebel succeeded in presenting management ideas and reforms as political commitments that supporters of the court could rally behind and aspire towards. This captures much of the enthusiastic tone of the exercise.

---

[87] Audit Report of the *Re*Vision project of the International Criminal Court's Registry, ICC-ASP/15/27, 9 November 2016, para. 14.

[88] Election of the Registrar of the International Criminal Court, Assembly of States Parties, 9 October 2012, ICC-ASP/11/19, Annex III, 49, available at: https://asp.icc-cpi.int/sites/asp/files/asp_docs/ASP11/ICC-ASP-11-19-ENG.pdf.

[89] Report of the CBF 7 June 2013, para. 64.

[90] ICC Interview 002, 13 July 2018 (on file with author).

[91] Statement of Registrar von Hebel during Ceremony for the Solemn Undertaking of the Registrar, International Criminal Court, 18 April 2013, para. 7.

The project was formally authorised by states parties in November 2013. ASP resolution 12/1 mandated von Hebel 'to reorganise and streamline the Registry's organisational structure within the envelope of the approved programme budget for 2014 and the maximum number of established posts and approved positions'.[92] The Assembly requested that the exercise 'achieve at least three per cent savings in the approved programme budget for the Registry'.[93] The five phases of *Re*Vision reflected this mandate while also redefining the Registry in management terms.

Phase 1, the set-up phase, saw the establishment of a Project Team and Project Board. The Project Team initially comprised three external experts 'experienced in working with international jurisdictions' and five Registry staff.[94] The team would later grow in size to fifteen members, and finance and human resources experts numbered among those recruited from the Registry.[95] The Project Board, which oversaw and offered guidance to the Project Team, was chaired by the registrar and comprised 'four representatives of the Registrar's users (the ASP, the Presidency and Chambers, the Office of the Prosecutor and a defence lawyer), [and] the President of the ICC's Staff Union'.[96] It also contained two members 'with leadership experience in an international judicial institution and/or extensive experience in one or more of the Registry functions'.[97] The first task of the Project Team was to publish *Re*Vision's Terms of Reference. By the end of Phase 1, the team had also provided a reorganisation plan covering the 'goals, scope, assumptions, deliverables, project team and governance structure, project methodology as well as detailed description of the phases and activities envisaged'.[98] The plan received the assent of the Project Board and was submitted to the CBF for approval in April 2014.

Phase 2 entailed the

> redefinition of the Registry's vision, mission and common values, a review
> of Registry mandates and inherent functions in order to identify areas of

---

[92] ASP Res 12/1 (27 November 2013) Part H, para. 3.

[93] Ibid.

[94] Audit Report on *Re*Vision, para. 46. See Comprehensive Report on Reorganisation, Executive Summary, 25.

[95] Ibid paras. 10 and 29.

[96] Ibid para. 11.

[97] Comprehensive Report on Reorganisation, paras. 49–50.

[98] Report of the Court on the Organisational Structure, ICC-ASP/13/16, 23 May 2014, para. 4.

6.4 FROM POLITICS TO TECHNIQUE 251

overlap or gaps, an analysis of existing and newly collected data, and a recommendation for a new organisational structure of the Registry.[99]

This preparation for organisational redesign required a review of existing information and collection of additional data from Registry staff throughout spring 2014.[100] The results of staff surveys revealed that '81 per cent of Registry staff participating in the May 2014 survey called for change in the Registry'.[101] The *Re*Vision team also consulted with judges and Registry managers on future models for the Registry's 'new high-level structure'.[102] This structure, based on three consolidated divisions within the organ, was formally announced to Registry and court staff in July 2014.

Towards the end of Phase 2, the *Re*Vision team commenced a detailed review of Registry functions. The *Re*Vision team's diagnosis was largely consistent with that of previous experts in the Registry, CBF, and external consultants:

> The results ... reveal fragmentation and inefficiency in several operational areas, leading to uneconomical use of resources, bureaucracy and sub-optimal operations. In particular, there is overlap or fragmentation of functions in field operations; victim participation; assistance and support to victims and victims' representatives; assistance and support to defence counsel; State co-operation and external relations; general legal function; and approval and certification of expenditure ... A number of gaps were also identified in areas such as internal communication; policy-making; organisational performance management; risk management practices; crisis management procedures; political analysis staff-management relations; and internal conflict resolution.[103]

The 2014 report further articulates *Re*Vision's 'guiding principles', which entrench the court's aspirations. These principles include the desire to establish management teams throughout the organ, make the Registry a good 'service provider' to its 'clients', and ensure 'effectiveness and efficiency'.[104]

The detailed review paved the way for the third phase of identifying urgent measures to be implemented 'swiftly without any structural

---

[99] Report on the Review of the Organisational Structure, para. 4(a).
[100] Comprehensive Report on Reorganisation, para. 55(a).
[101] Comprehensive Report on Reorganisation, Executive Summary 25.
[102] Ibid., 29.
[103] Report on the Review of the Organisational Structure, Executive Summary.
[104] Ibid., para. 11.

252 'IN A TECHNICAL AND POLITICAL VIEW'

changes'.[105] These measures included the adoption of principles and procedures concerning the rights and duties of Registry staff impacted by future reorganisation. At this stage, the *Re*Vision team also initiated the process of producing the Registry's new 'vision, mission and values', and centralising management of the court's budget.[106]

Phase 4, the 'Functions Performance Review', was the most lengthy and far-reaching.[107] The team reviewed the performance of each of the Registry's forty-six units and proposed measures to deal with underperformance, fragmentation, and duplication. In total, '18 detailed reports and 539 recommendations were put forward covering all functions of the Registry'.[108] The team then submitted this advice to the registrar and Registry section chiefs.[109]

Two substantive recommendations are worth mentioning since they were rejected at this stage. In March 2015, the Registry began to collect the views of judges and NGOs on a proposal to combine victim and defence functions into two consolidated offices. The Victims Office would merge the Victims Participation and Reparations Section and the Office of Public Counsel for Victims.[110] The office planned to enhance Registry involvement in the appointment of victims' counsel.[111] The Defence Office would amalgamate the Office of Public Counsel for Defence and the Court Services Section. In the end, neither proposal was implemented due to anxieties about the infringement of victims' and defendants' rights.[112] Given that the assent of judges was needed to amend the regulations dealing with victims and defence issues, these two proposals were abandoned.[113]

---

[105] Comprehensive Report on Reorganisation, para. 55(b).
[106] Audit Report on *Re*Vision, footnote 7.
[107] Report on the Review of the Organisational Structure, para. 4(c).
[108] Audit Report on *Re*Vision, para. 12(d).
[109] Comprehensive Report on Reorganisation, para. 55(d).
[110] Basic Outline of Proposals to Establish Defence and Victims Offices, 4.
[111] Fédération internationale des Ligues des droits de l'homme, FIDH Comments on the ICC Registrar's *Re*Vision Proposals in Relation to Victims, 18 November 2014, 2.
[112] Ex-ICC judge Adrian Fulford encapsulated judges' concerns about these changes, Joshua Rozenberg, 'UK's First ICC Judge Attacks Proposed Restructuring of International Court', *The Guardian*, 4 November 2014. Several NGOs also came out against aspects of the proposals, see International Bar Association, IBA Comments on Draft Registry *Re*vision Project Paper: Basic Outline of Proposals to Establish Defence and Victims Offices, December 2014, 8; Avocats sans frontières, ICC Registry *Re*Vision Project – Basic Outline Proposals to Establish Defence and Victims Offices, 22 April 2015, 2.
[113] Audit Report on *Re*Vision, para. 70.

6.4 FROM POLITICS TO TECHNIQUE 253

Bar these proposals, the Project Board approved the remainder of the team's recommendations in April 2015. In June, the registrar submitted the *ReVision* Outcome Report and an implementation roadmap, 'marking the end of the *ReVision* project'.[114] With the five phases complete, the Registry could now implement the team's recommendations. New structures and reporting lines were put in place by July 2015, while new divisions and sections were established throughout the following year. The Registry observed that implementation of the new structure was 'at its peak' by July 2016.[115]

After *ReVision* officially ended, the Registry began to implement staff alterations and, in some cases, redundancies. The Principles and Procedures for staff alterations were promulgated in 2014, before being circulated among Registry staff in June 2015. The Principles provided that posts would be abolished where functions were no longer required or where structural changes resulted in 'substantial changes' to the position necessitating staff redeployment elsewhere.[116] For those staff whose posts were being abolished, the Principles offered a choice between an 'Enhanced Agreed Separation Package' and priority candidacy for new positions at a similar level.[117] In July 2015, staff were notified if their post was to be abolished or substantially changed and by November all affected staff had vacated their positions.

As to the substantive changes enacted through *ReVision*, all 539 cannot be addressed here. Instead, I highlight those deemed most important by the *ReVision* team. The diagrams in Figures 6.1 and 6.2 offer a point of comparison between the Registry's organisational structure pre- and post-*ReVision*.

Key changes highlighted by the *ReVision* team included:

- *Restructuring*. The Registry's two existing divisions – Administrative Services and Court Services – were restructured. The most significant changes were that the new administration division, named the Division of Management Services, now encompasses security and safety, while

---

[114] Comprehensive Report on Reorganisation, Executive Summary, 32.

[115] Although the official end of *ReVision* was set at June 2015 with the publication of the final report, reforms continued to be implemented for 18 months thereafter. In November 2016, the court's External Auditor noted that the implementation had yet to be fully implemented, Audit Report on *ReVision*, para. 19.

[116] ICC Information Circular, Principles and Procedures Applicable to Decisions Arising from the *ReVision* Project, ICC/INF/2014/011/Rev.1, 13 June 2015, para. 9.

[117] Ibid., para. 17.

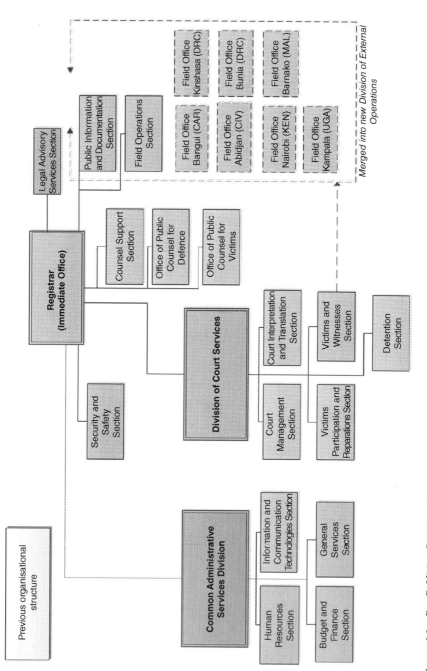

Figure 6.1 Pre-ReVision Registry structure
© ICC-CPI

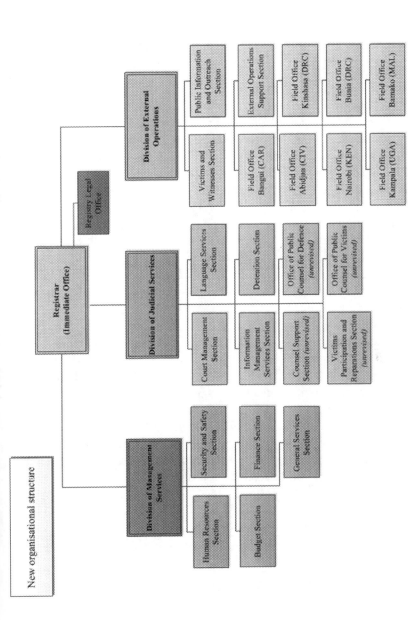

Figure 6.2 Post-ReVision Registry structure
© ICC-CPI

no longer including IT services. The new version of the court division, namely the Division of Judicial Services subsumed counsel support as well as the OPCV and OPCD, thereby centralising Registry control over appointment of victims and defence counsel without creating new Victims and Defence Offices. Rearrangement of sections was designed to 'facilitat[e] intra-Registry synergies and ensur[e] a cohesive Registry approach in all of its areas of responsibility and activities'.[118] All other sections in these two divisions went unchanged.

- *New 'Division of External Operations'*. To the two existing divisions, a third was added – the Division of External Operations (DEO) – combining sections such as field offices, public information and documentation, and the victims and witnesses section, which had previously operated outside a divisional structure. The DEO consolidated these functions to provide management oversight.[119]

- *Reduced number of Registry units*. The new Registry structure comprised thirty-nine units, down from forty-six. In most cases, this resulted from the merger of two or more units, as in the Human Resources Section, where the Entitlements and Payroll Unit, Staffing Unit, and Staff and Administration Unit merged into one Operations Unit.[120]

- *Reduced reporting lines to the Registrar*. Previously, the heads of the Common Administration Services Division, Division of Court Services, and seven isolated sections, reported directly to the Immediate Office of the registrar. This was said to have detracted from the registrar's strategic responsibilities and made lines of authority among Registry managers unclear.[121] Under the new structure, reporting lines to the registrar were reduced to four, primarily because of the DEO.

- *New management teams*. ReVision inserted new management teams with 'strategic leadership' and oversight functions into the Immediate Office, Divisions, and Sections of the organ.[122] The Registry Management Team in particular became the organ's 'highest-level forum to inform, advise and assist the Registry on strategic decisions, policies and major operational challenges'.[123] Within these new

---

[118] Comprehensive Report on Reorganisation, Executive Summary, 3.
[119] Ibid., Executive Summary, 13.
[120] Ibid., para. 265.
[121] Ibid., para. 212.
[122] Audit Report on *Re*Vision, para. 142.
[123] Comprehensive Report on Reorganisation, Executive Summary, 3.

6.4 FROM POLITICS TO TECHNIQUE

management teams, Division and Section heads were to focus on strategic guidance, while operational staff such as lawyers and translators would be left to perform core functions.[124]

- *Absorbing workload increases.* According to the Registry and *Re*Vision's auditors, Registry sections were much better placed to deal with increases in workload after the exercise ended. Although two sections – the Victims and Witnesses Section and the Language Services Section – still had limited capacity to absorb future workload increases post-*Re*Vision, this was attributed to their inherent dependence on the size and scale of investigations and trials.[125]
- *Financial benefits.* Among *Re*Vision's most-cited achievements, the Registry listed its short-term and long-term financial benefits. In 2016 alone, savings and efficiencies were calculated at €5.3 million. These were principally achieved through reductions in Registry staff, lower travel costs, and staggered recruitment of new staff.[126] The cost of reorganisation was €6.1 million and was said to have been offset by financial savings and efficiencies by the end of 2016.[127]
- *Reduction in staff numbers.* Officials calculated that approximately 120 Registry staff were affected by the staffing alterations either from relocation within the new structure or from post abolitions.[128] However, the project ultimately created a net reduction in Registry staff of just 10.4 full-time equivalent (FTE) posts, from 560.4 to 550 FTE staff. The vacancies resulting from *Re*Vision were gradually filled throughout late 2015/early 2016 via a policy of staggered recruitment.

For the experts and officials involved in the project, these were *Re*Vision's main achievements. In his foreword to the 2016 report, von Hebel asserted that 'the new Registry will indeed be a more efficient and effective service provider to all those who rely on it'.[129] This remark hints not only at the continuing importance of standards of efficiency and effectiveness to the project but also at the productive power of these management ideas. The following sections detail these constitutive effects

---

[124] Ibid., Executive Summary, 10.
[125] Comprehensive Report on Reorganisation, paras. 565–566.
[126] Ibid., Executive Summary, 21–23.
[127] Ibid., Executive Summary, 24.
[128] Ibid., para. 75.
[129] Ibid., Foreword, x.

258   'IN A TECHNICAL AND POLITICAL VIEW'

of *Re*Vision in enacting what von Hebel and others understood as a 'new Registry'.

6.5 Management Technique as Politics

Having outlined the context that *Re*Vision's architects fashioned, the previous section demonstrates some of the same patterns of narrowing as in earlier chapters. The following sections demonstrate the opposing set of dynamics that simultaneously emerged during the reform exercise. Having narrowed the extent of the Registry's political engagement down to the technically and institutional digestible, Registry reformers also made management and organisational reform the extent of the court's own policy engagement, or, in other words, the outer limits of its own politics. This reverse turn had significant inclusionary and exclusionary effects, entailing particular prioritisations of voice, the inculcation of certain management practices, and the documentary narration of the exercise. Together these moves by *Re*Vision's architects and collaborators permitted the representation of the Registry's main challenges and dilemmas not in terms of complexity and political contestation but as organisational deficiencies which, once rectified, would put the Registry back on course to fulfil its mandate.

6.5.1 *Voice and Representation*

Despite paeans to consultation, *Re*Vision was conducted from the outset in the voice and vocabulary of management. The pre-history of the exercise reveals the various events, processes, and actors that initiated, adjusted, and implemented reform: these were predominantly individuals who bore an affinity with optimising the institution. The 'advance review team' appointed by von Hebel in January 2014 comprised a director, legal adviser, and 'change facilitator ... all with extensive experience in the functioning of various other international courts and tribunals'.[130] Once the *Re*Vision team reached its full size of fifteen members, human resources, project support, and communications expertise were added to the group.

In parallel, a Project Board was also established 'to oversee the execution of the *Re*Vision project and to advise and support the Registrar in

---

[130] Ibid., para. 42.

6.5 MANAGEMENT TECHNIQUE AS POLITICS 259

the overall direction and management of the project'.[131] This group approved the project plan and the 'opening and closing of each phase, verifying that the project was on track'.[132] The Project Board comprised seven members, chaired by the registrar and consisting of ASP, Presidency/Chambers, and OTP representatives (as 'users' of the Registry), one Defence counsel, the Staff Union president, and two other members 'with leadership experience in an international judicial institution'.[133] Among other tasks, the Board approved the overall plan for the exercise in March 2014.

From the composition of these bodies, it emerges that those with greatest input over the eventual terms and institutional conditions of the exercise also happened to be those with most knowledge of and commitment to the goals of efficiency, optimisation, and planning. These were enhanced by the earlier studies and proposals of the internal auditors, CBF, PwC, and Mannet, which the ReVision bodies relied upon and took seriously as neutral, authoritative diagnoses of the Registry's problems.[134] In this regard, the furthest these experts were willing to revise the Registry was to address 'structural' and 'non-structural' deficiencies. They thereby affirmed the narrow, technical limits of the exercise as the extent of the court's own policy response to extant political dilemmas and contestations.

Several NGOs involved in ReVision consultations pointed towards the quite clear representational consequences arising from the heavy involvement of management experts. The International Federation for Human Rights (FIDH), one of the few anti-managerial voices against ReVision, observed that 'none of the members of the Project Board have direct experience working and interacting on a daily basis with victims of mass atrocities'.[135] Yet in their view, 'benefiting from the view of those who support victims and outside observers acquainted with the realities of victims in the situation countries is crucial'.[136] Another victim-facing NGO, REDRESS, regretted that 'external stakeholders, including NGOs and external Counsel representing victims ... were not meaningfully involved from an earlier stage in the process', having only been consulted

---

[131] Ibid., para. 49.

[132] Ibid.

[133] Ibid., para. 50.

[134] Johnson points to similar dynamics of reliance on managerial judgment in his studies: Gerry Johnson, *Strategic Change and the Management Process* (Blackwell 1987) 29.

[135] FIDH Comments, 1.

[136] Ibid.

260   'IN A TECHNICAL AND POLITICAL VIEW'

after the project plan was approved. They encouraged the Registry to 'take into account the views of those directly benefiting from the Registry's services', which they took to include not just other court organs but also victims and witnesses.[137] Even *Re*Vision's auditors observed that spending more time on recruiting experts 'would have made it possible to construct a more rounded team'.[138]

Failing a more representative team, *Re*Vision architects made much of the project's in-built consultation processes. Registry officials went to considerable lengths to consult with internal and external 'stakeholders' throughout the project. The project timeline contained in the Comprehensive Report reveals sustained periods of consultation with Registry managers, Hague- and field-based staff, as well as judges, NGOs, experts, and states parties. Internal reform proposals were discussed with staff during 'brown-bag lunch[es]' and 'town hall meetings'.[139] And the *Re*Vision team responded to staff proposals, as when it updated the organ's mission and common values 'following a Registry-wide consultation with staff members and with the active participation of the Staff Union'.[140] Externally, an expert conference was held to gauge NGO views on the proposed Victims and Defence Offices. From these consultative efforts, the registrar could point to a 'huge consensus on the big design' of the new Registry.[141] In an interview with *International Justice Monitor* in July 2014, von Hebel concluded that 'overall there is consensus for 70 to 80 percent as to what the new registry should look like'.[142]

Despite these frequent liaisons with staff and external parties, these consultations were not without context. The years leading up to the exercise had witnessed an expert convergence around managerial reform, and the members of the various *Re*Vision bodies adopted the diagnoses of previous Registry evaluators. What was put up for discussion during consultation was not the contextual assumptions and parameters of reorganisation itself but the best options for realising a largely settled

---

[137] REDRESS, Comments to the Registrar in Relation to the *Re*Vision Project as it Relates to Victims' Rights before the ICC, February 2015, 2–3.

[138] Audit Report on *Re*Vision, para. 28.

[139] Comprehensive Report on Reorganisation, Executive Summary, 29 and 31.

[140] Report on the Review of the Organisational Structure, para. 5.

[141] Taegin Reisman, 'ICC Registrar Discusses Restructuring and Need for Larger Budget', International Justice Monitor, 23 July 2014, available at: www.ijmonitor.org/2014/07/icc-registrar-discusses-restructuring-and-need-for-larger-budget/.

[142] Ibid.

6.5 MANAGEMENT TECHNIQUE AS POLITICS 261

set of organisational solutions within those assumptions. The project plan, which was based on the 2013 PwC report, was therefore approved by the Project Board without wider consultation, to the chagrin of REDRESS and others.[143] Following this, discussions with Registry directors and section chiefs centred on 'proposed models for the Registry's new high-level structure', leaving them with a choice between different types of managerial reform.[144] This constrained the available space for contesting the experts' own assumptions, as well as for reappraising the policy priorities and contexts that initially informed the exercise.

Consultations with staff members illustrate this dynamic. Surveys revealed that 81 per cent of Registry staff had 'called for change in the Registry'.[145] Yet this figure emerged from surveys conducted on a turnout of 60 per cent. Of these, only 59 per cent of participating staff believed a 'change in organisational structure' was 'necessary' with 37 per cent of respondents remaining 'neutral on this question'.[146] The team's consultations with Registry staff also centred on the relative strengths and weaknesses of 'three alternative organisational models'.[147] One of these was approved by the Project Board on 17 July 2014 and at a town hall meeting the following day, 'the Registrar announce[d] to all staff the new three-pillar structure of the Registry'.[148] It took a further three months after this announcement before the team began to present the reorganisation plans to a small pool of NGOs led by the Coalition for the ICC.[149]

The consensus which the registrar and others sought to build around the need for managerial reform was achieved only against a particular context assembled over the preceding years. By the time the *Re*Vision team began to collect feedback on the proposed changes, the options were severely restricted to different types of managerial reform. Rather than encompassing a much longer and deliberative process that accounted for the context and scope of reform, these attenuated moments of exposure to institutionally acceptable alternatives marked the extent of the court's willingness to confront contention and dilemma

---

[143] Comprehensive Report on Reorganisation, Executive Summary, 29.
[144] Ibid., Executive Summary, 29.
[145] Ibid., para. 16.
[146] Ibid.
[147] Ibid., para. 65.
[148] Ibid., Executive Summary, 29.
[149] Ibid., Executive Summary, 30.

among court participants.[150] To the extent that there were, as von Hebel later assured, only 'a few dissident voices on bits and pieces', such a finding needs to be assessed against this restricted discourse of reform.[151]

Prioritising managerial voices did not completely expunge alternatives to change, even if it severely curtailed opportunities for airing them. FIDH lamented the lack of wider consultation with those caught up in mass atrocities, particularly in proposed changes to victim representation processes. For FIDH, the right of victims to participate in proceedings would only be realised 'if legal representation is exercised in such a way that it puts victims at the centre of consultation initiatives and allows them to practically and really be a part of the proceedings, even through remote non-physical intervention'.[152] In their view, it was precisely the ReVision team's blinkered institutional view that got them to proposing a centralised system for the appointment of victims counsel in a new Victims Office. Challenging this view, FIDH asserted that 'the victims are where they ought to be, they are where the crimes were committed, they live in areas where they have always resided'.[153] Accordingly, '[w]hat is far is not the victims, but the seat of the Court', so '[t]he premise must be that the Court needs to adapt to victims; it is not for the victims to adapt to the Court'.[154] This is only a brief and rare glimpse into the alternative imaginaries of reform offered by consultees.

This brief intervention by FIDH offers a clear alternative to the narrow epistemic boundaries of ReVision. It not only foregrounds questions of representation but also suggests the imaginative possibilities accompanying perspectives that explicitly reject the blinkered gaze of the institution. Here, in a slightly reductive but dissident move, the ICC is provincialised within wider dynamics and actors involved in realising global justice.[155] Without pre-empting what forms of justice may emerge from such possibilities, it is enough that, as FIDH concludes, '[v]ictims have a

---

[150] This is consistent with the CBF's motivations for ReVision, which was to allow states and Registry officials like von Hebel to 'drive through reforms of this nature' rather than to meet the wider challenges posed by political actors; Report of the CBF 7 June 2013, para. 64.

[151] Reisman, 'ICC Registrar Discusses Restructuring and Need for Larger Budget'.

[152] FIDH Comments, 2.

[153] Ibid.

[154] Ibid. This should not be taken as a proposal for on-site court proceedings, which FIDH do not mention. See also Clark, 'Distant Justice'.

[155] Dipesh Chakrabarty, *Provincialising Europe: Postcolonial Thought and Historical Difference* (Cambridge University Press 2000).

6.5 MANAGEMENT TECHNIQUE AS POLITICS 263

myriad of needs and justice is one of them'.[156] That these and related political calls may demand a radical rethink of the Registry and court's place in that project (possibly even its extraction from it) is the price of directly confronting the political contestations and argumentative dilemmas facing the court.

6.5.2 Management Practices and ReVision

Consistent with prior reorganisations, *ReVision* saw the deployment of various management practices. As well as familiar tools of strategic planning and performance indicators, the exercise also saw the deployment of other management tools, and here I briefly discuss four. Although harbouring quite different aims and functions, these tools managed representations of risk, as well as the court's successes and failures. By these measures, contestation and dissent continued to be written out of the project of institutional change, and technical fine-tuning was reaffirmed as the extent of the court's own politics.

One tool which came to the fore during *ReVision* was the organisational chart or organigram. Organigrams have featured regularly as part of the court's management apparatus to depict the court's units, sections, divisions, and organs, as well as the linkages between them. Judged from the micro level, the organigram has also proven a useful pedagogical tool for 'onboarding' recent recruits and, as such, frames employees' professional commitments.

A similar but more explicit effect is visible in the use of organigrams during and after *ReVision*. The first sighting of such a tool came in PwC's 2013 report to the ASP. At this point, the organigram functioned not as a timeless depiction of the Registry but the opposite: a blueprint of a 'new Registry' intended to project future professional action. As the *ReVision* project commenced, versions of this new Registry no doubt circulated around the court and among consultees. Once the project and its implementation phase were completed, the Registry relied upon an updated organigram to contrast the new organ against the old. These depictions appear in sequence on the initial pages of the 2016 Comprehensive Report (see Figures 6.1 and 6.2).

As a 'before' and 'after' of the project, these organigrams reveal the extent of structural transformation to the court's many participants. Yet

---

[156] FIDH Comments, 6.

264   'IN A TECHNICAL AND POLITICAL VIEW'

both depictions go beyond capturing prior and new realities. Why, for example, is the old organigram colour-coded according to the new divisional structure? Why also does a dashed box frame nine old sections and offices as if they already existed within the structure of the new Division of External Operations? In fact, the illustrations give a clear sense of what was important to the *Re*Vision experts and, implicitly, what progress looked like to them. The old configuration was haphazard, overlapping, and with insufficient central oversight and hierarchy. The new offers clear and legible lines of authority, and logical groupings of sections and offices into the appropriate division. The Registry reveals that beyond individual measures, clarity, logic, and a sense of coherence were forefront in the reformers' minds.

There are many aspects of court life that necessarily do not feature in this diagrammatic. With no in-text explanation, the reader can hardly connect the work of, say, the Abidjan Field Office or the Court Management Section to contemporary activities. The only politics that such a depiction tolerates is an implicit link between the work of these sections and the achievement of the court's aims. Moreover, illustration of the old Registry structure represents not just the sub-optimal misalignment of divisions but also the confused, irrational, and uncontrolled aspects of the Registry's past. It is those irrationalities that *Re*Vision seeks to do away with. Other political complexities and tensions do not feature in these depictions.

A second technique was the project management tool known as PRINCE2. PRINCE2, short for 'Projects in Controlled Environments', was originally developed alongside the UK Office of Government Commerce at the height of British managerialism.[157] As a project methodology, it 'emphasises dividing projects into phases and established quality control to reduce risks inherent in projects during implementation'.[158] It also takes as its focus the long-term value of the organisation in which it is deployed. There is no indication as to why PRINCE2 was chosen over other possible tools but its emphasis on risk and staged reform also shaped experts' framings of liability, possibility, success, and failure.

---

[157] Audit Report on *Re*Vision, footnote 6. New managerialism and 'New Labour' politics defined the centre-left agenda of Tony Blair's first government; see Robert Protherough and John Pick, *Managing Britannia: Culture and Management in Modern Britain* (Imprint Academic 2003).

[158] Audit Report on *Re*Vision, footnote 6.

6.5 MANAGEMENT TECHNIQUE AS POLITICS   265

While risk already featured as its own sub-machinery within the court, PRINCE2 propelled concerns about institutional liability and reputation to the top of the agenda. In keeping with the experts' diagnosis, risk and liability were characterised largely in terms of organisational risk, whether to the financial viability of the Registry as the most expensive ICC organ, or to individual staff members, particularly those posted to field offices. Risks to victims or risks of not confronting political concerns raised by other actors were excluded. PRINCE2 further abstracted risk from these pressing concerns by identifying 'the main risks for each phase', thereby prioritising the *ReVision* team's concerns about timing and completion.[159] For the reformers, the key concern was to ensure each phase was completed in full and on time without risking delay.

PRINCE2's risk attitude also refined institutional definitions of success and failure. Those definitions were already being adapted through the more general management apparatus, and certainly from PwC's 2013 report. At that time, PwC consultants had noted that a successful Registry would implement modern methods, institute a new organisational chart, and define its tasks according to the strategic plan.[160] The Registry would also be deemed a success when it had clearer reporting lines, empowered managers, and when it could adapt to fluctuating workloads. Success meant 'One Registry' working together for the collective benefit of all 'clients'.[161]

The upshot of this redefinition was that PRINCE2 designated the completion of internal targets, deadlines, and management tweaks as successes in their own right, in a displacement of further transformation. The effectiveness of this redefinition is visible during and after *ReVision*. The registrar kept the ASP regularly updated on the project's progress and its compliance with deadlines. Proposing the 2015 annual budget to states parties, the registrar outlined the objective of 'finalis[ing] the Registry *ReVision* project by mid-2015'.[162] Officials noted that *ReVision* would be complete with the 'delivery of final *ReVision* report end June 2015'.[163] These indicia were later affirmed by the auditors. They found that 'the deadlines laid down for the end of each phase were met'

---

[159] Comprehensive Report on Reorganisation, para. 56.
[160] Report of the CBF 7 June 2013, para. 63.
[161] Comprehensive Report on Reorganisation, para. 39.
[162] Proposed Programme Budget for 2015, ICC-ASP/13/10, 18 September 2014, para. 273, Table 31.
[163] Ibid.

266 'IN A TECHNICAL AND POLITICAL VIEW'

and heralded this as a key achievement.[164] Recording these achievements, the timely and cost-effective completion of the reform project and its subsequent reporting became an important contribution of *Re*Vision to the ICC's global justice efforts.

Similarly, PRINCE2 redefined institutional failure as missing a deadline, going over budget, or failing to report findings. These priorities are to be expected from an organisation concerned with not only value for money but also perceptions of its own transparency and accountability. Although transparency and accountability could be linked to various groups or interests, here it is attached to internal processes. This occludes much of the wider context within which the Registry operated but allowed failure to be represented as constantly treatable and manageable. The kinds of failures – 'lessons learnt' – highlighted at the end of the Comprehensive Report point to the reformers' anxieties about the project's possible downsides.

The Registry cites only two deficiencies of *Re*Vision: the team's 'inability to communicate effectively' during the project and its length.[165] On the first, experts noted that communication with Registry staff and external constituencies could have been more effective during the process. This would apparently have avoided misperceptions about the exercise, damage to 'the reputation of the project and that of the Registry and the Court as a whole'.[166] It is telling here that the deficiencies identified are very similar to those the court identifies in its work in atrocity situations, where the problem of communication and misunderstanding is often offset to victim communities or uncooperative governments. Inside the institution, though, the solution to such problems in future should lie in more effective marketing of the project. Similarly, responsibility is passed onto those staff members who 'lack[ed] adequate or timely information'.[167] The possibility that the problem is not a failure of communication but a failure of that which is being communicated is not considered.

The second failure identified was the length of the process. Here, the problem is said to lie in the difficulty of balancing speed with fairness to those affected by the changes, which the court takes to mean Registry staff. The reformers point to the adverse consequences flowing from the

---

[164] Audit Report on *Re*Vision, para. 18.
[165] Comprehensive Report on Reorganisation, paras. 565 and 567.
[166] Ibid., para. 567.
[167] Ibid.

6.5 MANAGEMENT TECHNIQUE AS POLITICS 267

project's duration, namely low staff morale and job insecurity.[168] The problem of slow progress is attributed to the necessity of a 'fair, transparent and inclusive' consultation process and the registrar was adamant that the process was conducted to a 'high standard' of fairness even if 'different stakeholders' may have had different views about the correct balance between length and fairness.[169] Failure, namely staff anxiety, is not offset or displaced, as with communication failures but entirely removed as a point of critique. When the problem becomes one of a balancing act between speed and fairness, reasonable experts can disagree and the *Re*Vision team's particular balance may be posited as just one possible outcome, albeit with minor tweaking required in future. From both forms of failure – communication and duration – reformers offer a sense of what was prioritised but also how these failures represented all that was wrong with the exercise.

Two final tools of *Re*Vision – job reclassification and the Registry Core Values – show how the Registry professional became part of their own subjectivation through *Re*Vision. Practices such as onboarding, probation, and performance appraisal already fashioned the ICC professional as an institutionally responsible and efficient professional. *Re*Vision built on these micro-practices by identifying and arranging Registry staff according to their organisational value.

The process of staff redundancies demonstrates the individual effects of *Re*Vision. The procedure for dealing with employment decisions arising from *Re*Vision was laid down in an Information Circular on Principles and Procedures Applicable to Decisions Arising from the *Re*Vision Project. Subsequently, in June 2015, once the new structure had been decided,

> detailed job surveys were made for all new or modified positions, based on the recommendations of the *Re*Vision team and the Registrar's decisions. For modified positions, it was necessary to determine whether the changes in the job description amounted to a "substantial change". If there was no substantial change, the staff member occupying that position would continue in that same position. However, if there had been a "substantial change" in the position, the position was abolished and a new, or rather materially different, position was created.[170]

---

[168] Ibid., para. 565.
[169] Ibid.
[170] Ibid., para. 74.

Although the final decision as to post alterations and abolitions lay with the registrar, evaluations of 'substantial change' were made by 'an internal classification expert'.[171] From this expert analysis, Registry professionals found themselves characterised as either necessary for the new Registry and thus protected from the changes, or as less or even unnecessary and thus exposed to reallocation or redundancy. A recurring theme of *Re*Vision, particularly after its completion, was the lack of concern for the welfare of Registry professionals and failure to notify them in good time about the stability of their appointment. Although the number of Registry staff decreased by only ten full-time positions by the end, the confusion surrounding job reclassification meant that many more staff did not know whether they would remain employed until the exercise ended.

Beyond the clear material and emotional effects of the process, job reclassification also reconstituted the identity of professionals to align much more closely to the managerial ethos of the reformers themselves, whether as continuing employees or ex-employees with priority consideration for new posts. This dynamic is visible in the grounds for job reclassification and in the deliberations of the ILO Administrative Tribunal (ILOAT) in its hearings on certain complaints raised by Registry professionals about their treatment during *Re*Vision. Over twenty separate complaints were brought by Registry professionals against the organ and the court has since paid out in excess of €1 million to ex-employees in damages.[172]

In one case, *L. v. ICC*, the tribunal discussed the 'operative effect' of the Principles mentioned earlier, despite agreeing with earlier ILOAT findings that the Principles themselves 'were without legal foundation'.[173] In the course of this discussion, the tribunal discussed the consequences of a finding of 'substantial change' to positions, noting that 'the answer to the question of whether there had been a substantial change to the functions, duties and responsibilities of the position *influenced, indeed*

---

[171] Ibid., para. 75. The Registrar treated these determinations as binding.

[172] Kevin Jon Heller, 'ICC Labor Woes Part II: What's Two Million Euros Between Friends?', Opinio Juris blog, 30 June 2018, available at: http://opiniojuris.org/2018/06/30/the-iccs-labor-woes-part-ii/?utm_source=feedburner&utm_medium=email&utm_campaign=Feed%3A+opiniojurisfeed+%28Opinio+Juris%29.

[173] *L. (No. 3) v. ICC* (International Labour Organisation Administrative Tribunal Judgment) No. 3908 (24 January 2018) para. 9.

6.5 MANAGEMENT TECHNIQUE AS POLITICS

determined, the path the occupant of the position would take in order to secure ongoing employment with the ICC'.[174]

The tribunal was here referring to the decisions and actions of (ex-) professionals in seeking re-employment, including decisions about whether to enter a competitive re-recruitment process. Yet what is already apparent from our discussion of the court's recruitment practices is that such a process, however procedural, followed the standard practices for recruitment, including the use of job advertisements, interviews, and onboarding. While these may be somewhat attenuated due to the ex-professional's familiarity with the organ and position, the process of reapplying would nonetheless require them to redefine their professional selves according to criteria similar to those that resulted in their earlier dismissal. They might explain their value to the organ, describing past experience as a crucial asset and demonstrating their awareness of the new Registry's priorities. In this respect the court planned to offer affected staff 'relevant career transition workshops . . . how to source jobs, CV writing, preparing for interviews', and other training 'to enable them to better meet qualifications for suitable positions within the Court'.[175] Having been at the receiving end of a decision based on organisational need, the former and potential professional recommits to ideas of organisational need, efficiency, and service delivery.

A final management tool also implicated continuing staff. Whatever deficiencies arose from the project, its supporters dubbed Registry professionals 'the core stakeholders and clients of the new vision'.[176] On that basis, and consistent with its name, *Re*Vision attempted to instil a new vision among Registry professionals through a statement on core values (see Figure 6.3). This statement reiterated the mission of the Registry as well as the core values that ran through it. The Registry mission included managing human and financial resources and 'empower[ing] our staff to provide high quality services, in the fastest and most cost-effective way'.[177] Core values consisted of 'commitment', 'service-orientation', and 'collaboration'. The statement describes Registry professionals as 'hard-working, dedicated and . . . hav[ing] a sense of purpose'. They 'find

---

[174] Ibid., para. 11 (emphasis added).
[175] Report on the Review of the Organisational Structure, Annex II, para 47(d).
[176] Report on Phase 4 of the *Re*Vision Project, para. 24.
[177] Ibid., Annex V, The Registry Statements and Core Values.

Annex V

The Registry statements and core values

THE REGISTRY STATEMENTS AND CORE VALUES

VISION
A trusted Registry
Enabling the pursuit and delivery of justice through fair and transparent proceedings
Making the vision of the Rome Statute a reality

MISSION
The Registry is a neutral organ of the International Criminal Court. We support the other organs of the Court and its related bodies. We provide services to the judiciary, parties and participants to the proceedings, both at headquarters and in the field. We provide technical and operational assistance. We manage human and financial resources. We foster ties with the public and the international community. We empower our staff to provide high quality services, in the fastest and most cost-effective way.

VALUES

Respect: We exhibit a genuine human and professional respect for our colleagues, our clients. We treat all persons equally. We respect the judicial process. We earn the respect of those we interact with.

Commitment: We are hard-working, dedicated and "we go above and beyond" for the work that is required. We have a sense of purpose. People can count on us.

Constructive behaviour: We find solutions not problems. We are positive rather than negative in how we think, talk, and act.

Service-orientation: We are service and client-oriented. Our clients may be diverse, and our services may be complex, but our focus on service delivery is guaranteed. We will find a way within the boundaries of applicable rules.

Integrity: As civil servants working in a criminal court, integrity has special meaning. Rules are observed. Honesty and accountability prevail. In case of doubt, we are forthcoming and seek guidance. Everything we do is done for the right reasons. We are not driven by personal motives and personal agendas will not stand in the way of achieving results.

Collaboration: The Registry is One. We work together as a team at every level and we actively involve and inform each other. In providing services to our clients, we foster their active collaboration. The Registry promotes the One Court principle.

Figure 6.3   Registry Statements and Core Values
© ICC-CPI

6.5 MANAGEMENT TECHNIQUE AS POLITICS

solutions not problems' and 'are positive rather than negative in how [they] think, talk and act'. They are 'service and client-oriented' and '[e]verything [they] do is done for the right reasons'.[178]

Such individualised values evince a dual subjectivation. On one hand, their inclusion in the process is 'a deliberate choice enabling Registry staff to take ownership of the process and its outcomes'.[179] Registry professionals embody these values and thereby enact or 'live' them in their everyday activities. These quite vague phrases – designed to have the employee feel committed, service-oriented, and efficient – demand little else in the way of broader commitments or responsibilities beyond the institution. On the other hand, these values were later re-imposed on staff by the organ, notably through training programmes, performance management, and 'activities aimed at improving staff morale'.[180] These practices were deemed necessary 'to carry through an effective change management embraced by all Registry staff'.[181] The dynamic of professional regulation post-ReVision thus operated not coercively but relationally, between and within professionals.

6.5.3 Documenting ReVision

ReVision, like other organisational processes such as performance appraisal, was mediated via a range of expert documents. And like those processes, the documents entrenched a managerial 'way of seeing' the organ.[182] That lens is visible in the very layout of ReVision's main documents. The 'Report of the Registry on the Outcome of the ReVision Process', published in July 2015, provides an overview of each Registry section by 'identifying the major (i) issues; (ii) solutions; and (iii) costs'.[183] The Comprehensive Report published the following year offers a more elaborate division, outlining:

> (i) the main problems identified in the previous structure; (ii) the solutions found for these problems and the efficiencies achieved; (iii) an overview of the structural changes; (iv) staffing implications at the level

---

[178] Registry Statements and Core Values.
[179] Report on Phase 4 of the ReVision Project, para. 14.
[180] Comprehensive Report on Reorganisation, para. 278.
[181] Report on Phase 4 of the ReVision Project, para. 24.
[182] John Berger, *Ways of Seeing* (Penguin 2008).
[183] Report on Phase 4 of the ReVision Project, para. 10.

272 'IN A TECHNICAL AND POLITICAL VIEW'

of each post; (v) a detailed explanation of the staffing and work of the Section in the new structure; (vi) the capacity of the new structure to absorb workload increases; and (vii) organisational development plans.[184]

This step-by-step analysis is an apt metonym for the concerns included and excluded by the reformers. The layout of the project and of the section headings imply the major concerns as being whether efficiencies could be achieved, whether staffing implications could be minimised, and whether the new Registry could deal with workload increases. No further problems for the Registry appear. And whether or not these obstacles are overcome by the team is perhaps less relevant than assessing the organ through this lens. The Comprehensive Report also provides a detailed 'benefit–cost analysis', which allows all effects of the process, however complex, to be read through the binary of 'costs' and 'benefits' to the institution. Many of these are recorded in financial terms, while all benefits are registered as quantifiable statistics. According to this yardstick, unquantifiable benefits and costs are simply absent; officially, they did not happen. This creates a somewhat skewed reading of the project's consequences despite the clear material and emotional consequences of ReVision for many Registry staff. In fact, staff cuts are not recorded as costs but as benefits that reduced the court's 'budgetary needs'.[185] As von Hebel had put it to the ASP, the objective was not 'downsizing, but rightsizing'.[186] What the unquantifiable costs of ReVision were for failing to confront the ICC–AU relationship, or for victims, is far from the surface of such reports.

Nevertheless, Registry leadership admitted to some clear yet unquantifiable costs, even if these were left out of the initial table. In his foreword to the Comprehensive Report, von Hebel acknowledges that an ASP decision not to agree to the Registry's proposed budget for 2016 left the organ having to stagger the recruitment of new staff in the wake of ReVision, rather than recruit more rapidly as planned. Von Hebel notes that such staggering caused 'delays in the delivery of transcripts', 'delays in and postponement of missions to the field', and 'delayed investigations and proceedings'.[187] These costs are not recorded in the benefit–cost analysis while the only consequence of staggered recruitment is recorded as a benefit insofar as it produced savings of €3.4 million.

---

[184] Comprehensive Report on Reorganisation, para. 209.
[185] Report on Phase 4 of the ReVision Project, para. 41.
[186] Registrar Remarks to the ASP 12th Session, 8.
[187] Comprehensive Report on Reorganisation, Foreword, x.

6.5 MANAGEMENT TECHNIQUE AS POLITICS 273

Documents produced after *Re*Vision, ostensibly for the purpose of evaluating its procedures and effects, retrospectively affirmed and justified such an approach. In November 2015, the External Auditor was authorised to conduct a 'full assessment' of *Re*Vision.[188] They were to 'assess the compliance, efficiency and effectiveness of the approach followed [by the *Re*Vision team] and the measures adopted pursuant to the final report'.[189] These terms of reference were consistent with the auditor's mandate to 'make observations with respect to the efficiency of the financial procedures, the accounting system, the internal financial controls and, in general, the administration and management of the court'.[190]

Based on this framework, the two audits which followed *Re*Vision verified the context, parameters, and scope of the exercise even if they criticised some of the ways in which it was conducted. The 2016 report evaluated the project based on the comprehensiveness of the project plan and the justifications for reform, as well as the PRINCE2 methodology of compliance with deadlines and the structure of project phases. It concluded that since *Re*Vision redefined the Registry's values and principles, rationalised its divisions, and strengthened intra-organ co-ordination, it was 'justified in a technical and political view'.[191] The combination of the technical and the political is telling as a sign of their fusion within the imaginary of management experts involved in implementing and assessing *Re*Vision. A 2017 audit into the new Division of External Operations made a similar finding, observing the 'unanimous positive assessment among the major stakeholders'.[192] Both reports recommended that the organ go even further by instituting standard operating procedures for Registry staff and defining new working methods with the possible assistance of a 'firm of consultants or specialists'.[193]

From the early consultancies commissioned by the ASP to the post-project audit reports, *Re*Vision was mediated through expert documentation. The 2015 Outcome Report and the Comprehensive Report the following year represent the court's official history of the project, offering an insight into what was deemed important but also how the court

---

[188] ASP Res 14/1 (26 November 2015) Part J, para. 13.

[189] Audit Report on *Re*Vision, para. 4.

[190] Reg. 12.3, Financial Regulations and Rules, ICC-ASP/1/3, adopted 9 September 2002.

[191] Audit Report on *Re*Vision, para. 130.

[192] Final Audit Report on the Implementation of a Division of External Operations, ICC-ASP/16/27, 10 October 2017, para. 118(a).

[193] Audit Report on *Re*Vision, para. 5; Audit Report on DEO, para. 11.

reconstructed the more sensitive moments of the project and those unaddressed elements to states and other participants. Documenting *Re*Vision was a formulation of the Registry as it henceforth sought to be viewed and evaluated. Such documents left little room for the unquantified costs but also for appreciating or confronting the many contestations that by then circulated around and within the institution.

6.6 *Re*Vision as Professional Comfort

The *Re*Vision project sought to establish the terms of its own evaluation. The *Re*Vision team and Registry officials spearheading the project were largely successful in that endeavour. The two audit reports that followed the exercise adopted the terminology of efficiency, financial controls, and internal management as the basis for their assessment. The limited number of policy and scholarly engagements within the project also took many of these parameters for assessment at face value in order to analyse a specific set of changes.[194]

Nonetheless, approaching the project from the perspective of management practices brings to light a wider range of dynamics that 'effectiveness critiques' fail to transmit. These dynamics include, notably, the largely homogeneous voice in which the project was diagnosed and later conducted, the specific remit of terms adopted for analysis, such as 'risk', 'success', and 'failure', and the way in which effects were weighed on a scale of quantifiable benefits and costs. While it would be easy to read the cumulative effect of these dynamics as the fulfilment of the *Re*Vision team's mandate, an alternative account is possible. Under this view, *Re*Vision can be read as a dual project for replacing the political with the technical and equating the technical to the political. These are two quite different discursive processes that saw the court deal with a tumultuous time in its own history through an intense effort of professional renewal.

The first set of processes – of replacing or reducing the political to the technical – reflects some of the narrowing tendencies of management practices and experts described throughout this book. New dissent from political actors and enduring dilemmas of the court are effaced in favour of budget constraint and workload increases as context. These

---

[194] See above. See also Rachel Killean and Luke Moffett, 'Victim Legal Representation before the ICC and ECCC' (2017) 15 *Journal of International Criminal Justice* 713–740, at 739.

6.6 REVISION AS PROFESSIONAL COMFORT

assumptions were taken as the objective diagnosis of the Registry's ills. Although no mention is made of the wider political and discursive context of the time, reformers would no doubt have been cautious about importing overtly 'political' factors of African disenchantment into their calculations of organ reform, even as their own concerns introduced politics by managerial means.

Beyond constructing *Re*Vision as a purely technical project, its architects and executors simultaneously made technical fine-tuning a political project in its own right. *Re*Vision was heralded as a moment of institutional renewal and professional re-commitment to the Registry and court. In the almost one-sided evaluation of the project as a success, and the significant efforts made to avoid deep-seated criticism of its terms and results, *Re*Vision symbolises the expert's apolitical politics, characterised by a drive towards the institutional mission, arguments of pragmatism and necessity, and tools of management consultancy, organigrams, audits, and core value statements.

The *Re*Vision project demonstrates a politics of denial – both of other contestations, and of its own political character and effects. Although many scholars until now have sought to point out the evident politics and distributional implications of the court's work, very often this fails to rattle the court's supporters. Yet there are glimpses throughout the *Re*Vision project of individuals and groups attempting to articulate a response to the project outside the terms it set itself, thus disrupting its apolitical politics. The claims and provocations made by FIDH in shifting the situation in which knowledge is produced from the court's seat to a different gaze is one such attempt. Such an effort denies the taken-for-granted nature of contextual factors such as workload increases or budgetary constraints by the symbolic force of the voice which the court has, ironically, invested victims with. It accounts for the set of political choices involved in constructing a context, a set of problems, and a raft of organisational tweaks from the starting point of optimisation and institutional stability.

A second disruption came from the ICC bench. After *Re*Vision ended, it became clear that there had been considerable disagreement over the project among judges. The auditors later recalled that

> some of the judges complained of a lack of sufficient consultation during project implementation and criticised the consistency and relevance of certain of the project's proposals. Five of them (out of a total of 18) sent a number of collective messages of protest to the Presidency of the ICC at the end of the process on 24 June and reiterated them after the official

276 'IN A TECHNICAL AND POLITICAL VIEW'

closure of the *ReVision* Project, on 15 July and 7 September 2015, asking that the project be suspended.[195]

In email exchanges, pre-trial judge Cuno Tarfusser complained at having been 'systematically side-lined' and 'marginalised' alongside other judges who 'questioned the legality of the process, its methods and its costs'.[196] Tarfusser alleged that then-president, Silvia Fernández de Gurmendi, was partly responsible for not having raised these issues and instead 'peacefully awaiting the end of [her] mandate and leaving a mess for the next President'.[197] He asked her directly in his email: 'who will take the administrative and financial responsibility for what has happened?'.[198]

This rebuff to *ReVision* provides some reflections on which to conclude. On one level, Tarfusser's criticisms are little more than managerial concerns reflected back onto the process. His grievances relating to the project's cost and its possibly unlawful methods do not cast doubt on efficiency as a standard for evaluation and his attribution of blame to the registrar denies the wider expert work required to effect *ReVision*. Yet Tarfusser's criticism also points to complexity and failure as opposed to simplicity and inevitable success. He queries the managerial assumptions underpinning *ReVision* by forcing its architects to contemplate the political choices and costs that made the exercise possible. Even more so does FIDH demand this kind of contemplation in its effort to shift the vantage point from experts to purported beneficiaries. This is a matter of problematising *ReVision*, of 'begin[ning] to detect the very conditions that made it seem manifest: the familiarities that served as its support, the darknesses that brought about its clarity, and all those far-away things that secretly sustained it and made it "go without saying"'.[199] Indeed, by positing an alternative vantage point, FIDH inadvertently shows the difficulty of the epistemic shift. In the conclusion, I retrace some of the steps taken through the managerial thicket mapped out in this and preceding chapters to revisit these themes of flight, politics, and responsibility.

---

[195] Audit Report on *ReVision*, paras. 36–38.

[196] Stéphanie Maupas, 'ICC under Fire for Internal Management', Justice Info, 26 February 2018, available at: www.justiceinfo.net/en/36556-icc-under-fire-for-internal-management.html. Separately, Tarfusser asked von Hebel: 'Do you not think it is a waste of public money?'.

[197] Ibid.

[198] Ibid.

[199] Michel Foucault, 'For an Ethic of Discomfort' in Michel Foucault, *Power: Essential Works, 1954–1984* (Penguin Classics 2020) 443–448, at 447.

7

Conclusion

And I try
Oh my God, do I try
I try all the time
In this institution.[1]

7.1 Managerial Justice Continued

After over twenty years of institution-building and reform, court officials and supporters of the International Criminal Court (ICC) project are in no hurry to slow down. A retreat took place in the Netherlands in June 2019 to help members of the Bureau of the Assembly of States Parties (ASP) 'gain a better understanding of the current challenges facing the Court and to examine the ways forward'.[2] Among the various topics addressed at the retreat, participants considered fostering a 'strong management and governance culture', optimal use of human resources, and strengthened performance management.[3] In late 2019, the ASP convened in The Hague for its eighteenth annual session. Among other things, states agreed to launch an Independent Expert Review (IER) of the court and the wider Rome Statute system.[4] The review consisted of an in-depth study conducted by an independent panel of nine international criminal law (ICL) experts. Running until September 2020, the experts affirmed that their findings and recommendations would help officials in

---

[1] Four Non-Blondes, 'What's Up?' (Sony Productions 1992, lyrics by Linda Perry).

[2] Bureau of the Assembly of States Parties, Fifth Meeting: Agenda and Decisions, 7 June 2019, 2, available at: https://asp.icc-cpi.int/sites/asp/files/asp_docs/ASP18/ICC-ASP-18-Bureau-5.pdf.pdf.

[3] Summary of the Bureau of Assembly of States Parties Retreat, Santpoort, The Netherlands, 13 June 2019, 3.

[4] ASP Res 18/7 (6 December 2019).

278 CONCLUSION

'meeting the challenges of today for a stronger court tomorrow'.[5] If the IER is anything to go by, the discourses and techniques of management continue to be a fixture of institutional life for this central pillar of global justice.

The IER is indeed quite unique: it is the first such exercise to encompass the entire Rome Statute system and was largely driven by states, who decided upon the roster of experts and key themes. Yet the exercise also sounded a familiar song: the burst of energy and reformist zeal in its initial months, the diligent expert investigations into the court's functioning, and the spirit of efficiency guiding participants. Far from being unique, the IER emerges as rather routine, even banal, in its novelty. Expert consultations, consultancy reports, restructurings, and plans have been the court's modus vivendi for almost two decades. Before that, reliance on management as a discourse of repetitive renewal was apparent in the United Nations of the mid-late twentieth century, but also its interbellum antecedents. Back even further, we see ideas and techniques of efficiency fashioning the factory, the military-industrial complex, and the plantation.

The purported newness of the IER comes as a shock, therefore, to those who look back and around slightly further than ICC reformists. Management has been around for a long time. It has also been turned to by a range of groups including planters, factory engineers, technocrats, politicians, diplomats, and, yes, lawyers, as an innovative way of dealing with new problems. The chapter on the ICC's managerial present also showed how similar reform exercises have been made possible by the very claims to ahistoricity and political neutrality that its advocates and supporters rely upon. The Independent Expert Review was no different, with much being made of the experts' originality and impartiality both during investigations and after their work was done.[6]

Beyond allowing us to situate projects such as the IER, this book also brings together studies, consultations, reports, expectations, and constraints into an analysis of ICC management. We have seen how the

---

[5] Summary of ASP Bureau Retreat, 1.

[6] Independent Expert Review of the International Criminal Court and the Rome Statute System: Final Report, ICC, 30 September 2020, available at: https://asp.icc-cpi.int/sites/asp/files/asp_docs/ASP19/IER-Final-Report-ENG.pdf. Douglas Guilfoyle, 'The International Criminal Court Independent Expert Review: Questions of Accountability and Culture', EJIL Talk! Blog, 7 October 2020, available at: www.ejiltalk.org/the-international-criminal-court-independent-expert-review-questions-of-accountability-and-culture/.

7.1 MANAGERIAL JUSTICE CONTINUED

functionalist claims around management's optimising potential are its least interesting feature. Indeed, it is neither possible nor desirable to bundle the word 'management' into a homogeneous block with common traits or patterns of optimisation wherever it surfaces. Management makes the ICC, its professionals, and the argumentative field in various ways. Within the ICC alone, management has been deployed along at least three different scales – the macro level of large-scale organisational reform, the micro level of professional improvement, and the meso level of legal argument. While the IER has largely been assessed at the macro scale, it also permits of evaluation on the micro and meso scales. If the studies conducted in this book are anything to go by, macro-, micro-, and meso-management reveal the productive power of these ideas and practices for global justice ICC-style.

Together, though, this tripartite analysis shows what is lost in management's uptake. In reshaping the institution and its professionals, management demonstrates patterns of narrowing and broadening, inclusion and exclusion that may cause reformists to stop in their tracks before advocating more and better management.[7] Management ideas and practices facilitate a flight from the narrowings and exclusions it has itself occasioned. It leaves other contexts, problems, knowledges, and worlds on the cutting room floor, even while assuring its users that the leftovers will form tomorrow's agenda.

With this reading in mind, I end this book by asking how the terrain of management ideas and techniques, arguments and papers, might be navigated by those who wish to resist managerial justice at the ICC. In order to clarify the nature of such engagement, I briefly distinguish the intent here as ruptural in the mode of radical defence lawyer, Jacques Vergès. From this distinction, it is possible to account for the two most common responses to my diagnosis as forms of continuity, namely the call for removal and the call for renewal. Having done this, I then propose an alternative: a strategy of discomfort as professional posture. Drawing on Weber's ethic of responsibility, discomfort demands not only a recognition of one's own politics but also the realities of violence occluded by such politics. I end by sketching two strategies that may help us think productively against managerial justice at the ICC as we go in search of more just worlds.

---

[7] Luis Eslava and Sundhya Pahuja, 'Between Resistance and Reform: TWAIL and the Universality of International Law' (2011) 3 *Trade Law & Development* 103–130, at 113.

280 CONCLUSION

7.2 From Strategic Plan to Strategy of Rupture

A starting point is to salvage the term 'strategy' from the strategic planners. In ICL, there is no better aid than Jacques Vergès, the French-Algerian lawyer who defended high-profile individuals such as Klaus Barbie and Khieu Samphan. Throughout his career, Vergès was both theorist and practitioner of strategy, as detailed in his 1968 book *De la stratégie judiciaire*. Drawing on examples such as the trial of Socrates and the Dimitrov trial, Vergès distinguished two types of defence strategy pursued in criminal trials: connivance and rupture. The strategy of connivance is characterised by an adherence to the strictures and assumptions of the trial, including accepting the prosecution case on its own terms and the objectivity of the judicial bench. The aim of connivance is to obtain the best outcome for one's client. For Vergès, 'every characteristic of connivance trials espouses their fundamental need to respect the established order'.[8] This is the approach taken by the majority of defence counsel in criminal trials.

The contrasting strategy – *procès de rupture* – rejects the liberal premises of the criminal trial, including its self-presentation as apolitical and objective. The strategy of rupture treats the criminal trial as a 'confrontation with the system that is represented by the prosecution's case'[9] and aims not to 'obtain the acquittal of the accused, but to highlight his ideas'.[10] This approach to the criminal trial is crucial, according to Vergès, when there is no consensus between the judges and prosecution on one side and defence on the other over the terms and assumptions of the indictment. The strategy was partly on display during the trial of Slobodan Milošević at the International Criminal Tribunal for the former Yugoslavia (ICTY).[11] Vergès deployed the strategy by launching a *tu quoque* defence during the Barbie trial against French crimes in Algeria, and later in defending Khieu Samphan at the Extraordinary Chambers in the Courts of Cambodia (ECCC).[12]

---

[8] Jacques Vergès, *De la stratégie judiciare* (Minuit 1968) 31.
[9] Emilios Christodoulidis, 'Strategies of Rupture' (2009) 20 *Law & Critique* 3–26, at 5.
[10] Vergès, 'De la stratégie' 104.
[11] Milošević alleged that the ICTY was a 'false Tribunal' intended 'to produce false justification for the war crimes of NATO committed in Yugoslavia', *The Prosecutor v. Slobodan Milošević*, International Criminal Tribunal for the former Yugoslavia (Trial Transcripts) IT-02-54 (3 July 2001) 2, available at: www.icty.org/x/cases/slobodan_milosevic/trans/en/010703IA.htm. See John Laughland, *Travesty: The Trial of Slobodan Milošević and the Corruption of International Justice* (Pluto Press 2007) 69.
[12] Mikael Baaz and Mona Lilja, 'Using International Criminal Law to Resist Transitional Justice' (2016) 2 *Conflict & Society* 142–159. The dissenting opinion of Judge Pal at the

7.2 FROM STRATEGIC PLAN TO STRATEGY OF RUPTURE   281

Vergès' connivance/rupture distinction has since been taken up in international law more broadly. Emilios Christodoulidis calls the strategy of rupture a 'critical legal intervention in political-strategic terms'[13], while Brenna Bhandar finds it applicable in postcolonial settings beyond the criminal trial.[14] As Christine Schwöbel-Patel puts it, the strategy of rupture 'demonstrates an ironic stance towards the political power structures that constitute notions of legality, but is nevertheless focused on anti-imperial ends'.[15] It therefore has several advantages as a means of critical engagement with law. According to Christodoulidis, it can 'undercut and reconfigure the historical and didactic nature of the trial, increase its responsive range, re-negotiate past alliances [and] re-open wounds'.[16] It thereby disavows ameliorative tactics for failing to challenge institutional assumptions.[17]

Vergès' notions of connivance and rupture, deftly applied to criminal trials, are no less prescient for activities buttressing such trials. This book shows how the sites of legal struggle and professional engagement with the ICC project extend well beyond its 'core' prosecutorial and judicial tasks. Hence, as Golder argues, the strategy of rupture (and connivance) may be visible 'in a great number of everyday legal encounters'.[18] Considering management, this ranges from the grand reorganisation to the brief appraisal meeting. Such strategies are also not limited to courtroom lawyers but can and have been deployed by various legal and non-legal experts strategising, monitoring, and reshaping the ICC's management apparatus. Applying Vergès' theory to that apparatus, I now identify two obvious ways of engaging management – removal and renewal – as strategies of connivance.

Tokyo tribunal has been read as a ruptural strategy from the bench; see Latha Varadarajan, 'The Trials of Imperialism: Radhabinod Pal's Dissent at the Tokyo Tribunal' (2015) 21 *European Journal of International Relations* 793–815; John Reynolds and Sujith Xavier, '"The Dark Corners of the World": TWAIL and International Criminal Justice' (2016) 14 *Journal of International Criminal Justice* 959–983, at 962.

[13] Christodoulidis, 'Strategies of Rupture' 3.

[14] Brenna Bhandar, 'Strategies of Legal Rupture: The Politics of Judgment' (2012) 30 *Windsor Yearbook of Access to Justice* 59–78, at 66.

[15] Christine Schwöbel-Patel, *Marketing Global Justice: The Political Economy of International Criminal Law* (Cambridge University Press 2020) 261.

[16] Christodoulidis, 'Strategies of Rupture' 6.

[17] Ibid., 3.

[18] Ben Golder, *Foucault and the Politics of Rights* (Stanford University Press 2015) 127.

282   CONCLUSION

Option 1: Removal

Perhaps the most compelling counter to management practices is to advocate their removal from the institution. This may be an attractive prospect. The discursive grammar of efficiency, risk, and performance no longer available as mechanisms for narrowing, excluding, and disavowing wider political struggles and dilemmas. Such suspension of terminology might give those inside and outside the institution the room to formulate the organisation anew. Given the prioritisations of expertise that management entrenches within the institution, its removal might also permit the inscription of alternative knowledges that can highlight the political, structural, and affective dynamics of the anti-impunity project.[19]

One obstacle to this is the likely rationale for removal. Much in the way management is deployed within a context, its removal would be no less a situated effort. Indeed, in conversation with Vergès, Foucault pointed to the necessity of appreciating the theory's historical conjuncture.[20] Read this way, the hegemonic position of management ideas and practices within the institution is more likely to result in a removal justified for its failure to help meet the ICC's existing aims than for occasioning a flight from the political struggles and distributive stakes of the wider project. As much as some might invoke the latter justification, state, expert, and scholarly voices already overwhelmingly engage in a form of 'effectiveness critique', which would likely ensure management practices are evaluated and removed based on that standard.[21] In keeping with Vergès' notion of connivance, removal in this context would only reaffirm the centrality of effectiveness as a valid measure of court success and failure, ignoring the court's wider dilemmas.

A second problem with removal is that it is now extremely difficult to separate the vocabularies of anti-impunity and management within the ICC. This has been a core thread of the book. A call for anti-impunity today is a call for optimal performance of tasks, prudent allocation of resources, and constant improvement. A clean extraction of management is difficult to imagine: what would one be targeting exactly – a discourse, a language, a set of practices, a class of experts? Management turns out to

---

[19] See Kamari Maxine Clarke, *Affective Justice: The International Criminal Court and the Pan-Africanist Pushback* (Duke University Press 2019).

[20] Vergès, 'De la stratégie', Preface to the Second Edition.

[21] Christine Schwöbel, 'Introduction', in Christine Schwöbel (ed.), *Critical Approaches to International Criminal Law: An Introduction* (Routledge 2015) 1–14, at 3–4.

7.2 FROM STRATEGIC PLAN TO STRATEGY OF RUPTURE   283

be all of these things, and the chapter on micro-management of ICC professionals in particular demonstrates the imbrication of management thought by and through individual experts. If power works relationally, as I have argued, then removal would hardly address the professional commitment to management at a micro level.

Foucault's observations on reform caution against the removal and replacement of institutional practices. Replacement is less important than

> see[ing] how far the liberation of thought can go towards making these transformations urgent enough for people to want to carry them out, and sufficiently difficult to carry out for them to be deeply inscribed in reality ... Whatever the project of reform (and scrapping is also a kind of reform), its basis has not been thought working in itself; and if ways of thinking – which is to say, ways of acting – have not actually been modified, we know that it will be phagocyted and digested by behavioural and institutional modes that will always be the same.[22]

Option 2: Renewal

This book has pointed to the perils of reform as a cynical faith in renewal. But surely there are many managements, and among them management 'with a human face'? Responses to my study may follow similar argumentative patterns to those discussed throughout: management, and the institution, is a work-in-progress, which can only be improved through sustained effort; yesterday's failures are tomorrow's 'lessons'; the major constraints lie beyond institutional control. Yet the preceding chapters tell of the construction of these realities as contextual constraints, the power of each of these arguments and their variations to foreclose critique, narrow the imaginary of global justice, and discount the political struggles that comprise the ICC project.

Specific policy proposals may also be posited in a spirit of renewal, such as advocating for a more democratic institution guided by victims' priorities and substituting institution-centred notions of risk, success, and failure with those of victims and others. At the micro level, staff performance appraisals could additionally take account of the particular historical contexts of states and groups of the Global South. This has already been suggested for judicial decision-making during an ICC

---

[22] Michel Foucault, 'So Is It Important to Think?' in Michel Foucault, *Power: Essential Works, 1954–84* (Penguin Classics 2020) 454–458, at 457.

284 CONCLUSION

retreat and could easily be extended to individual staff. Meso-level experts may only need to do a better job at finding a balance between various argumentative poles and in putting management to work in realising it.

Attractive though these proposals are, it is precisely the work of turning anti-impunity into a problem-solving endeavour that this book has concerned itself with. Once we accept the terms management establishes, we become oriented around arguments of effective functioning and optimisation. These ideas and attendant practices demand evaluation on their own terms and make it much more difficult to move beyond extant institutional parameters. Indeed, the most recent update to the performance appraisal form reveals how easily the seemingly anti-managerial traits of creativity and critical judgment can be subsumed into the current apparatus.[23] To engage in such fine-tuning is thus also to adopt a connivance strategy.

Both removal and renewal thus fail to confront the deleterious sides of management. They do not challenge the narrowing and exclusionary dynamics of management nor the prioritisations of knowledge, voice, and politics that ensue from its use. In short, the difficulty of relying upon management as an elixir to institutional woes lies in how it heightens the field's 'aversion to contention' in the first place, as Schwöbel-Patel puts it, and thereby radically dilutes the court's political possibilities and emancipatory potential.[24] It is this aversion, which I also call 'flight' or 'escape' that captures the ICC's management apparatus. It offers comfort within expert discussions and glosses over difficult choices. To counteract this tendency, I channel an alternative strategy of rupture – a strategy of discomfort.

7.3 A Strategy of Discomfort

Is it desirable to make a court which has only prosecuted Africans *efficient*? Would a partial rendering of justice gain greater support were it *streamlined*?[25] Should an *outreach strategy* be the guide to professional

---

[23] See the updated annexes in the Administrative Instruction on the Performance Appraisal System, ICC/AI/2019/003, 26 February 2021, 7.

[24] Christine Schwöbel, 'The Comfort of International Criminal Law' (2013) 24 *Law & Critique* 169–191, at 170.

[25] Adapted from Christian De Vos, Sara Kendall and Carsten Stahn, 'Introduction' in Christian De Vos, Sara Kendall, and Carsten Stahn (eds.), *Contested Justice: The Politics*

7.3 A STRATEGY OF DISCOMFORT 285

contact with communities experiencing mass violence? These may be discomforting questions. Yet comfort, according to Tomas Maldonado, 'is a modern idea'.[26] Since the industrial revolution, it has come to signify a 'need' or even an entitlement to 'convenience, ease, and habitability' which, until then, was the preserve of the privileged few.[27] Comfort also signifies a phenomenological state experienced in relation to a thing-in-the-world.[28] It is a quality desired in relation to things in the world, particularly those things that comprise our immediate existence, such as material and physical needs, or indeed one's professional field. It is not difficult to witness the ICL expert's search for comfort through solutions and moral indignation in the face of global injustice.

Schwöbel-Patel has translated the idea of comfort to the field of international criminal law. She has described the uptake of ICL and the 'crowding out' of human rights law as a 'preference for comfort over discomfort'.[29] She identifies in the ICL field a 'contemporary desire for certainty over contention, action over discourse, and simplicity over complexity'.[30] In this book, the occluding dynamics of management and its preference for certainty, action, and simplicity over contention, discourse, and complexity also reveal it as a key source of comfort for international criminal lawyers and ICC experts.

In her article, Schwöbel-Patel thinks with several writers of discomfort, including Michel Foucault, whose brief piece, 'For an Ethic of Discomfort', offers a counterpoise to the comfort of management. Drawing on Merleau-Ponty, Foucault affirms the 'essential philosophical task' of 'never consent[ing] to being completely comfortable with one's own presuppositions'.[31] Here, assumptions become the object of (dis) comfort. Foucault continues that the challenge is 'never to let [our assumptions] fall peacefully asleep, but also never to believe that a

---

and Practice of International Criminal Court Interventions (Cambridge University Press 2015) 1–20, at 18.

[26] Tomás Maldonado, 'The Idea of Comfort', *Errant Journal*, Issue 3 (2022) 87.

[27] Ibid., 87.

[28] Edmund Husserl, *Logical Investigations* [1901]; Martin Heidegger, *Being and Time* [1927]. For a legal application of these ideas, see Duncan Kennedy, 'A Left Phenomenological Alternative to the Hart/Kelsen Theory of Legal Interpretation' in Duncan Kennedy, *Legal Reasoning: Collected Essays* (Davies Group Publishers 2008) 157.

[29] Schwöbel, 'Comfort' 169.

[30] Ibid.

[31] Michel Foucault, 'For an Ethic of Discomfort' in Michel Foucault, *Power: Essential Works, 1954–1984* (Penguin Classics 2020) 443–448, at 448.

286 CONCLUSION

new fact will suffice to overturn them'.[32] Comfort is not therefore desirable but subject to question and problematisation. Hence, lawyers' desire for comfort in ICL should be investigated, by adopting 'a distant view' as well as by 'look[ing] at what is nearby and all around oneself'.[33]

As Schwöbel-Patel demonstrates, Foucault's ethic treats discomfort as central to critical engagement. This is not surprising, given how discomfort has often featured at the heart of discussions on decoloniality.[34] In a recent issue of *Errant Journal*, a cultural theory publication, the editors convened around the theme of discomfort in relation to artists' engagements with another modern institution, the art gallery.[35] As noted by the editor-in-chief, 'the topic of discomfort is always present in the process of understanding structural inequalities in our societies, as well as our own role – and responsibilities – in these'.[36] Moreover, Saidiya Hartman speaks of the dynamics of 'white discomfort' and 'black freedom' in the context of American slavery.[37] Discomfort can therefore be experienced, sometimes viscerally, as an 'imbalance … of power relations' plotted along multiple economic, racial, and gender lines.[38] Similarly, in an effort to overcome such discomfort, one may experience the discomfort of shifting these power relations, or resisting the assumptions upon which comfortable thought rests. That sense may be keenly and unevenly felt within modern institutions such as the ICC. *Errant*'s editor-in-chief therefore proposes discomfort 'as a strategy, and consequently as an act

---

[32] Ibid.

[33] Ibid.

[34] Clare Land, *Decolonizing Solidarity: Dilemmas and Directions for Supporters of Indigenous Struggles* (Zed Books 2015). See also Sarah Hunt and Cindy Holmes, 'Everyday Decolonization: Living a Decolonizing Queer Politics' (2015) 19 *Journal of Lesbian Studies* 154–172, at 166; Sylvan Blignaut and Oscar Koopman, 'Towards an Embodied Critical Pedagogy of Discomfort as a Decolonising Teaching Strategy' (2020) 31 *Alternation* 81–96; Neha Shaji, 'Some Difficult Questions: On Discomfort, Institutional Activism and Anger', Exeter Decolonising Network, 21 March 2021, available at: http://exeterdecol.org/some-difficult-questions-on-discomfort-institutional-activism-and-anger/.

[35] Errant Journal, https://errantjournal.org/about/; Leon Moosavi, 'Turning the Decolonial Gaze towards Ourselves: Decolonising the Curriculum and "Decolonial Reflexivity" in Sociology and Social Theory' (2022) 00 *Sociology* 1–20.

[36] *Errant Journal*, Editor's note, 9.

[37] Saidiya Hartman, *Scenes of Subjection: Terror, Slavery, and Self-making in Nineteenth-Century America* (Oxford University Press 1997) 148.

[38] Irene de Craen, 'Editor's Note', Errant Journal, Issue 3 (2022) 9.

7.3 A STRATEGY OF DISCOMFORT

of resistance'.[39] This is the sense in which I carry the notion of discomfort forward 'against the grain' of managerial justice.[40]

To further flesh out discomfort, I draw on Max Weber's 'ethic of responsibility'. Weber sketched the ethic of responsibility in his 'Politics as a Vocation' lecture, delivered in Munich during the tumultuous month of January 1919. The Great War was lost, and Luxemburg and Liebknecht, leaders of the communist Spartacist movement, were dead not three weeks. In that context, Weber interpreted the speaking invitation by his audience as a 'desire for certainty . . . the desire to give some secure definition to human circumstances'.[41] Yet he treated that desire for comfort as dangerous and admitted to his audience that he was unlikely to satisfy them. Throughout his lecture, he derided the political machinations of those (including, indirectly, his audience) 'who do not genuinely feel what they are taking on themselves but who are making themselves drunk on romantic sensations'.[42] For Weber, such sensations reflected the certainties of the 'conviction politician', or the 'ethic of conviction', wherein the purity of one's intentions is all that matters regardless of the consequences likely to follow.[43] Such a stance fails to admit that the means of politics 'is the use of force' and that 'whoever makes a pact with the use of force, for whatever ends (and every politician does so), is at the mercy of its particular consequences'.[44]

This is where Weber's responsibility ethic becomes pertinent to discussions of dis/comfort. Weber counsels that

> anyone who wishes to engage in politics at all, and particularly anyone who wishes to practice it as a profession, must become conscious of these ethical paradoxes and of his own responsibility for what may become of

---

[39] Ibid., 10.

[40] Anshuman Prasad (ed.), *Against the Grain: Advances in Postcolonial Organisation Studies* (Universitetforlaget 2012).

[41] David Owen and Tracy B. Strong, 'Introduction' in David Owen and Tracy B. Strong (eds.), *Max Weber: The Vocation Lectures* (Hackett 2004, translated by Rodney Livingstone) xxxvi.

[42] Ibid., xxxix.

[43] Weber, 'Politics as a Vocation', in Owen and Strong, 'Max Weber: The Vocation Lectures' 32–94, at 84. Nouwen identifies the court as running on an ethic of conviction, Sarah Nouwen, '"As You Set Out for Ithaka": Practical, Epistemological, Ethical, and Existential Questions about Socio-Legal Empirical Research in Conflict' (2014) 27 *Leiden Journal of International Law* 227–260, at 252.

[44] Weber, 'Politics as a Vocation' 84–89.

288 CONCLUSION

him under the pressure they exert. For, I repeat, he is entering into relations with the satanic powers that lurk in every act of violence.[45]

This ethic of responsibility is, for Weber, a mark of maturity. As he postulates towards the end of his lecture,

> I find it immeasurably moving when a mature human being ... who feels the responsibility he bears for the consequences of his own actions with his entire soul and who acts in harmony with an ethics of responsibility reaches the point where he says, "Here I stand, I can do no other".

It is only those who 'can still say "Nevertheless!" despite everything' who have the vocation for politics, according to Weber. In settler colonial spaces, this position is well understood and inhabited:

> I just think you have to be able to endure the contradictions. I do not think there's answers. I think an attitude of acceptance of complexity, contradiction, discomfort, and all of those things, um, is the path, and you cannot escape it ... Basically you have to be able to maintain your self-respect. That might be a measure you can use – can I still respect myself and do this, or act in this way, or hold my tongue, or continue to listen, or continue to reflect, or even just continue to feel this discomfort?[46]

There are several important points to be drawn from this stance for a strategy of discomfort. First, a Weberian-inflected strategy of discomfort means admitting to the political stakes, including the potentially violent, unequal, and subordinating effects of professional activity. For Weber, this was the politician; for us, the anti-impunity expert working with or within the court. Such admission is a heady experience, and Weber is quick to admit that 'to use power is to play with the devil and risk always the Faustian loss of one's soul'.[47] Many scholars of the ICC, whether of a more or less critical persuasion, have commented upon the expert tendency to disavow politics and power within the seemingly apolitical sphere of judicial and prosecutorial activity. In the chapter on meso-management, I demonstrated how such apolitical claims are untenable in a field that is constantly susceptible to utopian and apologist arguments simultaneously. But beyond the critical legal intervention on this point, there is also the critical managerial one. The chapter tracing the ICC's managerial antecedents reveals the repudiation of politics as the *modus*

---

[45] Ibid., 90.
[46] Land, 'Decolonising Solidarity' 92.
[47] Owen and Strong, 'Introduction' xxxix.

7.3 A STRATEGY OF DISCOMFORT

operandi of institutional reform, and one of the key reasons for its recurring popularity across institutions.

To give up on apolitical claims would thus mean admitting to the politics of one's expert choices and claims made to produce them.[48] Management would become visible as the continuation of politics by institutional means, defenestrating those reformist projects that demand depoliticisation, and giving succour to those seeking to engage with the ICC as an explicitly political project.[49] In place of a depoliticised space, admitting to politics as part of the Weberian ethic entails its replacement. In that replacement, the expert accepts that 'humanity does not gradually progress from combat to combat until it arrives at universal reciprocity, where the rule of law finally replaces warfare [but] installs each of its violences in a system of rules and thus proceeds from domination to domination'.[50] The ICC, too, dominates – so says the discomforted expert – and management is part of that violence.

Second, admitting to politics will likely occasion deep discomfort for the expert. To confront the violent and exclusionary effects of one's professional-political articulations demands 'a kind of trained ruthlessness in looking at the realities of the world, a refusal to avoid anything'.[51] As Weber observed, anything that may amount to avoidance or denial marks out the individual as a 'political infant' or 'ideologist' concerned only with the purity of their own intentions.[52] Such 'realities' as are accepted by the discomforted ICC expert, then, are those that question the court's will to problem-solve, its understanding of progress and improvement, or its metrics of success and failure. Such questioning may also need to extend inwards. For Weber, maturity meant also taking a distance from one's own desires, indeed 'a distance on oneself'.[53]

For an idea of what such self-distance could entail, we can look to Kennedy's study of the laws of war and its uptake by international

---

[48] Sahib Singh, 'Narrative and Theory: Formalism's Recurrent Return' (2014) 84 *British Yearbook of International Law* 304–343, at 311.

[49] This of course paraphrases Clausewitz's famous line that war is 'merely the continuation of policy by other means', Carl von Clausewitz, *On War* (Princeton University Press 1989, edited and translated by Michael Howard and Peter Paret) 87. See also David Kennedy, *Of War and Law* (Princeton University Press 2006) 42.

[50] Michel Foucault, 'Nietzsche, Genealogy, History' in Paul Rabinow (ed.), *The Foucault Reader* (Pantheon Books 1984) 76–100.

[51] Owen and Strong, 'Introduction' xliii.

[52] Ibid., xliv.

[53] Ibid.

290 CONCLUSION

humanitarian professionals. One of Kennedy's main findings is that responsibility is lost when one adopts the language of law to talk about global suffering since international humanitarian law (IHL) not only restrains wartime violence but 'permits injury, as it privileges, channels, structures, legitimates, and facilitates acts of war'.[54] Kennedy hopes that such realisation 'might awaken our sense of responsibility for the terrible suffering of warfare' but is keenly aware that law itself 'dissolves the broader experience of political and ethical responsibility, while assuring everyone else in the war machine ... that they were, in one or another way, not responsible for the suffering, foreseen and unforeseen, that resulted'.[55] He continues: 'the problem is an unwillingness to [act] responsibly – facing squarely the dark sides, risks, and costs of what they propose'.[56] These remarks of Kennedy's are apt for the ICC expert who refuses to contemplate management's underbelly. And while the ICC expert remains further from the battlefield than IHL practitioners, responsibility is visible on an everyday level, when institutional goals are invoked, problems identified, and solutions proffered.

In response to 'comfortable interpretive routines', Kennedy proposes that experts 'embrace the exercise of power' and 'cultivate the experience of professional discretion and the posture of ethically responsible personal freedom'.[57] For the discomforted ICC expert, this means refusing to take comfort in justifications of budgetary restraint, workload demand, appraisal competencies, or future reform. These arguments are indeed highly sedimented over years of use, but they are nonetheless deployed frequently by various decision-makers at the ICC, ASP sessions, and academic conferences. Similarly, the will to escape the confrontation of law and politics or penal and victim-oriented justice may need to be resisted. One may have a choice in deploying them or not, feeling more or less constrained as one says the words. But to treat them as situated political avenues with potentially subordinating outcomes is already to feel the contingency and contestation of management.

Admittedly, denying this experience of freedom is perhaps what defines the expert in the first place.[58] Yet as Kennedy observes in his recent work, this is less likely to be experienced as existential crisis than

---

[54] Kennedy, 'Of War and Law' 167.
[55] Ibid., 167–168.
[56] Ibid., 169–170.
[57] Ibid., 170.
[58] Ibid., 171.

7.3 A STRATEGY OF DISCOMFORT

as the feeling of 'being persuaded' or 'knuckling under' as a momentary but never final 'loss of agency'.[59] Kennedy calls this 'yielding', or the moment when the expert 'abandons his position' and 'the felt necessity of the earlier position fades' with the realisation that 'things do not add up, that coherence fails, that incommensurability must be acknowledged'.[60] The argument or commitment 'gives way' and '[i]n that moment we may glimpse an alternative to rule by experts: rule by people deciding responsibly in a moment of unknowing'.[61] This is partly how 'to turn "expertise" into something that reverses systems of destitution, oppression, and inequality'.[62]

A final component of the Weberian strategy of discomfort concerns the unknown, which Kennedy already hints at in his 'moment of unknowing'. As Weber acknowledged, 'maturity ... is the recognition that any action taken under circumstances where the consequences of that action are not only not apparent but over the long term do not add up to make sense'.[63] Again, this is part of what it means to be concerned with the harmful sides of management. As Hannah Arendt noted of Adolf Eichmann, '[I]t does no good to say "I did not mean it"'.[64] But the opposite approach of only acting when one has gathered all information is equally paralysing. Rather, the discomforted ICC expert confronts the situation as they find it, having done the difficult work of mapping the wins and losses, while recognising that results may turn out differently, or not at all. That acceptance of working in the unknown is captured in the work of Janet Halley. Although speaking of law, we can imagine what it might look like for ICC experts to *manage* responsibly too:

> we cannot make decisions about what to do with legal power in its many forms responsibly without taking into account as many interests, constituencies, and uncertainties as we can acknowledge. To wield power responsibly, we need to fess up to the fact that, in deciding to advocate, negotiate, legislate, adjudicate, or administer one way or another, we spread both benefits and harms across social and ideological life – and

---

[59] David Kennedy, *A World of Struggle: How Power, Law, and Expertise Shape Global Political Economy* (Princeton University Press 2016) 166.

[60] Ibid., 166–167 and 255.

[61] Ibid., 166.

[62] Nouwen, 'As You Set Out for Ithaka' 260.

[63] Owen and Strong, 'Introduction' xliv.

[64] Ibid.

that some of these benefits and costs, however real, may be constituted by
our very practices of accounting for and attempting to redress them.[65]

The 'taking into account' that Halley mentions is the totting-up of rights, entitlements, wins, and losses required before the will to manage or reform is succumbed to. Accepting that even the best of intentions can curdle or boomerang back is part of what it means to approach one's task responsibly.[66] This understanding already takes us far beyond the current treatment of management at the ICC, where experts take up its assumptions and requirements in a near-total suspension of critical reflection. Together, the admission of politics, yielding, and unknowing form the contours of a professional posture or strategy of discomfort.

Having outlined this strategy, I further clarify what it is not, in the hope of avoiding additional displacements and denials. First, the strategy of discomfort is not the contrarian's blanket urge to shock. Discomfort is not an end in itself but is designed to prompt an awareness and either acceptance or rejection of alternative modalities for managing atrocities and people. Done for its own sake, discomfort is likely to stimulate, even exhilarate, its wielder and cause them to experience not a loss but a gain of agency. Moreover, discomfort as end depoliticises the space in which it is pursued, reducing all participants in the ICC project to targets of discomfort. Yet discomfort as a strategy means recognising the economy of discomfort among and between those participants, including who currently is permitted to remain comfortable and who is required to experience discomfort.

This raises the second non-strategy, which is that discomfort cannot resubordinate. Discomfort demands a capacious understanding of violence and the many ways in which discomfort for some can go hand in hand with violence of various kinds. This may amount to structural, symbolic, and epistemic violences based on structures of racialisation, patriarchy, and class. Such violences may equate to invisibilisation or forced visibilisation; refusal to engage or to accept incommensurability; attempts to authoritatively translate the claims of others; universalising oneself while particularising others; and the non-recognition of alternative bases of violence, including structural, symbolic, and slow violence.

---

[65] Janet Halley, *Split Decisions: How and Why to Take a Break from Feminism* (Princeton University Press 2006) 9.

[66] For an insightful conversation on this, see '140508 STD SW109 Professor Janet Halley', Conversation at King's College London, 15 May 2014, available at: www.youtube.com/watch?v=zs_yqY8NQsY&t=2022s.

7.3 A STRATEGY OF DISCOMFORT

A strategy of discomfort is, first and foremost, applied to oneself and not out of expectation that others will too.

Yet the economy of discomfort remains unevenly distributed. Alhaag and Ouédraogo highlight this unevenness in the *Errant* symposium on discomfort in the context of the art gallery. Similarly controlling of its substance, image, and access, the art gallery trades in its own comfort, and that of its audience. When the 'other' confronts the institution, discomfort becomes a key part of critical engagement for both insiders and outsiders. As Ouédraogo states, '[W]hen you are working with institutions and you are trying to do things differently, it creates a lot of discomfort for people'.[67] As has been revealed in recent examples of white fragility, the discomfort of some can end up getting expressed violently against others, mostly the institutional 'Other'.[68] International law also operates as a space for reinscribing discomfort among historically marginalised groups, and this continues to be experienced by Third World scholars, working-class academics, women, and disabled scholars when engaging with international law's institutions, societies, and experts.[69] Hence, it is important, as Ouédraogo recounts, to be cognisant of the differing valences of discomfort and its potential deployment as a weapon against others to merely reinforce existing arrangements of domination and exclusion. Calling for discomfort is thus to call for an ethic of expert responsibility that remains conscious of the economy of comfort from which some benefit and others lose out.

Finally, discomfort is not the self-conscious self-reflection that has largely powered and aggrandised international lawyers' engagements for the past decade or so. Many scholars have placed Weber's ethic of responsibility at the centre of a rejuvenated and actively self-conscious

---

[67] Irene de Craen in Conversation with Amal Alhaag and Rita Ouédraogo, 'Discomfort as (Curatorial) Strategy: A Funeral for Street Culture', *Errant Journal*, Issue 3 (2022) 33.

[68] Alternatively, it might get expressed as empathy or guilt for the other, which, as Rebecca Glyn-Blanco points out, also displaces discomfort by keeping it 'over there' as a vehicle for self-comfort. Empathy or guilt as responses 'limit[] the productive space that discomfort could offer, leading to empty performative political or personal gestures, simultaneously eroding social movements', Rebecca Glyn-Blanco, 'Discomfort against Empathy', *Errant Journal*, Issue 3 (2022) 54. On white fragility, *see* Robin DiAngelo, *White Fragility: Why It's So Hard for White People to Talk about Racism* (Penguin Books 2018).

[69] Mohsen al Attar, 'Tackling White Ignorance in International Law – "How Much Time Do You Have? It's Not Enough', Opinio Juris blog, 30 September 2022, available at: http://opiniojuris.org/2022/09/30/tackling-white-ignorance-in-international-law-how-much-time-do-you-have-its-not-enough/.

294   CONCLUSION

form of international legal work.[70] Yet there is a risk that such reflexivity uncritically takes the legitimation and functioning of the field as an end goal. This is perhaps borne out in ICL, where self-reflection has either failed to materialise or has ended all too prematurely. Reflection here has largely failed to pierce assumptions of the field's neutrality but has amounted to 'domestication[,] catharsis', and 'empowerment'.[71] This is also tantamount to a gain rather than loss of agency.[72]

A strategy of discomfort is not an end in itself. Nor can such a strategy be pursued if it ignores the economy of comfort and its uneven arrangement between institutional insiders and outsiders. Lastly, a strategy of discomfort, even if understood as a 'critical move' could still be relied upon to aggrandise international law, its institutions, and experts. The difficulty is that such a move is applied with the aim of minimising discomfort and subsequently re-entering professional comfort. With these ideas in mind, I consider what the strategy of discomfort might mean for experts working with and within the court's management apparatus.

Strategy 1: Outside In

The first strategy of discomfort entails 'taking a break', as Janet Halley has coined it, or as the editor of *Errant Journal* describes the

---

[70] Jean d'Aspremont, 'Jenks' Ethic of Responsibility for the Disillusioned International Lawyer', Amsterdam Law School Research Paper No. 2016-63, October 2016; Jochen von Bernstorff, 'International Legal Scholarship as a Cooling Medium in International Law and Politics' (2015) 25 *European Journal of International Law* 977–990, at 984; Gleider Hernández, 'The Responsibility of the International Legal Academic: Situating the Grammarian within the "Invisible College"' in Jean d'Aspremont et al. (eds.), *International Law as a Profession* (Cambridge University Press 2017) 160–188, at 188; Jean d'Aspremont, 'Martti Koskenniemi, the Mainstream, and Self-Reflectivity' (2016) 29 *Leiden Journal of International Law* 625–639, at 629–630.

[71] D'Aspremont, 'Martti Koskenniemi' 636. I have elsewhere described this as a form of ideology, see Richard Clements, 'International Law as a Belief System, by Jean d'Aspremont' (2018) 88 *British Yearbook of International Law* 1–4, at 3. The sense of empowerment of which d'Aspremont writes as a consequence of self-reflection is no coincidence – it is, after all, the individual who is empowered and has internalised responsibility that is treated as the ideal neoliberal subject, see Émilie Hache, 'Is responsibility a tool of neo-liberal governmentality?' (2007) 28 *Raisons politiques* 49–65, at 53. Responsibility here is not the experience of freedom and the vocation of politics, but a personal-psychological salve.

[72] Weber, 'Politics as a Vocation' 93.

7.3 A STRATEGY OF DISCOMFORT

process – 'letting-go'.[73] Halley has advocated taking a break in the context of feminist projects, particularly those that have seen feminist claims and policies incorporated into modern state and international apparatuses – what Halley and others have labelled 'governance feminism'.[74] Much in the way anti-impunity advocates have now become deeply implicated in the state and inter-state legal machinery, so too have certain feminist causes. And yet, Halley is concerned that the institutionalisation and acceptance of some feminisms have had unintended consequences both for feminism itself and other progressive projects. She therefore proposes taking a break from feminism in order to 'spend some time outside it . . . and imagin[e] political goals that do not fall within its terms'.[75] Halley is clear that taking a break does not mean to 'kill it, supersede it, abandon it; immure, immolate, or bury it'.[76] Rather, taking a break means avoiding the dogmatism of prescriptive ideology to instead adopt 'a posture, an attitude, a practice, of being in the problem'.[77]

The notion of taking a break powerfully disrupts the cycle of ICC suboptimality and managerial optimisation. It is a position that may be adopted any time an advocate, an expert, or a colleague proposes an updated strategic plan, better performance appraisal, or another lessons learnt exercise in response to the court's perceived ills. Taking a break is not about turning away but direct confrontation with assumptions, habits, and desires.[78] One might therefore take a break in an NGO report on victims' rights at the ICC by arguing against a 'lessons learnt' approach and instead confront the dilemma of victim participation as it currently stands. As defence counsel, one could take a break by challenging the institutional resourcing and workload concerns of judges as they articulate those arguments in court hearings and judgments. A break may also be warranted in the classroom or the managerial university. Given management's effect on professional thought and imagination, to notice and confront it is to render it contingent and contestable, whether for oneself, a community to which one is affiliated, or for the would-be yielder inside the court.

---

[73] Halley, *Split Decisions*; De Craen, 'Editor's Note' 9.
[74] Janet Halley et al. (eds.), *Governance Feminism: An Introduction* (University of Minnesota Press 2018).
[75] Halley, 'Split Decisions' 10.
[76] Ibid.
[77] Ibid., 7.
[78] De Craen, 'Editor's Note' 9. See Édouard Glissant, *Poetics of Relation* (University of Michigan Press 2010, translated by Betsy Wing) 189.

In addition, whether desirable or not, scholars of ICL and the ICC rival practitioners and court officials in number. Consequently, academic writing and teaching play an outsized role in the field.[79] Scholars, too, can therefore ill-afford to displace responsibility onto practitioners. Scholars can foster discomfort in refusing to engage with reform exercises (and explaining why), or in engaging with them in order to highlight their problematic assumptions and exclusionary effects.[80] This resembles Schwöbel-Patel's call to 'unplug' from global justice as a way to 'destabilise epistemological certainties'.[81] It may not feel like taking a break to spend precious research time on institutional skirmishes of this nature, but this may be what the strategy of discomfort requires. To recall Foucault's 'ethic of discomfort', challenging assumptions means that 'one must have a distant view, but also look at what is nearby and all around oneself'.[82] Taking a break may entail stepping back to see the bigger picture or to foreground others, or it might mean getting even closer to the object of critique or calling out assurances of future improvement. Whatever it looks like, taking a break means breaking with management's objectivity and the will to reform in an effort to stay with the institutional trouble.[83]

Strategy 2: Inside Out

What has been most difficult for critical scholars of ICL and the ICC is the question of how far or on what terms to engage with the institution. There is a rich critical debate about the extent of engagement with an institution that consistently fails to acknowledge its own politics, the political ramifications of its work, or contestation from others. The highly crafted image and messaging of the court have allowed it to double down on allegations of bias or selectivity in its investigations. Critique seems either not to stick or to be already built into the institutional

---

[79] Mikkel Christensen, 'Preaching, Practicing and Publishing International Criminal Justice: Academic Expertise and the Development of an International Field of Law' (2016) 17 *International Criminal Law Review* 1–20; Neha Jain, 'Teachings of Publicists and the Reinvention of the Sources Doctrine in International Criminal Law' in Kevin Jon Heller et. al. (eds.), *Oxford Handbook of International Criminal Law* (Oxford University Press 2020) 106–128.

[80] This draws on ideas of the 'practice of refusal'; see The Practicing Refusal Collective, www.thesojournerproject.org/about/.

[81] Schwöbel-Patel, 'Marketing Global Justice' 242.

[82] Foucault, 'Ethic of Discomfort' 448.

[83] Donna Harraway, *Staying with the Trouble: Making Kin in the Chthulucene* (Duke University Press 2016).

7.3 A STRATEGY OF DISCOMFORT

response.[84] The risk, of course, is that the critic who engages may find themselves lending succour to the institution or may find their critiques co-opted into the institutional status quo. This is a discomforting prospect that surely needs to be accounted for.

It may also be difficult to envisage rupture from within. I have shown how professional engagement with management ideas and practices is not imposed but personally mediated. There has already been a process of negotiation, adoption, and adaptation by experts as they chart a daily course through the institution. It is questionable whether those working within the court would either adopt a strategic goal that went against the court's own mission or be able to resist macro-, meso-, or micro-management in a hierarchical and often hostile institution such as the ICC.

Yet ICC staff are hardly expected to repudiate the court's mission, never mind lay down or break their management tools.[85] In this book, I have been careful not to identify one overarching target for managerial discontent – management is both a set of ideas with considerable productive power and a collection of multi-level practices with different effects on organisation, professional, and argument. However, the aforementioned commonality is the flight from the court's complexities and contestations. In that regard, the professional may find themselves frustrated at a colleague's failure to contemplate bigger issues; they may feel stuck between completing their contractual duties and the perceived futility of those duties; and they may wish to 'take a break' without risking professional opprobrium.

These experiences of the institution may prompt a desire to discomfort oneself, suspend givens, or push at the edges of comfortable office life. They may therefore find the most promising outlet for such a posture to be the management tools most proximate to them. If one is a non-lawyer, this may include those macro-management practices of onboarding, probation, and performance appraisal. If one is lucky, there will be an opportunity to engage with management proposals or reform exercises. Here, forming alliances among like-minded staff members, the Staff Union, and sympathetic outsiders may be necessary. This applies also to the ICC's legal experts – investigators, advisers, counsel, and even judges. As Judge Tarfusser's engagement with *Re*Vision attests, seniority is no bar to resisting management's claims. But lawyers are also in the

---

[84] Grietje Baars, 'Making ICL History: On the Need to Move Beyond Pre-fab Critiques of ICL' in Schwöbel, *Critical Approaches to International Criminal Law* 196–218, at 206.

[85] C.f. Gavin Mueller, *Breaking Things at Work: The Luddites were Right About Why You Hate Your Job* (Verso 2021).

298　　　　　　　　　　　　　CONCLUSION

position of engaging with, indeed constituting, the meso level of management as a systematic escape from argumentative dilemmas. Their urge to displace and delay in the name of institutional stability is resistible, though, as attested by *Re*Vision. Instead of relying on the wish for a brighter managerial future, lawyers can confront the multiple, complex, and contested realities of the managerial present as an admission of power and an engagement in politics.

7.4　(Not a) Conclusion

The effort to foster a strategy of discomfort comes as a response to the concerted management of global justice traced throughout this book. It is offered in place of a blanket solution to the management 'problem', if only because such a problem-solving mindset reinforces the interpretation of the ICC and, indeed, of global justice, as a factory. The opening epigraph of this book quoted the late Judge Antonio Cassese as stating that 'a court of law is not a factory'.[86] Such a proposition will hardly emerge through mere assertion but in the slow boring of holes by those concerned about managerial justice. However, the analysis in these pages also speaks to similar trends in other institutions. In the years before the outbreak of COVID-19, the World Health Organisation instituted a risk management approach to co-ordinating epidemic responses with national health agencies.[87] In 2021, the UN Environment Programme adopted a Medium-Term Strategy for 2022–2025 as a 'strategic approach' to transnational pollution.[88] It will therefore be not only anti-impunity and justice but human and planetary welfare that get filtered as management problems. This is already happening. The hope is that this book's analysis of one institution, and the proposed strategy of discomfort, will offer a word and mode of caution before international institutions and their experts embrace the will to manage once more.

---

[86] Report on the Special Court for Sierra Leone by the Independent Expert Antonio Cassese, 12 December 2006, para. 58, available at: www.rscsl.org/Documents/Cassese%20Report.pdf.

[87] World Health Organisation Health Emergency and Disaster Risk Management Framework (2019).

[88] United Nations Environment Assembly, For People and Planet: The United Nations Environment Programme Strategy for 2022–2025 to Tackle Climate Change, Loss of Nature and Pollution, UNEP/EA.2/3/Rev.1, 17 February 2021, para. 30, available at: https://wedocs.unep.org/bitstream/handle/20.500.11822/35162/Doc3%20Reve1%20EnglishK2100501.pdf?sequence=1&isAllowed=y.

SELECT BIBLIOGRAPHY

Books, Journals, Periodicals, Authored Newspaper Articles, Blogs, Web Articles

Abtahi, Hirad, and Charania, Shehzad, 'Expediting the ICC Criminal Process: Striking the Right Balance between the ICC and States Parties' (2018) 18 *International Criminal Law Review* 383–425.

Acker, Joan, 'Hierarchies, Jobs, Bodies: A Theory of Gendered Organisations' (1990) 4 *Gender & Society* 139–158.

'African Countries Back Away from ICC Withdrawal Demand', *Sudan Tribune*, 10 June 2009, available at: www.sudantribune.com/spip.php?article31443.

Ainley, Kirsten, Humphreys, Stephen, and Tallgren, Immi, 'International Criminal Justice on/and Film' (2018) 6 *London Review of International Law* 3–15.

Akande, Dapo, and de Souza Dias, Talita, 'The ICC Pre-Trial Chamber Decision on the Situation in Afghanistan: A Few Thoughts on the Interests of Justice', EJIL Talk! blog, 18 April 2019, available at: www.ejiltalk.org/the-icc-pre-trial-chamber-decision-on-the-situation-in-afghanistan-a-few-thoughts-on-the-interests-of-justice/

Akhavan, Payam, 'The Rise, Fall, and Rise of International Criminal Justice' (2013) 11 *Journal of International Criminal Justice* 527–536.

Alcock, Antony, *History of the International Labour Organisation* (Macmillan 1971) 121.

Alderman, Derek H., and Dobbs, G. Rebecca, 'Geographies of Slavery: Of Theory, Method, and Intervention' (2011) 39 *Historical Geography* 29–40.

Alvarez, José, 'The Proposed Independent Oversight Mechanism for the International Criminal Court' in Richard Steinberg (ed.), *Contemporary Issues Facing the International Criminal Court* (Brill Nijhoff 2016) 143–153.

Alvesson, Mats, and Deetz, Stanley, 'Critical Theory and Postmodernism: Approaches to Organisation Studies' in Chris Grey and Hugh Willmott (eds.), *Critical Management Studies: A Reader* (Oxford University Press 2005) 60–106.

Alvesson, Mats, and Willmott, Hugh, 'Identity Regulation as Organisational Control: Producing the Appropriate Individual' (2002) 39 *Journal of Management Studies* 614–644.

SELECT BIBLIOGRAPHY

Alvesson, Mats, Bridgman, Todd, and Willmott, Hugh, 'Introduction' in Mats Alvesson, Todd Bridgman, and Hugh Willmott (eds.), *The Oxford Handbook of Critical Management Studies* (Oxford University Press 2013) 1–28.

Ambach, Philipp, 'A Look towards the Future – The ICC and "Lessons Learnt"' in Carsten Stahn (ed.), *The Law and Practice of the International Criminal Court* (Oxford University Press 2015) 1277–1295.

'Performance Indicators for International(ised) Criminal Courts – Potential for Increase of an Institution's Legacy or "Just" a Means of Budgetary Control?' (2018) 18 *International Criminal Law Review* 426–460.

Ambach, Philipp, and Rackwitz, Klaus, 'A Model of International Judicial Administration?: The Evolution of Managerial Practices at the International Criminal Court' (2013) 76 *Law & Contemporary Problems* 119–161.

Anghie, Antony, 'Colonialism and the Birth of International Institutions: Sovereignty, Economy, and the Mandate System of the League of Nations' (2002) 34 *NYU Journal of International Law & Policy* 513–634.

Sovereignty, Imperialism, and the Making of International Law (Cambridge University Press 2004).

Anghie, Antony, and Chimni, B. S., 'Third World Approaches to International Law and Individual Responsibility in Internal Conflict' (2003) 2 *Chinese Journal of International Law* 77–103.

Annan, Kofi, 'Internal Oversight – A Key to Reform at the United Nations' (2003) 30 *International Journal of Government Auditing* 1–10.

Arsanjani, Mahnoush, 'Financing' in Antonio Cassese, Paola Gaeta, and John R. W. D. Jones (eds.), *The Rome Statute of the International Criminal Court*, Volume 1 (Oxford University Press 2002) 315–329.

al Attar, Mohsen, 'Tackling White Ignorance in International Law – "How Much Time Do You Have? It's Not Enough', Opinio Juris blog, 30 September 2022, available at: http://opiniojuris.org/2022/09/30/tackling-white-ignorance-in-international-law-how-much-time-do-you-have-its-not-enough/

Aufhauser, R. Keith, 'Slavery and Scientific Management' (1973) 33 *Journal of Economic History* 811–824.

Baars, Grietje, 'Making ICL History: On the Need to Move beyond Pre-fab Critiques of ICL' in Christine Schwöbel (ed.), *Critical Approaches to International Criminal Law* (Routledge 2015) 196–218.

Barnett, Michael, and Duvall, Raymond, 'Power in International Politics' (2005) 59 *International Organisation* 39–75.

Barnett, Michael, and Finnemore, Martha, *Rules for the World: International Organisations in Global Politics* (Cornell University Press 2004).

Bassiouni, M. Cherif, 'From Versailles to Rwanda in Seventy-Five Years: The Need to Establish a Permanent International Criminal Court' (1997) 10 *Harvard International Law Journal* 11–62.

SELECT BIBLIOGRAPHY

Bauman, Zygmunt, *Modernity and the Holocaust* (Polity Press 1989).

Benedetti, Fanny, Bonneau, Karine, and Washburn, John, *Negotiating the International Criminal Court: New York to Rome, 1994–1998* (Martinus Nijhoff 2014).

Benjamin, Todd, Interview with Luis Moreno Ocampo, International Bar Association, 1 February 2013, available at: www.ibanet.org/Article/NewDetail.aspx?ArticleUid=81213DCF-0911-4141-AD29-A486F9B03D37.

Berghahn, Volker, 'The Marshall Plan and the Recasting of Europe's Postwar Industrial Systems' in Eliot Sorel and Pier Carlo Padoan (eds.), *The Marshall Plan: Lessons Learned for the 21st Century* (OECD 2008) 29–42.

Bergsmo, Morten, Kaleck, Wolfgang, Muller, Sam, and Wiley, William H., 'A Prosecutor Falls, Time for the Court to Rise' (2017) 86 *FICHL Policy Brief Series* 1–4.

Bergsmo, Morten, Ling, Cheah Wui, and Ping, Yi (eds.), *Historical Origins of International Criminal Law*, Volume 1 (Torkel Opsahl Academic EPublisher 2014).

Bertrand, Maurice, 'The Historical Development of Efforts to Reform the UN' in Adam Roberts and Benedict Kingsbury (eds.), *United Nations, Divided World: The UN's Roles in International Relations* (2nd ed., Clarendon Press 1993) 420–436.

Bhandar, Brenna, 'Strategies of Legal Rupture: The Politics of Judgment' (2012) 30 *Windsor Yearbook of Access to Justice* 59–78.

Blignaut, Sylvan, and Koopman, Oscar, 'Towards an Embodied Critical Pedagogy of Discomfort as a Decolonising Teaching Strategy' (2020) 31 *Alternation* 81–96.

Boehme, Franziska, 'Exit, Voice and Loyalty: State Rhetoric about the International Criminal Court' (2018) 22 *International Journal of Human Rights* 420–445.

Boer, Lianne J. M., and Stolk, Sofia (eds.), *Backstage Practices of Transnational Law* (Routledge 2019).

Boisson de Chazournes, Laurence, 'Plurality in the Fabric of International Courts and Tribunals: The Threads of a Managerial Approach' (2017) 28 *European Journal of International Law* 13–72.

Bourdieu, Pierre, 'The Force of Law: Towards a Sociology of the Juridical Field' (1987) 38 *Hastings Law Journal* 805–853.

Bradney, Anthony, 'The Quality Assurance Agency and the Politics of Audit' (2001) 28 *Journal of Law & Society* 430–442.

Branch, Adam, 'Uganda's Civil War and the Politics of ICC Intervention' (2007) 21 *Ethics & International Affairs* 179–198.

Braverman, Harry, *Labour and Monopoly Capital: The Degradation of Work in the Twentieth Century* [1974] (Monthly Review Press 1998).

Brenneis, Don, 'Reforming Promise' in Annelise Riles (ed.), *Documents: Artifacts of Modern Knowledge* (University of Michigan Press 2006) 41–70.

Buchanan, Ruth, Byers, Kimberley, and Mansveld, Kristina, '"What Gets Measured Gets Done": Exploring the Social Construction of Globalised Knowledge for Development' in Mosche Hirsch and Andrew Lang (eds.), *Research Handbook on the Sociology of International Law* (Edward Elgar 2018) 101–121.

Burke-White, William, 'Complementarity in Practice: The International Criminal Court as Part of a System of Multi-Level Global Governance in the Democratic Republic of Congo' (2005) 18 *Leiden Journal of International Law* 557–590.

'Proactive Complementarity: The International Criminal Court and National Courts in the Rome System of International Justice' (2008) 49 *Harvard International Law Journal* 53–108.

Burley, Anne-Marie, 'Regulating the World: Multilateralism, International Law, and the Projection of the New Deal Regulatory State' in John Ruggie (ed.), *Multilateralism Matters* (Columbia University Press 1993) 125–156.

Burnham, James, *Managerial Revolution: What is Happening in the World* (The John Day Company Inc. 1941).

Campbell, Kirsten, 'The Making of International Criminal Justice: Towards a Sociology of the "Legal Field"'in Mikkel Christensen and Ron Levi (eds.), *International Practices of Criminal Law: Social and Legal Perspectives* (Routledge 2017) 149–169.

Carter, Linda, Ellis, Mark, and Jalloh, Charles C., *The International Criminal Court in an Effective Global Justice System* (Edward Elgar 2016).

Carter, William H., 'Elihu Root: His Services as Secretary of War' (1904) 178 *North American Review* 110–121.

Cascio, Wayne, 'How Does Downsizing Come About?' in Cary L. Cooper, Alankrita Pandey, and James Campbell Quick (eds.), *Downsizing: Is Less Still More?* (Cambridge University Press 2012) 51–75.

Cassese, Antonio, 'Is the ICC Still Having Teething Problems?' (2006) 4 *Journal of International Criminal Justice* 434–441.

Cayet, Thomas, 'The ILO and the IMI: A Strategy of Influence on the Edges of the League of Nations, 1925–1934' in Jasmien van Daele, Magaly Rodriguez Garcia, and Geert van Goethem (eds.), *ILO Histories: Essays on the International Labour Organisation and Its Impact on the World during the Twentieth-Century* (Peter Lang 2010) 251–270.

Chakrabarty, Dipesh, *Provincialising Europe: Postcolonial Thought and Historical Difference* (Cambridge University Press 2000).

Chandler Jr, Alfred D., *The Visible Hand: The Managerial Revolution in American Business* (Harvard University Press 1977).

Charlesworth, Hilary, and Chinkin, Christine, *Boundaries of International Law* (Manchester University Press 2000).

Chauvière, Michel, and Mick, Stephen S., 'The French Sociological Critique of Managerialism: Themes and Frameworks' (2011) 39 *Critical Sociology* 135–143.

SELECT BIBLIOGRAPHY

Chiam, Madelaine, Eslava, Luis, Painter, Genevieve R., Parfitt, Rose, and Peevers, Charlotte (eds.), 'Introduction: History, Anthropology and the Archive of International Law' (2017) 5 *London Review of International Law* 3–5.

Chimni, B.S., *International Law and World Order* (Cambridge University Press 2017).

Chinkin, Christine, *Women, Peace and Security and International Law* (Cambridge University Press 2022).

Christensen, Mikkel, 'The Emerging Sociology of International Criminal Courts: Between Global Restructurings and Scientific Innovations' (2015) 63 *Current Sociology Review* 825–849.

'Preaching, Practicing and Publishing International Criminal Justice: Academic Expertise and the Development of an International Field of Law' (2016) 17 *International Criminal Law Review* 1–20.

Christensen, Mikkel, and Levi, Ron, 'Introduction: An Internationalized Criminal Justice: Paths of Law and Paths of Police' in Mikkel Christensen and Ron Levi (eds.), *International Practices of Criminal Law: Social and Legal Perspectives* (Routledge 2017) 1–15.

Christodoulidis, Emilios, 'Strategies of Rupture' (2009) 20 *Law & Critique* 3–26.

Clark, Phil, *Distant Justice: The Impact of the International Criminal Court on African Politics* (Cambridge University Press 2018).

Clarke, Kamari Maxine, 'Rethinking Africa through Its Exclusions: The Politics of Naming Criminal Responsibility' (2010) 83 *Anthropological Quarterly* 625–651.

Fictions of Justice: The International Criminal Court and the Challenge of Legal Pluralism in Sub-Saharan Africa (Cambridge University Press 2010).

Affective Justice: The International Criminal Court and the Pan-Africanist Pushback (Duke University Press 2019).

Clements, Richard, 'Near, Far, Wherever You Are: Distance and Proximity in International Criminal Law' (2021) 32 *European Journal of International Law* 327–350.

'"Efficiency Is Paramount in This Regard": The Managerial Role of the ICC Presidency from Kirsch to Fernández' (2022) 21 *Law and Practice of International Courts & Tribunals* 342–368.

Cooper, Robert, and Burrell, Gibson, 'Modernism, Postmodernism and Organisational Analysis: The Contribution of Michel Foucault' in Alan McKinlay and Ken Starkey (eds.), *Foucault, Management and Organisation Theory* (SAGE Publishing 1998) 14–28, at 25.

Crawford, James, 'The ILC Adopts a Statute for an International Criminal Court' (1995) 89 *American Journal of International Law* 404–416.

Çubukçu, Ayça, *For the Love of Humanity: The World Tribunal on Iraq* (University of Pennsylvania Press 2018).

Cummings, Stephen, Bridgman, Todd, Hassard, John, and Rowlinson, Michael, *A New History of Management* (Cambridge University Press 2019).

SELECT BIBLIOGRAPHY

d'Aspremont, Jean, 'Martti Koskenniemi, the Mainstream, and Self-Reflectivity (2016) 29 *Leiden Journal of International Law* 625–639.

d'Aspremont, Jean, Gazzini, Tarcisio, Nollkaemper, André, and Werner, Wouter (eds.), *International Law as a Profession* (Cambridge University Press 2017).

de Cooker, Chris (ed.), *International Administration: Law and Management Practices in International Organisations* (Martinus Nijhoff 2009).

Davenport, David, 'International Criminal Court: 12 Years, $1 Billion, 2 Convictions', *Forbes*, 12 March 2014, available at: www.forbes.com/sites/daviddavenport/2014/03/12/international-criminal-court-12-years-1-billion-2-convictions-2/?sh=4d2e0b672405.

Davis, Cale, 'Political Considerations in Prosecutorial Discretion at the International Criminal Court' (2015) 15 *International Criminal Law Review* 170–189.

'Challenges in Charge Selection: Considerations Informing the Number of Charges and Cumulative Charging Practices' in Agirre Aranburu, Xabier, Bergsmo, Morten, De Smet, Simo, and Stahn, Carsten (eds.), *Quality Control in Criminal Investigation* (Torkel Opsahl Academic EPublisher 2020) 703–734.

Davis, Kevin, Kingsbury, Benedict, and Engle Merry, Sally 'Indicators as a Technology of Global Governance' (2012) 46 *Law & Society Review* 71–104.

Davis, Mike, 'The Stopwatch and the Wooden Shoe: Scientific Management and the Industrial Workers of the World' in James Green (ed.), *Workers' Struggles, Past and Present: A "Radical America" Reader* (Temple University Press 1983) 83.

de Silva, Nicole, 'International Courts' Socialization Strategies for Actual and Perceived Performance' in Squatrito, Theresa, Young, Oran R., Follesdal, Andreas, and Ulfstein, Geir (eds.), *The Performance of International Courts and Tribunals* (Cambridge University Press 2018) 288–323.

de Vos, Christian, *Complementarity, Catalysts, Compliance: The International Criminal Court in Uganda, Kenya, and the Democratic Republic of Congo* (Cambridge University Press 2020).

Dehm, Sara, 'Accusing "Europe": Articulations of Migrant Justice and a Popular International Law' in Andrew Byrnes and Gabrielle Simm (eds.), *Peoples' Tribunals and International Law* (Cambridge University Press 2017) 157–181.

Delagrange, Mikel, 'The Path towards Greater Efficiency and Effectiveness in the Victim Application Processes of the International Criminal Court' (2018) 18 *International Criminal Law Review* 540–562.

Dezalay, Yves, and Garth, Bryant G. (eds.), *Lawyers and the Construction of Transnational Justice* (Routledge 2012).

DiAngelo, Robin, *White Fragility: Why It's So Hard for White People to Talk about Racism* (Penguin Books 2018).

SELECT BIBLIOGRAPHY

Dijkzeul, Dennis, and Beigbeder, Yves, 'Introduction' in Dennis Dijkzeul and Yves Beigbeder (eds.), *Rethinking International Organisations* (Berghahn 2006) 1–23.

Drucker, Peter, *Management: Tasks, Responsibilities, Practices* [1974] (Harper Collins 2008).

Management Challenges for the Twenty-First Century (Harper 2001).

du Plessis, Max, and Gevers, Chris, 'The Sum of Four Fears: African States and the International Criminal Court in Retrospect – Part I', Opinio Juris blog, 8 July 2019, available at: http://opiniojuris.org/2019/07/08/the-sum-of-four-fears-african-states-and-the-international-criminal-court-in-retrospect-part-i/.

Dugard, John, 'Obstacles in the Way of an International Criminal Court' (1997) 56 *Cambridge Law Journal* 329–342.

Düsterhöft, Isabel, and Kennedy, Dominic, 'How to Manage the Defence – Experiences from the ADC-ICTY' in Mayeul Hiéramente and Patricia Schneider (eds.), *The Defence in International Criminal Trials: Observations on the Role of the Defence at the ICTY, ICTR and ICC* (Nomos 2016) 227–244.

Enteman, Willard F., *Managerialism: The Emergence of a New Ideology* (University of Wisconsin Press 1993).

Esch, Elizabeth, *The Color Line and the Assembly Line: Managing Race in the Ford Empire* (University of California Press 2018).

Eslava, Luis, and Pahuja, Sundhya, 'Between Resistance and Reform: TWAIL and the Universality of International Law' (2011) 3 *Trade Law & Development* 103–130.

Eslava, Luis, *Local Space, Global Life: The Everyday Operation of International Law and Development* (Cambridge University Press 2015).

Eslava, Luis, Fakhri, Michael, and Nesiah, Vasuki (eds.), *Bandung, Global History, and International Law: Critical Pasts and Pending Futures* (Cambridge University Press 2017).

Fanon, Franz, *The Wretched of the Earth* (Grove Press 1963).

Ferencz, Ben, *An International Criminal Court: A Step to World Peace* (Oceana Publications 1980).

Fernández de Gurmendi, Silvia, 'Final Reflections: The Challenges of the International Criminal Court' in Hector Olásolo (ed.), *Essays on International Criminal Justice* (Hart Publishing 2012) 194–198.

'Introductions to the Third Edition' in Otto Triffterer and Kai Ambos (eds.), *The Rome Statute of the International Criminal Court: A Commentary* (3rd edn., C.H. Beck Hart Nomos 2016) xvi–xvii.

'From the Drafting of the Procedural Provisions by States to Their Revision by Judges' (2018) 16 *Journal of International Criminal Justice* 341–361.

Findlay, Patricia, and Newton, Tim, 'Re-framing Foucault: The Case of Performance Appraisal' in Alan McKinlay and Ken Starkey (eds.),

306   SELECT BIBLIOGRAPHY

Foucault, Management and Organisation Theory (SAGE Publishing 1998) 211, at 214–215.

Fiti Sinclair, Guy, *To Reform the World: International Organisations and the Making of Modern States* (Oxford University Press 2017).

Foucault, Michel, *The Will to Knowledge: The History of Sexuality Volume 1* [1976] (Penguin 1998).

     Discipline and Punish: The Birth of the Prison [1977] (Penguin Books 1991).

     '8 January 1978' in *Security, Territory, Population: Lectures at the Collège de France 1977–1978* (Michel Snellart ed., Palgrave Macmillan 2009) 29–53.

     'The Subject and Power' (1982) 8 *Critical Inquiry* 777–795.

     'Nietzsche, Genealogy, History' in Paul Rabinow (ed.), *The Foucault Reader* (Pantheon Books 1984) 76–100.

     'Governmentality', in Graham Burchell, Colin Gordon, and Peter Miller (eds.), *The Foucault Effect: Studies in Governmentality* (University of Chicago Press 1991) 87–104.

     'For an Ethic of Discomfort' in Michel Foucault (ed.), *Power: Essential Works, 1954–1984* (Penguin Classics 2020) 443–448.

     'So Is It Important to Think?' in Michel Foucault (ed.), *Power: Essential Works, 1954–1984* (Penguin Classics 2020) 454–458.

Franda, Mark, *The United Nations in the Twenty-First Century: Management and Reform Processes in a Troubled Organisation* (Rowman & Littlefield Publishers 2006).

Freedman, Lawrence, *Strategy: A History* (Oxford University Press 2013).

Gaeta, Paola, 'Does President Al Bashir Enjoy Immunity from Arrest?' (2009) 7 *Journal of International Criminal Justice* 315–322.

Gardner, Richard, 'Can the United Nations be Revived?', *Foreign Affairs*, July 1970, available at: www.foreignaffairs.com/articles/1970-07-01/can-united-nations-be-revived.

Garland, David, 'What Is a "History of the Present"? On Foucault's Genealogies and their Critical Preconditions' (2014) 16 *Punishment & Society* 365–384.

Geuss, Raymond, 'Genealogy as Critique' (2002) 10 *European Journal of Philosophy* 209–215.

Gevers, Christopher, 'Africa and International Criminal Law' in Kevin Jon Heller, Frédéric Mégret, Sarah M.H. Nouwen, Jens David Ohlin, and Darryl Robinson (eds.), *Oxford Handbook of International Criminal Law* (Oxford University Press 2020) 154–194.

Glissant, Édouard, *Poetics of Relation* (University of Michigan Press 2010, translated by Betsy Wing).

Glyn-Blanco, Rebecca, 'Discomfort against Empathy' (2022) issue 3 *Errant Journal*, 54.

Golder, Ben, *Foucault and the Politics of Rights* (Stanford University Press 2015).

SELECT BIBLIOGRAPHY

Gordon, Colin, 'Governmental Rationality: An Introduction', in Graham Burchell, Colin Gordon, and Peter Miller (eds.), *The Foucault Effect: Studies in Governmentality* (University of Chicago Press 1991) 1–52.

Grey, Christopher, 'Career as a Project of the Self' (1994) 28 *Sociology* 479–497.

Grey, Chris, and Willmott, Hugh, 'Introduction' in Chris Grey and Hugh Willmott (eds.), *Critical Management Studies: A Reader* (Oxford University Press 2005) 1–6.

Grey, Chris, *A Very Short, Fairly Interesting and Reasonably Cheap Book about Studying Organisations* (SAGE Publishing 2005).

Grey, Rosemary, *Prosecuting Sexual and Gender-Based Crimes at the International Criminal Court* (Cambridge University Press 2019) 128–142.

Guilfoyle, Douglas, 'The International Criminal Court Independent Expert Review: Questions of Accountability and Culture', EJIL Talk! Blog, 7 October 2020, available at: www.ejiltalk.org/the-international-criminal-court-independent-expert-review-questions-of-accountability-and-culture/.

Gupta, Priya S., 'From Statesmen to Technocrats to Financiers: Development Agents in the Third World' in Luis Eslava, Michael Fakhri, and Vasuki Nesiah (eds.), *Bandung, Global History, and International Law: Critical Pasts and Pending Futures* (Cambridge University Press 2017) 481–497.

Hache, Émilie, 'Is Responsibility a Tool of Neo-Liberal Governmentality?' (2007) 28 *Raisons politiques* 49–65.

Halley, Janet, *Split Decisions: How and Why to Take a Break from Feminism* (Princeton University Press 2006).

Halley, Janet, Kotiswaran, Prabha, Rebouché, Rachel, and Shamir, Hila (eds.), *Governance Feminism: An Introduction* (University of Minnesota Press 2018).

Hancock, Philip, and Tyler, Melissa, '"MOT Your Life!": Critical Management Studies and the Management of Everyday Life' (2004) 57 *Human Relations* 619–645.

Harper, Richard, *Inside the IMF: An Ethnography of Documents, Technology and Organisational Action* (Routledge 1998).

Hartman, Saidiya, *Scenes of Subjection: Terror, Slavery, and Self-Making in Nineteenth-Century America* (Oxford University Press 1997).

Heikkilä, Mikaela, 'The Balanced Scorecard of International Criminal Tribunals' in Cedric Ryngaert (ed.), *The Effectiveness of International Criminal Justice* (Intersentia 2009) 27–54.

Heller, Kevin Jon, and Simpson, Gerry (eds.), *The Hidden Histories of War Crimes Trials* (Oxford University Press 2013).

Heller, Kevin Jon, 'ICC Labor Woes Part II: What's Two Million Euros Between Friends?', Opinio Juris Blog, 30 June 2018, available at: http://opiniojuris.org/2018/06/30/the-iccs-labor-woes-part-ii/?utm_source=feed burner&utm_medium=email&utm_campaign=Feed%3A+opiniojurisfeed +%28Opinio+Juris%29.

SELECT BIBLIOGRAPHY

Hewes.Jr, James E., *From Root to McNamara: Army Organisation and Administration, 1900–1963* (Center of Military History 1975).

Hoffmann, Stanley, 'No Choices, No Illusions' (1976–77) 25 *Foreign Policy* 97–140.

Hogan, Michael, *The Marshall Plan: America, Britain and the Reconstruction of Western Europe, 1947–1952* (Cambridge University Press 1987).

Hohmann, Jessie, and Joyce, Daniel (eds.), *International Law's Objects* (Oxford University Press 2019).

Hough, Jill, and White, Margaret, 'Using Stories to Create Change: The Object Lesson of Frederick Taylor's "Pig-Tale"'(2001) 27 *Journal of Management* 585–601.

Hoxie, Robert, *Scientific Management and Labour* (Appleton-Century-Crofts 1915) Appendix II, 140–149.

Hüfner, Klaus, 'Financing the United Nations: The Role of the United States' in Dennis Dijkzeul and Yves Beigbeder (eds.), *Rethinking International Organisations: Pathology and Promise* (Berghahn Books 2003) 29–53.

Hull, Matthew, 'Documents and Bureaucracy' (2012) 41 *Annual Review of Anthropology* 251–267.

Hunt, Sarah, and Holmes, Cindy, 'Everyday Decolonization: Living a Decolonizing Queer Politics' (2015) 19 *Journal of Lesbian Studies* 154–172.

Irene de Craen in Conversation with Amal Alhaag, and Rita Ouédraogo, 'Discomfort as (Curatorial) Strategy: A Funeral for Street Culture', Errant Journal, Issue 3 (2022).

Jacobs, Dov, 'ICC Pre-Trial Chamber Rejects OTP Request to Open an Investigation in Afghanistan: Some Preliminary Thoughts on an Ultra Vires Decision', Spreading the Jam Blog, 12 April 2019, available at: https://dovjacobs.com/2019/04/12/icc-pre-trial-chamber-rejects-otp-request-to-open-an-investigation-in-afghanistan-some-preliminary-thoughts-on-an-ultra-vires-decision/.

Jain, Neha, 'Teachings of Publicists and the Reinvention of the Sources Doctrine in International Criminal Law' in Kevin Jon Heller, Frédéric Mégret, Sarah M.H. Nouwen, Jens David Ohlin, and Darryl Robinson (eds.), *Oxford Handbook of International Criminal Law* (Oxford University Press 2020) 106–128.

Jessup, Philip, *Elihu Root, Volume 1* [1938] (Archon 1964).

Johns, Fleur, *Non-Legality and International Law: Unruly Law* (Cambridge University Press 2013).

Johnson, Gerry, *Strategic Change and the Management Process* (Blackwell 1987).

Jones, Annika, 'A Quiet Transformation? Efficiency Building in the "Fall" of International Criminal Justice' (2019) 19 *International Criminal Law Review* 445–474.

Jones, John R.W.D., 'The Registry and Staff' in Antonio Cassese, Paola Gaeta, and John R.W.D. Jones (eds.), *The Rome Statute of the International Criminal Court, Volume 1* (Oxford University Press 2002) 280.

SELECT BIBLIOGRAPHY

Jordan, Robert, 'What Has Happened to Our International Civil Service?' (1981) 41 *Public Administration Review* 236–245.

Kaplan, Laurence, *The United States and NATO: The Formative Years* (University Press of Kentucky 1984).

Kaul, Hans-Peter, 'The International Criminal Court: Current Challenges and Perspectives' (2007) 6 *Washington University Global Studies Law Review* 575–582.

Kendall, Sara, and Nouwen, Sarah M.H. 'Representational Practices at the International Criminal Court: The Gap Between Juridified and Abstract Victimhood' (2013) 76 *Law & Contemporary Problems* 235–262.

Kendall, Sara, 'Commodifying Global Justice: Economies of Accountability at the International Criminal Court' (2015) 13 *Journal of International Criminal Justice* 113–134.

'Beyond the Restorative Turn: The Limits of Legal Humanitarianism' in Christian De Vos, Sara Kendall, and Carsten Stahn (eds.), *Contested Justice: The Politics and Practice of International Criminal Court Interventions* (Cambridge University Press 2017) 352–376.

Kennedy, Carol, *Guide to the Management Gurus* (Random House 2012).

Kennedy, David, 'The Move to Institutions' (1987) 8 *Cardozo Law Review* 841–988.

'Background Noise?: The Underlying Politics of Global Governance' (1999) 21 *Harvard International Review* 52–57.

'When Renewal Repeats: Thinking Against the Box' (1999–2000) 32 *NYU Journal of International Law and Politics* 335–500.

'The Politics of the Invisible College: International Governance and the Politics of Expertise' (2001) 5 *European Human Rights Law Review* 463–497.

'Challenging Expert Rule: The Politics of Global Governance' (2005) 27 *Sydney Law Review* 1–24.

Of War and Law (Princeton University Press 2006).

A World of Struggle: How Power, Law, and Expertise Shape Global Political Economy (Princeton University Press 2016).

Kennedy, Duncan, 'The Three Globalizations of Law and Legal Thought: 1850–2000' in David M. Trubek and Alvaro Santos (eds.), *The New Law and Economic Development: A Critical Appraisal* (Cambridge University Press 2006) 19–73.

'A Left Phenomenological Alternative to the Hart/Kelsen Theory of Legal Interpretation' in Duncan Kennedy (ed.), *Legal Reasoning: Collected Essays* (Davies Group Publishers 2008).

Keohane, Robert, 'The Demand for International Regimes' (1982) 36 *International Organisation* 325–355.

Kettl, Donald, *The Global Public Management Revolution: A Report on the Transformation of Governance* (Brookings Institution Press 2000).

SELECT BIBLIOGRAPHY

Khan, Karim, 'Article 34: Organs of the Court' in Otto Triffterer and Kai Ambos (eds.), *The Rome Statute of the International Criminal Court: A Commentary* (3rd edn., C.H. Beck Hart Nomos 2016) 1197–1203.

Khurana, Rakesh, *From Higher Aims to Hired Hands: The Social Transformation of American Business Schools and the Unfulfilled Promise of Management as a Profession* (Princeton University Press 2007).

Killean, Rachel, and Moffett, Luke, 'Victim Legal Representation before the ICC and ECCC' (2017) 15 *Journal of International Criminal Justice* 713–740.

Kiyani, Asad, 'Al-Bashir and the ICC: The Problem of Head of State Immunity' (2013) 12 *Chinese Journal of International Law* 467–508.

Klikauer, Thomas, *Managerialism: Critique of an Ideology* (Palgrave 2013).

Knop, Karen, 'The Tokyo Women's Tribunal and the Turn to Fiction' in Fleur Johns, Richard Joyce, and Sundhya Pahuja (eds.), *Events: The Force of International Law* (Routledge 2010) 145–164.

Koh, Harold Hongju, 'International Criminal Justice 5.0', Remarks at the Vera Institute of Justice, New York City, 8 November 2012, available at: www .state.gov/s/l/releases/remarks/200957.htm.

Koskenniemi, Martti, 'The Politics of International Law' (1990) 1 *European Journal of International Law* 4–32.

'Letter to the Editors of the Symposium' (1999) 93 *American Journal of International Law* 351–361.

The Gentle Civilizer of Nations: The Rise and Fall of International Law 1870–1960 (Cambridge University Press 2001).

'Global Governance and Public International Law' (2004) 37 *Kritische Justiz* 241–254.

From Apology to Utopia: The Structure of International Legal Argument (Reissued with a new epilogue, Cambridge University Press 2005).

'International Law: Constitutionalism, Managerialism and the Ethos of Legal Education' (2007) 1 *European Journal of Legal Studies* 8–24.

'The Fate of Public International Law: Between Technique and Politics' (2007) 70 *Modern Law Review* 1–30.

'The Politics of International Law – Twenty Years Later' (2009) 20 *European Journal of International Law* 7–19.

Kosofsky Sedgwick, Eve, 'Paranoid Reading and Reparative Reading, Or, You're So Paranoid, You Probably Think This Essay Is about You' in Eve Kosofsky Sedgwick (ed.), *Touching Feeling: Affect, Pedagogy, Performativity* (Duke University Press 2003) 123–151.

Kotecha, Birju, 'The ICC'S Office of the Prosecutor and the Limits of Performance Indicators' (2017) 15 *Journal of International Criminal Justice* 543–565.

'The International Criminal Court's Selectivity and Procedural Justice' (2020) 18 *Journal of International Criminal Justice* 107–139.

SELECT BIBLIOGRAPHY 311

Kotschnig, Walter, 'The United Nations as an Instrument of Economic and Social Development' (1968) 22 *International Organisation* 16–43.

Kraines, Oscar, 'Brandeis' Philosophy of Scientific Management' (1960) 13 *Western Political Quarterly* 191–201.

Krever, Tor, 'Quantifying Law: Legal Indicator Projects and the Reproduction of Neoliberal Common Sense' (2013) 34 *Third World Quarterly* 131–150.

Labuda, Patryk I., *International Criminal Tribunals and Domestic Accountability: In the Court's Shadow* (forthcoming, Oxford University Press).

Laing, Aislinn, 'International Criminal Court is "hunting" Africans', *Daily Telegraph*, 27 May 2013, available at: www.telegraph.co.uk/news/world news/africaandindianocean/10082819/International-Criminal-Court-is-hunting-Africans.html.

Lake, Milli, 'Organising Hypocrisy: Providing Legal Accountability for Human Rights Violations in Areas of Limited Statehood' (2014) 58 *International Studies Quarterly* 515–526.

Land, Clare, *Decolonizing Solidarity: Dilemmas and Directions for Supporters of Indigenous Struggles* (Zed Books 2015).

Langer, Maximo, 'The Rise of Managerial Judging in International Criminal Law' (2005) 53 *American Journal of Comparative Law* 835–910.

Latour, Bruno, *The Making of Law: An Ethnography of the Conseil d'État* (John Wiley & Sons 2010).

Lauterpacht, Hersch, *The Function of Law in the International Community* [1933] (Oxford University Press 2011).

Lee Ashcraft, Karen, 'Gender and Diversity: Other Ways to "Make a Difference"'in Mats Alvesson, Todd Bridgman, and Hugh Willmott (eds.), *The Oxford Handbook of Critical Management Studies* (Oxford University Press 2013) 304–327.

Lee, Roy S., 'Introduction: The Rome Conference and Its Contribution to International Law' in Roy S. Lee (ed.), *The International Criminal Court: The Making of the Rome Statute* (Kluwer Law International 1999) 1–40.

Legg, Stephen, '"The Life of Individuals as well as of Nations": International Law and the League of Nations' Anti-Trafficking Governmentalities' (2012) 25 *Leiden Journal of International Law* 647–664.

Leonardi, Paul, and Jackson, Michele H., 'Technological Determinism and Discursive Closure in Organisational Mergers' (2004) 17 *Journal of Organisational Change Management* 615–631.

Lepawsky, Albert, 'Technical Assistance: A Challenge to Public Administration' (1956) 16 *Public Administration Review* 22–23.

Lepore, Jill, 'Not So Fast', *The New Yorker*, 12 October 2009, available at: www .newyorker.com/magazine/2009/10/12/not-so-fast.

Locke, Robert R., and Spender, J.-C., *Confronting Managerialism: How the Business Elite and Their Schools Threw Our Lives Out of Balance* (Bloomsbury Academic 2011).

SELECT BIBLIOGRAPHY

López, Rachel, 'Black Guilt, White Guilt at the International Criminal Court' in Sirleaf, Matiangai (ed.), *Race and National Security* (Oxford University Press 2023).

Lowen, Mark, 'Greeks Seek Austerity Trial at The Hague, *BBC News*, 24 April 2012, available at: www.bbc.com/news/world-europe-17811153.

Lowenkron, Laura, and Ferreira, Letícia, 'Anthropological Perspectives on Documents: Ethnographic Dialogues on the Trail of Police Papers' (2014) 11 *Vibrant: Virtual Brazilian Anthropology* 76–112.

Luban, David, 'After the Honeymoon: Reflections on the Current State of International Criminal Justice' (2013) 11 *Journal of International Criminal Justice* 505–515.

Maldonado, Tomás, 'The Idea of Comfort', *Errant Journal*, Issue 3 (2022) 87.

Mamdani, Mahmood, *When Victims Become Killers: Colonialism, Nativism and the Genocide in Rwanda* (Princeton University Press 2001).

'The New Humanitarian Order', *The Nation*, 29 September 2008, available at: www.thenation.com/article/new-humanitarian-order/.

Maupas, Stéphanie, 'ICC under Fire for Internal Management', *Justice Info*, 26 February 2018, available at: www.justiceinfo.net/en/36556-icc-under-fire-for-internal-management.html. Separately, Tarfusser asked von Hebel: 'Do Not You Think It Is a Waste of Public Money?'.

Mazower, Mark, *No Enchanted Palace: The End of Empire and the Ideological Origins of the United Nations* (Princeton University Press 2009).

Governing the World: The History of an Idea (Penguin 2012).

Mbeki, Thabo, and Mamdani, Mahmood, 'Courts Cannot End Civil Wars', *New York Times*, 5 February 2014.

McDermott, Yvonne, *Fairness in International Criminal Tribunals* (Oxford University Press 2016).

'The International Criminal Court's Chambers Practice Manual: Towards a Return to Judicial Law Making in International Criminal Procedure?' (2017) 15 *Journal of International Criminal Justice* 873–904.

McKenna, Christopher, *The World's Newest Profession: Management Consulting in the Twentieth Century* (Cambridge University Press 2006).

Mégret, Frédéric, 'International Criminal Justice: A Critical Research Agenda' in Christine Schwöbel (ed.), *Critical Approaches to International Criminal Law: An Introduction* (Routledge 2015) 17–53.

'What Sort of Global Justice Is "International Criminal Justice"?' (2015) 13 *Journal of International Criminal Justice* 77–96.

'International Criminal Justice as a Juridical Field' (2018) 13 *Champ Pénal* 1.

Mégret, Frédéric, and DelFalco, Randle, 'The Invisibility of Race at the ICC: Lessons from the US Criminal Justice System' (2019) 7 *London Review of International Law* 55–87.

SELECT BIBLIOGRAPHY

Meierhenrich, Jens, 'The Practice of International Law: A Theoretical Analysis' (2013) 76 *Law & Contemporary Problems* 1–83.

Meltzer, Ronald, 'Restructuring the United Nations System: Institutional Reform Efforts in the Context of North–South Relations' (1978) 32 *International Organisation* 993–1018.

Mendes, Errol, 'The Important Role of the IMF and External Creditors in Case of Arrest Warrants from the ICC – the Case of Sudan', OTP Guest Lecture Series (2009).

Merkle, Judith, *Management and Ideology: The Legacy of the International Scientific Management Movement* (University of California Press 1980).

Miller, Peter, and O'Leary, Ted, 'Accounting and the Construction of the Governable Person' (1987) 12 *Accounting, Organisations and Society* 235–265.

Mitrany, David, 'The Functional Approach to World Organisation' (1948) 24 *International Affairs* 350–363.

Moffett, Luke, *Justice for Victims before the International Criminal Court* (Routledge 2014).

Moosavi, Leon, 'Turning the Decolonial Gaze towards Ourselves: Decolonising the Curriculum and "Decolonial Reflexivity" in Sociology and Social Theory' (2022) 00 *Sociology* 1–20.

Morden, Tony, *Principles of Management* (McGraw-Hill 1996).

Moreno-Ocampo, Luis, 'The International Criminal Court: Seeking Global Justice' (2007) 40 *Case Western Reserve Journal of International Law* 215–225.

    'From Brexit to African ICC Exit: A Dangerous Trend', Just Security blog, 31 October 2016, available at: www.justsecurity.org/33972/brexit-african-icc-exit-dangerous-trend/.

    'The International Criminal Court' in David Crane, Leila Sadat, and Michael Sharf (eds.), *The Founders: Four Pioneering Individuals Who Launched the First Modern-Era International Criminal Tribunals* (Cambridge University Press 2018) 94–125.

Moretti, Franco, and Pestre, Dominique, 'Bankspeak: The Language of World Bank Reports' (2015) 92 *New Left Review* 75–100.

Morgan, Glenn, and Spicer, André, 'Critical Approaches to Organisational Change' in Mats Alvesson, Todd Bridgman, and Hugh Willmott (eds.), *Oxford Handbook of Critical Management Studies* (Oxford University Press 2013) 251–266.

Moyn, Samuel, 'Anti-Impunity as Deflection of Argument', in Karen Engle, Zina Miller, and D.M. Davis (eds.), *Anti-Impunity and the Human Rights Agenda* (Cambridge University Press 2016) 68–94.

Moynihan, Daniel P., 'The United States in Opposition', *Commentary*, March 1975, available at: www.commentarymagazine.com/articles/the-united-states-in-opposition/.

Muhammad, Samaria, 'Reimagining the ICC: Exploring Practitioners' Perspectives on the Effectiveness of the International Criminal Court' (2021) 21 *International Criminal Law Review* 126–153.

Müller, Joachim, *Reforming the United Nations: New Initiatives and Past Efforts, Volume 1* (Brill 1997).

(ed.), *Reforming the United Nations: A Chronology* (Brill Nijhoff 2016).

Müller, Philipp, 'Promoting Justice Between Independence and Institutional Constraints: The Role of the Office of the Public Counsel of the Defence at the ICC' in Mayeul Hiéramente and Patricia Schneider (eds.), *The Defence in International Criminal Trials: Observations on the Role of the Defence at the ICTY, ICTR and ICC* (Nomos 2016) 245–268.

Mutua, Makau, 'Africans and the ICC: Hypocrisy, Impunity, and Perversion' in Kamari Maxine Clarke, Abel S. Knotterus, and Eefje de Volder (eds.), *Africa and the ICC: Perceptions of Justice* (Cambridge University Press 2016) 47–60.

Mwangi, Wambui, and Mphepo, Tiyanjana, 'Developments in International Criminal Justice in Africa during 2011' (2012) 12 *African Human Rights Law Journal* 254–282.

Naldi, Gino, and Magliveras, Konstantinos, 'The International Criminal Court and the African Union: A Problematic Relationship' in Charles Chernor Jalloh and Ilias Bantekas (eds.), *The International Criminal Court and Africa* (Oxford University Press 2017) 111–137.

Nelson, Richard, 'Current Developments: International Law and U.S. Withholdings of Payments to International Organisations' (1986) 80 *American Journal of International Law* 973–983.

Nesiah, Vasuki, 'Doing History with Impunity' in Karen Engle, Zina Miller, and D.M. Davis (eds.), *Anti-Impunity and the Human Rights Agenda* (Cambridge University Press 2016) 95–122.

'Local Ownership of Global Governance' (2016) 14 *Journal of International Criminal Justice* 985–1009.

Newton, Michael, 'A Synthesis of Community-Based Justice and Complementarity' in Christian De Vos, Sara Kendall, and Carsten Stahn (eds.), *Contested Justice: The Politics and Practice of International Criminal Court Interventions* (Cambridge University Press 2017) 122–144.

Nouwen, Sarah M.H., 'Justifying Justice' in Martti Koskenniemi and James Crawford (eds.), *Cambridge Companion to International Law* (Cambridge University Press 2012) 327–351.

Complementarity in the Line of Fire: The Catalysing Effect of the International Criminal Court in Uganda and Sudan (Cambridge University Press 2013).

'"As You Set Out for Ithaka": Practical, Epistemological, Ethical, and Existential Questions about Socio-Legal Empirical Research in Conflict' (2014) 27 *Leiden Journal of International Law* 227–260.

SELECT BIBLIOGRAPHY

Nouwen, Sarah M.H., and Wouter Werner, 'Monopolising Global Justice: International Criminal Law as Challenge to Human Diversity' (2015) 13 *Journal of International Criminal Justice* 157–176.

Nuremberg Academy, 'Power in International Criminal Justice: Towards a Sociology of International Justice', Istituto degli Innocenti, 28–29 October 2017, available at: www.nurembergacademy.org/fileadmin/user_upload/170912_Programme_and_concept_note_Florence_conference_20171028-29.pdf.

O'Donohue, Jonathan, 'Financing the International Criminal Court' (2013) 13 *International Criminal Law Review* 269–296.

Okafor, Obiora, and Ngwaba, Uchechukwu, 'The International Criminal Court as a "Transitional Justice" Mechanism in Africa: Some Critical Reflections' (2014) 9 *International Journal of Transitional Justice* 90–1086.

Orford, Anne, 'Muscular Humanitarianism: Reading the Narratives of the New Interventionism' (1999) 10 *European Journal of International Law* 679–711.

'In Praise of Description' (2012) 25 *Leiden Journal of International Law* 609–624.

Osborne, David, and Gaebler, Ted, *Reinventing Government: How the Entrepreneurial Spirit is Transforming the Public Sector* (Penguin 1993).

Otto, Dianne, 'Beyond Legal Justice: Some Personal Reflections on People's Tribunals, Listening and Responsibility (2017) 5 *London Review of International Law* 225–249.

Özsu, Umut, 'Neoliberalism and the New International Economic Order: A History of "Contemporary Legal Thought"' in Justin Desautels-Stein and Christopher Tomlins (eds.), *Searching for Contemporary Legal Thought* (Cambridge University Press 2017) 330–347.

Pahuja, Sundhya, *Decolonising International Law: Development, Economic Growth and the Politics of Universality* (Cambridge University Press 2011).

Parker Follett, Mary, 'The Giving of Orders' in Henry Metcalf and Lyndal Urwick (eds.), *Dynamic Administration: The Collected Papers of Mary Parker Follett* (Harper & Brothers Publishers 1942) 23–45.

Parker, Martin, *Organisational Culture and Identity: Unity and Division at Work* (SAGE Publishing 2000).

'Managerialism' in Mark Tadajewski, Pauline Maclaren, Elizabeth Parsons, and Martin Parker (eds.), *Key Concepts in Critical Management Studies* (SAGE Publishing 2011) 155–159.

Phillips, Nelson, and Dar, Sadhvi, 'Strategy' in Mats Alvesson', in Todd Bridgman and Hugh Willmott (eds.), *The Oxford Handbook of Critical Management Studies* (Oxford University Press 2013) 414–432.

Piiparinen, Touko, 'Law versus Bureaucratic Culture: The Case of the ICC and the Transcendence of Instrumental Rationality' in Jan Klabbers and Touko Piiparinen (eds.), *Normative Pluralism and International Law: Exploring Global Governance* (Cambridge University Press 2013) 251–283.

SELECT BIBLIOGRAPHY

Power, Michael, *The Audit Society: Rituals of Verification* (Oxford University Press 1997).

Prahalad, C.K., and Hamel, Gary, 'The Core Competence of the Corporation', *Harvard Business Review*, May–June 1990, 1–15.

Prasad, Anshuman (ed.), *Against the Grain: Advances in Postcolonial Organisation Studies* (Universitetforlaget 2012).

Protherough, Robert, and Pick, John, *Managing Britannia: Culture and Management in Modern Britain* (Imprint Academic 2003).

Pues, Anni, *Prosecutorial Discretion at the International Criminal Court* (Hart Publishing 2020).

Raad Al Hussein, Zeid, Stagno Ugarte, Bruno, Wenaweser, Christian, and Intelman, Tiina, 'The International Criminal Court Needs Fixing', *New Atlanticist*, 24 April 2019, available at: www.atlanticcouncil.org/blogs/new-atlanticist/the-international-criminal-court-needs-fixing.

Rajagopal, Balakrishnan, *International Law from Below: Development, Social Movements and Third World Resistance* (Cambridge University Press 2000).

Rajkovic, Nik, '"Global Law" and Governmentality: Reconceptualizing the "Rule of Law" as Rule "through" Law' (2010) 18 *European Journal of International Relations* 29–52.

'The Space Between Us: Law, Teleology and the New Orientalism of Counterdisciplinarity' in Wouter Werner, Marieke de Hoon, and Alexis Gálan (eds.), *The Law of International Lawyers: Reading Martti Koskenniemi* (Cambridge University Press 2017) 167–196.

Rao, S. Rama, 'Financing the Court, Assembly of States Parties and the Preparatory Commission' in Roy S. Lee (ed.), *The International Criminal Court: The Making of the Rome Statute* (Kluwer Law International 1999) 399.

Reiley, Alan Campbell, and Mooney, James D., *Onward Industry!: The Principles of Organisations and Their Significance to Modern Industry* (Harper & Bros 1931).

Reisman, Taegin, 'ICC Registrar Discusses Restructuring and Need for Larger Budget', International Justice Monitor, 23 July 2014, available at: www.ijmonitor.org/2014/07/icc-registrar-discusses-restructuring-and-need-for-larger-budget/.

Resnik, Judith, 'Managerial Judges' (1982) 96 *Harvard Law Review* 374–448.

'Managerial Judges and Court Delay: The Unproven Assumptions' (1984) 23 *Judges Journal* 8–11 and 54–55.

Reynolds, John, and Xavier, Sujith, '"The Dark Corners of the World": TWAIL and International Criminal Justice' (2016) 14 *Journal of International Criminal Justice* 959–983.

Ricoeur, Paul, *Freud and Philosophy: An Essay on Interpretation* (Yale University Press 1970).

SELECT BIBLIOGRAPHY

Riles, Annelise, 'Introduction: A Response' in Annelise Riles (ed.), *Documents: Artifacts of Modern Knowledge* (University of Michigan Press 2006) 1–40.

'[Deadlines]: Removing the Brackets on Politics in Bureaucratic and Anthropological Analysis' inAnnelise Riles (ed.), *Documents: Artifacts of Modern Knowledge* (University of Michigan Press 2006) 71–94.

Robinson, Darryl, 'Inescapable Dyads: Why the International Criminal Court Cannot Win' (2015) 28 *Leiden Journal of International Law* 323–347.

Roediger, David, and Esch, Elizabeth, *The Production of Difference: Race and the Management of Labor in US History* (Oxford University Press 2012).

Roele, Isobel, *Articulating Security: The United Nations and Its Infra-Law* (Cambridge University Press 2021).

Rose, Nikolas, and Miller, Peter, 'Political Power Beyond the State: Problematics of Government' (1992) 43 British Journal of Sociology 173–205.

Rosenthal, Caitlin, *Accounting for Slavery: Masters and Management* (Harvard University Press 2018).

Ryngaert, Cedric (ed.), *The Effectiveness of International Criminal Justice* (Intersentia 2009).

Salomons, Dirk, 'Good Intentions to Naught: The Pathology of Human Resources Management at the United Nations' in Dennis Dijkzeul and Yves Beigbeder (eds.), *Rethinking International Organisations* (Berghahn 2006) 111–139.

Sander, Barrie, 'The Expressive Turn of International Criminal Justice: A Field in Search of Meaning' (2019) 32 *Leiden Journal of International Law* 851–872.

Doing Justice to History: Confronting the Past in International Criminal Courts (Oxford University Press 2021).

Sands, Philippe, *From Nuremberg to The Hague: The Future of International Criminal Justice* (Cambridge University Press 2009).

Savino, David, 'Louis D. Brandeis and His Role Promoting Scientific Management as a Progressive Movement' (2009) 15 *Journal of Management History* 38–49.

Schabas, William, 'Victor's Justice: Selecting "Situations" at the International Criminal Court' (2010) 32 *John Marshall Law Review* 535–552.

Schachter, Oscar, 'Dag Hammarskjold and the Relation of Law to Politics' (1962) *American Journal of International Law* 1–8.

Scherer, Andreas Georg, 'Critical Theory and Its Contribution to Critical Management Studies' in Mats Alvesson, Todd Bridgman, and Hugh Willmott (eds.), *The Oxford Handbook of Critical Management Studies* (Oxford University Press 2013) 29–51.

Schilling, Elaine, 'Core Competencies and their Role in Performance Appraisal', Webchat Presentation on Performance Management, University of California Merced, 3 May 2016, available at: https://hr.ucmerced.edu/files/page/documents/webchat_slide_-_core_competencies.pdf.

318 SELECT BIBLIOGRAPHY

Schwöbel-Patel, Christine, 'The Comfort of International Criminal Law' (2013) 24 *Law & Critique* 169–191.

'Spectacle in International Criminal Law: The Fundraising Image of Victimhood' (2016) 4 *London Review of International Law* 247–274.

Marketing Global Justice: The Political Economy of International Criminal Law (Cambridge University Press 2021).

Sekhon, Nirej, 'Complementarity and Post-Coloniality' (2013) 27 Emory International Law Review 799–828.

Selznick, Philip, 'Foundations of the Theory of Organisation' (1948) 13 *American Sociological Review* 25–35.

Sending, Ole Jacob, and Neumann, Iver B., 'Governance to Governmentality: Analyzing NGOs, States, and Power' (2006) 50 *International Studies Quarterly* 651–672.

Shaji, Neha, 'Some Difficult Questions: On Discomfort, Institutional Activism and Anger', *Exeter Decolonising Network*, 21 March 2021, available at: http://exeterdecol.org/some-difficult-questions-on-discomfort-institutional-activism-and-anger/.

Shany, Yuval, *Assessing the Effectiveness of International Courts* (Oxford University Press 2014).

Shelton, Jeffery, 'Tennessee Valley Authority: The Establishment of a System for the Development of Agency Objectives', Unpublished MPA thesis, Atlanta University, July 1981.

Shoamanesh, Sam Sasan, 'Institution Building: Perspective from within the Office of the Prosecutor of the International Criminal Court' (2018) 18 *International Criminal Law Review* 489–516.

Shore, Cris, and Wright, Susan, 'Coercive Accountability: The Rise of Audit Culture in Higher Education' in Marilyn Strathern (ed.), *Audit Cultures: Anthropological Studies in Accountability, Ethics and the Academy* (Routledge 2000) 57–89.

Simpson, Gerry, *Law, War and Crime: War Crimes, Trials and the Reinvention of International Law* (Wiley 2007).

'The Conscience of Civilisation, and Its Discontents: A Counter History of International Criminal Law' in Philipp Kastner (ed.), *International Criminal Law in Context* (Routledge 2018) 11–27.

Singh, Sahib, 'Narrative and Theory: Formalism's Recurrent Return' (2014) 84 *British Yearbook of International Law* 304–343.

Skouteris, Thomas, 'The New Tribunalism: Strategies of (De)Legitimation in the Era of International Adjudication' (1999) 17 *Finnish Yearbook of International Law* 307–356.

Slobodian, Quinn, *Globalists: The End of Empire and the Birth of Neoliberalism* (Harvard University Press 2018).

SELECT BIBLIOGRAPHY

Smith, James, *The Ideas Brokers: Think Tanks and the Rise of the New Policy Elite* (Free Press 1993).

Stahn, Carsten, 'Between "Faith" and "Facts": By What Standards Should We Assess International Criminal Justice?' (2012) 25 *Leiden Journal of International Law* 251–282.

Stokes, Peter, *Critical Concepts in Management and Organisation Studies* (Palgrave 2011).

Stoler, Ann, 'Colonial Archives and the Arts of Governance' (2002) 2 *Archival Science* 87–109.

Stone, Donald C., 'Organising the United Nations' (1946) 6 *Public Administrative Review* 115–129.

  'Administrative Management: Reflections on Origins and Accomplishments' (1990) 50 *Public Administration Review* 3–20, at 8.

Strathern, Marilyn, *Audit Cultures: Anthropological Studies in Accountability, Ethics and the Academy* (Routledge 2000).

  'Bullet-Proofing: A Tale from the United Kingdom' in Annelise Riles (ed.), *Documents: Artifacts of Modern Knowledge* (University of Michigan Press 2006) 181–205.

Tallgren, Immi, 'The Sensibility and Sense of International Criminal Law' (2002) 13 *European Journal of International Law* 561–595.

Tan, Celine, *Governance through Development: Poverty Reduction Strategies, International Law and the Disciplining of Third World States* (Routledge 2011).

Taylor, Frederick W., *Principles of Scientific Management* [1911] (Dover Publications 1998).

Tellmann, Ute, 'Catastrophic Populations and the Fear of the Future: Malthus and the Genealogy of Liberal Economy' (2013) 30 *Theory, Culture and Society* 135–155.

Terry, Nicholas, and Moles, Peter, *Oxford Handbook of International Financial Terms* (Oxford University Press 2005).

'The scandal of the UN "lost" millions', *Sunday Times*, August 1993.

Townley, Barbara, 'Foucault, Power/Knowledge, and Its Relevance for Human Resource Management' (1993) 18 *Academy of Management Review* 518–545.

  Reframing Human Resource Management: Power, Ethics and the Subject at Work (SAGE Publishing 2014).

Tzouvala, Ntina, *Capitalism as Civilisation: A History of International Law* (Cambridge University Press 2020).

Ullrich, Leila, 'Beyond the "Global–Local Divide": Local Intermediaries, Victims and the Justice Contestations of the International Criminal Court' (2016) 14 *Journal of International Criminal Justice* 543–568.

van den Meerssche, Dimitri, The World Bank's Lawyers: The Life of International Law as Institutional Practice (Oxford University Press 2022).

van Sliedregt, Elies, 'International Criminal Law: Over-Studied and Underachieving?' (2016) 29 *Leiden Journal of International Law* 1–12.

Varadarajan, Latha, 'The Trials of Imperialism: Radhabinod Pal's Dissent at the Tokyo Tribunal' (2015) 21 *European Journal of International Relations* 793–815.

Vasiliev, Sergey, 'The Crises and Critiques of International Criminal Justice' in Kevin Jon Heller, Frédéric Mégret, Sarah M.H. Nouwen, Jens David Ohlin, and Darryl Robinson (eds.), *Oxford Handbook of International Criminal Law* (Oxford University Press 2020) 626–651.

Verges, Jacques, *De la stratégie judiciare* (Minuit 1968).

von Bernstorff, Jochen, and Dann, Philipp (eds.), *The Battle for International Law: South-North Perspectives on the Decolonisation Era* (Cambridge University Press 2019).

von Clausewitz, Carl, *On War* (Princeton University Press 1989, edited and translated by Michael Howard and Peter Paret).

Walleyn, Luc, 'Victims' Participation in ICC Proceedings: Challenges Ahead' (2016) 16 *International Criminal Law Review* 995–1017.

Wasser, Solidelle, and Dolfman, Michael, 'BLS and the Marshall Plan: The Forgotten Story', *Monthly Labour Review*, June 2005 44–52.

Weber, 'Politics as a Vocation', in David Owen and Tracy B. Strong (eds.), *Max Weber: The Vocation Lectures* (Hackett 2004, translated by Rodney Livingstone) 32–94.

Weil, Simone, *Oppression and Liberty* [1933] (Routledge 1988).

Werner, Wouter, 'Justice on Screen – A Study of Four Documentary Films on the International Criminal Court' (2016) 29 *Leiden Journal of International Law* 1043–1060.

Whyte, William H., *The Organisation Man* (Simon & Schuster 1961).

Williams, Abiodun, 'Strategic Planning in the Executive Office of the UN Secretary-General' (2010) 16 *Global Governance* 435–449.

Witcher, Ellis, 'Doing History to Justice: Theory and Historiography in the History of International Criminal Law', PhD Dissertation, University College Dublin, May 2022, available at: https://researchrepository.ucd.ie/bitstream/10197/13169/1/103255081.pdf.

Wolcott, Harry, *Ethnography: A Way of Seeing* (AltaMira Press 1999).

Wren, Daniel A. , and Bedeian, Arthur G., *The Evolution of Management Thought* (Wiley 2017).

Zacklin, Ralph, 'The Failings of Ad Hoc International Tribunals' (2004) 2 *Journal of International Criminal Justice* 541–545.

Zavala, Osvaldo 'The Budgetary Efficiency of the International Criminal Court' (2018) 18 *International Criminal Law Review* 461–488.

SELECT BIBLIOGRAPHY 321

International Materials

African Union

African Union Assembly Decision 264(XIII), Decision on the Abuse of the Principle of Universal Jurisdiction, Doc. Assembly/AU/11(XIII), Thirteenth Ordinary Session of the Assembly of the Union, 1–3 July 2009, available at: https://au.int/sites/default/files/decisions/9560-assembly_en_1_3_july_2009_auc_thirteenth_ordinary_session_decisions_declarations_message_congratulations_motion_0.pdf

African Union Assembly decision 622(XXVIII), Decision on the International Criminal Court, Doc. EX.CL/1006(XX), Twenty-Eighth Ordinary Session of the Assembly of the Union, 30–31 January 2017, available at: https://au.int/sites/default/files/decisions/32520-sc19553_e_original_-_assembly_decisions_621-641_-_xxviii.pdf

African Union Assembly Decision on the Progress Report of the Commission on the Implementation of the Decision on the International Criminal Court, Assembly/AU/Dec.493(XXII), 30–31 January 2014

African Union Commission, Press Release No. 002/2012 (9 January 2012)

Cases

Combined Decision on the Impact of the Budgetary Situation on Cases 003, 004, and 004/2 and Related Submissions by the Defence for Yim Tith, Office of the Co-Investigating Judges of the Extraordinary Chambers in the Courts of Cambodia, 004/2/07-09-2009-ECCC-OCIJ (11 August 2017) available at: www.eccc.gov.kh/sites/default/files/documents/courtdoc/%5Bdate-in-tz%5D/D349_6_EN.PDF (ECCC Combined Decision)

L. (No. 3) v. ICC (International Labour Organisation Administrative Tribunal Judgment) No. 3908 (24 January 2018)

New State Ice Co. v. Liebmann 285 US 262 at 308 (1932)

Situation in Islamic Republic of Afghanistan (Decision Pursuant to Article 15 of the Rome Statute on the Authorisation of an Investigation into the Situation in the Islamic Republic of Afghanistan) ICC-02/17-33 (12 April 2019)

Situation in the Republic of Kenya (Victims' Request for Review of Prosecution's Decision to Cease Active Investigation) ICC-01/09-154 (3 August 2015)

The Prosecutor v. Al Hassan Ag Abdoul Aziz Ag Mohamed Ag Mahmoud (Decision on the Procedure for the Admission of Victims to Participate in Proceedings for the Purposes of Trial) ICC-01/12-01/18-661 (12 March 2020)

The Prosecutor v. Callixte Mbarushimana (Decision Requesting the Parties to Submit Observations on 124 Applications for Victims' Participation in the Proceedings) ICC-01/04-01/10-265 (4 July 2011)

322 SELECT BIBLIOGRAPHY

The Prosecutor v. Jean-Pierre Bemba Gombo (Prosecutor's Submission of Additional Information Demonstrating the Existence of an Objectively Identifiable Risk) ICC-01/05-01/08-122-Redacted (26 September 2008)

The Prosecutor v. Jean-Pierre Bemba Gombo (Registry Submission on the Installation of Additional Software in the Courtrooms and Certain Modalities of Evidence Presentation) ICC-01/05-01/08-920 (1 October 2010)

The Prosecutor v. Joseph Kony (Decision on the Admissibility of the Case under Article 19(1) of the Statute) ICC-02/04-01/05-377 (10 March 2009)

The Prosecutor v. Laurent Gbagbo and Charles Blé Goudé (Consolidated Response to Laurent Gbagbo's and Charles Blé Goudé's Appeals Against the 'Decision on the Prosecutor's Application to Introduce Prior Recorded Testimony under Rules 68(2)(b) and 68(3)') ICC-02/11-01/15-644 (1 August 2016)

The Prosecutor v. Ntaganda (Decision Concerning the Organisation of Common Legal Representation of Victims) ICC-01/04-02/06-160 (2 December 2013)

The Prosecutor v. Omar Hassan Ahmad Al Bashir (Decision on the Cooperation of the Democratic Republic of the Congo regarding Omar Al Bashir's Arrest and Surrender to the Court) ICC-02/05-01/09-195 (9 April 2014)

The Prosecutor v. Omar Hassan Ahmad Al Bashir (Decision Pursuant to Article 87 (7) of the Rome Statute on the Failure by the Republic of Malawi to Comply with the Cooperation Requests Issued by the Court with respect to the Arrest and Surrender of Omar Hassan Ahmad Al Bashir) ICC-02/05-01/09-139 (12 December 2011)

The Prosecutor v. Omar Hassan Ahmad Al-Bashir (Judgment in the Jordan Referral re Al-Bashir Appeal) ICC-02/05-01/09-397 (6 May 2019)

The Prosecutor v. Saif Al-Islam Gaddafi (Decision on the 'Admissibility Challenge by Dr. Saif Al-Islam Gadafi pursuant to Articles 17(1)(c), 19 and 20(3) of the Rome Statute') ICC-01/11-01/11-662 (5 April 2019)

The Prosecutor v. Slobodan Milošević, International Criminal Tribunal for the former Yugoslavia (Trial Transcripts) IT-02-54 (3 July 2001) available at: www.icty.org/x/cases/slobodan_milosevic/trans/en/010703IA.htm

The Prosecutor v. Thomas Lubanga Dyilo (Decision on the Prosecutor's Application for a Warrant of Arrest, Article 58) ICC-01/04-01/06-1 (10 February 2006)

International Criminal Court Documents

Address by Prince Zeid Raad Zeid Al Hussein President of the ASP, Assembly of States Parties 3rd Session, 6 September 2004, available at: https://asp.icc-cpi.int/iccdocs/asp_docs/library/asp/060904_PZ_ASP_English.pdf

Address of Hans-Peter Kaul at the 6th Annual International Humanitarian Law Dialogues, 'The ICC of the Future', Robert H. Jackson Centre, 28 August 2012, available at: www.icc-cpi.int/NR/rdonlyres/8572B9B0-B827-466C-B67A-3C9C

SELECT BIBLIOGRAPHY

06A5E46E/284994/30082012_ChautauquaSpeech_THEICCOFTHEFUTURE_provis.pdf

Administrative Instruction on the Performance Appraisal System, ICC/AI/2019/003, 26 February 2021

Annual Report of the Head of the Independent Oversight Mechanism, ICC-ASP/20/16, 17 November 2021

Annual Report of the Head of the Independent Oversight Mechanism, ASP-ICC/17/8, 8 November 2018

Annual Report of the Head of the Independent Oversight Mechanism, ICC-ASP/16/8, 17 October 2017

'Arresting ICC Suspects at Large: Why it Matters, What the Court Does, What States can Do', International Criminal Court, January 2019, available at: www.icc-cpi.int/news/seminarBooks/bookletArrestsENG.pdf

Assembly of States Parties Resolution 1/10 (9 September 2002)

Assembly of States Parties Resolution 1/4 (3 September 2002)

Assembly of States Parties Resolution 12/1 (27 November 2013)

Assembly of States Parties Resolution 12/6 (27 November 2013) Annex: Operational Mandate of the Independent Oversight Mechanism

Assembly of States Parties Resolution 13/5 (17 December 2014) Annex 1, para. 7 (b).

Assembly of States Parties Resolution 14/1 (26 November 2015)

Assembly of States Parties Resolution 18/7 (6 December 2019)

Assembly of States Parties Resolution 5/2 (1 December 2006)

Assembly of States Parties Resolution 9/2 (10 December 2010)

Audit of the Registry's Field Operations - Organisational Structure, Office of Internal Audit, OIA.08-A09, 31 May 2010

Audit Report of the ReVision project of the International Criminal Court's Registry, ICC-ASP/15/27, 9 November 2016

Basic Outline of Proposals to Establish Defence and Victims Offices (Draft), International Criminal Court, 15 September 2014, available at: http://michaelgkarnavas.net/files/140954-outline-defence-proposals.pdf

'Building a Future on Peace and Justice', Address by Mr Luis Moreno-Omcapo, Nuremberg, 24/25 June 2007, available at: www.icc-cpi.int/sites/default/files/NR/rdonlyres/4E466EDB-2B38-4BAF-AF5F-005461711149/143825/LMO_nuremberg_20070625_English.pdf

Bureau of the Assembly of States Parties, Fifth Meeting: Agenda and Decisions, 7 June 2019, available at: https://asp.icc-cpi.int/sites/asp/files/asp_docs/ASP18/ICC-ASP-18-Bureau-5.pdf.pdf

Chambers Practice Manual, Third Edition, International Criminal Court, May 2017

Clark, Helen, Keynote Address to the 11th Session of the Assembly of States Parties to the International Criminal Court: Human Development and International

324   SELECT BIBLIOGRAPHY

Justice', 19 November 2012, available at: https://asp.icc-cpi.int/sites/asp/files/NR/rdonlyres/E10A5253-DA2D-46CE-90B8-7497426E9C39/0/ICCASP11_COMPKeynote_Remarks_HCENG.pdf

Comprehensive Report on the Reorganisation of the Registry of the International Criminal Court, Registry, ICC, August 2016, available at: www.icc-cpi.int/sites/default/files/itemsDocuments/ICC-Registry-CR.pdf

Development of a Human Resources Strategy: Progress Report, ICC-ASP/7/6, 26 May 2008

Discussion paper submitted by the Coordinator concerning Part 4. Organisation and composition of the Court, ICC Preparatory Commission Working Group on Rules of Procedures and Evidence, PCNICC/1999/WGRPE(4)/RT.2/Add.1, 14 December 1999

Draft Financial Regulations, ICC Preparatory Commission, PCNICC/2001/1/Add.2, 8 January 2002, available at: www.legal-tools.org/doc/396a35/pdf/

Draft Paper on Some Policy Issues before the Office of the Prosecutor for Discussion at the Public Hearing in The Hague on 17 and 18 June 2003, Office of the Prosecutor, 18 June 2003

Election of the Registrar of the International Criminal Court, Assembly of States Parties, 9 October 2012, ICC-ASP/11/19, available at: https://asp.icc-cpi.int/sites/asp/files/asp_docs/ASP11/ICC-ASP-11-19-ENG.pdf.

Final Audit Report on the Implementation of a Division of External Operations, ICC-ASP/16/27, 10 October 2017

'Flexibility must be Cornerstone of Administration of International Criminal Court, Preparatory Commission told', Press Release L/2976, 6 March 2001, available at: www.legal-tools.org/uploads/tx_ltpdb/doc41976.htm

ICC Information Circular, Principles and Procedures Applicable to Decisions Arising from the ReVision Project, ICC/INF/2014/011/Rev.1, 13 June 2015

ICC Report on the Court Capacity Model, ICC-ASP/5/10, 21 August 2006

ICC, Job Description for Human Resources Assistant (G-5), International Criminal Court, ID 18427 (posted on 19 July 2018)

Indictment of Sitting Heads of State and Government and Its Consequences on Peace and Stability and Reconciliation: Informal Summary by the Moderator, Assembly of States Parties, ICC-ASP/12/61, 27 November 2013

'International Criminal Court "Now a Fully Functional Judicial Institution", Assembly of States Parties Told as It Begins One-Week Session', Press Release no. ASP2004.003-EN, 6 September 2004, available at: https://asp.icc-cpi.int/iccdocs/asp_docs/library/asp/ICC-ASP20040906.003-E.Rev.21.pdf

International Criminal Court Rules of Procedure and Evidence, ICC-PIDS-LT-02-002/13_Eng

International Criminal Court Strategic Plan 2013–2017, 13 April 2013

International Criminal Court Whistleblowing and Whistleblower Protection Policy, ICC/PRESD/G/2014/003, 8 October 2014

SELECT BIBLIOGRAPHY

325

Judge Sang-Huyn Song Remarks to the Assembly of States Parties, ASP 10th Session, 12 December 2011, available at: https://asp.icc-cpi.int/iccdocs/asp_docs/ASP10/Statements/ASP10-ST-Pres-Song-Remarks-ENG.pdf

'Judges of the ICC Visit Auschwitz-Birkenau at the End of Their Retreat on Efficiencies' (Press Release) ICC-CPI-20170626-PR1314 (26 June 2017), available at: www.icc-cpi.int/news/judges-icc-visit-auschwitz-birkenau-end-their-retreat-efficiencies

Office of the Prosecutor Strategic Plan June 2012–2015, 11 October 2013, available at: www.legal-tools.org/doc/954beb/pdf/

Paper on Some Policy Issues before the Office of the Prosecutor: Referrals and Communications, Office of the Prosecutor, September 2003

Performance Appraisal Rebuttals and Procedures, ICC/AI/2010/002, 22 December 2010

Performance Appraisal System, ICC/AI/2013/003, 6 March 2013, Annex: The Core Competencies of the ICC

Performance Appraisal System, ICC/AI/2019/003, 22 February 2019

Performance Appraisal System, ICC/AI/2019/003, 22 February 2019, Annex II: Performance Appraisal Form

Performance Appraisal System, ICC/AI/2021/001, 26 February 2021, Annex 1: The Core Competencies of the ICC

Philippe Kirsch Address to the Assembly of States Parties, Assembly of States Parties 7th Session, 14 November 2008, available at: https://asp.icc-cpi.int/NR/rdonlyres/EB40944C-C250-4466-B99A-2F5ACDC8C941/0/ICCASPASP7GenDebePresident_Kirsch.pdf

Policy Paper on Case Selection and Prioritisation, Office of the Prosecutor, 15 September 2016

Policy Paper on Victims' Participation, Office of the Prosecutor, April 2010

Presidential Directive on Audit Committee, ICC/PRESD/G/2009/1, 11 August 2009

Probationary Period and Performance Appraisal, ICC/AI/2013/004, 5 April 2013

Proposed Programme Budget for 2015, ICC-ASP/13/10, 18 September 2014

Prosecutorial Strategy 2009–2012, Office of the Prosecutor, 1 February 2010

Provisional Estimates of the Staffing, Structure and Costs of the Establishment and Operation of an International Criminal Court, Preliminary Report of the Secretary-General, Ad Hoc Committee for an International Criminal Court, A/AC.244/L.2, 20 March 1995

Registrar Herman von Hebel Remarks to the 14th Session of the Assembly of States Parties, Herman von Hebel, Assembly of States Parties 14th Session, 21 November 2015, available at: https://asp.icc-cpi.int/iccdocs/asp_docs/ASP14/ASP14-BDGT-REGISTRAR-ST-ENG-FRA.pdf

Registrar Presentation of the 2014 Proposed Programme Budget, Assembly of States Parties 12th Session, 23 November 2013

326   SELECT BIBLIOGRAPHY

Registry Strategic Plan 2019–2021, International Criminal Court, 17 July 2019, available at: www.icc-cpi.int/sites/default/files/itemsDocuments/190717-reg-strategic-plan-eng.pdf

Report of the Ad Hoc Committee on the Establishment of an International Criminal Court, UN General Assembly, A/50/22, 7 September 1995

Report of the Bureau on the Establishment of an Independent Oversight Mechanism, ICC-ASP/8/2, 15 April 2009

Report of the Bureau on the Strategic Planning Process of the ICC, ICC-ASP/7/29, 6 November 2008.

Report of the Bureau on the Study Group on Governance, ICC-ASP/10/30, 22 November 2011

Report of the Committee on Budget and Finance on the Work of Its 4th Session, ICC-ASP/4/2, 15 April 2005

Report of the Committee on Budget and Finance on the Work of Its 8th Session, ICC-ASP/6/2, 29 May 2007

Report of the Committee on Budget and Finance on the Work of Its 11th Session, ICC-ASP/7/15, 31 October 2008

Report of the Committee on Budget and Finance on the Work of Its 21st Session, ICC-ASP/12/15, 4 November 2013

Report of the Committee on Budget and Finance on the Work of Its 17th Session, ICC-ASP/10/15, 18 November 2011

Report of the Committee on Budget and Finance on the Work of Its 20th Session, ICC-ASP/12/5/Rev.1, 7 June 2013, available at: https://asp.icc-cpi.int/iccdocs/asp_docs/ASP12/ICC-ASP-12-5-Rev1-ENG.pdf

Report of the Committee on Budget and Finance on the Work of Its 22nd Session, ICC-ASP/13/5, 18 August 2014

Report of the Committee on Budget and Finance on the Work of Its 19th Session, ICC-ASP/11/15, 29 October 2012

Report of the Court on Human Resources Management, ICC-ASP/17/6, 11 May 2018

Report of the Court on Measures to Increase Clarity on the Responsibilities of the Different Organs, ICC-ASP/9/34, 3 December 2010

Report of the Court on the Basic Size of the Office of the Prosecutor, International Criminal Court, ICC-ASP/14/21, 17 September 2015

Report of the Court on the Development of Performance Indicators for the International Criminal Court, 12 November 2015, available at: www.icc-cpi.int/sites/default/files/itemsDocuments/Court_report-development_of_performance_indicators-ENG.pdf

Report of the Court on the Organisational Structure, ICC-ASP/13/16, 23 May 2014

Report of the Office of Internal Oversight Services on the Audit and Investigation of the International Criminal Tribunal for Rwanda, A/51/789, 6 February 1997

SELECT BIBLIOGRAPHY

Report on Programme Performance of the International Criminal Court for the Year 2004, ICC-ASP/4/13, 6 September 2005, available at: https://asp.icc-cpi.int/iccdocs/asp_docs/library/asp/ICC-ASP-4-13_English.pdf

Report on Programme Performance of the International Criminal Court for the Year 2008, ICC-ASP/8/7, 6 May 2009, available at: https://asp.icc-cpi.int/sites/asp/files/asp_docs/ASP8/ICC-ASP-8-7-ENG.pdf

Report on the Activities of the Court, ICC-ASP/12/28, 21 October 2013

Report on the Activities of the International Criminal Court, ICC-ASP/13/37, 19 November 2014

Report on the Review of the Organisational Structure of the Registry, ICC-ASP/13/26, 28 October 2014

Report on the Review of the Organisational Structure of the Registry: Outcomes of Phase 4 of the ReVision Project, ICC-ASP/14/18, 4 May 2015

Response of the ICC Office of the Prosecutor to an Outcome Report and Recommendations from Open Society Justice Initiative and Amsterdam Law School, 8 May 2020, available at: www.icc-cpi.int/itemsDocuments/200508-OTP-response-to-OSJI-UoA-report.pdf

Rome Statute of the International Criminal Court (signed 17 July 1998, entered into force 1 July 2002) A/CONF.189/9

Sang-Hyun Song Remarks to the 11th Session of the Assembly of States Parties, Assembly of States Parties 11th Session, 14 November 2012, available at: www.icc-cpi.int/sites/default/files/NR/rdonlyres/0EEEED0E-5BA8-4894-8AB5-3C2C90CD301B/0/ASP11OpeningPICCSongENG.pdf.

Second Court's Report on the Development of Performance Indicators for the International Criminal Court, ICC, 11 November 2016, available at: www.icc-cpi.int/sites/default/files/itemsDocuments/ICC-Second-Court_report-on-indicators.pdf

Silvana Arbia Registrar Address to the Assembly of States Parties, Assembly of States Parties 7th Session, 17 November 2008, available at: https://asp.icc-cpi.int/NR/rdonlyres/6FFBBDCD-313D-4765-A603-0CCE900B4B83/0/ICCASPASP7StatementRegistrar.pdf

Staff Regulations for the International Criminal Court, adopted in ASP Res 2/2 (12 September 2003)

Staff Rules of the International Criminal Court (as amended), ICC/AI/2015/004/Corr.1 (entered into force 27 July 2015)

Statement by Luis Moreno-Ocampo, Prosecutor of the International Criminal Court, Assembly of States Parties 4th Session, 28 November 2005, available at: www.icc-cpi.int/NR/rdonlyres/0CBFF4AC-1238-4DA1-9F4A-70D763F90F91/278514/LMO_20051128_English.pdf

Statement of the Prosecutor of the International Criminal Court, Fatou Bensouda: 'The Public Deserves to know the Truth about the ICC's Jurisdiction over Palestine', 2 September 2014, available at: www.icc-cpi.int/news/statement-pros

328   SELECT BIBLIOGRAPHY

ecutor-international-criminal-court-fatou-bensouda-public-deserves-know-truth

Strategic Plan 2019–2021, Office of the Prosecutor, 17 July 2019

Strategic Plan for Outreach, ICC-ASP/5/12, 29 September 2006

Strategic Plan of the International Criminal Court, ICC-ASP/5/6, 4 August 2006

Study Group on Governance, Lessons Learnt: First Report of the Court to the Assembly of States Parties, ICC-ASP/31/Add.1, 23 October 2012

Summary of Proceedings of the Ad Hoc Committee during the Period 3–13 April 1995, A/AC.244.L.2

Summary of the Bureau of Assembly of States Parties Retreat, Santpoort, The Netherlands, 13 June 2019

Third Court's Report on the Development of Performance Indicators for the International Criminal Court, 15 November 2017, available at: www.icc-cpi .int/sites/default/files/itemsDocuments/171115-Third-Report-performance-indi cators-ENG.pdf

United Nations

A New United Nations Structure for Global Economic Co-operation: Report of the Group of Experts on the Structure of the United Nations System, E/AC.62/9, 28 May 1975

A Study of the Capacity of the United Nations Development System, Volume 1, United Nations, DP/5, 1969, available at: https://digitallibrary.un.org/record/ 695860?ln=en

'Development of a Twenty-Year Programme for Achieving Peace through the United Nations', UN General Assembly, A/1525, 17 November 1950

Group of High-Level Intergovernmental Experts to Review the Efficiency of the Administrative and Financial Functioning of the UN, General Assembly Official Records 41st Session, Supplement No. 49, A/41/49, 15 August 1986

Human Resources Management Reform: Report of the Secretary-General, A/55/ 253, 3 August 2000

Management in the United Nations: Work in Progress, Joint Inspection Unit, JIU/ REP/95/8, 4 August 1995

Report of the Commission to the General Assembly on the Work of Its 46th Session, A/CN.4/SER.A/1994/Add.1, 2 May-22 July 1994, Volume II.II

Report of the International Civil Service Commission, General Assembly 34th Session, Supplement No. 30, A/34/30, 4 October 1979, available at: https://icsc .un.org/Resources/General/AnnualReports/AR1979.pdf

Report of the International Law Commission on the Work of Its 2nd Session, A/ CN.4/34, Volume II.IV, 5 June–29 July 1950

'Secretary-General Says Establishment of International Criminal Court is Major Step in March towards Universal Human Rights, Rule of Law' (Press Release) L/

SELECT BIBLIOGRAPHY

2890 (20 July 1998), available at: www.un.org/press/en/1998/19980720.l2890 .html

Sixth Report of the Technical Assistance Board, ECOSOC, 18th Session, E/2566E/ TAC/REP.3, 24 (1954)

Statute of the Joint Inspection Unit, Annex to United Nations General Assembly Resolution 31/192 (22 December 1976)

Towards a New System of Performance Appraisal in the United Nations Secretariat: Resources for Successful Implementation, Joint Inspection Unit Report, JIU/REP/94/5, June 1994, available at: https://documents-dds-ny.un .org/doc/UNDOC/GEN/GL9/904/68/pdf/GL990468.pdf?OpenElement

United Nations Development Programme: Report of the Governing Council, Sixth Session, E/4545, 11–28 June 1968, available at: https://digitallibrary.un.org/ record/1298171?ln=en

United Nations General Assembly Declaration on the Establishment of a New International Economic Order, General Assembly Sixth special session, 3201(S-VI), 1 May 1974

United Nations General Assembly Resolution 198 (III) (4 December 1948)

United Nations General Assembly Resolution 40/237 (18 December 1985)

United Nations General Assembly Resolution 45/237 (21 December 1990)

United Nations General Assembly Resolution 48/221 (23 December 1993)

United Nations General Assembly Resolution 50/213C (7 June 1996)

United Nations Security Council Resolution 1593 (31 March 2005)

United Nations Security Council Resolution 1970 (26 February 2011)

Other Documents

Amnesty International, 'The International Criminal Court: Making the right choices – Part IV: Establishing and financing the court and final clauses', March 1998, available at: www.amnesty.org/en/library/asset/IOR40/004/1998/ en/6b9d9776-f000-40e2-ae29-2006d9785e2c/ior400041998en.html

Avocats sana drontières, ICC Registry ReVision Project – Basic Outline Proposals to Establish Defence and Victims Offices, 22 April 2015

Coalition for the International Criminal Court, 'Independent Oversight Mechanism Team: Comments and Recommendations to the Ninth Session of the Assembly of States Parties', 26 November 2010, available at: www.iccnow .org/documents/CICC_IOM_Team_Paper.pdf

Comments of the United States of America, Comments received pursuant to paragraph 4 of General Assembly Resolution 49/53 on the Establishment of an International Criminal Court', Report of the Secretary-General, Ad Hoc Committee for an International Criminal Court, A/AC.244/1/Add.2, 31 March 1995

330 SELECT BIBLIOGRAPHY

Déclaration de M. Jean-François Blarel (France), Assembly of States Parties 7th Session, 14 November 2008, available at: https://asp.icc-cpi.int/iccdocs/asp_docs/library/asp/ICC-ASP-ASP7-GenDebe-France-ENG.pdf

Expert Initiative on Promoting Effectiveness at the International Criminal Court, December 2014, available at: https://asp.icc-cpi.int/sites/asp/files/asp_docs/ASP19/Ind_Exp_Initiative.pdf

Fédération Internationale des Ligues des Droits de l'Homme, FIDH Comments on the ICC Registrar's ReVision Proposals in Relation to Victims, 18 November 2014

High Representative of the European Union for Foreign Affairs and Security Policy, Joint Staff Working Document on Advancing the Principle of Complementarity, 31 March 2013, SWD(2013)26 final

Human Rights Watch, The Strategic Plan of the International Criminal Court: A Human Rights Watch Memorandum, July 2006, available at: www.hrw.org/sites/default/files/related_material/The%20Strategic%20Plan%20of%20the%20ICC.pdf

International Bar Association, 'Enhancing Efficiency and Effectiveness of ICC Proceedings: A Work in Progress', January 2011

—, IBA Comments on Draft Registry Revision Project Paper: Basic Outline of Proposals to Establish Defence and Victims Offices, December 2014

O'Connell, James, Official Circular No. 12, Office of the International President, International Association of Machinists, 26 April 1911 (reprinted in Hearings to Investigate the Taylor System, Volume 2, 1222–1223)

REDRESS, Comments to the Registrar in Relation to the ReVision Project as it Relates to Victims' Rights before the ICC, February 2015

Report on the Special Court for Sierra Leone by the Independent Expert Antonio Cassese, 12 December 2006, para. 58, available at: www.rscsl.org/Documents/Cassese%20Report.pdf

Statement of the Government of Japan, Assembly of States Parties 6th Session, 3 December 2007, available at: https://asp.icc-cpi.int/iccdocs/asp_docs/library/asp/Japan_gd_statement_en_6thasp.pdf

US Comptroller-General, U.S. Participation in International Organisations, ID-77-36, 24 June 1977, available at: www.gao.gov/assets/120/119000.pdf

War Crimes Research Office, Investigative Management, Strategies, and Techniques of the International Criminal Court's Office of the Prosecutor, Washington College of Law, American University, October 2012

INDEX

accounting, 41–42
Ad Hoc Committee, 95–96
ad hoc tribunals, 26, 91, 94, 97, 105
  jurisprudence of, 188
administrative instruction, 152, 154,
  158, 162
Afghanistan, 11, 124, 178–181, 187,
  191, 226, 232
African Union, 15, 127, 209–211,
  234–235
Al Hussein, Zeid, 102
Al Bashir, Omar, 119, 189, 209–211
Ambach, Philipp, 216
ameliorationists, 43
Amnesty International, 98
amnesty laws, 188
Annan, Kofi, 2, 83–87
anti-African bias, 15, 22, 193, 234
anti-imperialism, 281
anti-impunity, 109–111, 138
  discourse of, 12
  ideals of, 37–38
  language of, 1–2, 282
anti-racism, 17
applicable law, 189
  management arguments and, 189–192
applicant, 138–147
appraisee, 152
appraiser, 152
Arbia, Silvana, 119–121, 135
Arendt, Hannah, 291
argumentative dilemmas, 10, 12, 30,
  181, 182–187, 213, 223–226,
  233, 263, 298
  framework of evaluation, 186
  case selection, 192–200
  complementarity, 200–207

cooperation, 208–213
  sources, 187–192
  victim participation, 213–223
arrest and surrender, 209
  model procedures, 212
art gallery, 286, 293
Assembly of States Parties, 2, 102, 120,
  124, 174, 197, 221, 238, 241,
  250, 277
audit, 81–83, 172–174
  ICC infrastructure, 118
  infrastructure, 103
  language of, 103
  national offices, 103
Audit Committee, 122
audit society, 81
auditors, 82, 104, 173–174, 239, 257
Auschwitz, 3
austerity, 123
  as context, 245–247
  trial, 237

background norms, 23
backlash, 237
banality, 278
Barbie, Klaus, 92, 280
Basic Size model, 197–198
Bemba, Jean-Pierre, 190
Bensouda, Fatou, 232
Bertrand, Maurice, 81
best practices, 205, 212, 220
Bethlehem Steel Company, 49
Brandeis, Louis, 52–53
Braverman, Harry, 50
budget, 79, 245, 250
  results-based, 21, 108
  zero-growth, 179

331

INDEX

budgetary constraint, 180
  as context, 205
bullet-points, 110, 156
bullying, 148
bureaucracy, 101, 205, 217
Business Schools, 6

capacity
  arguments, 196, 197
  Court Capacity Model, 11, 112–115
capitalism
  managers, 8
  post-war, 63
  UN management, 74
career, 137, 269
Cassese, Antonio, 4, 108, 208, 298
Cathala, Bruno, 107
Central African Republic, 107
Chambers, 220–222
Chambers Practice Manual, 191,
  219–222
Chandler, Alfred, 41
Christodoulidis, Emilios, 281
Clarke, Kamari, 133, 236
Clinton administration, 83
Coalition for the International
  Criminal Court, 261
Cold War, 27, 63, 66
colonial administration, 58
colonial relations, 15
comfort, 141, 285–286
Committee on Budget and Finance, 20,
  103, 108–109, 118–122, 228, 249
communication, 266
competencies, 143, 146, 160
  diagram, 157
  ICC model, 140, 154–158, 171
  interview, 146, 238
complementarity, 13, 13, 14, 23, 105,
  183, 202–207
  management practices, 204, 206
complexity, 162, 230–231
  administrative, 240
confession, 153
cooperative systems, 60
Corporate Governance Statement, 122
cosmopolitanism, 37, 90, 137, 201
cost-effectiveness, 96, 107, 207

Côte d'Ivoire, 107
cover letter, 139
Crawford, James, 94
crimes against humanity, 1
Critical Management Studies, 5, 6–7
critique
  deferral of, 186–187, 198, 225
  effectiveness-type, 274
curriculum vitae, 139, 141
customary law, 188, 210

data management, 219
deadlines, 265
Decade of International Law, 90
decoloniality, 286–287
defence, 125, 213, 215, 241
Defence Office, 241, 252
dehistoricisation, 32, 278
del Ponte, Carla, 195
Democratic Republic of the Congo,
  107, 115, 195, 207, 209–211
depoliticisation, 32, 35, 79, 278, 289
  claims to, 192
development, 17, 17, 40, 66–70
discomfort, 285–298
  political economy of, 293
documents, 103–104, 271–274
  access to, 175
  ethnography of, 33–34
  materiality of, 33–34, 158
domestic courts, 92, 105, 203
domination, 115
  colonial forms of, 14
downsizing, 240
Drucker, Peter, 5, 8

ecocide, 2
effectiveness and efficiency, 2, 21, 78,
  85, 180, 220
  as evaluation criteria, 14
efficiency, 84, 217, 274, 282
  savings, 125, 222, 228, 246, 257
efficient communities, 58
Eichmann, Adolf, 291
Elements of Crimes, 102
emancipation, 89
employee file, 163, 170
employment contract, 148, 152

INDEX 333

*e*Recruitment, 138–145
ethic of conviction, 287
Eurocentrism, 4
evidence, 198
exclusion, 30, 113, 132, 245, 258, 279, 284, 293
expectations management, 117
experimentation, 53
expertise
  axioms of, 19–28
  historical paradox of, 26–27
  productive power of, 26
  as truth effect, 28
Extraordinary Chambers in the Courts of Cambodia (ECCC), 21, 280

factory, 1, 46
  court of law as, 4
  history of, 29
  ICC as, 91, 114–116, 298
  in management theory, 45
  post-war performance reports, 62
failure, 110, 115, 266
fair trial, 132
fairness, 130, 267
  conflict with efficiency, 126
  discourse of, 215–216
Fernández de Gurmendi, Silvia, 37–40, 88, 276
Financial Regulations and Rules, 103
flowchart, 129
forms, 86, 162, 165, 168
  materiality of, 161
Foucault, Michel, 11, 86, 176
  ethic of discomfort, 285–286
  genealogy, 31–33
  governmentality, 9
  law as tactic, 11
  power, 10
  power/knowledge, 7
  productive power, 9–10
  on reform, 283
fragments. *See* style
fraud, 175

Gaddafi, Muammar, 124
Gaddafi, Saif, 188
Gantt, Henry, 41

Gardner, Richard, 75, 82
Gbagbo, Laurent, 190
Gender and Children Unit, 139, 145, 148, 172
genocide, 1
Global Financial Crisis, 120–122, 246
global governance, 204
global justice
  practices of, 12
  apparatus, 12
  imaginary of, 13, 29, 161, 273, 283
  sites of, 13
Global North, 73, 79, 97–98
Global South, 15, 64–65, 97–99
  as management problem, 66–70
governance
  good-, 174
  regimes, 23
  scales of, 30, 32–35, 279
governance feminism, 295
Gross Domestic Product, 76, 99
Group of 77, 29, 66, 72–73, 75, 79
  counter-strategy against, 66, 74–79
growth, 69, 245

habitus, 149
Hague Conference, 45
Halley, Janet, 31, 291–292, 294–295
Heritage Foundation, 78
hermeneutics of suspicion, 4
human resources
  practices, 136
  strategic approach to, 118
  strategy, 118
Human Resources Section, 118, 145, 148
human rights, 40
Human Rights Watch, 125
humanitarianism, 202
hypertextual reading, 31

ideal candidate, 140, 143, 146
immunity, 127, 189, 209–211, 234
impunity
  gap, 12
  as management problem, 12

INDEX

incentive scheme, 41, 46
incrementalism, 187
Independent Expert Review, 277–279
Independent Oversight Mechanism,
    122–123, 174–176
indeterminacy, 22, 183
individual responsibility, 15
information circular, 267
information-sharing, 212
inspection, 174–176
institution-building
    rationale of, 3
interests of justice, 178, 191
intermediaries, 14
Internal Auditor, 118
international authority, 13
International Bank for Reconstruction
    and Development, 67
International Bar Association, 125, 215
International Civil Service
    Commission, 84
international community, 184, 189
    tension with national, 200–207
International Court of Justice, 93
International Criminal Court (ICC)
    African states parties to, 15, 29, 124,
        126–127, 196, 233–236
    alternative interpretations of, 17
    application process, 138–147
    as argumentative field, 35
    budget, 97–99
    building, 147
    centrism, 110–111
    as criminal tribunal, 213–216
    critiques of, 14–15
    deterrent effect of, 19
    dispositif, 12–18
    as infant institution, 14
    as institutional experiment, 14
    instrumentalisation of, 196
    lawyer, 9, 33
    as non-standing body, 94–96
    opposition to, 13
    staff members, 135
    staff morale, 267
    and subordination, 14
    value-for-money of, 13, 120
    victim-centrism, 213–216

international criminal law, 184
International Criminal Tribunal for the
    former Yugoslavia, 25, 280
International Criminal Tribunal for
    Rwanda, 99–101
International Federation for Human
    Rights (FIDH), 259, 262–263
international institutions, 54–59
International Labour Organization,
    54–57
International Labour Organization
    Administrative Tribunal,
    268–269
International Law Commission, 93–96
international legal work, 10
International Management Institute, 55
International Military Tribunal at
    Nuremberg, 93, 195
International Monetary Fund, 75
iron cage, 142
irony, 3

Jackson, Sir Robert, 70
job advertisement, 142, 154
job description, 140
job evaluation, 106
job interview, 145–147
Jordan, 189
judicial
    decision-making, 11, 179
    expediency, 215–217, 219–223
    independence, impartiality, 208
    process, 126
    self-perception, 21
justice, 132, 142, 263
    ICC version of, 123, 183
    institutionally palatable, 112, 177
    office-based, 136
    quality of, 112

Kammarskjold, Dag, 68–69
Kendall, Sara, 184
Kennedy, David, 19, 22–25, 244,
    289–291
Kenya, 127, 190, 236
Kenyatta, Uhuru, 190
Kirsch, Philippe, 119
Koh, Harold Hongju, 202

INDEX

Kony, Joseph, 218, 232
Koskenniemi, Martti, 18, 22, 24, 27,
   182–184

labour, 46, 57
   conflict with capital, 46, 52–53
   division of, 45–46, 50
   Schmidt (worker), 49, 56
   Watertown strikes, 49
   withholding of, 48, 49
law
   administration and, 58
   management and, 40, 54
   distinction, 12
   relationship, 11
law of nations, 45
leadership, 171
League of Nations, 29, 58, 63
legal adviser, 169
legal argumentation, 181–187
legal officer, 139
legal personality, 208
legal reasoning, 178–182
   extra-legal factors in, 180–181
   state-based, 193
legalism, 193–196, 199
legitimacy, 194
lessons learnt, 82, 129, 205, 221–223,
   295
   Working Group, 222
Libya, 188
Lie, Trygvie, 67
Lord's Resistance Army, 107, 195, 232
Lubanga Dyilo, Thomas, 107, 124, 232

Malawi, 210, 234
management
   claims of political neutrality, 21–23
   as class war, 50
   as constraining/liberating, 224–225
   consultancy, 121
   critical reading of, 10
   definitions, 5
   discourses of, 29
   effectiveness claim of, 19–20
   as expert practice, 10, 11
   flight to, 182, 187, 192, 215, 223–227,
   238, 276, 297

functionalist claims of, 23–26
hierarchy, 142
historical claims of, 26–28
human relations school, 56–57, 59
as knowledge technique, 133
language of, 2, 90, 282
listed practices of, 29
mainstream reading, 6
by objectives, 69
as problem-solving, 30
productive power of, 10
professionalisation of, 47
removal of, 282–283
as remover of distance, 42
renewal of, 283–284
tactics, 9
technologies of the self, 167, *See*
   professional self-discipline
timelessness of, 39
turnover rate of, 20
manager, 41, 46, 58, 64, 172, 174
   figure of, 7–9, 52
   as moral guide, 46
   plantation overseer as, 41
   professional, category of, 169–176
   responsibilities, 169–176
managerial judging, 25–26
managerial university, 295
managerial work, 10
managerialism
   international law definitions of, 19
   in international legal scholarship,
   18–19
Mannet (management consultancy), 3,
   248
marketing, 12
Marshall Plan, 60, 62–63
Mavi Marmara, 236
Mayo, Elton, 56
measurement, 20, 130, 146
   partiality of, 113, 131
Merleau-Ponty, Maurice, 285
method
   deconstruction, 35
   genealogy as, 31–32
   notes on, 30–31
Midvale Steel Works, 47
Millennium Declaration, 88

336 INDEX

Mindua, Antoine, 179
mismanagement, 91, 99–101, 179, 181
mission, 110, 129, 143, 155, 252, 297
 civilising, 150
Moreno-Ocampo, Luis, 16, 104–107, 206
motion study, 48
Moynihan, Daniel Patrick, 74–75
multidivisional form (M-form), 41, 67

narrowing, 23, 29, 91–92, 109, 156,
 243–248, 262, 274, 279, 284
neo-colonialism, 4, 127, 194, 234
neoliberalism, 80
New Deal, 53, 59–62
New International Economic Order, 29,
 66, 72–73, 79–80
New Public Management, 80–87
new tribunalism, 87, 195
Nouwen, Sarah, 20, 132, 204
Ntaganda, Bosco, 232
Nuremberg, 26

Obama administration, 178, 232
Office of Internal Audit, 103, 239
Office of the Prosecutor, 2, 88, 231
 case selection and prioritisation,
  196–199
 Executive Committee, 106, 170
 Integrated Teams, 199
 investigation, 2, 23, 124, 200
 investigatory approach, 198
 policy paper, 105, 196, 204
 preliminary examination, 105, 197,
  200
 as start-up, 104–105
onboarding, 148–150
one Court principle, 149
Oppenheim, Lassa, 45
Orford, Anne, 39
organisational chart, 42, 150, 263
organisational context, 140, 141
organisational sustainability, 178, 181,
 245
outreach, 10, 12, 42, 237
Outreach Strategy, 116–117

Palestine, 236
Paschke report, 99–101

Paschke, Karl, 99, 103
people's tribunal, 17
performance
 appraisal, 2, 85–86, 162–172,
  238
  documents, 86
  form, 165
  report, 163
 individual objectives, 160
 individual report, 158–162
 informal meetings, 165
 management, 85–86, 121
 meeting, 152–154
 rating, 160–161, 165, 168
 under-, 167
Performance Appraisal System,
 162–172
 appeals process, 168–169
 non-compliance, 167
performance indicators, 2, 38, 116, 132,
 200, 221
Permanent Mandates Commission,
 57–59
phenomenology, 285
Philippines, The, 101
planning, 59–64
plantation, 29, 40–43
politics, 35, 298
 admission of, 288
 as force, 287
 of international law, 22, 192–200
positive complementarity, 204–207
power, 18, 39, 89, 167, 174, 192, 199,
 279, 283, 286, 298
pragmatism, 76, 77
Preparatory Commission, 102
Presidency, 100
presidential directive, 176
PricewaterhouseCoopers, 3, 84, 239,
 247, 263
PRINCE2 (project management),
 266
probation, 10, 86, 148, 150–163, 238
production line, 4, 46, 113
professional
 action, limits of, 142
 anxiety, 100
 faith, 200

INDEX

freedom, 225
ideal, 155
identity work, 136, 149, 162–164, 167, 268
imaginary, 161
misconduct, 175
optimisation, 136
responsibility, 86, 142, 289–292
self-discipline, 145, 151–162, 175–176
sensibility, 10, 27, 119, 141, 146, 150, 154–156, 185
socialisation, 137–138
trauma, 240
progressivism (movement), 50–52
promotion, 167
prosecutor, 172, 190, 203
prosecutorial discretion, 199–200
Prosecutorial Strategy, 205
public administration, 81, 111

race
advantage claims, 76
discomfort, 286
superiority, 49, 52
undertones, 76
racialisation, 292
Reagan, Ronald, 78
recruitment panel, 145–147
redescription, 230
REDRESS (non-governmental organisation), 259, 261
Registry, 100, 190, 217–220
alternative imaginaries of, 262
Core Values document, 267, 269
Division of External Operations, 256, 264, 273
Immediate Office of the Registrar, 229
management teams, 256
reparations, 12
Resnik, Judith, 25
resolution, sense of, 186
resource constraints, 11
responsibility, 197, 241
allocation of, 112, 116
ethic of, 287–289, *See* also Max Weber

flight from. *See* management flight to
scholarly, 296
restructuring, 9, 35, 73, 77, 79, 84–85, 106, 199, 218, 253
Registry, *See* ReVision
of states, 206–207
United States Army, 43–45
United States executive, 60
results, 129
ReVision, 35
Comprehensive Report, 271–272
consultation, 251, 260–262
context-creation, 244–247
deficiencies, 266–267
dispositif, discourse, 231–238
dissent, 262, 275
documentation, 271–274
experts, 250–251, 258–263
job classification, 267–269
justifications of, 238–243
length of, 266
methodology, 264
phases, 249–253
politics of, 231, 249, 264, 275
problem-identification, 247–248
redundancies, 240, 253, 267–269
results of, 253–257
as site of management, 229
staff alterations, 253
Terms of Reference, 250
risk
discourse of, 81–83, 121–124, 190, 265
institutional, 110
management, 3, 122, 130
techniques of, 57
Robinson, Darryl, 182–186
Rome Conference, 96–102
Rome Statute
drafting of, 93–102
ecosystem, 12, 60
global justice and, 13
Root, Elihu, 43–45, 54
rule of thumb, 48–49
Rules of Procedure and Evidence, 102, 236
Ruto, William, 190

338 INDEX

Samphan, Khieu, 280
Schwöbel-Patel, Christine, 229, 281,
    285–286
scientific management, 47–56
self-referral, 195
self-reflexivity, 293–294
Serbia, 195
sexual and gender-based crimes, 141,
    190
sexual harassment, 148
Simpson, Gerry, 201
skills, 139, 143, 146
slavery, 29, 41–43
    management as, 49
slippage, 110–111, 115–116, 119, 129,
    142
SMART goals, 118
soldiering, 48
Song, Sang-Hyun, 124–125
Spanish-American War, 43–44
Special Court for Sierra Leone, 249
Special Tribunal for Lebanon, 249
spectacle, 137, 292
Staff Rules and Regulations, 118, 151
Staff Union, 250, 260, 297
state
    cooperation, 13, 209
    court dependence on, 23, 208–213
    donor, 22, 76, 97–99, 116, 120, 123,
        192
    non-cooperation, 179
    sovereignty, 13, 201–213
Stone, Donald, 59–60, 65
strategic goals, 110–112, 116, 154
    indeterminacy of, 19
Strategic Plan, 2, 19, 87, 109–112,
    115–116, 120, 127, 138, 180,
    190, 198, 205, 211
strategic planning, 86–88, 108–119
strategy of connivance, 280–281
strategy of discomfort, 29, 36, 279,
    284–298
    institutionally, 296–298
    as taking a break, 294–296
    negative definitions of, 292–294
strategy of rupture, 280–281
streamlining, 38, 76, 198
structural bias, 22

struggle
    expert, 183
    institutional, 27, 235
Study Group on Governance, 222
style, 36
success, 110–111, 115
    meaning of, 265
    professional, 2
Sudan, 15, 209–211
supervisor, 150, 151–154
supply and demand, 198, 238, 244

tables, 156
Tarfusser, Cuno, 276, 297
targets, 265
task management, 49
Taylor, Frederick Winslow, 40, 47–53
Taylorism. See scientific management
technical assistance, 57, 64–65
Tennessee Valley Authority, 61–62
termination of employment, 159, 167
tick-box, 111
training, 129, 168, 269
transitional justice, 17
transparency, 199
treaties, 188
Treaty of Versailles, 54
trigger mechanism, 196

Uganda, 15, 107, 115, 195
United Nations
    1960s, 66–72
    1970s, 72–78
    1980s, 78–80
    audit culture, 79
    civil servants, 85, 88
    common budget, 98
    common system, 106
    Congo peacekeeping mission,
        68
    creation of, 63–64
    decentralisation of, 75
    decolonisation period, 70
    democratisation of, 66
    Gardner report, 75–77
    Group of 18 (expert panel), 79
    Jackson report, 70–72
    management criticism of, 74–79

INDEX

managerial struggle, 79
Office of Human Resources
    Management, 79
post-war period, 66
recruitment, 77
Secretary-General, 64, 68–69
specialised agency structure, 63
United Nations Conference on Trade
    and Development, 69
United Nations Development
    Programme, 67, 70–71
United Nations Economic and Social
    Council, 67, 75
United Nations Efficiency Board, 84
United Nations Environment
    Programme, 298
United Nations General Assembly, 67,
    69–71, 81, 82–83, 93, 98
United Nations Industrial
    Development Organisation,
    69
United Nations Joint Inspection Unit,
    81–83
United Nations Office of Internal
    Oversight Services, 83, 122
United Nations Security Council, 99,
    107, 124, 196, 209
United Nations Strategic Planning
    Unit, 88
United States, 78
universal jurisdiction, 94
unknowing, 291
Urwick, Lyndall, 55
utopianism, 194

Vergès, Jacques, 280–282
victim
    application, 124, 218–220
    application form, 219
    hierarchy, 214
    participation, 14, 129, 214, 244

reparations, 14, 214
statistical, 242
victim communities, 117, 125, 262
Victims and Witnesses Unit, 102, 218
Victims Office, 216, 242, 252
Victims Participation and Reparations
    Section, 2, 218
Victims Strategy, 129
victor's justice, 14, 195
violence, 289
    psycho-social, 115
    slow, structural, 14, 156, 292
    transgenerational, 14, 115
voice, 258–263
    institutional, 158
    managerial, expert, 239
    of victims, 239
voluntarism, 188
voluntary contributions, 99
von Hebel, Herman, 228–229, 240, 246,
    257–258
    election as Registrar, 249

Wall Street crash, 47
war crimes, 1
Weber, Max, 287–289
whistleblowing, 176
white fragility, 293
will to manage, 29, 298
work
    layout, 49
    ledger, 42
    plan, 160
workload, 257
    arguments, 295
    increase as context, 244–245
World Bank, 75
World Health Organisation, 298
Wright, Quincy, 58

yielding, 291–292

CAMBRIDGE STUDIES IN INTERNATIONAL AND COMPARATIVE LAW

Books in the Series

181 *A Communitarian Theory of WTO Law*
Chi Carmody

180 *Drones and International Law: A Techno-Legal Machinery*
Rebecca Mignot-Mahdavi

179 *The Necessity of Nature: God, Science and Money in Seventeenth Century English Law of Nature*
Mónica García-Salmones

178 *Making the World Safe for Investment: The Protection of Foreign Property 1922–1959*
Andrea Leiter

177 *National Governance and Investment Treaties*
Josef Ostřanský and Facundo Pérez Aznar

176 *Who Owns Outer Space? International Law, Astrophysics, and the Sustainable Development of Space*
Michael Byers and Aaron Boley

175 *Intervening in International Justice: Third States before Courts and Tribunals*
Brian McGarry

174 *Reciprocity in Public International Law*
Arianna Whelan

173 *When Environmental Protection and Human Rights Collide*
Marie-Catherine Petersmann

172 *The International Law of Sovereign Debt Dispute Settlement*
Kei Nakajima

171 *The Everyday Makers of International Law: From Great Halls to Back Rooms*
Tommaso Soave

170 *Virtue in Global Governance: Judgment and Discretion*
Jan Klabbers

169 *The Effects of Armed Conflict on Investment Treaties*
Tobias Ackermann

168 *Investment Law's Alibis: Colonialism, Imperialism, Debt and Development*
David Schneiderman

167 *Negative Comparative Law: A Strong Programme for Weak Thought*
Pierre Legrand

166 *Detention by Non-State Armed Groups under International Law*
Ezequiel Heffes

165 *Rebellions and Civil Wars: State Responsibility for the Conduct of Insurgents*
Patrick Dumberry

164 *The International Law of Energy*
Jorge Viñuales

163 *The Three Ages of International Commercial Arbitration*
Mikaël Schinazi

162 *Repetition and International Law*
Wouter Werner

161 *State Responsibility and Rebels: The History and Legacy of Protecting Investment Against Revolution*
Kathryn Greenman

160 *Rewriting Histories of the Use of Force: The Narrative of 'Indifference'*
Agatha Verdebout

159 *The League of Nations and the Protection of the Environment*
Omer Aloni

158 *International Investment Law and Legal Theory: Expropriation and the Fragmentation of Sources*
Jörg Kammerhofer

157 *Legal Barbarians: Identity, Modern Comparative Law and the Global South*
Daniel Bonilla Maldonado

156 *International Human Rights Law Beyond State Territorial Control*
Antal Berkes

155 *The Crime of Aggression under the Rome Statute of the International Criminal Court*
Carrie McDougall

154 *Minorities and the Making of Postcolonial States in International Law*
Mohammad Shahabuddin

153 *Preclassical Conflict of Laws*
Nikitas E. Hatzimihail

152 *International Law and History: Modern Interfaces*
Ignacio de la Rasilla

151 *Marketing Global Justice: The Political Economy of International Criminal Law*
Christine Schwöbel-Patel

150 *International Status in the Shadow of Empire*
Cait Storr

149 *Treaties in Motion: The Evolution of Treaties from Formation to Termination*
Edited by Malgosia Fitzmaurice and Panos Merkouris

148 *Humanitarian Disarmament: An Historical Enquiry*
Treasa Dunworth

147 *Complementarity, Catalysts, Compliance: The International Criminal Court in Uganda, Kenya, and the Democratic Republic of Congo*
Christian M. De Vos

146 *Cyber Operations and International Law*
François Delerue

145 *Comparative Reasoning in International Courts and Tribunals*
Daniel Peat

144 *Maritime Delimitation as a Judicial Process*
Massimo Lando

143 *Prosecuting Sexual and Gender-Based Crimes at the International Criminal Court: Practice, Progress and Potential*
Rosemary Grey

142 *Capitalism As Civilisation: A History of International Law*
Ntina Tzouvala

141 *Sovereignty in China: A Genealogy of a Concept Since 1840*
Adele Carrai

140 *Narratives of Hunger in International Law: Feeding the World in Times of Climate Change*
Anne Saab

139 *Victim Reparation under the Ius Post Bellum: An Historical and Normative Perspective*
Shavana Musa

138 *The Analogy between States and International Organizations*
Fernando Lusa Bordin

137 *The Process of International Legal Reproduction: Inequality, Historiography, Resistance*
Rose Parfitt

136 *State Responsibility for Breaches of Investment Contracts*
Jean Ho

135 *Coalitions of the Willing and International Law: The Interplay between Formality and Informality*
Alejandro Rodiles

134 *Self-Determination in Disputed Colonial Territories*
Jamie Trinidad

133 *International Law as a Belief System*
Jean d'Aspremont

132 *Legal Consequences of Peremptory Norms in International Law*
Daniel Costelloe

131 *Third-Party Countermeasures in International Law*
Martin Dawidowicz

130 *Justification and Excuse in International Law: Concept and Theory of General Defences*
Federica Paddeu

129 *Exclusion from Public Space: A Comparative Constitutional Analysis*
Daniel Moeckli

128 *Provisional Measures before International Courts and Tribunals*
Cameron A. Miles

127 *Humanity at Sea: Maritime Migration and the Foundations of International Law*
Itamar Mann

126 *Beyond Human Rights: The Legal Status of the Individual in International Law*
Anne Peters

125 *The Doctrine of Odious Debt in International Law: A Restatement*
Jeff King

124 *Static and Evolutive Treaty Interpretation: A Functional Reconstruction*
Christian Djeffal

123 *Civil Liability in Europe for Terrorism-Related Risk*
Lucas Bergkamp, Michael Faure, Monika Hinteregger and Niels Philipsen

122 *Proportionality and Deference in Investor-State Arbitration: Balancing Investment Protection and Regulatory Autonomy*
Caroline Henckels

121 *International Law and Governance of Natural Resources in Conflict and Post-Conflict Situations*
Daniëlla Dam-de Jong

120 *Proof of Causation in Tort Law*
Sandy Steel

119 *The Formation and Identification of Rules of Customary International Law in International Investment Law*
Patrick Dumberry

118 *Religious Hatred and International Law: The Prohibition of Incitement to Violence or Discrimination*
Jeroen Temperman

117 *Taking Economic, Social and Cultural Rights Seriously in International Criminal Law*
Evelyne Schmid

116 *Climate Change Litigation: Regulatory Pathways to Cleaner Energy*
Jacqueline Peel and Hari M. Osofsky

115 *Mestizo International Law: A Global Intellectual History 1842–1933*
Arnulf Becker Lorca

114 *Sugar and the Making of International Trade Law*
Michael Fakhri

113 *Strategically Created Treaty Conflicts and the Politics of International Law*
Surabhi Ranganathan

112 *Investment Treaty Arbitration As Public International Law: Procedural Aspects and Implications*
Eric De Brabandere

111 *The New Entrants Problem in International Fisheries Law*
Andrew Serdy

110 *Substantive Protection under Investment Treaties: A Legal and Economic Analysis*
Jonathan Bonnitcha

109 *Popular Governance of Post-Conflict Reconstruction: The Role of International Law*
Matthew Saul

108 *Evolution of International Environmental Regimes: The Case of Climate Change*
Simone Schiele

107 *Judges, Law and War: The Judicial Development of International Humanitarian Law*
Shane Darcy

106 *Religious Offence and Human Rights: The Implications of Defamation of Religions*
Lorenz Langer

105 *Forum Shopping in International Adjudication: The Role of Preliminary Objections*
Luiz Eduardo Salles

104 *Domestic Politics and International Human Rights Tribunals: The Problem of Compliance*
Courtney Hillebrecht

103 *International Law and the Arctic*
Michael Byers

102 *Cooperation in the Law of Transboundary Water Resources*
Christina Leb

101 *Underwater Cultural Heritage and International Law*
Sarah Dromgoole

100 *State Responsibility: The General Part*
James Crawford

99 *The Origins of International Investment Law: Empire, Environment and the Safeguarding of Capital*
Kate Miles

98 *The Crime of Aggression under the Rome Statute of the International Criminal Court*
Carrie McDougall

97 *'Crimes against Peace' and International Law*
Kirsten Sellars

96 *Non-Legality in International Law: Unruly Law*
Fleur Johns

95 *Armed Conflict and Displacement: The Protection of Refugees and Displaced Persons under International Humanitarian Law*
Mélanie Jacques

94 *Foreign Investment and the Environment in International Law*
Jorge E. Viñuales

93 *The Human Rights Treaty Obligations of Peacekeepers*
Kjetil Mujezinović Larsen

92 *Cyber Warfare and the Laws of War*
Heather Harrison Dinniss

91 *The Right to Reparation in International Law for Victims of Armed Conflict*
Christine Evans

90 *Global Public Interest in International Investment Law*
Andreas Kulick

89 *State Immunity in International Law*
Xiaodong Yang

88 *Reparations and Victim Support in the International Criminal Court*
Conor McCarthy

87 *Reducing Genocide to Law: Definition, Meaning, and the Ultimate Crime*
Payam Akhavan

86 *Decolonising International Law: Development, Economic Growth and the Politics of Universality*
Sundhya Pahuja

85 *Complicity and the Law of State Responsibility*
Helmut Philipp Aust

84 *State Control over Private Military and Security Companies in Armed Conflict*
Hannah Tonkin

83 *'Fair and Equitable Treatment' in International Investment Law*
Roland Kläger

82 *The UN and Human Rights: Who Guards the Guardians?*
Guglielmo Verdirame

81 *Sovereign Defaults before International Courts and Tribunals*
Michael Waibel

80 *Making the Law of the Sea: A Study in the Development of International Law*
James Harrison

79 *Science and the Precautionary Principle in International Courts and Tribunals: Expert Evidence, Burden of Proof and Finality*
Caroline E. Foster

78 *Transition from Illegal Regimes under International Law*
Yaël Ronen

77 *Access to Asylum: International Refugee Law and the Globalisation of Migration Control*
Thomas Gammeltoft-Hansen

76 *Trading Fish, Saving Fish: The Interaction between Regimes in International Law*
Margaret A. Young

75 *The Individual in the International Legal System: Continuity and Change in International Law*
Kate Parlett

74 *'Armed Attack' and Article 51 of the UN Charter: Evolutions in Customary Law and Practice*
Tom Ruys

73 *Theatre of the Rule of Law: Transnational Legal Intervention in Theory and Practice*
Stephen Humphreys

72 *Science and Risk Regulation in International Law*
Jacqueline Peel

71 *The Participation of States in International Organisations: The Role of Human Rights and Democracy*
Alison Duxbury

70 *Legal Personality in International Law*
Roland Portmann

69 *Vicarious Liability in Tort: A Comparative Perspective*
Paula Giliker

68 *The Public International Law Theory of Hans Kelsen: Believing in Universal Law*
Jochen von Bernstorff

67 *Legitimacy and Legality in International Law: An Interactional Account*
Jutta Brunnée and Stephen J. Toope

66 *The Concept of Non-International Armed Conflict in International Humanitarian Law*
Anthony Cullen

65 *The Principle of Legality in International and Comparative Criminal Law*
Kenneth S. Gallant

64 *The Challenge of Child Labour in International Law*
Franziska Humbert

63 *Shipping Interdiction and the Law of the Sea*
Douglas Guilfoyle

62 *International Courts and Environmental Protection*
Tim Stephens

61 *Legal Principles in WTO Disputes*
Andrew D. Mitchell

60 *War Crimes in Internal Armed Conflicts*
Eve La Haye

59 *Humanitarian Occupation*
Gregory H. Fox

58 *The International Law of Environmental Impact Assessment: Process,
Substance and Integration*
Neil Craik

57 *The Law and Practice of International Territorial Administration:
Versailles to Iraq and Beyond*
Carsten Stahn

56 *United Nations Sanctions and the Rule of Law*
Jeremy Matam Farrall

55 *National Law in WTO Law: Effectiveness and Good Governance in the
World Trading System*
Sharif Bhuiyan

54 *Cultural Products and the World Trade Organization*
Tania Voon

53 *The Threat of Force in International Law*
Nikolas Stürchler

52 *Indigenous Rights and United Nations Standards: Self-Determination,
Culture and Land*
Alexandra Xanthaki

51 *International Refugee Law and Socio-Economic Rights: Refuge from
Deprivation*
Michelle Foster

50 *The Protection of Cultural Property in Armed Conflict*
Roger O'Keefe

49 *Interpretation and Revision of International Boundary Decisions*
Kaiyan Homi Kaikobad

48 *Multinationals and Corporate Social Responsibility: Limitations and
Opportunities in International Law*
Jennifer A. Zerk

47 *Judiciaries within Europe: A Comparative Review*
John Bell

46 *Law in Times of Crisis: Emergency Powers in Theory and Practice*
Oren Gross and Fionnuala Ní Aoláin

45 *Vessel-Source Marine Pollution: The Law and Politics of International
Regulation*
Alan Khee-Jin Tan

44 Enforcing Obligations *Erga Omnes* in International Law
Christian J. Tams

43 *Non-Governmental Organisations in International Law*
Anna-Karin Lindblom

42 *Democracy, Minorities and International Law*
Steven Wheatley

41 *Prosecuting International Crimes: Selectivity and the International
Criminal Law Regime*
Robert Cryer

40 *Compensation for Personal Injury in English, German and Italian Law:
A Comparative Outline*
Basil Markesinis, Michael Coester, Guido Alpa, and Augustus Ullstein

39 *Dispute Settlement in the UN Convention on the Law of the Sea*
Natalie Klein

38 *The International Protection of Internally Displaced Persons*
Catherine Phuong

37 *Imperialism, Sovereignty and the Making of International Law*
Antony Anghie

36 *Principles of the Institutional Law of International Organizations*
C. F. Amerasinghe

35 *Necessity, Proportionality and the Use of Force by States*
Judith Gardam

34 *International Legal Argument in the Permanent Court of International
Justice: The Rise of the International Judiciary*
Ole Spiermann

33 –

32 *Great Powers and Outlaw States: Unequal Sovereigns in the
International Legal Order*
Gerry Simpson

31 *Local Remedies in International Law* (second edition)
C. F. Amerasinghe

30 *Reading Humanitarian Intervention: Human Rights and the Use of
Force in International Law*
Anne Orford

29 *Conflict of Norms in Public International Law: How WTO Law Relates
to Other Rules of International Law*
Joost Pauwelyn

28 –

27 *Transboundary Damage in International Law*
Hanqin Xue

26 –

25 *European Criminal Procedures*
Edited by Mireille Delmas-Marty and J. R. Spencer

24 *Accountability of Armed Opposition Groups in International Law*
Liesbeth Zegveld

23 *Sharing Transboundary Resources: International Law and Optimal Resource Use*
Eyal Benvenisti

22 *International Human Rights and Humanitarian Law*
René Provost

21 *Remedies against International Organisations*
Karel Wellens

20 *Diversity and Self-Determination in International Law*
Karen Knop

19 *The Law of Internal Armed Conflict*
Lindsay Moir

18 *International Commercial Arbitration and African States: Practice, Participation and Institutional Development*
Amazu A. Asouzu

17 *The Enforceability of Promises in European Contract Law*
James Gordley

16 *International Law in Antiquity*
David J. Bederman

15 *Money Laundering: A New International Law Enforcement Model*
Guy Stessens

14 *Good Faith in European Contract Law*
Reinhard Zimmermann and Simon Whittaker

13 *On Civil Procedure*
J. A. Jolowicz

12 *Trusts: A Comparative Study*
Maurizio Lupoi and Simon Dix

11 *The Right to Property in Commonwealth Constitutions*
Tom Allen

10 *International Organizations before National Courts*
August Reinisch

9 *The Changing International Law of High Seas Fisheries*
Francisco Orrego Vicuña

8 *Trade and the Environment: A Comparative Study of EC and US Law*
Damien Geradin

7 *Unjust Enrichment: A Study of Private Law and Public Values*
Hanoch Dagan

6 *Religious Liberty and International Law in Europe*
Malcolm D. Evans

5 *Ethics and Authority in International Law*
Alfred P. Rubin

4 *Sovereignty over Natural Resources: Balancing Rights and Duties*
Nico Schrijver

3 *The Polar Regions and the Development of International Law*
Donald R. Rothwell

2 *Fragmentation and the International Relations of Micro-States:
Self-Determination and Statehood*
Jorri C. Duursma

1 *Principles of the Institutional Law of International Organizations*
C. F. Amerasinghe

Printed in the United States
by Baker & Taylor Publisher Services